HOW TO BE A
Great Parent
to Your
Inner Child

ACUDRAGON® WELLNESS SYSTEM'S
ENLIGHTENED LIVING 101 SERIES

HOW TO BE A
Great Parent to Your Inner Child

Connect With Your Heart and Higher Purpose

WILLIAM J. KAPLANIDIS, L.Ac., M.S., M.A.

How To Be A Great Parent to Your Inner Child:
Connect To Your Heart and Higher Purpose

The content of this book is for general instruction only. Each person's physical, emotional, and spiritual condition is unique. The instruction in this book is not intended to replace or interrupt the reader's relationship with a physician or other professional. Please consult your doctor or healthcare professional for matters pertaining to your specific health and diet.

ISBN: 978-0-9835634-1-9

To my teachers, patients, students, colleagues, friends and family who encouraged me to persevere and share my gifts and experiences with all of you.

To my inner wounded children who made themselves known to me over the years and gave me the opportunities to heal, find my path and be fortunate enough to help others.

Table of Contents

PREFACE

My entire adult life has been spent in the helping and healing professions. However, this was not what I had envisioned as a young child. I had a passion for martial arts, team sports, music, and the hard sciences like chemistry and physics. Although I had some natural talent at listening and massage skills that many of my family and friends enjoyed, I basically was a misanthrope who wanted to work in a laboratory. As an early teen, I was enrolled in a gifted youth program at a college in New York City where I studied nuclear physics and laser theory. I remember a French documentary film crew came to a class and asked if they could interview some of the students for their film, which would be aired in France shortly thereafter. They were particularly excited to interview me because I could speak French. I told them I wanted to be a scientist when I grew up but did not know which kind. I had been particularly interested in different types of energy and had an uncle who not only encouraged this pursuit but used his connections to help me. I was given a private tour of the Indian Point Nuclear Power Plant in New York and visited the fusion reactor at Princeton University before I entered high school.

I did my best to excel in my other passions but often suffered from injuries because of a congenital weakness with my joints and connective tissue. With a little help, I was usually able to walk off an injury and keep playing. I knew I would continue playing sports, music, and possibly be a martial arts instructor as an adult but also knew from what doctors told me that careers in these passions were not likely. However, I had hoped for an athletic scholarship to help pay for college. As I pushed my body to meet this goal, I finally had the accident that I could not walk off. As I attempted to score my third goal and impress the varsity soccer coach, I was stopped by a defender who kicked my kicking leg. He had at least 50 lbs on me, and my foot stretched so far back that I tore most of the ligaments that hold your foot to your leg.

This injury led to a series of other joint injuries, and not only was there no hope for any scholarship but I was also told after a year of being bedridden and on crutches that I would never walk independently again. You can imagine how devastating this would be for any relatively healthy 17-year-old to hear. Medicine has evolved leaps and bounds from that time, but my options for treatment back then were not only limited but not promising in the long term. I was then told that I would be crippled with arthritis by the time I reached 40.

My focus began to shift as I contemplated what a life would be without being able to do what I loved. I went through all of Elisabeth Kübler-Ross's stages of grief—denial, anger, bargaining, depression, and acceptance—that are part of the framework that make up our learning to cope with losing someone. In my case, it was the loss of my inner-child athlete. The first four stages were relatively immediate. The acceptance became part of my life's journey as did living with constant, excruciating pain.

In an attempt to bring back my lost inner child and to understand the connection between the body, mind, and spirit, I began to study T'ai Chi, Zen Buddhism, philosophy, psychology, hypnotherapy, and meditation. I worked with athletes as an athletic trainer's assistant providing physical and emotional support to injured athletes and worked under a psychologist at a state psychiatric hospital doing counseling, psychological testing, and teaching T'ai Chi. I later continued to work in hospitals, had a private practice, and taught both here and abroad.

My journey took me to China, India, Nepal, and Tibet where I studied acupuncture, acupressure, T'ai Chi, martial arts, qigong, meditation, and even taught T'ai Chi and psychology. My own self-cultivation and my calling to help others heal and transform on many levels at once continued and continues to evolve. I take my responsibility to help others and to practice what I preach very seriously. Eventually, I founded the Acudragon® Wellness System to give a name to the work I do and the training I provide.

From the very beginning, I was on a quest to learn the best techniques from the East and West. For over three decades, one of the things I discovered was that whether I was working with professional athletes or dancers with injuries; lawyers or corporate executives with never-ending stress; couples trying to get pregnant or having relationship difficulties; people with addictions or with behaviors they wanted to change; people feeling depressed, anxious, or scared; people trying to figure out what they want to be when they grow up; or people looking for guidance on their spiritual path, they all had one thing in common—learning how to be a great parent to their inner child.

WARNING: Continuing to read this book may increase your awareness and accelerate your healing and transformation.

The Western Perspective

In Western psychology, the idea of the "inner child" is often connected to a part or parts of us that got wounded or hurt at different points in our developmental stages as children. These "inner children" are often connected to specific emotions and survival instincts and may come out in specific situations when we are adults: in intimate relationships, stressful situations at work, or sometimes as a way to help us heal and find our path.

The Eastern Perspective

In ancient Eastern traditions, it is understood that the body, mind, and spirit are interconnected not only within the individual but also with the environment around us.

Each of our organs not only has a physical function but is also connected to specific emotions and archetypes that guide and protect us. As humans, we are a microcosm of the macrocosm, meaning everything that is in nature is also within us. Each season can be seen as a stage in our lives. For example, spring can be seen as the time of our birth and early childhood. Summer can be seen as young adulthood. Fall or autumn can be seen as midlife, and winter as old age and our return to the earth.

The development of your inner child during the spring season of your life will affect how the other seasons play out. Understanding how past experiences from your childhood affect you as an adult on a physical, mental/emotional, and spiritual level can help you not only have a deeper understanding of yourself but also help you live a more enlightened life. You can feel more whole, more complete, and find inner peace and freedom to fully express who you are in this life.

For each of us, there may be one or more emotions that

we had difficulty feeling and expressing as a child. This pattern can continue into adulthood. For example, many women are conditioned as children not to express anger, while many men are conditioned not to cry or be sad. We often push down these feelings and can even disconnect from them. Sometimes, it is easier to see that someone else is overreacting emotionally to a situation and not be aware when we are doing the same thing. It may appear as if a child is hurt or throwing a tantrum.

For example, imagine someone who suffered many losses as a child. Perhaps the person lost a parent or loved one, moved to a new neighborhood and lost friends, had a pet die, or an older brother moved out to go away to school. For many years, this person never learned how to grieve these losses and release the accompanying sadness. Now 40-ish, while at work, this person notices a favorite pen that was a gift from a lost loved one is missing. After a quick scan of the desk, the drawers, and the cubicle, the person begins crying hysterically. Coworkers are alarmed and come to offer support. They seem perplexed that someone would have such a reaction about losing a pen. What they fail to see or understand is that their coworker is no longer the 40-year-old assistant manager but a six-year-old child releasing many years of grief and loss. The pen was the straw that broke the camel's back.

Similar patterns can be seen with other emotions like anger, fear, anxiety, worry, and even excess joy. You may be thinking of several examples you have seen of people over-reacting to a situation with anger, fear, anxiety, worry, or joy. These reactions are usually connected to one of their inner children. The age and developmental stage at which someone suffers a significant trauma or insult will help determine both the behavior pattern and the physical manifestation in the body. For example, a young girl who is abused at the time she is beginning to get her menses may have later difficulties with certain intimacies as well as her menstrual cycle, especially if the emotions related to the abuse are suppressed and not expressed and healed.

In this book, I hope to provide you with an East-West perspective to expand your knowledge of connecting with your heart and life purpose and how to be a great parent to your inner child. Fasten your seatbelt and enjoy the ride!

OVERVIEW

CHAPTER 1

The Seasons of Life

To be a great parent to your inner child, many factors need to be considered. A more general place to start is to understand the seasons of life. Much of Chinese medicine theory stems from Taoist philosophy of understanding man's relationship with nature. There are many references and analogies made to different aspects of nature, like the weather and the different energies of each season.

Our normal life span can be seen as beginning in the spring as a newborn and a young child. Then summer is associated with our expansive and expressive young adulthood. As we reach middle age, we enter the autumn and begin bringing the energy back inside us. And finally in winter, with old age setting in, our bodies generally slow down as we approach the end of our life cycle.

The part of the life cycle of spring represents birth and new beginnings. Children are conceived and born into this world. Completely dependent, children are at the mercy of those around them as they begin interacting with the world. It is at this time when animal instincts of both parent and child unfold. As humans, we are complex animal and spiritual beings. And as with all beings, even some of the most basic instincts can become complicated because of a host of reasons.

For example, a single mom living in poverty may have different challenges compared to a middle-class or wealthy intact family. However, there are some basic experiences, like bonding with our mothers, breast-feeding, and being held shortly after birth that can be considered common for all humans. Different cultures, religions, and age groups may have their own ideas about parenting a baby. Whether they are in their home country or living as immigrants can also influence their experiences.

Children given up for adoption or children who were not planned or abandoned in other ways have their own challenges. Children forced to grow up in environments in which their parents may have serious mental health or substance abuse issues or other forms of abusive behaviors have their share of challenges as well.

Regardless of the unique challenges each of you has faced, the time from ages zero to eight is when you are learning the basics of survival. You learn how to eat, poop, crawl, speak, walk, and begin to learn what is safe and what is dangerous. For example, you are encouraged not to touch a hot stove or run out into the street. As with certain animals— like big cats that model hunting for their young— there are times in which you are expected to learn certain skills like walking, speaking, reading, and sharing.

Most parents or caretakers have a basic understanding of these needs of small children and do their best to help their children learn and grow. What might be less obvious to parents, and those involved in raising and teaching children, is that children are also picking up how to relate to others in intimate relationships and relationships in general.

When you are young, your body and mind are picking up on both the obvious and the subtle behaviors and cues exhibited by the adults around you. When you are young, your liver is relatively large for your small body. In a way, you grow into your liver. The liver in Chinese medicine acts like radar, picking up and registering the energy and information around you, and is associated with the spring season.

During this early springtime of your life from ages zero to eight, your subconscious is being imprinted with vital information that is connected to how to survive in this world. Some of this imprinting may already be passed down to you in your DNA from previous generations. However, the early years generally give you the guidelines on how to survive both literally and figuratively in your relationships.

Your emotions—sadness, anger, fear, anxiety, worry, and joy—are all intimately involved in your early process of learning how to survive and be in this world. Each emotion is a natural part of being human and can serve many important functions. Think about each emotion and how you would react to a small child exhibiting that emotion. As little children, we will learn how to cope with these emotions, which hopefully will evolve with time. For example, if you felt very angry as a young child, you may

> Your emotions—sadness, anger, fear, anxiety, worry, and joy—are all intimately involved in your early process of learning how to survive and be in this world.

have thrown something or lashed out and hit someone. Hopefully as an adult you have other ways to express and channel your anger that are not potentially harmful to yourself or others.

What does your parenting instinct tell you to do when you see a sad child, sitting alone, crying?

Do you approach the child and try to cheer him or her up?

Maybe offer something sweet or fun?

Maybe let the child know that it's okay to cry?

Maybe, gently or assertively, tell the child to stop crying?

Or, maybe do nothing and wait for the child to stop crying on his or her own?

Now, take a moment and ask yourself the same questions about an angry child, a scared child, an anxious child, or a happy child. Are your answers similar to how your parents treated you? Or, are they the *extreme opposite* of how your parents acted? Or, are they somewhere in the middle? Knowing the answers to these questions can assist in helping you parent your own inner child.

As you continue to grow into your second half of the spring phase of your life, you begin to develop a critical mind. From around the age of nine to your teenage years, you become less open to the survival imprinting and begin to critically look at and examine the information you have received thus far. Again, this is a natural process. Depending on your life and how you were treated, you may look outside of your immediate family for role models of critical minds. Or in most cases, a part of you will adopt the most critical aspects of your parents. Based on how you perceived your treatment from ages zero to eight will largely determine your early feelings of self-worth and self-esteem. For example, if you were abandoned in some way or hurt, you may conclude that you were not good enough or that something must be wrong with you.

> Based on how you perceived your treatment from ages zero to eight will largely determine your early feelings of self-worth and self-esteem.

Now, as you enter the latter part of the spring into adolescence and teenage years, you often struggle with your identity. You have some innate ideas of your heart's desires and who you are deep inside. You also try to make sense of and integrate the feedback and messages you get from your family, teachers, friends, and peers. It is a time to become more independent and decide how to express your true self in the world.

As the teenage years come to an end, you begin the summer phase of your life. This is the time to expand and let your heart shine. In general, your body is strong, and you can explore things that are fun and bring you joy. For some, this may be traveling and being more creative with music or the arts; others might pursue a more practical path and choose to work more than play. Everyone's circumstances will be different. Some of you may not have the support or luxury to play as you would like and decide you should be responsible and focus on work or education. Others may follow their hearts and struggle making a living by being more like "starving" artists. And some will be able to balance both work and play and be happy.

As the summer season continues, you usually reach a crossroads around the age of 29. In astrology, this time is known as "Saturn's return." It is a time of a shift in maturity, wisdom, and connecting with your life's path. If you have been following your heart with the support of your other parts, it will be a time of expanding your path. If your heart was blocked or overindulged without boundaries or skills of responsibility, this can be a time of career change or a serious wake-up call to get your life together. Some of you find your calling and begin more firmly on your path. Others may not heed the call out of fear or prior conditioning. Or, you may choose a path that feels more comfortable or safe, which may or may not be in line with your destiny. Looking back at my life, I found that certain milestones coincided with astrology and planets in transit.

In your 30's, as you move toward autumn, you are building yourself up in all areas of your life. You may have a strong sense of self-identity, in your relationships, with your family, at work, and with your life's purpose. As your life begins to feel more stable, some of your previously hurt inner children that are still hiding may begin to show themselves. Have you ever suddenly felt depressed or overwhelming emotion like sadness, fear, anger, or anxiety during a time in your life when things were going well and felt more stable than ever? These are the inner children that either went into hiding on their own, or were locked away, or disassociated because you were too busy in survival mode to deal with them.

> As your life begins to feel more stable, some of your previously hurt inner children that are still hiding may begin to show themselves.

Early autumn can be a time to harvest some of your rewards of being on your path. For example, you may be in good health, you may be in a good relationship, raising a family, doing well at work, and feeling satisfied overall. As autumn continues, you reach what is known as the "midlife crisis." (The word "crisis" comes from the Greek *krino,* which means a time for decision.) As we approach the late 40's, early 50's, we are at the peak of the autumn ("fall") season. This is a natural progression, and there are changes to our bodies and shifts in our energies. Both men and women experience changes in their bodies and their hormones. For women, it is the menopause transition; for men, it is often issues with their prostate and a decline in testosterone.

In Chinese medicine, this shift of energy for both

women and men is connected to the kidney's energy, which is like your batteries and is connected to your aging process. The kidneys directly connect to your libido, sexual and reproductive functions, your bones, and the hair on your head. They also connect to your teeth, your hearing, your lower back, knees, brain function, and memory. They also support the functions of all your other organs. Some of the physical changes you may experience include things like hair loss, frozen shoulder, the beginnings of arthritis, or just some general aches and pains.

In addition to all these not-so-fun physical changes, that we begin to experience with getting older, it is a time of reflection similar to that of age 29. This time, astrologically, it is not Saturn but the smaller planet called Chiron that returns. I am not an expert in astrology, but as I was having some life changing experiences a friend told me it was connected to my Chiron return. In mythology, Chiron was the Centaur known as the "Wounded Healer". Nothing he tried could fully heal his wound. Through his suffering he gained knowledge and wisdom and was able to counsel, teach and help heal others. His journey as a teacher and a healer resonated deeply for me. Accepting that there may be something you cannot heal completely can be difficult. However, choosing to do your best to heal your deepest wounds can propel you forward on your life's path.

By now, most of your forgotten, suppressed inner children in hiding make themselves known to you loudly and hopefully clearly. Many of the physical symptoms, ailments, illnesses, and diseases you experience may be directly connected to past "incompletions" in your life that began with a wounded inner child. The initial trauma may have been an insult or some type of abuse or mistreatment. It may first manifest as "stuck energy," or not being able to process emotions or complete an experience. As a child, you may not have had the tools to cope with these incompletions or traumas. If they are ignored or suppressed, stuck energy will try to get your attention by turning into a physical ailment or intense, emotional feelings or expressions. Let's go back to example of the very angry young child. Now instead of throwing some-

> Many of the physical symptoms, ailments, illnesses, and diseases you experience may be directly connected to past "incompletions" in your life that began with a wounded inner child.

thing or hitting someone you hold in your anger. Maybe you are afraid of the consequences of letting it out or you don't want to hurt the feelings of the person who has said or done something to anger you. Regardless of why, this anger inside you becomes stuck energy that you may initially feel as tightness in particular muscles. Over time, this and other unexpressed anger stuck in your body can manifest as chronic pain or have some other negative effect on your body's functioning. Sometimes throwing a tantrum is a quick way to release the anger energy, but becomes less ideal as you get older. Much of the work that I do in my practice helps people discover how stuck emotions affect their bodies. After going into a deep state of relaxation you can quickly release pain and tension, and complete past experiences. By removing these energetic blockages you can find healthier ways to move forward on your path.

Your "fall" season can manifest as a health crisis, job loss, divorce... but it is also an opportunity to fully recognize the areas of your life and the inner children that need you to step up and fill in the parenting gaps to be more integrated and whole. Whichever parts of us that did not fully express in the spring and summer seasons, tend to come out at this time and demand attention. For men, it may be dating younger women or getting that red, convertible sports car. Or maybe it is learning how to open your heart and be more sensitive to others. For women, it may be getting Botox injections or other body modifications and a new trendy wardrobe to look younger. It may also be stepping into a role of power and reconnecting with your passions.

In any case, it is a time of both reflection and looking into the future. Although we tend to have negative associations with the word "crisis," remember it is the time for decision-making. It is a significant time for insights and transformation, as we can choose to find the positive within the negative. It is also a time when we can choose, if we want to, to help others with the knowledge and wisdom we have gained. Or if we wish to, we can retreat into a cave as we move into the winter season of life. Either way, we have the opportunity to be more present and free to express who we are on all levels.

As you enter winter, you are becoming an elder or senior citizen and may feel your body is not what it used to be. Around the age 59-60 is the second return of Saturn, which gives you a chance at peace of mind. As you enter into your last season of life, there is often an appreciation and gratitude for the wisdom you have gathered over the years. You may begin to accept and respect your body's limitations and appreciate moderation and discipline in its care. Again, you are faced with a choice on how to live out this season. You can choose to be rigid in body and mind and gradually fade away, or you can choose to continue to find purpose and freely express all that you are.

Your abilities in certain physical or work areas may begin to slow down, but your opportunities to connect with spirit, God, Tao, the universe, or whatever you call the energy greater than you can emerge like never before. Even those of you who did not feel you were on a spiritual path earlier in life often have a shift in perception and consciousness. It is a time where you can truly embody any of the virtues you strived to live up to earlier in life, as well as a time you can allow your inner children to be truly free to enjoy life consciously. Depending on your culture, society, and upbringing, there is a level of respect for elders and their wisdom. As you approach death, healing any remaining inner children may help you find peace of mind in your last, earthly transition. You can have fun and use the energy of your inner children to be one with yourself and in the environment around you. If you had a near-death experience (or two or three in my case) before this winter season of life, you may have come to the time of recovery of your core individuality sooner. Sometimes a near-death experience wakes you up and gives you the motivation to reflect on your life and see what is important to you. You don't need a near-death experience to have this revelation. However, things like getting a serious medical diagnosis or losing someone close to you often spark the question of how you want to live your life.

As you continue reading, I will ask you questions that will give you more insight into your inner children and other parts of yourself. You may want to take some notes along the way to help you keep track of your parts as you learn ways to heal yourself. These notes can also be useful to track your insights and share with your therapist/healthcare practitioner. Awareness is the first step to healing and living a more enlightened life.

EARLY SPRING

CHAPTER 2

The Divine Child Is Born

The beginning of your life and childhood is the spring season of your life cycle. From the moment of conception, a complex process of cells generates and begins forming based on your parents' DNA and the energies of heaven and earth at that moment. The former seems logical in that you inherit certain genetic traits based on your parents and family lineage. The latter may seem more esoteric and is usually connected to astrology whether East,

West, or both. Science has shown that your existence is interconnected with the universe, from the bees that pollinate your food to the gravitational pull of the planets and the rays of the sun.

Inside the womb, the child is essentially one with the mother. Her overall health, state of mind, habits, and environment will all have some influence on the growing fetus. If you are born to relatively healthy parents in a stable environment, you will have a different starting point then, let's say, if you are born to a parent who is addicted to drugs and does not have a stable home. Those of you born in an unstable environment may have some kind of illness, deformity, or addiction.

When I worked on locked psychiatric wards, I saw an incredible range of people whose childhood traumas were so severe and ongoing that they struggled into adulthood not being able to care of themselves. They were, in a sense, little children in adult bodies who needed a parental do over. Some of them had children hoping to experience the love they never received.

I remember there was a 21-year-old, pregnant, crack-addicted, homeless patient about to give birth to her sixth child. This child would be her third to be born addicted to crack cocaine. Despite her circumstance and past history, she believed she would be able to keep this one and give and receive the love she so craved. Needless to say, this child, like the five before her, was immediately placed in foster care. The mental health system and other social services provide various levels of care and support but often fall short in helping heal the myriad of difficult cases.

Despite how a child comes out of the gate—whether it was a home birth in a tub or at a high-tech hospital—I think we can all agree there is a certain innocence that all children have. For many, there are feelings of love, joy, and an opening of the heart despite how painful and difficult the birth process may have been. It is up to the parents and caretakers to accept and unconditionally love their children. Much of our emotional struggles are rooted in our desire to give and receive love.

> Many of our emotional struggles are rooted in our desire to give and receive love.

In Chinese medicine, certain energies develop while you are in the womb. These reservoirs of energies are connected to what are called the Eight Extra Channels. The energy of your main organs develops once you are born and are connected to the 12 Main Meridians. Using acupuncture you can access both the deeper reservoirs of energy through the Eight Extra Channels and the energies of your organs through the 12 Main Meridians for deep healing. Practices, like qigong ("chee-gung") or energy cultivation, provide meditative, therapeutic exercises that can also empower you to heal on many levels. According to Chinese medicine, your organs are divided into Yin and Yang pairs. Each organ is responsible for different body functions and is associated with different emotions, archetypes, virtues, seasons, colors, and other energies found in nature. The Yin organs—Liver, Heart, Spleen, Lungs, and Kidneys—are responsible for the major functions of your body, mind, and spirit and are supported by their Yang pair.

Each Yin/Yang pair is associated with Five Elements or Phases: Wood (Liver/Gallbladder); Fire (Heart/Small Intestine); Earth (Spleen/Stomach); Metal (Lungs/Large Intestine); and Water (Kidneys/Urinary Bladder). These elements individually have specific relationships to each other and to the environment and work together to keep you healthy and balanced. (See figure 2-1.)

Five Elements or Phases

Figure 2-1. Five Element Correspondences

	Wood	**Fire**	**Earth**	**Metal**	**Water**
Yin Yang Organ Pairs	Liver /Gallbladder	Heart / Small Intestine	Spleen / Stomach	Lungs / Large Intestine	Kidneys / Urinary Bladder
Emotions	Anger	Joy	Pensive / Anxiety / Worry	Grief / Sadness	Fear /Fright
Colors	Green	Red	Yellow	White	Black /Dark Blue
Seasons	Spring	Summer	Late Summer	Fall	Winter
Virtues	Kindness / Benevolence	Propriety	Faithfulness /Fairness	Righteousness / Courage	Wisdom / Gentleness

In Western medicine doctors generally look at the body and its organs by their measurable and observable physical functions, much like a mechanic looks at a car. For example, it is obvious that the heart pumps your blood through your body. As technology evolves we are able to get more details of how our organs function. More and more research is demonstrating how mind and body are connected. Western medicine being very reductionist with many specialties often seems to ignore relationships between physical and mental/emotional systems. However, Chinese medicine as well as other ancient medicine traditions observed these relationships and created treatments to connect with you and help on all levels. That said, both Eastern and Western medicine have their strengths and weaknesses. This topic will be covered in more detail in a future book. For now, I would like to share some of the relationships and connections.

The Heart is not only connected to the physical body by pumping blood but with all the emotions, especially with love and joy. It is considered the home of your Spirit and is the Ruler of your Inner Kingdom. Although there are other organs and their associated emotions, when people speak of

> When people speak of the inner child, they are often referring to your Heart.

the inner child, they are often referring to your Heart. In some ways, it is similar to Carl Jung's archetypes of the Divine Child (symbol of your true self that connects you to the higher power within and leads you towards wholeness) and the Wonder Child (part of you that is curious, creative and loves to explore).

Whether it is from the East or the West, literal or metaphysical, all cultures and humans can agree on the primal importance of the Heart. Sayings like, "follow your heart," she or he is a "heartbreaker," and "what does your heart want to do?" all imply that the Heart connects to your core. (We explore this further in the next chapter.)

The Liver, which is relatively large in the body when you are young, is in charge of the smooth flow of energy throughout your body. The Liver influences your connective tissues and helps the body's digestive and menstrual processes. In the West it is primarily known for its detoxification function. Early on, it acts like radar, picking up on the environmental cues around you. It can be considered the General or Warrior and not only protects the Heart but also assists the Heart by following its orders to help the Heart accomplish what it wants to do in life. It is associated with the emotion of anger and the virtue of kindness.

The Kidneys are like your batteries. You are born with a certain "charge" given to you by your parents, heaven and earth. This charge is connected to your aging process, sexual energy, hormones, bones, and brain function. In the West it is involved with detoxification as well. The Kidneys are like the Wise One or Philosopher and have the initial blueprint of who you are and all you potentially can become. A Western analogy may be like how Merlin the Wizard was to Prince and later King Arthur. The Spirit of the Heart is closely connected to the essence of the Kidneys. (We talk more about how this connection helps the body, mind, and spirit in later chapters.) The Kidneys are associated with fear and fright (shock) as well as willpower, wisdom, and the virtue of gentleness.

The Lungs in Western medicine are primarily associated with breathing and the exchange of oxygen and carbon dioxide. In Eastern medicine they control breathing and bring in heaven's energy and air into the body. Together, they are considered a High Minister located next to the Heart. They not only discern and extract what is valuable in life from the air to energize the body but help protect it from outside pathogens. The archetype of the lung is generally very organized, disciplined, methodical and efficient. The Lungs are associated with sadness and grief and the virtues of righteousness and justice.

The Spleen connects to Mother Earth and is nurturing. In Western medicine, it is known to filter the blood and store platelets and white blood cells, primarily assisting the immune system. In Chinese medicine, the Spleen is in charge of digesting the food to nourish all the other organs. The Lungs get energy from air, while the Spleen gets energy from food and helps the Heart make blood. As a child, the Spleen is like the Peacemaker in the family. Later, it grows into the Nurturer and Caretaker. It is associated with pensiveness/worry and the virtue of fairness.

Most of you are already aware that you are made up of different parts inside you. For example, you may have an athlete part, a mother or parent part, a responsible and organized worker part, a religious or spiritual part, and a little kid part that likes to have fun or feels hurt sometimes. So, depending on where you are, a different part of you may come forward. Whether you are at work, with your family, at the gym, or at a party with friends, different parts of you will act appropriately, or not, for each of these situations. Each of these archetypes and parts of your personality are connected to your body and are strongly influenced by your Heart. How you interact with your environment, whether appropriately or not, will be determined by the state of your Heart.

There are dozens of archetypal parts inside us. Take a moment and think about all the different parts of yourself. Some of them may make you feel strong and alive, while you may feel others are better off hidden and out of sight. Regardless of what you call these parts or feel about them, there is one thing I have found that holds true, which is: Once a part is formed inside you, it is there to stay. Often, you may spend years trying to hide or get rid of a part of yourself you don't like. For those of you familiar with certain traditions, it is often said that you need to "get rid of your ego" to become enlightened and achieve a higher spiritual level of being. While there is some truth to this, getting rid of your ego or any of your inner children creates an inner battle. Those parts are usually connected to your Heart and to your survival and will not go without a fight. There are other traditions that believe in "possession," in which an outside force gets inside and influences you; these traditions believe those parts are better removed.

> Once a part is formed inside you, it is there to stay.

I found through my work that the process to self-healing and more enlightened living begins with healing the inner child/children, accepting all of your parts, and understanding your ego. Finding the strengths of the parts you don't like and giving them new jobs to help the whole is more productive than fighting and trying to get rid of those parts of yourself. Once you feel more whole and complete, it is easier to allow your Higher Spiritual Self to lead the way. As a human, you are born as a divine child, both spiritual and animal, both separate from and one with everything, all at the same time.

In this book, we focus on some of your main players that make up your inner kingdom. The more adult, evolved parts of yourself can help your inner wounded children heal, grow, and be more productive on your life's path. Take a moment now and think about some of the key players that can help your inner child. What do they look like to you, and how well are they doing their job?

> Finding the strengths of the parts you don't like and giving them new jobs to help the whole is more productive than fighting and trying to get rid of those parts of yourself.

Reflections

The Liver/General/Warrior/Protector:

- What parts of you act as protector? Think of the different levels, from animal to spiritual. How do you protect yourself?

The Spleen/Mother/Nurturer/Caretaker:

- What parts of you nurture yourself? How do they take care of you? Do you feel balanced?

The Lung/High Minister/Organizer/Transformer:

- What parts of you are organized and disciplined? How do you take in what is pure and good and stand up for your moral values?

The Kidney/Wise Sage/Wizard/Philosopher:

- What parts of you are wise and have a larger perspective on life? Do you have an inner truth seeker that helps you see conventional, as well as the ultimate reality?

CHAPTER 3

The Heart as Ruler

et's take a closer look at the Heart and why it is so important. As I stated earlier, your Heart is your Ruler, your King or your Queen. Imagine before you were born, your parents were told that you were the next king, queen, president, or prime minister. Or, what if shortly after your birth, you were recognized for being the next Jesus, Dalai Lama, or other spiritual leader? How do you think your upbringing would have been different if your parents knew they had the responsibility of raising the ruler of their country or a significant spiritual leader in the world?

Now, imagine how you would treat that child knowing everything you know. Imagine a child is the ruler. The parents, the advisers, and all the caretakers are expected to help this child grow into being the best ruler he or she can be. You would probably love and respect the child and teach the child various age-appropriate skills like self-care, discipline, and compassion.

At first, you learn basic survival skills and how to be more and more independent. Your heart connects you with your purpose from within and from the outside environment. As your being and your purpose continue to unfold, you learn how to connect with the people and the world around you. Your body (mind and spirit) is always trying to heal and find balance. For example, if you fall down and cut yourself, your body will automatically heal the cut. You do not have to speak to your body and command the white blood cells to ward off any infection or command the skin cells to heal. It just happens automatically. Your mind and

> Your heart connects you with your purpose from within and from the outside environment.

spirit work in a similar way. They are automatically trying to heal and express who you are. The more relaxed and balanced you are, the quicker and easier

> Your body (mind and spirit) is always trying to heal and find balance.

things heal. Creating a safe, nonjudgmental space for your Heart is important. It allows your Heart to be free to express and guide you with love and wisdom.

As a child, your Heart does its best to give and receive love, find joy, and connect happily with your environment. Any insults, injury, illness, or trauma can make your happy, little Ruler want to hide. Imagine your little King or Queen being hurt in some way. You may feel sad, angry, scared, or anxious and decide to hide in the tower. When this happens, the other parts of you may have to take over to ensure that you survive and continue to go to school or live your life at whatever stage it is. Early traumas that may be experienced in the womb or shortly after birth are more difficult to understand cognitively but may be stored in the body and reveal themselves with specific "triggers." (A trigger is any stimulus that sets off a flashback or past traumatic memory. It is very personal and can be something that affects one your senses like a particular smell, color, touch, taste or sound. During a trauma your senses are heightened. Particular stimuli may then get associated with the trauma.) The trigger may cause a tight feeling in your chest or some other bodily reaction. You may be aware of how your body reacts, but not the cause. Whether from abuse or neglect, these traumas may manifest later as not feeling good enough, having abandonment fears, and issues with trust.

I had a 35-year-old female patient who was diagnosed with generalized anxiety disorder who I will call Betty. As I did the intake, Betty stated she had suffered from anxiety as far back as she could remember but could not understand why. The anxiety usually manifested with a tight feeling in her chest and what felt like a racing heart. She worked for herself and had a successful business but could not shake this feeling. Having tried conventional psychotherapy and Western medications in the past with no resolution, she decided to try Chinese medicine. Betty was open to trying any and all of the tools of the Acudragon® Wellness System. Her Heart and Kidney energies were not in harmony, and we did a combination of acupuncture and acupressure from the Eastern perspective and hypnotherapy and other mind-body techniques from the Western perspective. In the first session, we were able to identify the root cause of the anxiety and help her complete and release it from her body.

It turned out that her parents got divorced when she was four years old, forcing her mother to get a full-time job. Her mother left Betty with her neighbor who was a stay-at-home mom with her own young children. At first, Betty thought it was a play date and had fun. But as the hours passed, she began to feel scared and wondered where her mother was. Her mother returned after work and picked Betty up. The next day, her mom left her again. She became fearful and anxious again, trying to be strong. It was not until the third day, when her mom sensed her anxiety, that she sat her down and explained that she had to work and that she would be back later. Betty seemed to understand, but the anxiety of being abandoned and losing her mother was already imprinted in her.

After just one session, Betty was free from the anxiety because she found the root and completed the experience. We allowed the child to speak to her mom and say what she could not say at age four. Then, Betty's adult, inner mom reassured her inner child that she was loved and would be safe.

Most of us have a series of traumatic events that get imprinted early on, but sometimes it is just one that lingers into adulthood. Let's say you are four years old and while you're eating dinner with your family, you are insulted or made fun of and your feelings are hurt. Your Heart may retreat inside you to feel safe. Let's say your mother or another family member then offers you sweets to make you feel better. Your Spleen or Inner-Mother part may come forward and learns to nurture your Heart with food and sweets. Now as an adult, you may turn to sweets when your feelings are hurt in a similar way you did when you were four. Often food, especially sweets, can become a way of showing yourself love. Almost every culture has their version of comfort foods.

Or maybe you are 10 years old, and you are the victim of sexual abuse or some other type of physical abuse and the Heart retreats into the tower. You are scared and confused and are afraid to tell anyone. Or maybe you seek help but get dismissed and no one believes you. Initially, you feel sad, but this can turn to anger or fear to cover the sadness. The Liver or the Inner General/Warrior part may come out and try to protect you with anger. Sometimes this anger can be directed outward toward people that remind you of the perpetrator or those who did not believe you. And sometimes the anger can be directed inward, in which case your Liver may be angry at the Heart, or at itself, for not being able to protect the Heart.

If you were physically abused, and especially if you were sexually abused as a child, you might often feel a myriad of emotions that can be very confusing and painful to process. You, like many children, may disassociate from the experience and bury the memories deep inside. This is the equivalent to the Inner Ruler hiding in the tower or deep in the dungeon. The unresolved confusion and pain can make it difficult to express your love or receive love in intimate relationships. Addressing these different emotions, how they affect your body and how they affect your perception of love, can lead to finding inner peace and balance.

As children, we all have had experiences where our Hearts get hurt. This can happen at different times throughout our childhood. In our culture, we may call this the "wounded inner child." However, if we have suffered multiple traumas, illnesses, injuries, and insults, we may end up with "multiple inner children." Through my decades of working with people by fusing Chinese medi-

> If you are significantly hurt at different ages throughout your childhood, your Heart or Inner Ruler gets broken into pieces.

cine and Western psychology, I discovered that most of our inner wounded children are actually broken pieces of the Heart. As adults, we are all familiar with the saying that he/she has "a broken heart." We usually say this when someone is hurt by the one they love. If you are significantly hurt at different ages throughout your childhood, your Heart or Inner Ruler gets broken into pieces.

Let's say you were hurt at ages 4, 8, 12, and 14, and you were not able to heal or complete the experiences. You not only have four inner-wounded children, but each of them is connected to your Heart and is your King or Queen. And while other parts of you may have taken control to help guide you in deciding what you studied in school or what type of work you did, the Heart is ultimately in charge. As an adult, different situations and experiences may trigger the wounds of your Heart. This may lead one of your inner wounded children to come forward and take charge depending on the situation. You may now have a four-year-old, an eight-year-old, or a 12- or 14-year-old taking the lead. Their intention is to help you heal and reconnect with your Heart, but often their actions are not appropriate for the current situation. Having some ice cream when you were four years old might have made you feel better, but now maybe it is part of a trigger for your eating disorder or a food that does not help with your diabetes. Our other parts may know better and may try to stop the inner child from doing something that is harmful or inappropriate for the current situation. But because this wounded child is your Ruler, King or Queen, the other parts have no choice but to step aside.

Sometimes, the young child is often seen as the "shadow side" of us. It has been my clinical experience that this shadow part, which we often fear or dislike, is actually a wounded part of our Heart; it is a very young child in an alleyway casting a very big shadow on the wall. Our adult parts are afraid of going into the alley because this large shadow is scary. However, if you're able to walk into the alley and get past your fear, you will see a young child who just wants to be loved and healed.

How your Heart was treated, and how the other parts of you perceive and act toward your Heart, will influence your decisions and life choices. Choosing foods, clothes, partners, careers, hobbies, and other interests will reflect the state of your Heart and its quest to heal and express the true you. Think about some of your choices that made you happy in the long run; your Heart probably made them. However, sometimes the Heart can go to extremes and go overboard, for example, by buying large amounts of the things you love whether they are sweets, fancy clothes, or things that are expensive or addictive.

When I worked with patients with both mental health and substance abuse issues, I learned about the concept of "harm reduction." The idea was to give clean needles to heroin addicts to reduce the spread of HIV/AIDS and hepatitis. While this seemed like a bandage and was not addressing the roots causing someone to shoot heroin, I understood its immediate value. I began to adapt and use this concept with my private patients who had certain obsessive or addictive behaviors; it not only gave them immediate gratification but also relieved them from some stress to their bodies or finances.

So, if your Inner Ruler indulges in food that is not good for you or chooses retail therapy that is maxing out your credit card, you can try harm reduction. In the case of food, let's say sweets, you can find sweets that are more natural, like fruit, or are made with stevia instead of processed sugar or artificial sweeteners. Sometimes, slowly eating a medjool date or stevia-sweetened chocolate does the trick for me. Depending on your food of choice, you can find a healthier substitute while you are working on the root cause and finding out what the underlying need of your Heart is.

The same goes for any type of "retail therapy." Finding cheaper but good-quality items may be a place to start as you address the deeper needs of your inner child. Getting your other parts involved may include setting some boundaries regarding quantity and when you can get your fix. Once you are able to make healthier and wiser choices, you can then turn them into rewards for doing some of the more important work. As you learn more about which inner children are involved and how to meet their true needs, the need for sweets or clothes no longer have the addictive appeal and can become a *conscious* choice.

:ctions

Let's check in with your Inner Ruler with the following questions:

1. How connected do you feel to your Heart?

2. Do you feel confident listening to your Heart and the choices you make?

CHAPTER 4

Animal Instincts

You can better get an idea of the age and needs of your inner children by understanding some of the basics of child development. As humans, we are both animals and spiritual beings. Coming into the world, we have the DNA of all life—plant and animal. From a single cell in the womb, the embryo goes through the evolutionary stages of fish, amphibian, and lower mammals until a very evolved, complex baby is born. In Deepak Chopra's *Rein-*

venting the Body, Resurrecting the Soul, he points out that we share 60% of the same genes as a banana, 90% with a mouse, and more than 99% with a chimpanzee. This is a more literal way of understanding that all of nature is within us.

For some species, once you are hatched or born, you are on your own. You may be programmed like a turtle to follow the moonlight and run for the ocean. For animals higher in the evolutionary chain, you may be parented for a few years while you learn how to hunt and be in your environment, as it is with some of the big cats, like tigers. Think about birds, their nests, and monkeys and apes and their social networks. As humans, babies are dependent for many years and cannot survive without support. Psychologists have studied and theorized about babies' bonding with their mothers early on and the developmental stages of childhood. Freud, Jung, Piaget, Maslow, and many others have described how we develop and interact in the world.

Early on, we begin with breathing, eating, sleeping, and eliminating waste. The oral stage may be instinctual in that we automatically begin sucking when something touches our mouths. While this and other stages—like grasping, crawling, and eventually walking—may be natural instincts, we are also learning and adapting to our environment at the same time. We may learn that to get attention or to get our food, we need to cry and be heard. Different genes get activated based on our developmental stages, our desires, and our environment. How to survive in our environment is being imprinted on many levels.

Although the exact ages may vary a year or two, through my studies and clinical experience, a significant amount of survival and imprinting happens between the ages of zero and eight. From infancy to about eight, you are learning the basics of your body and how to take care of yourself. Much of what you experience through all of your senses is programmed into your subconscious as your survival tools. Some of these tools relate to body basics: You learn about food, how to eat, and go to the bathroom. You also learn about hygiene, like bathing and brushing your teeth. When there are traumas very early on, this can have an effect on your body and your ability to take care of your basic needs.

As an adult, you may have trouble with eating or maintaining personal hygiene when you feel depressed or when some other strong emotion is triggered. Many times, the reaction in your body is like an uncontrollable reflex. When I worked on the inpatient psychiatric wards, patients were judged on their activities of daily living (or ADLs). We would often see severely depressed or otherwise severely disturbed patients having trouble with ADLs like self-hygiene. Many did not shower or bother combing their hair or keeping themselves clean.

I remember this being an issue with a young man who I will call Freddie. Freddie was in his 30's and was assigned to me as one of my primary cases. He had a history of psychiatric problems and cocaine abuse. On the surface, he was handsome, in shape, and an amateur boxer. He was severely depressed but had been making steady progress. Freddie generally was quiet and kept to himself. You could feel his anger and rage just below the surface, which became more apparent after a visit with his mother. Besides individual counseling, he participated in a work activities program that allowed him to spend some time off the ward to do some work that was outsourced by a nonprofit agency, like stuffing envelopes. Although he participated and was making progress, I received complaints that the other patients in the work program were getting agitated because he had bad body odor.

My team told me that I needed to address this with him if he wanted to continue having the work program as a privilege. They also told me that his poor ADLs could affect his discharge planning, and that I had to speak to him. This was the first time I had to counsel someone about poor hygiene and struggled with how to bring up the subject. Part of me knew he was potentially a ticking time bomb and was hesitant to insult or irritate him. After meeting with him, he assured me he was showering and was clean. However, the complaints about his body odor continued. Now I was told that if he did not shower, he would be physically forced to do so. I knew that would not go well for anybody involved. While he dressed appropriately and combed his hair before going off the locked ward to the work program, I could see after a few days that his hair was greasy and unwashed. When he told me he was showering after our third meeting on the subject, I pointed out my observation of his hair.

He began to get irritated and told me he could not shower because the water was too cold. Initially, I thought to myself that I showered daily without hot water for over five weeks on my first trip to China, and it could be done with the right mind-set. I then shifted my thoughts to be more compassionate and get more clarification. He then proceeded to tell me how he was tortured as a child by his brother, and one of the times included cold water. He said he had been hospitalized many times as a result of his brother's torture and neglect from his mother. I did some research in the basement medical records room and found his chart from when he was a young child. There were several hospitalizations that were due to his brother inflicting some sort of torture. Besides the one that included the cold water, another described how his brother tied him to a chair at age four and burned paper between his toes.

Having even more empathy for my patient, I shared my findings with my team. While they were sympathetic, they reminded me that he did not have a choice, and that he would be physically forced to shower if necessary. After another counseling session and offering my support, he was able to overcome his fears and muscle memories and began showering and consistently improved his hygiene. Pointing out his strengths and helping him parent his inner child gave him more confidence. Using basic counseling techniques, I helped him accept his boxer part and reinforced his self-discipline, strength and athleticism. I also acknowledged his progress on the ward and how his self-control and improvements communicating had earned him certain privileges, like going off the ward to work. He was soon discharged.

As you become a toddler, you begin to learn about boundaries. You begin separating yourself from others while at the same time you are learning how to relate to others. You have been observing the behaviors of the adults around you and have been imprinting these behaviors inside your subconscious as the appropriate way to survive in this world.

In the beginning, your mere cute presence may have been enough for you to give and receive love. As you get older, giving and receiving love can become more complicated depending on how your caregivers were conditioned and how they behaved and acted. Although you are still dependent on your caregivers in many ways, you begin to express your independence and test different boundaries. The traumas, insults, and confusion you ex-

> As you get older, giving and receiving love can become more complicated depending on how your caregivers were conditioned and how they behaved and acted.

perience from birth to age eight get imprinted into your subconscious and can affect everything from ADLs to relationships. You begin to develop "buttons" that when pushed, can elicit an emotional response. Some of you are more aware of what your buttons are— a child being bullied, a racist comment, or a child being molested. Sometimes, the button is closer to home and can be pushed very easily, for example, by criticism from your mother or father. One of the reasons they are masters at pushing your buttons is because they had a part in creating them.

Your emotions and the emotions of your parents, caretakers, siblings, and others close to you in your early years play a key role in your survival. Emotions like joy, sadness, anger, fear, anxiety, worry are basic emotions that connect with your body, your energy, your behaviors, and your ability to be successful in life. Emotions are a natural part of being human, and just like learning how to eat and bathe; we must learn appropriate and healthy ways of managing our emotions. Feeling love and joy tend to be what everyone wants and are connected to the energy of your Heart (your Inner King/Queen). While the other emotions may correspond to other organs—for example, anger is often connected to the Liver (your Inner General/Warrior)—all the emotions affect your Heart. Other correlations are sadness and grief with the Lungs (Inner High Minister); pensiveness and worry with the Spleen (Inner Peacemaker/Nurturer); and fear and fright with the Kidneys (your Inner Philosopher/Wise Sage) (see figure 2-1 in chapter 2). Each of these emotions may serve a purpose in your survival. For example, anger may protect you and help you take action, while fear may stop you from taking part in a dangerous situation. Unresolved, extreme emotional states are often paired with traumas, insults, and negative experiences you have as a child.

> Unresolved, extreme emotional states are often paired with traumas, insults, and negative experiences you have as a child.

As you get older, one or two of these basic emotions may continue to haunt you because you never learned how to cope with or resolve the emotional trauma. For instance, after love, the first emotion you may experience is grief and loss. The birth process takes us away from our comfortable, no-maintenance womb to a brightly lit, cold, loud environment where we are often met with a slap on the rear end to get us to breathe. This may also anger us and make us cry. Your emotions can be the gateway to identifying your wounded inner child and getting the help that part needs. Being aware of which emotions you feel most often, or feel are the strongest, and how they affect your thinking and your body, are good first steps.

Feeling strong emotions is one way your inner child tries to get your attention for love and healing. Eventually, the emotions may go from being stuck energy and turn into behaviors that no longer serve you. As an adult, these energies may also become physical symptoms or ailments. Your innate instincts combine with your experiences and become *reflexive behaviors*. These behaviors, habits, and reactions to different stressors and triggers are programmed into your subconscious and are difficult to change because they are connected to what your inner child sees as your survival.

> Feeling strong emotions is one way your inner child tries to get your attention for love and healing.

I once treated a couple that seemed like the perfect match. The wife, who had found numerous benefits from treatments, told me about her husband's anger issues and encouraged him to work with me. Usually, when one partner pushes another to get help, there is often resistance. In this case, however, her husband, who I will call Barry, came willingly and wanted to do whatever he could to heal himself. Barry seemed like a gentle giant who, after 30 years of marriage, was still very much in love with his wife. What his wife described to me sounded like fits of dissociative rage, so I began by using acupuncture points to help release the Liver energy and explore any issues with anger.

At first, Barry stated he did not have any anger and was not aware of his outbursts with his wife. This confirmed that he was indeed dissociated and disconnected when his anger surfaced. As we explored further, we discovered that Barry's mom had been very critical of him throughout his childhood. Nothing he did or achieved seemed good enough. Barry also felt alone and ignored and learned how to keep a low profile and be with himself. Because they lived in the suburbs, he was dependent on his mom for driving him to things. He often wanted to participate in a sporting or social event, but stayed home alone because his mom would not take him.

As we began to get in touch with his anger toward his

mother, it intensified, and rage began to surface. I asked Barry if there were an animal associated with that rage, what would it be? Without hesitation, he said, "A bear!" and then quickly asked if we should kill it. I explained that the bear was a part of him and that we needed to work with it. Barry saw how the bear was there to protect his inner child especially when he felt his wife was criticizing him in a similar way as his mother had. He also realized that his bear was very powerful, and he did not mean to direct such a strong force toward his wife.

In the next few weeks, his inner child was able to complete and express his anger issues virtually to his mom, and he became more present and kind toward his wife. Part of his daily routine was to check in with his bear, which now became a power animal and companion for his inner child. The bear seemed content, often walking through the woods and eating berries. His inner child now looked to his more evolved adult part to screen situations that could potentially push his buttons, and he felt safe knowing his bear was there for him in case of emergency.

Creating a safe time and place for your inner children to express their emotions is also important. Of course one obvious place may be with your therapist. If you don't have a therapist or you'd like a homework assignment, you can write a letter from the voice of your inner child to whoever needs to hear it. For example, you may have a sad, inner child who needs to express his or her disappointment to a parent. Do your best to let this child write from the sad part's voice without censoring or adding other parts. Each child/emotion needs to fully express. You can also choose to let that part draw, paint or use another art medium to express.

For some of you speaking or writing may not do the trick. You may need or want more of a physical release. For the sad part, that may mean making time to cry. For an angry inner child you can make time to do some exercise with the intention of releasing your anger. Perhaps you can use music and beat a drum or dance to let it out. Acupuncture and other alternative treatments provide ways to help your inner children and emotions release and balance themselves. Sometimes this can happen without you even being consciously aware of what happened to your inner child. This is one of the reasons I became an acupuncturist. I wanted to find a way to help those who had trouble expressing verbally heal on the physical, mental, emotional and spiritual levels.

Reflections

Now think about what kinds of things push your buttons and what emotions they bring out.

- What are your reflex feelings, emotions, and reactions? Do you feel angry and want to punch a wall? Do you feel hurt, sad, and want to cry?
- Who is best at pushing your buttons? Is it your mom, dad, brother, sister, friend, partner?

Do your best to pause whenever a button is pushed, so you can choose how to act in the moment and not just react reflexively. Take time to think about the source of the button and the reaction of your inner child. Sometimes, those parts will feel strongly about their purpose and initially will not want to change. However, once you identify the age of that part, you can use logic and your virtues, like compassion and wisdom, to help that part change to a more age-appropriate behavior.

Understanding and accepting your animal instincts can help you use them more consciously and transform them to a more enlightened life.

CHAPTER 5

Look What I Can Do!

Around age five, we begin getting exposed to more people and topics as we begin school. Do you remember what kind of things you were interested in? Did you like sports, music, art, science, language, math, reading, writing, or anything else? Perhaps you liked everything. Or maybe there were a few things that you had an affinity for and seemed to be a natural doing.

From ages five to eight, whatever you're passionate

about is a hint to what your inner purpose and future skills might be. You are relatively fearless and present as you express yourself. Your imagination is strong, and you may be very creative. You may like to get dressed up and sing into a brush, pretending it is a microphone as you perform for your family. You may turn a towel into a cape and be a superhero showing off your abilities. Or, maybe you are creative in some other way, drawing pictures or building things.

One of my cousins is a role model for many as she is someone who never stopped following her Heart. From a young age, she sang in a band and was a visual artist. I remember her cool, red-leather motorcycle jacket and accompanying her to paint supply stores. She merged her passion for visual arts with her education and her career and has been teaching art for over 30 years. Everyone who meets her or works with her feels her passion and the love that emanates from her Heart.

Whatever your dreams and imagination can see connect with your Heart energy. As mentioned earlier, your Heart is your Ruler, but it is also the part of you that connects with your passion and your environment. It is the source that connects you to your Kidneys, which hold your blueprint of who you are. It also connects you with heaven's energy, which connects to your Higher Self and your potential. All the other organs and parts of you are responsible for different duties but ultimately fall under the rule of the Heart.

> When all of your parts work in harmony and support the Heart, your path in life becomes clearer.

When all of your parts work in harmony and support the Heart, your path in life becomes clearer. Following your Heart typically translates to long-term happiness.

Now think about something you really liked doing or that you were really good at as a young child. Often at this age, we love to show off, especially if we are getting positive feedback. Did your parents, teachers, and caregivers reinforce what you were doing? Or were you shut down for some reason? Did you find yourself trying to please your caregivers, or were you simply expressing your passions? At this young age, the reactions of our parents, teachers, caregivers, and peers can get imprinted into our subconscious.

Maybe as a boy you were good at sports, and your parents reinforced this. Perhaps you played on teams and won championships, or you competed individually and won medals. Being an athlete was both natural and reinforced by your environment. Now, imagine a young girl whose father wanted an athletic boy. The young girl does her best to be athletic to please her father. However, her father feels she should focus her energy on something else more feminine and does not reinforce her athletic attempts. Conversely, the father may be happy his girl is interested in sports and does not mind that she is considered to be a tomboy by others.

You can see how a child's interests and passions interact with and how they are received or reinforced by the environment. An only child expressing his or her passion may be treated differently than a child who has to compete and be compared to brothers and sisters. For example, the parents of an only child may pay particular attention to what their child is interested in and reinforce it. Or they may impose what they think is important onto the child. In the case of my cousin, her parents always encouraged her to follow her Heart.

If you grew up with brothers and sisters, you might have felt that you were compared to them or felt competitive with them. Imagine your older sister is a talented dancer, and she receives a lot of positive attention both at home and at school. You are more interested in science and animals, and perhaps your body is a little overweight and is less toned than your sister's. For some of you, this may not be a problem. However, some of you may develop negative emotions depending on how you are treated.

When I was young, I loved to move, had a need for speed, and had trouble sitting still. I was good at school and did well in all subjects. I did not consider myself the best at any one thing, but I worked hard and finished all my homework on Friday so I could play hard all weekend. Struggling with joint problems from a young age made it difficult at times to fully express my Heart through movement and sports. The older kids in the neighborhood always cheered me on as I performed stunts on my tricycle, trying to emulate Evel Knievel.

However, I knew at a young age that I wanted to be a scientist, a musician, and a martial arts instructor and saw Mr. Spock from *Star Trek*, Jimi Hendrix, and Bruce Lee as models. I also looked for models in my family and neighborhood. My family reinforced my interests in science, music, and martial arts and gave me toys/tools/instruments, extra classes and lessons in what interested me. I loved running, skateboarding, and playing team sports, basketball being my favorite. Although I played basketball about four hours a day, I knew being short for my age and my joint problems would keep me from becoming a professional athlete.

As I got older, I considered many different possible careers based on my many talents and passions. I was leaning toward becoming a scientist and having music and martial arts as hobbies. At age 13, my parents enrolled me in a gifted youth program at a college in New York City. There, I took courses on nuclear energy and laser theory. My uncle, who was an engineer and vice president of operations at an electrical company, reinforced my interest in energy and science and provided me with many tools and information to help guide me.

It would take very traumatic accidents to eventually guide me in the direction that coincided with my Heart and my whole Inner Kingdom. There were many signs that I did not understand that were meant to guide me into the helping professions. The practical part of me was interested more with working with energy and physics and less with people. However, helping people feel better both by touch and listening was natural for me. My traumas and experiences soon pushed me into learning to find the positive in the negative and how this can help you tune into your life's purpose.

 You are probably very familiar with the T'ai Chi symbol of Yin and Yang. The white/yang/ positive side has a small black/yin/negative circle within it and the black/yin/negative side has a small white/yang/positive circle within it. The meanings behind this symbol explain much of our daily life and reality. One idea is that there is always a little negative in the positive and always a little positive in the negative. Many of you may have no problem finding the negative in the positive, but may find it harder to find the positive in the negative.

You must be patient, persistent and have great faith that the burdens you carry will eventually lead to blessings. This will connect you to your higher purpose in life and can help you realize that there is always positive in the negative. Although I suffered unimaginable pain daily for many years, God or the universe always sent signs of hope and direction. Once I began to open my mind and accept more parts of myself, my life's purpose became clearer. After not being able to walk independently for over seven years, and told by some of the top doctors I would never walk without some aid ever again, I got in touch with my

> You must be patient, persistent and have great faith that the burdens you carry will eventually lead to blessings. This will connect you to your higher purpose in life can help you realize that there is always positive in the negative.

Heart and learned ways to heal myself with the best methods from East and West. I began to do things the doctors deemed impossible, and now as an adult I get to say, "Look what I can do!"

Reflections

What kinds of things you were interested in or good at between the ages of five and eight?

- What did you want to be when you grew up?
- Did you see yourself as a leader, a performer, an athlete, or some kind of superhero?
- Were there any adults, real or fictional, who you modeled yourself after?
- Was there someone you looked up to and thought, "I'd like to be like that person"?
- How did everyone in your environment react to your interests/passions?
- How did that affect you in terms of pursuing your interests?

In the next chapter, we explore how and why we don't always follow our Hearts.

LATE SPRING

CHAPTER 6

_____

There Is No Santa

Up till now, your Heart has been doing its best to express itself and relate to the environment. At around age nine, you begin to develop a critical mind. It is a time where you reflect on your life thus far. You begin to try to make sense of your life and develop mental constructs to help organize your thoughts and feelings. You consider how you were treated and what it all means. You begin to question things that you once took for granted. Parts like your Liver and your Lungs may get stronger as they analyze the worth of the Heart. Your feelings of self-worth and your self-esteem get more defined. You start using logic and reasoning along with rationalization to explain some of the things that might have happened to you that were not in line with your Heart.

In the United States and some other parts of the world, many children—including you— get excited thinking about getting gifts for Christmas. As Christmas approaches, however, you begin to worry about whether you were naughty or nice. You make your Wish List and hope Santa gives you what you want. As a younger child, you don't think twice and can't wait to see what gifts you get. But as you get older, you may begin to question whether Santa Claus really exists. You may have heard from a classmate that he does not exist. Or maybe you recognized your relative dressed up as Santa.

For me, I noticed the handwriting on the gifts from Santa looked similar to the handwriting from the gifts from my mother. I began to wonder how Santa Claus got into our apartment. We had no chimney, and the windows and doors were locked and secure. I even remember trying to stay up one Christmas Eve to see if I could hear

Santa coming into the apartment. Needless to say, it did not take me long to realize there is no Santa.

For those of you who do not celebrate Christmas, see if you can remember something you believed as a young child but began to question around age nine. At this time, you continue to have more interaction with your peers and the adults outside of your family. You also begin to have a better understanding of what is considered right and what is considered wrong. Your Heart may still be looking for unconditional love, but as your critical mind develops, it may form judgments and place conditions on love and emotions.

For example, if you were told you were fat when you were younger, this may have gotten imprinted as something negative. You may then believe you need to starve yourself or purge after eating to become thin and loved. Or, perhaps like others, food becomes a reward or a way to make you feel better when you are sad or upset. How many times were you or someone you know offered something sweet, like chocolate for good behavior or to help you feel better? What are some of your comfort foods?

I choose food as an example because for many of us, dinnertime is when the whole family is together. It is also

the time when you were a child where you may have gotten scolded or praised for something like your grades or
behavior at school or at home. These judgments not only
affect your self-esteem, but also may now be associated
with eating and certain foods. If you had many traumas
as a child or were mistreated in some ways, your broken
Heart may go into hiding and have difficulty navigating
your life.

The Liver may take over to guide you, much like a military coup. As the General and as the organ connected to
anger, the Liver may be angry at the Heart and begin leading you. The General may remember what your Heart was
interested in and choose a path that is related in some way.
However, the Liver may look to your parents, especially
the father energy, to figure out the best way to go.

For example, let's say you loved art and demonstrated
skills as a painter when you were younger, but your Heart
went into hiding in the tower after being humiliated by a
family member. The Liver, being practical, may take over
so you finish school and get a job. Years later, you find
yourself working in a textile design firm. The Heart, seeing things are stable, comes out, and you begin painting at
home in private. A coworker drops by one day and notices

the paintings on the wall and is extremely impressed. She asks where did they come from and says they should be in a gallery. You shyly say they were your creations and dismiss the compliment.

If the Liver takes on the mind of a critical father, putting down the Heart for being artsy, it may take a more practical path completely unrelated to the Heart's desires. For example, if your father says you should work in the family business or become a doctor or a lawyer, you may just push yourself and follow that path. Perhaps your Lung energy takes the lead and you get a job that requires organizational skills and stands for righteousness. Or maybe your Spleen energy leads you to working as a teacher or in the helping/healing professions. You may be very competent at your job and even appreciate its worth to you and others. However, if it is not aligned with your Heart, there may always be an underlying feeling of dissatisfaction. You may have mixed feelings about yourself and the choices you make. (In a future chapter, we see how this can manifest for you later in life.)

Usually, you feel bad when you do or say something that goes against what you think you "should" have done or said. The "should" is usually related to what others think is right and may not align with your Heart. However, another part of you may have internalized this "should" based on what you learned as you developed your critical mind. Teasing out what comes from your Heart and what is imposed on you can be helpful in navigating life and finding your purpose. In any case, your inner child is usually under the age of eight and is your Inner Ruler, so it may not be the best idea to call it negative names. It has a way of pulling the rug out from under you when you think you are doing the right thing based on others' expectations.

> The "should" is usually related to what others think is right and may not align with your Heart.

I have worked with many patients with chronic conditions who were not getting better with conventional treatments. Many of them were quite accomplished in their fields and chose careers encouraged by their fathers. Often, these fathers were critical of their children's passions, saying they were not practical and that they should be lawyers or doctors, for example.

In many instances, we tend to *throw out the baby with the bath water.* Your critical parts may transfer your negative feelings of your parents to your inner child. When this happens, you may take an extreme stance and not see the skills or positive attributes of the part of you that you despise.

I have had many patients who grew up in a household with an abusive, alcoholic father. The little girl just wants daddy to love her. Before the age of nine, she can't seem to do anything to please her father and gets confused by his unpredictable reactions. After the age of nine, she may appear needy and manipulative not only by others, but she may also have her own critical part that agrees with this observation. She may find ways to criticize or even punish herself for feeling needy, as she gets older.

Finding the positive in the negative can help you gain access to the power of this part of you. When you get in touch with this younger part of your Heart, you may be able to see how highly developed your observation skills are. Having walked on eggshells your whole childhood has now made you really good at interpreting subtle body language, tone, inflection, and reading people in general.

This idea of finding the positive in the negative can be applied in many circumstances when working with your inner child. Your inner critical part may have picked up the habit of telling your inner child, don't do this or that, or you can't do or achieve that. Your mind, especially that of your inner child, does not have a picture for "not". If I told you to think about anything you like, except *don't* think of an elephant. See what happens? The same thing happens when you tell a child don't hit your sister, don't jump on the bed, don't run.... Children at times will not only continue doing the things you don't want them to do, but they may increase or magnify the behavior. Finding a positive way to express what you want could be, play nice with your sister, come down from the bed, walk slowly....

Using positive phrasing is also important when you want to change your behavior or manifest something in your life. Instead of telling yourself not to eat that cake, tell yourself to have some tea. Instead of saying, I don't want an abusive partner; you can say I want someone who treats me with kindness and respect. How about, I can't exercise today, I'm too tired; even though I'm tired, I can do this one simple exercise today.

Reflections

- How does your critical mind speak to your inner child? (Imagine you did something wrong or made a mistake.)

- What are the first words you call yourself? Are you quick to call yourself *stupid? Idiot? Dummy?* (Sometimes, you may use stronger words when we are angry or disappointed in yourself in some way.)

- Where did the words come from? Are they the same things your father, mother, or sibling called you?

- What are some of the positive traits/qualities of the parts you may not like about yourself?

- What are some of your negative thoughts and phrasing that you can change to positive?

EARLY SUMMER

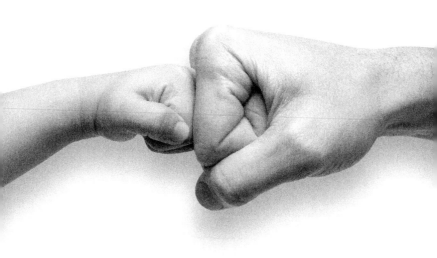

CHAPTER 7

The Force Is Strong

Around age 13, you enter the summer stage of your life; you must deal with puberty and the other challenges you face in your teenage years. For girls, this is usually a bit earlier. Your growth and body changes may feel awkward and may bring unwanted attention to yourself. Your emotions and sexual energy become strong, and you may be challenged trying to control them. It is a time where you are becoming even more independent.

Some cultures have rituals at this time as a rite of passage to acknowledge their children are transitioning into becoming adults. Many Native American tribes practice the rite of Vision Quests. The specifics of the ritual vary depending on the tribe and whether it is a boy or a girl who is transitioning into adulthood. The child spends time away from the tribe as he/she connects with the spirit world. Upon return, the transition into adulthood is celebrated and they move forward to pursue their life's journey. In the Jewish religion, a boy or girl become a Bar or Bat Mitzvah, respectively, and are accountable for their actions which includes a moral responsibility and the practice of their religion.

As a teenager, you begin to further define your identity and connect with some of the things that bring you joy, like music, art, sports, dance, and social events. Your increased energy may make you feel more powerful and invincible. For some of you, a rebel may be born to deal with your situation at home or school. You may go against your parents' wishes and stay out late, or you may cut school or act out in some other way.

Connecting with your peers, fitting in with different crowds, and having an increased social life outside of school may pose new challenges for you, the teenager. The risk-taker part of you may get involved in situations like dating, trying drugs and alcohol, and other extra-curricular activities both legal and illegal. Peer pressure usually becomes more intense during the teenage years, and setting self-boundaries based on your self-esteem and your beliefs are necessary. Different types of bullying also become more intense as groups form based on looks, intelligence, athleticism, money, race, ethnicity, sexuality, and social norms of the times. Riding the waves of your teenage years can be both exhilarating and scary at the same time.

As a teenager, your Kidney energy and sexual energy grow stronger, and so does your Inner Philosopher. The emotions connected to the Kidneys are fear and fright. The Kidneys are also connected to your willpower, wisdom, and the virtue of gentleness. The color associated with the Kidney is black, representing the depths of the ocean, where the light of the sun cannot reach. How many teenagers do you know who wear mostly black? For many teenagers—perhaps for you—the Inner Philosopher is seeking truth, wisdom, and the information of what your destiny will be. Although your teenage years may have been tumultuous in many ways, certain seeds from your birth have sprouted while others are planted for your future.

Now take a moment and check in to see if one of your inner children is a teenager. Do you have a rebel inside you? What about a risk taker or a competitor? Do you have hobbies or desires that were started or became strong during your teenage years? Being a parent to your inner teen can be just as challenging as your actual teenage child. As with all your inner children you need to help that part express while setting appropriate boundaries.

Because I was seriously injured at the age of 16 playing soccer and told at 17 that I would never walk independently again, I decided to revisit many of my study and career plans. Although it took many years before I was able to heal myself and prove the doctors wrong, I have always had to be mindful of my risk taking. My inner 15-year-old athlete and my 17-year-old inner rebel both have the need for speed. Driving a car was the quick fix to being able to run again. However, my inner risk taker loves riding a bike and a skateboard even more. Occasionally, I do not set the appropriate boundaries with that part of myself and am painfully reminded of my body's limitations and past injury history. One hopes that wisdom grows with age.

Having a *philosophy* (Greek for "love of wisdom") can give you a framework for understanding knowledge, values, logic, reasoning, metaphysics, and existence. As a teenager, I had formed my own thoughts about life and existence. When I began my formal study of philosophy in college, I noticed many of my thoughts coincided with Taoist and Buddhist philosophy as well as several ancient Greek and other later Western philosophers. As I later traveled throughout the East, I opened my mind further, was given hope, and saw how important and useful philosophy could be in helping to cope with many of life's challenges.

Throughout your life, you may be faced with challenges and even contemplate killing yourself. In my late teens, I was devastated at the thought of never being able to do the things that I loved and wondered if I should go on living. My Inner Ruler contemplated suicide and enlisted all my parts to think of the most effective and least messy ways to end my life. While I knew the act of suicide could be considered extremely selfish, I wanted to be considerate to those who would have to deal with my body. Several of my friends sensed my depression and anger and tried to help me see that there were many worthy parts of myself and that I was not only an athlete. They pointed out many of my qualities, like my sense of humor, but the hurt Inner Ruler had trouble receiving any compliments.

At the same time that I was struggling with severe and constant pain and contemplating existence, several people who I barely knew shared with me that they wanted to kill themselves, too. I found myself counseling them and finding reasons for them to live. I did not appreciate that these incidents perhaps were reflections from the universe to help me find my own reasons for living. I remember the first time I was faced with someone pouring out his soul to me and how intense it was.

I was 17, and it was the summer before I went away to college. I had stepped out to get dinner for my little brother and me. As I was returning home, I bumped into a man who I had spoken to once in the local deli a few months earlier. He was using a cane at the time and had made a comment that I was young to be walking with a cane. I explained that I was told I would need at least a cane for the rest of my life and that surgery did not seem like a viable option, but I would wait and see. He told me that he had a minor sprain and would not need his cane long and wished me luck. For the weeks that followed, I saw him almost daily at a local bar from where he waved to me as I passed on my way to the train.

Then on that summer day, he stood outside the deli as I approached and began calling to me. He was about 6'3" and at least 230 lbs. At the time, I was about 5'8" and 130 lbs. We stood facing each other as he began ranting about different things. I could see he was drunk and did my best to calmly listen as I held the McDonald's bag in my left hand and my deceased grandmother's cane in my right. I mention the cane because it was before I had my own extensive cane collection. I was concerned that the food was getting cold and that my brother was hungry and probably wondering where I was.

As I proceeded to walk, he blocked my path and began to tell me he dreamt about me and had sexual fantasies about me. I was taken aback and tightened my grip on my cane as my martial arts part assessed the situation. He began to cry and told me that his dog just died and that he was going to go home and jump off the roof of his apartment building. Keeping my martial part on hand, a curious and compassionate part came forward, as I could feel his torture and his pain. He then told me that as a gay, alcoholic, Irish Catholic he felt alone and trapped with no family support.

I began exploring his family situation with him and looked for anything that could help. He stated that no one knew he was gay and that they would not accept him. I asked if there were anyone in his family that he felt loved him and that would still love him, even if they knew. He said he had a young niece and nephew whom he loved and that they loved him. I did my best to help him see how they would be hurt if they lost him. It seemed to shift his suicidal thoughts, but I still felt uneasy walking away. I then asked him if he remembered that I might get surgery, and he said of course. I explained that I did not know when I was going to get the surgery, but I had no one to be there for me in the hospital.

He quickly affirmed that he would be there for me and for me not to worry. I repeated that I did not know when I would be in the hospital and that I was counting on him to be there. He again assured me not to worry and that he would be there as he started crying again. He then firmly hugged me as he cried and reassured me. My martial part stepped aside, realizing this guy was a giant teddy bear who could probably kick my butt, and I received the hug. When he let go, I started to walk home and continued telling him that I would call on him when

I needed him. He waved and continued to reassure me as I walked away.

A few days later, the bar where he sat daily closed, and I had no idea what happened to him. Then, many months later, I had returned from college to visit for a weekend. As I was driving in the neighborhood with a friend, I saw the man walking with whom I assumed to be his niece and nephew. They were all smiling as they walked around one of the shopping and restaurant areas in the 'hood. I was so excited to see him looking happy and I told my friend the story. I decided not to stop and keep driving, learning from Zen Buddhism to leave no trace.

Having a philosophy that helps us understand life's challenges can often give us some relief and hope. Over the years as I contemplated suicide, I had many experiences in which I gained more insights and was able to help many others and myself when feeling hopeless. One thing I realized is that our lives are relatively short anyway, so we might as well do our best to live them out and see what happens.

> Having a philosophy that helps us understand life's challenges can often give us some relief and hope.

When I worked on a rehabilitation medicine ward in a hospital in New York City, my supervisors helped me see that I could choose to *survive* or I could choose to *live* life. The famous Yin/Yang symbol helped me see that everything was relative and that there was always a little bad in the good and a little good in the bad. We had the choice of how to focus our minds and finding the positive in the negative. When you are in a dark place, it can be difficult to see any light at the end of the tunnel. However, knowing that nothing is constant except transiency helps me ride the waves of life. Whatever may be causing the storm inside you will pass. It is up to you to learn from your experiences and harness your inner teenager's power to get you through. The force is strong with this one.

Reflections

Your upbringing, your earlier experiences, and how you have perceived them will contribute to how your teenager develops.

- How grounded did you feel as a teenager?
- What tools did you have that were helpful, and what did you rebel against?
- Did you take risks to shine, or did your Heart continue to hide and lay low?
- Did you feel supported by your caretakers, or were you still in survival mode?
- Did you experience any traumas or significant insults that may have changed the course of your life in some way?

LATE SUMMER

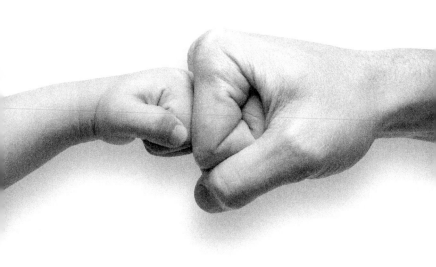

CHAPTER 8

Making Sense of It All

Being in our 20's is like the summer solstice giving us a chance to shine brightly. We continue transitioning to being more independent and continue to explore life. For some of us, it is a time to further our studies. For others, we begin working or start a family; and for some, it is a time to travel and wander about enjoying our youth and vitality. As we approach age 29, there is a planetary transit known as your "Saturn return." Some of you may be familiar with this astrological transition or may want to be if you are reading this and you are around that age.

As you enter into your 30's, there may be a feeling that you really have to face becoming an adult and being responsible for your life. I see this time similar to age nine, in that it is a time when you look back and reflect on your life thus far. It is a time to "check in" and see if you have been following your Heart/Ruler. What tools/skills do you have to survive on your own and live as an adult? Have you chosen your career path based on your Heart, or was one chosen for you? If for whatever reason you are not on your Heart's path or fulfilling your inner purpose, this is a time when the universe may slap you in some way to get your attention. If, because of traumas or other issues, your Inner Ruler is still an injured child, you may not have seen the signs that the universe reflected along the way. Sometimes, we find our path through our traumas; however, we need to have some part of us that can see the signs to help the Heart.

> Sometimes, we find our path through our traumas; however, we need to have some part of us that can see the signs to help the Heart.

For me, the universe sent many signs before it did more than slap me. By the time I was 28, I felt relatively confident that I was well on my life's path helping people heal themselves from physical and emotional traumas, and empowering people to reach their full potential. I had over 10 years of clinical experience working with severe cases on locked psychiatric wards. I also had experience working with injured athletes, people with developmental disabilities, spinal cord injuries, head trauma, stroke, and other life-changing events.

In addition, I had a successful private hypnotherapy practice and was studying and teaching Asian methods of healing and self-defense. My passion for T'ai Chi and martial arts led me to go to China, and my injuries led me to the study of acupuncture, herbs, tui na massage/acupressure, qigong, and other healing arts. I felt happy that I not only healed myself against all odds, but that I was also making a difference in people's lives. I was content with my Western work at the hospital by day and my Eastern work by night. My acupuncturist, with whom I apprenticed, often encouraged me to become a licensed acupuncturist, saying it was what my Heart wanted to do. My Liver/General did not see it as a realistic or practical way of making a living, so it continued to be more of a hobby and self-healing tool. After seven years of not being able to walk, I was happy to be not only walking again, but also doing things like jumping and kicking. Although I still had physical challenges, I steadily walked without any cane or aids for three years.

At the age of 28, on my third trip to Asia, I traveled to India, Nepal, and Tibet. A friend with whom I taught meditation in New York City organized the trip. He told me when we first met a few years earlier that I was a teacher and a healer. I told him I was a counselor and that I taught people about themselves and hoped they healed. He said, "No, you are an acupuncturist and teach a movement art that is important to you." I just figured he tuned into my past trips to China and my T'ai Chi practice.

After traveling to India, Nepal, and Tibet, we returned to Nepal via Tibet. A problem at the border delayed us, and our driver drove recklessly to get us to the airport. The driver would not listen to our pleas to be more careful and eventually crashed, leaving us to fend for ourselves. I suffered eight serious injuries and was in a wheelchair for months, and once again was told that it was unlikely I would walk independently again. All this to say, that I believe it was the universe's way of saying you are close but you are not fully on your life's path. This accident led to many changes in my life, but the most important may have been not having enough energy to lead the double work life I was living. It forced me to make a choice, and my Heart seemed clear about my choice to go back to school and become a licensed acupuncturist.

For most of us, our wounded inner child is primarily our Heart/Ruler. As mentioned earlier, another part of you, like the Liver/General or the Lungs/High Minister, may have taken over and has been driving the bus. The Heart wants to heal and become a Great Ruler, but may not have the tools to do so. For instance, imagine you felt you were not good enough, smart enough, or "whatever" enough as a child and struggled to feel love and acceptance from your parents. At the same time, your father may have been abusive toward your mother, and you felt helpless not being able to come to her aid.

Your Heart is wounded, and your Inner Ruler struggles with what to do. Your Liver/General pushes you to do well in school, and your Lungs/High Minister decide you should be a lawyer to fight for justice. These parts work together hoping to get recognized and provide some safety in the household. However, no matter how high your grades or how prestigious your schools, your parents fail to recognize your accomplishments or give the Heart the love and acceptance it yearns for. You continue to work hard and be disciplined to no avail and are left feeling a deep sadness. Your Heart decides you want to find a partner who appreciates you and becomes open to finding people to help you heal and explore a new career. (We address what to do in these situations more in the next chapter.)

If you have been following your Heart into your 20's in a more balanced way, your Saturn return may be relatively smooth. Instead of having some life-changing trauma to get your attention, the Universe may support you at this time by giving you the push you need to continue further on your path.

For example, let's say you knew as a child you wanted to be a doctor and help people. You did well in school and all of your parts growing up were in line with your Heart's desires. You were able to have fun while having the discipline to study and excel. Your practice is going well, and as you go through your Saturn return, you have an opportunity to be involved in some research that will not only help your career, but will also help many more people than you imagined. This may be a way the Universe is reinforcing that you are on your path.

The late-summer phase of life is a good time to assess your strengths and weaknesses and see what challenges, if any, you are having living on your own.

Reflections

- Are you meeting the expectations of your parents, friends, teachers, religion, or culture?

- Are those expectations more like what you "should" be doing versus what your Heart wants to do? What healing do your inner children need?

- Do you feel confident in your survival tools?

- What are your major concerns, if any, of becoming more of an adult?

FALL / AUTUMN

CHAPTER 9

Leave No Child Behind

L ate summer and the fall seasons of life bring us into our 40's and 50's. If you have been giving your power away throughout your life and have been on autopilot not delegated by your Heart, this change in season can be tougher than your previous challenges. Once again, it is a time to reflect and make a choice if you are willing to take 100% responsibility for your life. This includes your choices affecting your health, relationships, emotions, career, and the world around you.

Usually, this time in your life is more stable on the outside but may not be on the inside. Because you are no longer in survival mode, any inner children that were hiding or pushed down may now feel safe to come out. You may experience this by having strong emotional feelings that don't clearly correspond with your current life. You could begin feeling very sad and depressed for no apparent reason.

On the surface, you have everything you thought you wanted in life—a good job, a great family, a wonderful home, and financial stability. Now all of a sudden, you find yourself overreacting emotionally to your partner, children, or someone close to you. Perhaps you are confronted with a serious health problem that has no easily identifiable cause or realize you have had some chronic pain that nothing doctors offer seems to help. Or maybe you keep getting close to meeting a goal and some part of you pulls the rug out from under you. Some of this may have happened in earlier adulthood, but it gets revisited or more intense as we get older. These inner children have wanted to heal for decades.

All of the above may have some environmental factors, but oftentimes it is the way your wounded inner children are trying to get your attention. Even seemingly environmental factors can have their roots in our incomplete emotions and need to heal. Something as common as a sprained ankle may have underlying causes that contributed to the injury.

Imagine you just had an argument with your partner, and you were feeling sad and unsupported. Being upset and distracted, you did not pay attention to the crack in the sidewalk and end up spraining your ankle. Although you may not have this insight as you limp around for a week, the injury and pain you are experiencing may be connected to a wounded inner child who did not feel support from your mother.

I know for some of you this may sound far-fetched, but I have seen both acute and chronic pain conditions resolve instantly once the root causes were identified emotionally and physically. The inner child is given a safe place to heal the old wound and given assurance and hope from your more evolved parts. These evolved parts are committed to helping you move forward in harmony. I can give many examples that continue to amaze me even after all these years. One of my specialties has been to help people connect their physical pain or illness to the related emotions, discover the inner wounded children, and finally heal and feel free.

Although much of my work has helped people heal from unthinkable abuse and neglect, sometimes I am surprised when an ailment or pain issue is connected to a one-time incident in which an authority figure like a teacher or doctor says something that hurts the Heart. In chapter 4, I wrote about how things are imprinted into your subconscious from birth to around age eight. While this time period sets certain survival tools in place, words from an authority figure or experiencing an unforeseen trauma like a bad car accident can imprint into the subconscious at any age.

There are many cases that I will never forget, but here are two that I love sharing because they illustrate both the East and the West in understanding and treating people.

First, a tall, dark, handsome man came into my office complaining of lower back pain that he has had for 20 years. As I conducted the intake, I noticed that he had amazing pulses, a normal tongue, and nothing I could put my finger on to illustrate a reason for the back pain. He told me that he never had an accident or any trauma to his back. Doctors had performed extensive medical tests that came out normal. Odd, I thought to myself, no herniated discs, no injuries, just chronic back pain for 20 years. I realized that in these cases the pain is caused by stuck energy involving the Liver energy and sometimes has not manifested in a physical way that can be seen by X-rays and MRIs. After two acupuncture treatments, he felt some relief lasting for about one week. I knew he was moving out of the country to start a business and that we would only have one or two more sessions before he left. I asked if he was open to exploring any emotional connections to his pain.

He said he was open to anything that might help. I now call this part of treatment "going down the rabbit hole." It was our third session and down the hole we went. He identified that the emotion, anger, was connected to the back pain. He saw it as a large red ball. As we continued, he recalled that at age 11 he had tried out for the choir. The choir teacher told him he couldn't sing and rejected him. At first I thought, the choir teacher? Really? Could that be the cause of 20 years of back pain? Usually going down the rabbit hole reveals something more objectively traumatic. But doing my best not to judge, I followed along and guided him and his inner child. Part of the process was allowing his inner child to confront the teacher. In order for his inner child to feel safe, his adult self accompanied him in the visualization. The child proceeded to call the teacher a jerk, tell him he was wrong and that he could sing. His angry inner child continued and got to say everything that he could not at the time he was 11, and was protected by his adult self in the process. Once complete, there was a process of helping the child feel more whole and allow forgiveness as a way of letting go. The adult self then assured the child that he was talented and could safely express himself freely.

As we continued through the mind-body steps of healing and completing, he checked in with his lower back. A part of me was expecting to go back further in time to something more traumatic, but he said things were clear and he no longer felt the pain. In most cases, the large red ball may change to something smaller with a different color and different feeling. This would indicate we made progress but did not reach the root. He got up and moved around in different positions, checking to see if he could feel the pain. He seemed as surprised as I was. I told him we could squeeze in one more session if the pain came back before he left, and I wished him good luck on his new venture. He called to say he did not need the additional treatment. About a year later, his wife came to me for treatment. She told me that her husband's back pain never returned. He told her that sometimes it got tight when he was stressed, but it was easily relieved with yoga and stretching.

The second case was a 68-year-old woman who just returned with her husband from visiting their son in South America. They stopped in New York to see their daughter before returning home to California. Unfortunately, her lungs had filled with fluid, and she was unable to fly home. She was receiving respiratory therapy three days a week at a local hospital, and her daughter recommended she see me.

She was immediately open to the mind-body connection and *going down the rabbit hole*. She explained that her husband and son have had a strained relationship, and she had hoped the visit would resolve some of their past difficulties. Instead, they fought more, and the trip ended on a negative note. She felt very sad and held back her tears. She remained silent the whole trip back not to further upset her husband. In Chinese medicine, sadness and grief are associated with the lungs, so what she said made sense to me.

As we went down the rabbit hole, she remembered when she was 11 that she had her tonsils removed. She recalled crying after the surgery, trying to eat ice cream in her hospital bed. Her doctor entered the room and said, "Stop crying, you cry baby!" She immediately stopped crying and realized she has had difficulty crying and expressing her sadness her whole life. She felt intimidated speaking her truth to the doctor and told other stories until we ran out of time. I asked where she would like to put the doctor so we could continue the next session, and her inner child quickly responded, "In the washing machine!"

Again, not judging, we put him in the washing machine until the next visit. In her next visit, she spoke about some issues with her daughter that were more pressing at the moment. I listened and continued my meditative acupressure process as she lay with the acupuncture needles inserted. She then screamed out, "Oh no!" I nearly jumped off my stool as I quickly scanned her body to see if something had happened with the needles. I asked if she was okay, and she said, "Oh no; we left the doctor in the dryer." I smiled to myself and told her it was okay, and we could take him out now. I guess she must have put him in the dryer sometime between sessions. She told me the doctor had shrunk to about 11 inches. She then proceeded to say everything she couldn't before and allowed herself to cry. Now that he had shrunk, she felt safe and empowered to speak her truth. That week, her lungs completely cleared much to the surprise of the hospital staff, and she was on a plane back home.

In both cases, physical manifestations correlated to ancient Chinese medicine theory and were resolved with combining Eastern and Western methods. Also in both cases, the insults happened at 11 years old and were imprinted by authority figures. As I stated earlier, these are relatively rare cases in that there were not earlier traumas associated with their symptoms. Oftentimes, there are multiple traumas throughout childhood and young adulthood that are associated with a group of symptoms. Symptoms improve when you clear the later traumas first, but some remain until you find the root. However, if you find the root first, the later traumas are usually healed automatically.

The autumn or fall season is also sometimes regarded as the "midlife crisis," the "empty-nest syndrome" for those with older children, or simply the "change of life" because of natural hormonal changes. Your reactions to this time in your life will give you clues as to any inner children that were left behind and are ready to come forward and heal. Instead of feeling bad about yourself, you can see your emotional reactions as opportunities to heal.

Some of you who may have married at a young age and worked to support your family, may feel like you missed out on certain parts of your life. You may now have the money and stability to satisfy some of what your inner children had wanted to do decades ago. Some of you may have been able to let your inner children come out as you played with your actual children and have found a nice balance. There are many variations of family from single parents on their own to multigenerational extended families. You may be single at this stage and continue to be busy working. In whatever way it plays out, it is a time to open and connect to your Heart, especially if one of your more practical parts, like the Liver, has been guiding you thus far.

Or maybe you spent the last 20 years or so being a super mom, and now your child is going away to start a life in a different city. Part of you wants another child but may settle for a dog or two. As you struggle with your perceived loss, your Heart now has a chance to do something she wants to do. Perhaps you had a career in mind or a subject you wanted to study that you put aside to raise your child/children. Now is your chance to give your Inner Queen the attention she deserves. It is a time to come into your power. You have both male (yang) and female (yin) energies inside you. Each of you needs to accept and find the balance of expression that is right for you.

Look at your relationships and others as reflections. Is there something you see in someone else that you don't like or wish you could change? Ask yourself, how does that something reflect in me? Is it similar to something in you that you don't know how to change,

> Look at your relationships and others as reflections.

or is it the extreme opposite of who you are or want to be? Oftentimes our wounded inner child struggles with not wanting to be like our parents. Sometimes in our relationships with our family, we find ourselves saying or doing things just like our parents even though we don't like or want to. Another possibility is that we are so afraid of being like our parents that we put a lot of energy in doing the extreme opposite. Oftentimes this means *throwing out the baby with the bath water*. In other words, we are trying so hard to be the opposite that we may overlook or not accept any of the positives are parents offered. One of my friends used to say, "God gives you friends to apologize for your family."

Getting in touch with your Heart and identifying the

ages, the emotions, and the behaviors of your wounded inner children are important steps toward healing. Also, appreciating the power of your Inner Ruler and getting the best help possible can truly transform your life. Listen to your body and your mind. Both physical and mental/emotional issues can often be linked to your Inner Ruler trying to get your attention. From the moment you are born, your body, mind, and spirit are always trying to heal. As an adult your inner child or Heart may choose people to try to help you work through things, but often gets stuck in a loop choosing people that cannot help you. Instead of getting angry or critical of that part of yourself that keeps making poor choices, understand that the inner child, your Ruler, is trying to heal.

Listen to your body and your mind.

Part of the problem is that the younger wounded part does not have the tools to make better choices or cope with the feelings. For example, if you were abused as a child by a parent who was an alcoholic, you may have not only felt hurt and confused, but at times you may have had to play more of an adult role. Part of your Heart may be attracted to someone with addiction problems and abusive tendencies in an attempt to heal the past relationship with your parent. You may try very hard to help your partner get treatment and therapy. You may also feel like you are the adult

> **From the moment you are born, your body, mind, and spirit are always trying to heal.**

in the relationship and start to resent that you cannot be vulnerable with your partner. Now once again you are left feeling hurt and confused. Sometimes this can become a pattern even if your adult parts know better. You may say I don't know why I keep picking this type of partner, I deserve better than this.

If you work on becoming more aware and healing that inner child, then you may see improvements in your partner choices. This can be a slow but steady process. For instance, you may pick someone who is not overtly addicted to a substance and is less abusive. Sometimes it hits like an epiphany and you take charge and full responsibility of your care. As your inner child begins to feel loved and safe, you can help your Heart make even better choices.

I worked with a young lady who we will call Jodie that had been physically and sexually abused as a child. Jodie had a child with someone she thought was the one. He was handsome, intelligent and strong. Unfortunately, he was also abusive physically and emotionally to her, to her three-year-old son and even to his elderly parents. Other than his parents, with whom they all lived, she did not have any outside support and was financially and otherwise dependent on them. Through the work, she became empowered and more capable of protecting herself and her child. She also became better at visualizing and getting what she wanted, but fell short when it came to choosing men. I asked her if she ever made a "checklist" of qualities she wanted in a man. Jodie said, "Of course" and began describing the ideal partner. I asked, "How old were you when you came up with this list?" and she replied, "13". Her description was that of a good-looking, teenage "bad boy". She basically described her child's father. We both realized that she needed to update her "checklist". Once she refined her checklist and added some of her more mature desires, she met someone who was kind and supportive. Jodie was able to break the negative pattern and moved on to a much better living situation.

I have worked with many women (and men) who were sexually and physically abused as children. Each case had its unique challenges and the abuse manifested differently for each of them as adults. For those of you that have personal and/or clinical experience with serious forms of abuse, you know how complex healing can be. The myriad of emotions and conflicting feelings often breaks the Heart into many inner children. Each one needs a safe space to heal.

Depending on your situation, you may need a team of different types of helpers to assist you in identifying and healing any broken pieces of your Heart. See if you can connect and listen to each part. How old is the wounded part crying out for help? Speak to that inner child and give an age-appropriate intervention. For example, if your inner wounded child is very young she or he may just need to hear that it's ok or you may just imagine hugging or holding the child. A slightly older inner child may need to hear that it was not his or her fault. Tell the child he or she did the best he or she could do given the situation. Let the child know that you will protect him or her going forward. Perhaps a teenage part needs help setting some boundaries. Maybe that part has an addictive nature that gets excessive with the things that bring pleasure. You can set up the thing or the behavior as a reward for the teenage part and limit where and when. Let's say that part loves to play video games but can get lost for hours.

Maybe something important does not get done and you feel bad about yourself. Instead of trying to deny or punish yourself, make a conscious plan. Let the teenager part know that he or she can play on Saturday for three hours if certain things are completed that week.

Connect with your Higher Self, your most evolved self, and any and all parts that are willing to help heal your Heart. Be aware of any parts that are critical or dislike any part of your Heart. Perhaps there are parts of you that are angry at the childish behavior, or have internalized some belief that your Heart is not worthy, or is scared at the enormous shadow it is casting on the alley wall. See if you can talk with those parts and get them to understand that your Heart is ultimately your Ruler. Let them know that it would be in their best interests to either participate in helping the Heart heal or at least get out of the way until such time they come around.

Being a great parent to your inner child usually means filling in the gaps yourself that were left by your parents. You must realize that you cannot expect your parents, if they are still alive, or your partners, or even your children to provide your Heart with what you deserved to receive from your parents as a child. You must do your best to "retire" your parents or others from their parenting role to you and take responsibility for providing the love, protection, joy, and care to yourself. Of course, your parents will always be your parents. However, by retiring them, you

> Being a great parent to your inner child usually means filling in the gaps yourself that were left by your parents.

can still respect their rank as parents but not expect them to meet your inner child's needs. For example, you would respect the rank of a retired general but not expect him to lead the current army.

Look inside to all your parts as you rebuild your inner family, kingdom, or tribe. Some of your parts may be more developed than others because you did not get all the tools you needed to love yourself. Sometimes, you need to look outside yourself for role models. They will have the skills or characteristics you need to heal and be able to balance work and fun. In fact, you can have fun thinking about what some of the skills or characteristics you need are to be a better parent to yourself. Do you need more mother/ nurturing energy; do you need more protective/warrior energy; do you need more discipline/organizer energy, or more assertive/decisive energy? Who do you feel has the type of energy you need? It can be someone you know or even a fictional character. You don't even have to mimic the whole person but just the specific part that fills in the gap you need.

I had a female patient in her 50's who I will call Lucy. Lucy was stuck in a loop in a long distance relationship that ultimately left her feeling bad. She was in love with a married man who had made it clear that he was not leaving his wife. They met every few months and would have a very deeply moving experience each time. One of her inner children was being satisfied at the expense of several other more adult parts. Part of her Heart felt attractive, alive and very satisfied, while another craved that he would leave his wife for her. After each brief but intense meeting was over, Lucy would feel bad about herself as she returned to her daily life.

She realized there was an internal conflict between parts of her Heart. One part of her Heart was overjoyed at being wanted and with the intense intimacy. However, another part felt used and not good enough since he would not leave his wife for her. Another part felt guilty that she "should" not be with a married man. Ultimately, Lucy hoped she could find a more available man that could connect with her with the same intense passion. Given her prior dating experiences she was not optimistic that such a man would be easy to find. Lucy knew it would take time and was not in a rush to give up her intense affair. However, she wanted to find a way not to feel bad after each encounter and to accept her actions without guilt. This was a new experience for her and she did not have the tools or immediate role models to help her quickly resolve her inner conflict.

When we explored the type of energy she needed to get through the next encounter with her lover without feeling bad afterwards, she said James Bond. Lucy needed to both protect herself and be nonattached and chose to channel James Bond. She thought James Bond had a way of being intimate and present in the moment, and at the same time able to walk away feeling good. We also had a meeting of the different parts of her Heart to help console and support the part of her that wanted more. After her next encounter with her lover, she reported back that it worked. Lucy enjoyed and appreciated the time with her lover and then went back to her daily life feeling happy and confident. She accepted her inner children, felt empowered and now was ready to go deeper into healing. If she were to meet her lover again, she would speak to the parts that wanted more and felt guilty beforehand. Lucy no longer was attached to her lover leaving his wife. She began dating more available men, in her search of a more meaningful relationship.

It is never too late to heal and transform your life. Sometimes, if parts of us feel very evolved and mature, it can become difficult to admit or face a young inner child that we may see as needy, ugly, stupid, or just not worthy of the effort. When that child is your Inner Ruler, you will have some reminder, whether in your body or expressed in your behaviors, that may leave you feeling incomplete in some way. I believe that true happiness and fulfillment is being able to express fully who you are, which means— *leave no child behind.*

Reflections

- Are there any inner conflicts? Are there conflicts with the environment?

- What behavior patterns no longer serve you as an adult?

- Do you feel you missed out on something your Heart wanted when you were younger?

- What can you say to that inner child who was left behind to welcome him or her?

- Are you willing to take 100% responsibility for your choices, your life?

WINTER

CHAPTER 10

You're a Teacher and a Healer

As you continue to age, you enter into the winter season of your life. You hope that with age comes a certain level of awareness and wisdom. The batteries you were given at birth usually have less of a charge than in your youth. And while your body may have some wear and tear, you have one last chance to heal and express the unique self that you are. Those of you who have been actively pursuing your path will continue to have increased awareness.

Parenting your inner child becomes easier because you are wiser and have a bigger perspective on life. Some of you may continue your work as it has been aligned with your Heart and destiny, while some of you may move toward retirement and pursue interests that resonate with your Heart. If you have not considered dying before now, this might be the time to think about your legacy.

As you transition from late fall to early winter, you may have the experience of still parenting your now-adult children. Some of you may also find yourselves having to parent your parents in their late-winter stage. For those of you who have a strong Spleen/Nurturer or Mother Earth energy, this can be challenging. Your inner children by now will be expressing themselves and demanding your attention, especially if you have ignored them earlier in your life.

Learning how to put your oxygen mask on first before your children or your parents can be difficult. Accepting what is your karma, and what is the karma of others comes into play even more than before. Because of your life experience and wisdom, you may have strong urges to help others learn from your mistakes so they can avoid the potential pain and problems you experienced. But everyone must do his or her own work. You can be supportive, but you cannot do the work for them. Whether you are a parent and/or a practitioner in the helping and healing professions, you sometimes need a reminder to care for yourself.

Although the body, mind, and spirit are one and work together, we tend to focus on one part at a time. Perhaps when you

> The body, mind, and spirit are one and work together

were younger, it was easy to exercise and be quick-witted, but you found it more difficult to be spiritual. Being spiritual can be a different experience for everyone; however, I believe there are certain Universal Principles and practices that are considered spiritual across the board. For example, meditation is a practice that can help give your nervous system and brain some rest and promote deep healing. It can also give you a clearer perspective on life, as well as help you understand the oneness and interrelatedness of all things. Meditation, as a self-help tool, can uncover any remaining, hidden inner children that need to be healed.

Your body, mind, and the universe will continue to give you signs to guide you on your path. Having a philosophy

Meditation is a practice that can help give your nervous system and brain some rest and promote deep healing. It can also give you a clearer perspective on life, as well as help you understand the oneness and interrelatedness of all things. Meditation, as a self-help tool, can uncover any remaining, hidden inner children that need to be healed.

or some spiritual guidelines can be useful as you approach death. My philosophy is that we need to give attention to all our parts and how they translate to our body, mind, and spirit. Making time to nurture each part and allowing them to have time to express their feelings and thoughts, helps keep your energy flowing and keeps you healthy. As humans, we generally have a potential life span of approximately 100 years. There are many environmental factors that affect our health and life span that are often out of our control. However, understanding who you are and being able to express all of you, tends to be important whether you reach 100 or not.

"You're a teacher and a healer." One of my teachers said these words to me when I was doing counseling on locked psychiatric wards and hypnotherapy in private practice. I assumed that a counselor could be considered a teacher and a healer, and was content that I was on my path. However, there was always a part of me that felt dissatisfied with the limitations of counseling, and the limitations the hospital put on me in terms of my job description. I had tools that I felt could help some of the patients, but was not allowed to use them. I found ways to use those tools in my private practice and through teaching. As I mentioned earlier, a car accident in Nepal, along with continued signs from the universe, guided me to go back to school to make Chinese medicine my career.

While I went to school full time, I eventually had to leave the full-time hospital job. I was carrying my résumé, but had been too busy to send it out and look for part-time jobs. I had a very strict routine of waking up early to do my qigong/T'ai Chi practice, go to work, get a fresh-squeezed juice, and go to class. I had given up many aspects of my life in order to maintain a 6 a.m. to 11 p.m. schedule Monday-Friday (6 a.m. to 6 p.m. Saturdays). One Friday while waiting for my juice, I recognized a woman walking toward me and smiled. She smiled back as we both recalled being psychology majors in college. I remembered her from several of my classes, but we had never really spoken.

As we caught each other up on our current lives, I mentioned I was looking for a part-time job. She said she was looking to hire someone part-time and said to send her my resume if I was interested. Without hesitation, I reached into my backpack and pulled out my resume. That Monday, I had a formal interview and was hired to do social work outreach with the homeless population of New York City.

My office was less than five blocks from my school, and my boss was amazingly supportive as I continued to go to school full time, six days a week. The universe seemed to be making it easy for me to continue on my path. As I became a licensed acupuncturist, I was able to use all of my tools to help people heal and transform their lives. Simultaneously, more people asked me to teach, and I soon was very busy teaching and maintaining my private practice. My Heart was fulfilled, and I had the luxury of doing something I loved—helping people heal along their path—and continuing to work on myself.

Although I have been called many names besides William over the years, many referred to me as their teacher and healer. It took me a while to embrace the idea of being a teacher, and I still have a little trouble with the word "healer" because I feel it implies someone doing the heal-ing for you. In my view, all healing is self-healing and hap-pens when you are ready.

The healer is there to create a safe and optimal environ-ment for you to heal yourself. That said, we are all teach-ers and healers. My dear friend who helped me make my five Acuformula® topical blends once said everyone was his teacher. With time, I understood this on deeper and deeper levels. At the very least, everyone you cross paths with has something you can learn. And in the same way, those closest to you usually offer insights on how you can heal. Many of the martial and healing arts I have studied have their roots in observing nature, animals, and how your body, mind, and spirit are connected to each other and the universe.

At this stage, your Heart or Inner Ruler joins forces with your Kidney or Wise Sage and connects you even deeper to who you are and to your environment. Often, you may find yourself wanting to share what you have learned and experienced with others to help make the world a better place. Conversely, you may feel it is time to retreat into your cave of solitude. For me, this life seems to be finding the balance of doing both. Either way, allow the Kidney/Wise Sage to be gentle as it continues to support all of you. The Sage can use wisdom to help your Protector, Nurturer and other parts do their jobs from a higher place.

Throughout your journey as an adult, you may often make promises to your inner children trying to appease or comfort them. It is important to keep your word to your inner children so that they can trust you and be part of the solution. So if you tell your inner child that you are going to go to the gym twice a week, or enroll in an art or acting class or stand up to the bully at work by speaking to them and your supervisor, it is very important that you demonstrate that you mean what you say. Your follow through will help build trust with your inner child and make it more likely to get that part's support. If you overpromise or do not deliver, your inner child may make your life more difficult in some way. Choose something you know you can do for sure that meets your inner child's needs, whether that is related to nurturing, protecting or just having fun.

> It is important to keep your word to your inner children so that they can trust you and be part of the solution.

By the winter stage, you probably have a good idea of who you are, what you are passionate about, and what things continue to provoke a reaction in you. Those things that continue to push your buttons and illicit emotional responses give you the opportunity to heal any remaining inner children. One way is to recognize the inner child, the primary emotion, and learn how to transform that emotion into a higher virtue. This not only helps your inner child heal and grow, but can also help those around you. For example, let's say your Liver part is impatient and quick to anger at times. Sometimes, if you can switch your mind to be kind and compassionate, it can transform the anger.

One day, I was third on line at the supermarket. I noticed a woman, probably in her early 70's, who was buying about 20 boxes of a popular frozen dinner. She seemed in a hurry and dumped all the boxes on the counter, as she reached in her bag for her coupons. The cashier was a young man in his late teens or early 20's, and was new at this supermarket. He looked at the coupons and told the lady they were for the smaller sized-version of her frozen dinner, and not for the larger boxes that she had chosen. The woman became irate and began yelling at the cashier.

He did his best to remain calm and polite as he offered her options. This seemed to only fuel her anger further, and she continued yelling at him and being disrespectful. I could see the mercury rising in the young man, as he did his best not to explode like an overheated thermometer.

As the person ahead of me and I began getting impatient, I quickly saw the opportunity to practice a spiritual approach. I imagined that her husband was sick and home alone, and that the coupons were necessary for her to be able to afford feeding herself and her husband. My Liver or Inner Warrior/General chose to be kind and have compassion for her. The lady ended up buying only two of the boxes and continued yelling and mumbling as she left the store. As I got to the cashier, I could feel his Liver energy still stuck as if he was pressing on the brake and accelerator of a car at the same time.

I told him I was impressed about how he had handled the situation and kept his cool. Almost instantly, he took a deep breath and took his foot off the gas pedal. The tires stopped spinning, and the engine cooled down. He seemed grateful to have been acknowledged. Most of our reactions are based on how some part(s) of us perceive the situation. We often have a go to video or make a story in our head and react to the video or story. Your inner children are usually the ones reacting with strong emotions. We can make up a scenario in our minds that helps transform a lower, emotional reaction to a higher, vir-

> We can make up a scenario in our minds that helps transform a lower, emotional reaction to a higher, virtuous one.

tuous one. I find this very helpful in day-to-day interactions like riding the train, driving my car, waiting on lines, watching the news, or dealing with people who may have a different opinion than mine on what is important. I have mentioned the correlations in earlier chapters, but here is a quick review:

- Transform Anger to Kindness/Compassion
- Transform Sadness to Righteousness/Justice
- Transform Worry/Pensiveness to Fairness/Reciprocity
- Transform Fear/Fright to Gentleness/Wisdom
- Transform Anxiety to Joy

Take a moment and think about a daily annoyance, whether at home, in your neighborhood, or at work. Pick something relatively minor, like someone pushing you to get on that crowded train, or cutting you off while driving so he or she could catch the light, causing you to miss it. Make note of your initial reaction. If it stimulated a negative emotion, see if you can make up a story that shifts it to a virtue. Maybe the person who pushed you to get on the train is a single parent and was late to work twice this week. Her boss said one more time and you're fired. Perhaps you can find some compassion as long as she did not hurt you or step on your nice shoes. Or maybe you can make up an even better story that puts your fancy shoes second. I have a few different go-to stories to keep any potential road rage in check. After I quickly blurt out the appropriate curse word (releasing the emotion), I may think that the driver's wife is going into early labor, and he is rushing to the hospital (finding compassion). Commuting in New York City provides plenty of opportunities to practice transforming emotional responses into virtuous ones.

You don't have to be in your winter stage to be more spiritual. There are certain milestones at each season of life. Remember from the time you are born, you are both an animal and a spiritual being. As a human, you can choose how to express yourself. In each situation you have

a choice. Applying any and all of the virtues to yourself
and others can go a long way in helping heal your inner
children as well as those around you. Buddhism is well
known for compassion and wisdom and Christianity for
forgiveness. While embodying and practicing these principles is both powerful and healing, it is also important
to help your inner children who may be hiding, stuck or
incomplete in some way. Allow those inner children to
express themselves as fully as possible. Now let's say your
inner children were abused in such a way that there is no
way you can forgive the abuser. You try real hard to forgive, knowing some forgiveness is better than none. What
do you do?

In Dan Millman's, *The Laws of Spirit*, there is a chapter
on the law of compassion. The protagonist is confronted
with his inability to have compassion and forgive a person
who he thinks is better off dead. The Sage says, "Then you
can forgive yourself for not forgiving them..." Through
forgiveness and compassion you can release and let go of
various types of pain you are holding in your body.

Many who come to me say the Acudragon® Wellness
System is like one stop shopping. It is a fusion of Eastern
and Western healing approaches that can help you heal

your body, mind and spirit. While each person receives a very individualized treatment session, you can choose from an extensive menu. All of the above virtues as well as other therapeutic and spiritual practices like acceptance, gratitude, integrity, empathy, non-judgment, faith, presence, hope, and love are all part of and incorporated into my being a teacher and a healer.

After just a few individualized sessions or classes, many of my patients and students are able to use many of the tools at home to heal and be a great parent to their inner child.

Reflections

- What is your calling?
- Are you expressing your Heart's passions through your work or play?
- Imagine all the different parts that make up who you are. Who (that is, which part) has been driving the bus?
- What are some things you can do today to bring joy and responsibly meet the needs of your inner children?

EPILOGUE

Socrates and others shared the philosophy to "Know Thyself." I believe this is the first step to healing, but it may be more appropriate to say, "Know Thy *Selves*." To be whole and complete, you really need to know all of your parts, especially your inner children/Heart. Confucius said, "Wherever you go, go with all your heart."

The inner child is connected to your Heart or Inner Ruler. Connecting with all of your Heart can bring you joy, help you feel and be younger, and even help you live a healthier, longer, and more fulfilling life. Your Heart connects you to your intuition, your creativity, and your passions; together with connecting you to your environment and early childhood experiences, you can realize your higher purpose. Getting all of your parts to work together in harmony can bring inner peace and peace with others. Many of you have been on a path of healing and enlightenment long before reading this book. Some of you are at the beginning of your journey, while others have an interest but are not sure about leaving your comfort zone, even if it is not the life you had hoped for.

Even though we are all one and interconnected in many ways, everyone is unique and must find what works for them. After more than 30 years of study and practice, I founded the Acudragon® Wellness System, which is a fusion of some of the best Eastern and Western approaches to healing and transformation. A *system* is an approach in which a set of parts work together and form a complex whole. *Wellness* is a state or condition of being in good physical and mental health. Acudragon® combines "acu" (*acupuncture*, *acupressure*) with "dragon" (an Eastern, mythical creature made up of different parts symbolizing power, courage, and transformation).

The system will continue to evolve as I continue my self-cultivation and refining of what helps people heal and transform quickly and safely. Many have traveled from around the world to work with me privately. Others have done some long-distance sessions by phone and with energy work. I have also traveled to teach and work with people here and abroad. My quest to help people connect with their Hearts and be as whole, independent, and complete as possible has always been the motivating force behind all my work. I also do my best to practice what I preach, and I am grateful to all of you who have helped me continue to move forward.

Like the expanding universe, I have been asked by teachers, students and patients to expand in order to serve more people. The Acudragon® Wellness System provides tools to help the body, mind, and spirit. Included in the system are acupuncture, acupressure, herbs, counseling, therapeutic exercises such as qigong (ch'i kung) and taiji (T'ai Chi) and other mind-body techniques to reduce stress and accelerate healing and peace of mind. Through my own experiences and the experiences of my patients and students, I have seen firsthand what works.

One of my unique tools that can help you take charge

of your health are my Acuformulas (five proprietary blends of essential oils, herbs, and homeopathic dilutions used topically to provide relief and healing for many common imbalances). Each Acuformula® corresponds to the Five Elements and can help you with the physical, mental, emotional and spiritual aspects of the organs, their functions and their associated emotions and archetypes. Your inner child usually knows which one is best for you simply by the aroma. You can then apply the oils to a specific acupuncture point or area of your body. Many acupuncturists, massage therapists and chiropractors have been using the Acuformulas for years with amazing results. With a little instruction, you can use them at home on your own. The roll-on bottles are portable and easy to use, just "shake and roll".

- Acuformula® T5-Green Dragon-Wood-Warrior-For Trauma, Pain, Anger, Kindness
- Acuformula® A7-Bronze/Red Dragon-Fire-Ruler-For Anxiety, Insomnia, Joy, Calm
- Acuformula® N6-Yellow Dragon-Earth-Nurturer-For Digestion, Worry, Fairness
- Acuformula® R5-White Dragon-Metal-Organizer-For Respiration, Sadness, Courage

- Acuformula® H5-Blue Dragon-Water-Sage-For Headaches, Cramps, Fear, Wisdom

This book on being a great parent to your inner child is the first of my *Enlightened Living 101* series. Be on the lookout for my self-help guide to healing the body, mind, and spirit. In addition I will be writing my memoir, which I am sure, will inspire and empower you not only to heal yourself but also free yourself to reach your full potential. Go to Acudragon.us and join my mailing list to receive seasonal self-help tips and info about classes and products. While you're on the site, check out my blogs and videos and see which self-help products resonate with you. Order directly from the site or from distributors that sell my products. You can also e-mail me if you have any questions, want to set up an appointment in person or long-distance, or are interested in hiring me for a speaking engagement or leading a workshop. Feel free to let me know if this book has been helpful to you in any way. My inner child loves to help people, and getting feedback helps me keep going, riding the waves of life. You can also check out Acudragon® Wellness System and William Kaplanidis on Facebook, YouTube, and LinkedIn and follow me on Twitter @acudragonnyc.

As long as you live, there is room to heal and grow. Heal your Heart and listen to it. I wish you all the best as you continue on your path to healing and transformation.

About the Author

William healed himself from the depths of physical and emotional pain and as a result, embodies a deep understanding of Western psychology and Eastern medicine approaches. He has a wonderfully intuitive and effective way of practicing the healing arts that led to the creation of the Acudragon® Wellness System. The various tools of the Acudragon® Wellness System is customized for each person. The system works rapidly and safely to help you heal from pain, injury or illness, prevent disease, cope with stress, and connect with your heart.

Through teaching and energetic healing, William guides others along an enhanced path and excels at changing the trajectory of people's lives. His tranquil demeanor, frank openness and sense of humor help create a safe space that has helped many move from pain, poor health and victim consciousness to recovery and enlightenment in one lifetime. Daily challenges remain but each patient is empowered to change the drama, the trauma, the patterns, and the results in their lives. In this way they experience greater self-love, good health, wholeness, happiness, and financial success.

William J. Kaplanidis is recognized for his work as a healer, counselor, professor, public speaker, author and entrepreneur. He has over 30 years of training and clinical experience, and has degrees in psychology, counseling, and traditional Oriental medicine. To complement his academic work, he has traveled to China, India, Nepal and Tibet to study and apprentice with masters of the healing and martial arts. William has also worked in various hospitals and has published in the fields of mental health, Chinese medicine, and martial arts. He has spoken at conferences, universities, corporations and has made numerous multimedia appearances (including television, radio and the Internet).

For more information:
www.Acudragon.us and
www.threetreasuresinc.com

Printed in Great Britain
by Amazon

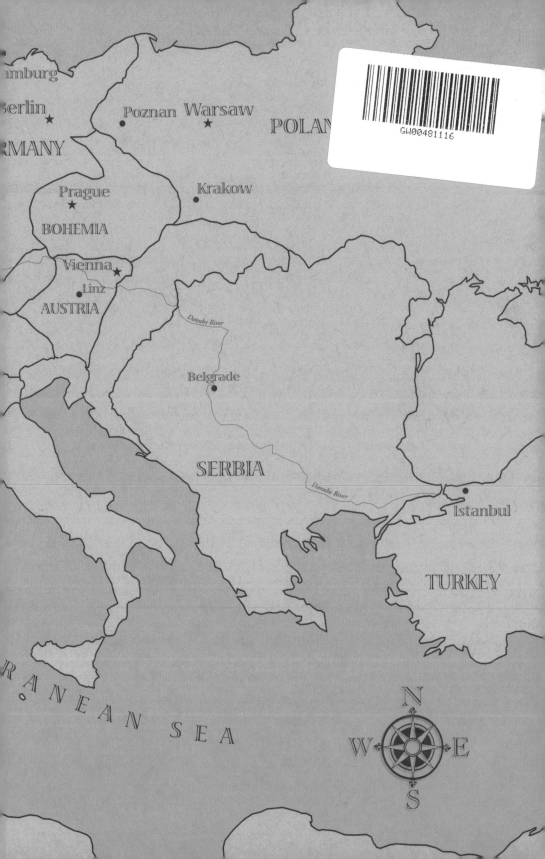

TO FREEDOM

AVNER GOLD

FIRST EDITION
First Impression … August 2008

Published and Distributed by
MESORAH PUBLICATIONS, LTD.
4401 Second Avenue / Brooklyn, N.Y 11232

Distributed in Europe by
LEHMANNS
Unit E, Viking Business Park
Rolling Mill Road
Jarow, Tyne & Wear, NE32 3DP
England

Distributed in Australia and New Zealand by
GOLDS WORLDS OF JUDAICA
3-13 William Street
Balaclava, Melbourne 3183
Victoria, Australia

Distributed in Israel by
SIFRIATI / A. GITLER — BOOKS
6 Hayarkon Street
Bnei Brak 51127

Distributed in South Africa by
KOLLEL BOOKSHOP
Ivy Common
105 William Road
Norwood 2192, Johannesburg, South Africa

ARTSCROLL SERIES®
THE LONG ROAD TO FREEDOM
© Copyright 2008, by MESORAH PUBLICATIONS, Ltd.
4401 Second Avenue / Brooklyn, N.Y. 11232 / (718) 921-9000 / www.artscroll.com

---

ISBN 10: 1-4226-0833-6 / ISBN 13: 978-1-4226-0833-3

Typography by CompuScribe at ArtScroll Studios, Ltd.

Printed in the United States of America by Noble Book Press Corp.
Bound by Sefercraft, Quality Bookbinders, Ltd., Brooklyn N.Y. 11232

CONTENTS

THE LONG ROAD TO FREEDOM

AUTHOR'S NOTE

TWENTY YEARS HAVE PASSED since I wrote *The Marrano Prince*, the eighth in my series of historical novels about Jewish life in the early modern era. During this time, many of my readers, some of whom knew the books practically by heart, have asked me why I discontinued the series. I always answered that the series was not discontinued but only suspended and that I intended someday to pick up the thread and carry it forward until the present.

For various personal reasons, that day was many years in coming, and now that it has come, I want to express my deepest gratitude to the Almighty for granting me this opportunity once again.

The first eight books in the series — *The Promised Child, The Dream, The Year of the Sword, Twilight, The Impostor, The Purple Ring, Envoy from Vienna,* and *The Marrano Prince* — were all set in seventeenth-century Europe, from 1610 to 1680. The newest book in the series, *The Long Road to Freedom,* spans the years 1680 through 1683. Directly connected to the ending of *The Marrano Prince*, it tells the story of Sebastian Dominguez's electrifying escape from a Spanish prison, his perilous journey to be reunited with his family in Paris, and their struggles to reach the Portuguese community in Amsterdam.

The story takes place against the backdrop of the European continent groping toward the modern era. King Louis XIV, the most powerful and forward-looking monarch in Europe, is locked in a struggle for supremacy with the emperor of the reactionary Austro-Hungarian Empire. At the same time, the Turkish Empire is projecting its power into Europe as it sends a vast army to besiege and capture the Austrian capital, Vienna. Poland and Germany are drawn into the defense of the city, but France stands aloof, refusing to come to the aid of its archrival even if means the Muslim conquest of central Europe. The story reaches its climax during the historic Siege of Vienna in 1683.

The political and economic changes sweeping across Europe are particularly important to the Jewish communities of the West. The progress of commerce and industry and the intensification of economic competition have enhanced the importance of the Jewish people to the respective governments. Persecution and expulsions are more and more becoming a thing of the past. Only Spain persists in its relentless hostility. The Jewish community of Vienna, expelled in 1670, is slowly returning and reestablishing itself. Although Jews are still officially banned from France, many are returning unofficially after an absence of hundreds of years, and the flourishing communities of Metz in Lorraine and Strasbourg in Alsace enjoy the favor and protection of the French crown.

Most of all, it is the glittering Dutch city of Amsterdam that is providing the Jewish people with almost unlimited toleration and opportunity. It has become the home of two important Jewish communities — the Sephardic community of Portuguese and Spanish Jews fleeing the Inquisition and the Ashkenazic community founded by refugees from the Cossack massacres in Poland, Lithuania, and the Ukraine.

In our story, the Dominguez family, having escaped from Spain, aspires to settle in Amsterdam, but numerous obstacles must first be overcome. The next book in the series, *Scandal in Amsterdam*, takes place when they finally reach their goal and discover that their troubles are far from over.

Before closing, I would like to extend a note of personal thanks to my old friend Rabbi Nosson Scherman, my new friend Rabbi Meir Zlotowitz, and the rest of the staff at Mesorah Publications for their enthusiastic embrace of the revival of the series and the gracious consideration with which they have treated me personally. May the Almighty grant us an enjoyable and stimulating relationship in good health for many years to come.

A.G.

Lakewood, NJ.

15 Av 5768 (2008)

THE HOLY HERMIT · 1

THE MIDSUMMER SPANISH sun beat down mercilessly on the shoulders of the old man and the donkey trudging up the mountainside toward Avila. The air was perfectly still, as if paralyzed by the heat, and the silence was unbroken but for the crunch of their footsteps on the gravelly road. The white stucco houses along the roadside were shuttered and still. Even the forest crawlers lay motionless in their shaded retreats waiting resignedly for the respite that evening would bring.

The old man wore the shabby brown cassock of a Dominican friar, his cowl pushed back from his head into a dusty pile around his shoulders. He had been riding on the donkey earlier that morning, but as the heat rose ever higher, he took pity on the poor beast and dismounted. A sheen of sweat covered his red-splotched face, and his longish white hair was brittle and tangled. His chin and cheeks were overgrown with sparse stringy white hairs that were not quite a beard. His back was bent over nearly double, causing his large rough-hewn wooden crucifix to dangle free from his neck, like a weight that was too heavy to bear while standing upright. In his hand he held an oak branch that had been fashioned into a walking stick.

Gripping the donkey's halter in one hand and his staff in the other, the old friar placed one foot in front of the other with dogged determination, speaking no word and uttering no sound, not even the slightest grunt, until the walls of the fortress monastery came into view.

As he approached the massive gates of the monastery, he pulled the cowl over his head and wiped his face with the coarse cloth of his sleeve. He lifted the heavy brass knocker on the gate and let it fall. There was no response. He waited for a minute or two and did it again. Still no response. Exasperated, he banged on the gate with his heavy staff again and again until he finally heard some movement inside.

A small metal panel in the center of the gate slid open, and a pair of eyes peered out at the old friar and the donkey.

"What's going on here?" a sleepy voice called out. "Who are you?"

The old friar did not speak.

"Please identify yourself," said the voice from the other side of the gate.

The old friar remained silent and immobile.

A key turned in the lock and the gate swung open. A barefoot corporal in an unbuttoned tunic stood there rubbing his eyes. The old friar surveyed the corporal up and down and turned away. He said nothing.

"A thousand apologies for my appearance, good father," said the corporal as he rapidly buttoned his tunic. "I was just taking my siesta in the guardroom when you knocked. We do not usually have visitors in the middle of hot summer mornings. I thought there was an emergency, and I came running before I had a chance to dress properly. I didn't even take the time to pull on my boots. Please come in."

He stepped aside and let the old friar lead his donkey into a small courtyard from which a number of passageways radiated outward. There was a water trough to the right of the gateway. The old friar led his donkey to it and watched as the donkey slaked its thirst.

"What do you need, good father?" said the corporal.

"How can I be of service to you on this fine morning?"

The old friar remained motionless and said nothing.

"Good father, why don't you speak?" asked the corporal.

The old friar looked at him and said nothing.

"Are you mute?" asked the corporal.

The old friar grimaced, revealing that two of his front teeth were missing. He shook his head.

"Are you hungry? Do you need assistance? A place to lodge?"

The old friar shook his head again.

"Then why are you here? What do you want?"

The old friar reached into his cassock and pulled out a letter.

"You are here to deliver a letter?"

The old friar nodded.

"For whom is the letter?"

The old friar pointed to the name written on the envelope.

The corporal blushed. "I'm sorry, good father, but I cannot read. Is it for Father Jorge de Megala, the abbot of the monastery?"

The old friar shook his head.

"Is it for one of the friars?"

The old friar shook his head again. He thrust his finger in a downward direction.

"Down?"

The old friar nodded.

"Under the ground?"

The old friar nodded again.

"You want someone who is under the ground? You want to deliver the letter to one of our friars who is dead and buried?"

The old friar squinted in frustration. He made a motion as if he were grabbing two imaginary poles and shaking them vigorously.

"The dungeon!" cried the corporal. "You want someone in the dungeon?"

The old friar was about to nod but stopped himself. Instead, he rolled his head slightly from side to side.

"Yes, but not quite," said the corporal. "Aha! I've got it. You want to see the warden of the dungeon. Captain Carlos Parran."

One corner of the old friar's mouth twitched in a semblance of a smile, and he nodded vigorously.

"I will take you to him immediately, good father," said the corporal. "Just wait here for a moment or two while I make sure he is properly attired to receive you. His office is just down this last passageway on the left."

The moment or two became a quarter-hour, but the old friar waited patiently. Presently, the corporal returned followed by an officer in a well-cut uniform.

"Welcome, good father," said the officer as he extended his hand.

The old friar studied the officer's hand briefly, then he thrust out his own clawlike hand, grabbed the officer's hand with the tips of his fingers and dropped it immediately.

"My name is Captain Carlos Parran. I am the warden of the military prison attached to the monastery. It is my honor to make your acquaintance. And you name is …?"

The old friar fixed the warden with a baleful stare and remained silent. The captain looked at the corporal, who shrugged in response.

The corporal leaned over and whispered in the warden's ear. "It is as I told you, sir. The old fellow has not spoken a word since he got here. I asked him if he is mute, and he shook his head. It's probably some kind of religious thing, like a vow of silence or something."

The warden nodded and turned to the old friar.

"Diego here tells me you have a letter for me. Would you

like to give it to me here or would you rather come to my office?" He stretched out his hand.

The old friar made no move to give him the letter.

"I gather then that you want to give it to me in my office," said the warden. "Come with me, good father."

He turned to go, but the old friar held back. He pointed to his donkey.

"Don't worry," said the warden. "Diego will take your donkey to the stables and take care of him."

The old friar shook his head vehemently. He pointed to the ground in front of the trough and stamped his foot.

"You want the donkey to remain here?"

The old friar nodded.

"Very well," said the warden. "Here he remains, waiting for you whenever you are ready to depart. Diego will see to it that he is fed right here. Come, let us go to my office where we can … uh … talk."

The warden ushered the old friar into the passageway with an elaborate flourish and a bow. Then he rolled his eyes at the corporal and hurried ahead to lead the way.

The warden's office was a large room. In the center were six upholstered chairs and a table covered with an orange cloth upon which a carafe of water, a tray of glasses and a bowl of figs had been placed. The room was otherwise bare.

"Please sit down, father," said the warden. "Take something to eat and a little cold water to wet your throat. Can I offer you a glass of wine?"

The old friar shook his head as he sat down. Without changing his contorted posture, he poured himself a glass of water and drank deeply. Then he ate a few figs, chewing them slowly and deliberately before he finally swallowed. Satisfied, he reached into his cassock and extracted the letter once again. He handed the letter to the warden and motioned upward with his upturned palm.

"You want me to read the letter aloud in front of you, father?"

The old friar nodded.

The warden broke the seal on the envelope and extracted a single folded sheet. He cleared his throat, but before he began to read he glanced down at the signature.

"Ah, I see that this letter is from Father Rodrigo Arias Davila," he said, "of the Holy Office of the Inquisition in Madrid. He made a personal visit here about a year ago, a most gracious and learned person, a man who brings honor to the Holy Church and our sacred motherland." He picked up the envelope and looked more closely at the broken seal. "Yes, it is the seal of the Inquisition. I recognize it, of course, since we do a lot of business with the Inquisition here."

The old friar nodded and pointed to the letter.

"Yes, of course," said the warden. "Father Rodrigo begins with an overly generous salutation which I shall not bother to read aloud, and then he writes, 'I put my pen to paper on this day, 3 July 1680. This letter is to introduce to you Father Miguel Gutierrez, an old and dear friend of mine, a man of profound wisdom and surpassing holiness. Father Miguel is a holy hermit. He has taken a vow of silence many years ago, but from time to time, he will make an exception when there is an urgent need. He has agreed to represent me in a matter of great urgency in Avila. Please cooperate with him fully and without question. He has the full authority of the Queen and the Holy Office of the Inquisition. Your faithful servant, Rodrigo Arias Davila.' That is the letter."

He raised his eyes and gave the old friar a questioning look.

"Listen carefully, Captain Parran," said the old friar, finally breaking his silence. He spoke in a hoarse, froglike croak as if every word was being across a bed of gravel. "I have no words to waste. You have a prisoner here named Sebastian

Dominguez, the son of Don Pedro Dominguez, the Duke of Monteverde."

"Yes, of course," said the warden. "We had Don Pedro here as well last year before he was moved to the Palace of the Inquisition at Madrid. Who would have believed that they are dirty Jews?"

"They are not Jews, Captain," snapped the old friar. "They were all duly and voluntarily baptized as Christians. That makes them Christians, not Jews. If they behave as Jews in secret, that makes them heretics, not Jews. There is a world of difference between them. Do you understand? They are not accursed Jews."

"Yes, father, I understand. I stand corrected."

"The members of the Dominguez family are our Christian brothers and sisters, and we want them reconciled to the Church. Don Pedro stubbornly refused to repent. He did not ask to be taken back into the loving embrace of the Church, so he suffered the fate he deserved. Originally, Sebastian was to have shared his father's fate in Madrid, but the Queen ordered that he remain here. She cares about him because he is her kinsman, and because he was always one of her favorites. She believes he was led astray by his father's influence, but now that his father is gone, she believes he can be induced to repent and be reconciled with the Church. She is ready to return his titles and estates to him and to extend her protection to his mother, sister and brother. Do you understand?"

"Yes, father, I do. I mean, I really don't. What are you trying to say?"

"I am not *trying* to say anything. I am *saying* it. My mission, for the Queen and for Father Rodrigo, is to convince the young man to save his life, his family and, most important, his immortal soul from everlasting damnation. I need your cooperation."

"Of course, Father Miguel. Whatever you wish."

The old friar stood up and gazed around the room. He began to breathe deeply, and a strange, almost maniacal light was kindled in his eyes. He fixed his gaze on the warden and slammed his fist onto the table with such force that the figs jumped out of their dish.

"I have fought the Devil all my life," he hissed between clenched teeth, at least those that he still had. "I have fought him in my prayers. I have fought him in my devotions. I have fought him in my incantations. I have won some battles and lost others. But this time I will not be denied. The Devil has come too close to the heart of Christendom. These people he has trapped in his snare are not some Portuguese peddlers from Toledo. They are close kinsmen to the royal family. The blood of emperors flows in their veins!"

He slammed his fist onto the table again. His breath came in short gasps, and his voice rose to a trembling shout. "By all the saints in Heaven, I will not allow him to gain a victory in this battle! I will not! I will not! He will not win, I swear it! He will not —"

The old friar stopped in midsentence and clutched his chest. The warden leaped to his side and helped him sit down. He poured a glass of water and handed it to him.

"Father Miguel, are you all right? You are an old man, and you must take care of your heart. Please drink a little water. You will feel better. You must not agitate yourself, especially not on hot days like these."

The old friar waved him away. "I am not agitated, you small-minded little man. My heart is not endangered. It is bursting with faith and love. I burn with the fury of Christian righteousness. I don't need water. I need confessions! I need repentance! I need reconciliation! I need the capitulation of the Devil!"

"Of course, Father Miguel. I meant no offense. I am at your service. What do you want me to do?"

"I need to speak to Sebastian. I need to penetrate to his heart of hearts. I need to find that deeply buried mother lode of pure faith and let it burst forth into every fiber of his being. Listen closely, Captain Parran. I want you to find me a secure room here in the monastery, a room in which Sebastian and I can be completely alone but from which he cannot escape. I need to scream and yell and cajole and plead and shout and scream some more. I need to bring this proud young fellow to tears. I need to break him down with remorse so that he bawls like a little child. And I don't want curious ears loitering about. This is between him and me and the angels in Heaven. Find me a room with bars on the windows at the end of a long passageway from which there is only one door to the outside. Post double guards at the entrance to the passageway but let no one come near the room where the battle with the Devil is taking place. Do you have such a room in this monastery, captain?"

"Oh yes, Father Miguel. We have several. You can take your pick."

"I don't want to climb stairs. My knees are sore."

"There are two such rooms right here on the ground level. You can have your pick."

"You choose. It does not matter to me."

"Do you want me to supply the room with food and drink?"

The old friar scratched at the stringy stubble on his chin. "Maybe a pitcher of water, some glasses and a hand towel. Nothing else. Except for a chamber pot."

"How much time will you need?"

"Hah! A question from the Devil himself. How much time? How much time? A moment? A day? A thousand years? Don't ask me such silly questions. I will sit with him, and I will go out to give him time to think, and I will come back, and I will wear him down and wear him down until he has no resistance left. Then he will give himself over into my hands and I will snatch him away from the Devil, and like a precious little fledgling, I will bring his sacred soul back to its mother, the holy Church, from which it was torn away."

"When do you want to start, good father?"

"Right now. Do you understand what I need?"

"Yes, perfectly."

"Then I shall talk to you no more. I have wasted enough words. I have allowed myself to speak to you, and I have foolishly spoken too many words. The rest of my words here in Avila will be spoken to Sebastian Dominguez and no one else."

The warden stood up. "I will give you the use of the interrogation room, Father Miguel. One of the passageways coming off the inner courtyard leads directly to it. The passageway is not very long, but it should give you the privacy you seek. Two of my men will be posted at the entrance to the passageway. Shall I get the prisoner now?"

The old friar rose to his feet and nodded. Then he motioned with his hand that they should go right away. He did not speak another word.

THE INTERROGATION ROOM · 2

DEEP IN THE DUNGEON, Sebastian Dominguez marched back and forth in his small cell. The stone walls were glazed with rancid moisture, and the air was damp and putrid. A tiny aperture high on the back wall allowed a few rays of dusty sunlight to illuminate the hard-packed earthen floor on which Sebastian trod. Five paces took him from the wall beside the pail that served as his chamber pot to the wall beside the narrow pallet on which he slept. Then he turned around and walked the five paces back. Again and again, he repeated this routine so that his muscles would not atrophy from inactivity and his mind would not atrophy from boredom.

Sebastian had been languishing in this cell for over a year. By the grace of Father Rodrigo, he had been allowed to speak with his father two weeks after they had been arrested, right before Don Pedro was transferred to Madrid. But ever since, he had enjoyed no human contact other than a few trivial words exchanged with his guards from time to time. During this time, he had not seen a printed word nor held a pen in his hand. He had not been allowed a single step out of his cell. His world had been condensed to a tiny brutish speck below the ground that he shared with nothing but the unwashed clothes upon his back and the thoughts and memories in his mind.

But Sebastian did not allow himself to succumb to despair and madness. Every day, without exception, Sebastian marched back and forth a thousand times in the morning and

another thousand times in the evening, meticulously counting every step he took. He devised word and number games
he could play in his mind. On occasion, he would take a long
Spanish or German word and calculate how many short ones
he could form out of its letters. He would then memorize the
number he had found and, some time later, revisit that word
and try to equal or better his earlier score.

Many times throughout the day, he would spend a few
minutes praying to the Almighty. He tried to repeat from
memory a few of the psalms he had learned, but for the
most part, he composed his own prayers for deliverance and
salvation for himself, his father and his entire family in this
time of their dire peril. In the evenings, exhausted from his
physical, mental and emotional exertions, he would lean
back, close his eyes and sing popular Spanish ballads and
the military marching songs of his regiment. When he felt
especially inspired, he would compose poems about the
beautiful world he recalled from before his captivity. Then
he would repeat them innumerable times until they became
so deeply burned into his memory that he could recall them
instantly.

On this oppressive summer morning, with the damp air
in his cell practically scalding the skin of his face, he finished
his thousand paces and lay down on his pallet to catch his
breath. He closed his eyes and tried to transport himself to a
world of beautiful thought and beautiful words.

The sound of footsteps outside his cell intruded into his
thoughts. Ordinarily, there was only one set of footsteps
signaling that the guard would momentarily slide his food
through the opening in the bottom of the door. But this
time there were two or perhaps even three sets of footsteps.
Sebastian sat bolt upright. Was this a cause for terror or could
this mean a reprieve?

The key turned in the lock and the door swung open.

Sebastian was momentarily blinded by the weak torchlight in the corridor, which seemed as bright as the noonday sun in comparison to the gloom of his cell. When his eyes adjusted somewhat to the light, he discerned a corporal and two guards in full uniform.

"Come with us, Dominguez," said the corporal.

"Where are you taking me?" asked Sebastian.

"Come of your own will or we will drag you. No talking."

"Am I going to be tortured?"

One of the guards snickered, and the corporal laughed.

"Yes, Dominguez," he said. "You are about to be tortured, but not in the way you think." He laughed again, then he grew serious. "No more talking, I mean it. Not a single word. You will have plenty of opportunity to talk later."

When they emerged into the courtyard, Sebastian recoiled from the bright light and the sudden blast of heat. He had felt nothing like it for over a year. From the upper floors of the monastery, the sounds of monks and friars chanting in their chapels floated down to him.

They crossed the courtyard and entered another passageway. That led to a single door at the end. The door was slightly ajar.

The corporal knocked on the door. Hearing a guttural grunt from inside, he opened the door.

"Bring in the prisoner," he said to the guards.

The guards led Sebastian into the center of the room and left him there. Sebastian surveyed the room. There were oil lamps on the walls. On a table in the center of the room were an earthenware jug, two glasses and a towel. A straight-backed chair stood on either side of the table. In the corner stood a chamber pot, a strange sight to find in what seemed like some kind of office. An old Dominican friar stood against the far wall. He was bent over, and his face was partially obscured by the cowl of his cassock.

"Is everything to your satisfaction, good father?" said the corporal.

The old friar grunted and nodded.

"Do you need anything else?"

The old friar grunted again and shook his head.

"I've brought you a chamber pot as you requested," said the corporal, "in case this takes a long time."

The old friar growled impatiently.

The corporal turned to Sebastian. "Do not even think about trying to escape. There is no way out of here but the passageway, and there are armed guards posted at the door. This is Father Miguel Gutierrez, an emissary of the Holy Office of the Inquisition in Madrid. You will, of course, give him your complete cooperation. He is a holy hermit who has taken a vow of silence, but he has come to speak with you, so you can well imagine how —"

The old friar could contain himself no more. He let out a piercing howl of frustration and motioned with both hands for the corporal and his men to get out. When they hesitated, he hurled his heavy walking stick in their direction.

The guards retreated toward the passageway, but even before they were out of the room, the old friar had dismissed them from his mind and turned his attention to Sebastian.

"I feel the fires of Purgatory raging around you," he screamed at Sebastian, and he reeled back with his forearm raised across his brow as if to shield himself from the searing heat. "I smell the sulfurous breath of the Devil hanging over your head like a stinking cloud. Repent! Get on your knees and plead for forgiveness, you foolish wayward child!"

After the door closed, the old friar bent down to pick up his fallen stick. Then he whirled around, lifted his stick high in the air and screamed, "Repent, you sinner! Repent right now before the Devil drags your immortal soul into the fires of Purgatory."

Then the old friar fell silent and remained standing still, his back bent over grotesquely, his staff gripped in his right hand, his eyes riveted to the ground.

Sebastian stared in amazement at the frozen figure of the old friar. Who was this gargoyle of a man? What did he want?

The old friar breathed a long sigh. He uncoiled his back, straightened his shoulders and rose to his full height, which was considerable. He threw back the cowl from his head and relaxed the contorted muscles of his face. Except for his white stringy hair and beard, the layers of age and decrepitude seemed to fall away from him. He turned and looked Sebastian full in the face.

Sebastian gasped and clutched at his throat. The monk had suddenly taken on a strong resemblance to one of the cavaliers who had attended his father loyally for many years. "Gonzalo?" he breathed. "Gonzalo Sanchez? Is it really you?"

"It is I, Don Sebastian. I have come to liberate you from this place."

"I cannot believe it! Oh, praise the Almighty." He fell to his knees and bowed his head. "Oh, thank you, Merciful Lord. Thank you for answering my prayers."

"I think you should stand up, Don Sebastian," Gonzalo remarked. "I don't think that Jews pray on their knees."

Sebastian scrambled to his feet. "My father, Gonzalo. What about my father? Do you have any news of my father? Is my father still alive?"

Gonzalo shook his head. "He gave up his soul a month ago in Madrid. He died a hero's death."

"Did you speak to him at the end?"

"Yes, I did."

"Tell me about his last moments. Please. I want to hear every word."

"There is no time to talk now, Don Sebastian. We have to get out of here. There will be time to talk later if the Almighty performs a miracle and we can get away safely."

"Of course, Gonzalo, but tell me one thing. Were his thoughts about me at the end? Was he worried for me?"

Gonzalo shook his head. "I lied to him. I told him that you had escaped and had already sailed safely from Valencia. He was relieved."

Sebastian nodded gravely. "You did the right thing. He did not need to be distracted by worries about the safety of his family when he was about to return his soul to its Creator. So tell me, Gonzalo, what is the plan? How do you intend to get me out of here?"

"Just follow my lead, Don Sebastian. Play your role, and I will play mine. I am the holy hermit come to save your immortal soul, and you are the intransigent heretic who stubbornly refuses to see the light of truth. I scream and shout and cajole, and you insist that you are a good Christian and that to the best of your knowledge everyone in your family is a devout, faithful child of the Church."

"All right."

"Ask me no questions. I will tell you what you need to know when you need to know it. Understood?"

"Yes."

"Good. Now we've been through our first session, and I have not succeeded. Remain standing near the table. Do not sit down. Let your head hang onto your chest. I will go out for a while to vent my frustrations, but I will be back soon."

Gonzalo took a deep breath and curled himself back into the contorted figure of the old friar. His eyes regained their hint of madness, and his face once again presented the ravages of age and distemper. He grabbed his walking stick, stamped out of the room and headed down the passageway. He banged on the door at the far end with his stick, and the corporal opened it. The two guards stood right behind him.

"Are you finished, Father Miguel?" asked the corporal.

The old friar glared at him as if he had lost his mind. Then he shook his head, partly to signal that he was absolutely not finished and partly in wonderment at the lunacy of the corporal who could even ask such a question. He brandished his stick at the men, and they fell back.

Grunting and growling, the old friar stamped on the ground and marched around the courtyard in no particular pattern, muttering wordlessly to himself and waving his stick at unseen demons that surrounded him. When he had calmed down a bit, he stopped beside his donkey and patted its flank. Then he glared at the guards again, motioned to them with his stick to open the door and disappeared down the passageway.

When he came back into the interrogation room, Sebastian was exactly where he had left him, standing perfectly still with his head slumped on his chest. This time, Gonzalo did not uncoil himself or relax his facial features for Sebastian's benefit. He remained hunched over and contorted, a bitter, ill-tempered old friar on the edge of hysteria and madness.

"If you don't mind, Don Sebastian," said Gonzalo, "I will remain in character until we are out of here. I've shown you who I am; now I must play my role so completely so that it becomes my identity. Every word I speak to you as an old friend takes me away from the authenticity of my impersonation, so I will say as little as possible."

"I understand."

"Here is the plan. The warden and his guards know me as a holy hermit. They know that I have made a vow of silence and that I do not speak to them. When I give you the signal, you will put on my cassock, get on my donkey and ride out of the monastery. You'll find bread and money in the pockets."

Sebastian gave him a puzzled look. "Just like that?"

"Just like that."

Sebastian took a deep breath. "I think you were right. It will take a miracle for this plan to succeed."

"No, it will not. What it will take is flawless execution. We will do it, don't worry. Do you know the pond behind the Coreillas farm?"

"Yes, I do. It is not far from here."

"A fast horse is tethered there in a stand of tall pines. Set the donkey loose, and take the horse. On the road going west toward Saragossa, near a large dead oak split by lightning, there is a small trail that heads into the forest. Leave me a sign by the roadside, then take the trail. It will lead you to an abandoned cabin high on a hillside."

Sebastian nodded. "I know the place."

"Good. I will meet you there. Right now, I think I need another break from this grueling session we are having. I think I will go outside for some fresh air."

When the old friar reappeared in the courtyard, the guards immediately stepped back to give him room for his manic shenanigans, and he did not disappoint them. This time he had his cowl pulled well over his head so that only his febrile eyes and the wispy white strands of his beard showed from the shadows within. Once again, he ranted and raved without uttering a word, stamping on the ground and swinging his stick at the demons that surrounded him. At last, he stopped at the gate to the outside and pointed.

The corporal came running. "What do want, Father Miguel?" he asked.

The old friar did not even turn to look at him. He just stared at the gate and pointed.

"Do you want me to open the gate, good father?"

The old friar tapped on the gate with his stick and waited.

"As you wish, good father," said the corporal. He extracted a key from his pocket and opened the gate.

The old friar grunted again and walked out into the bright sunlight. He marched off in the direction of the city and disappeared around a bend in the road. The corporal stared after his receding back and shrugged his shoulders.

"Do you think he's gone away, Corporal?" asked the taller of the guards. The other guard just kept dabbing with his sleeve at the sweat that was puddling on his forehead. He didn't particularly care if the old friar returned or not.

"He'll be back," said the corporal. "He's just gone out to blow off some steam. The man is mad as a bat, and he's determined to wring a confession out of Dominguez. I could have told him he would not have an easy time of it. He won't leave here until he does it. I'll lay you a wager that he'll be back. And very soon."

The guards laughed and declined to accept the wager. And indeed, not more than ten minutes later, the old friar was back, pounding the ground with his staff and snorting and muttering to himself. One of the guards went to close the gate behind him, but the old friar stamped on the ground and brandished his stick at the guard. The guard backed away and resumed his position near the entrance to the passageway.

The old friar wandered about the courtyard, his back deeply bent and the cowl of his cassock hanging over his head so that he looked more like a giant brown beetle than a man. Every once in a while, he looked up at the sky and let loose such a bloodcurdling howl that the corporal and the guards shrank back into the shadows.

Finally, a certain sense of serenity seemed to descend on the troubled hermit, and he began to hum tonelessly as he ambled around the courtyard. He glanced for a moment at the passageway from which he had emerged. Then he apparently thought better of it. Instead of returning to his prisoner, he mounted his donkey, rode out into the open and turned in the direction of the city.

"What do you think now, Corporal?" asked the tall guard. "Do you think he's coming back or have we seen the last of this madman?"

The corporal shook his head and smiled. "We really shouldn't call him a madman, *muchachos*. Do you think you would be any different if you lived the life of a holy hermit and never uttered a word unless it was in the service of the Lord? He is obviously not of this world, but he is a holy man, and we must respect him. Will he come back? Absolutely! Does anyone want to lay a wager?"

No one did, and minutes later, the old friar was back. He dismounted, and whistling merrily, he disappeared back into the passageway. The door closed behind him, and the guards resumed their positions.

The old friar had been away for quite a while, and when he opened the door to the interrogation room, he saw that Sebastian was desperately worried.

"Calm yourself, Don Sebastian," he said. "It goes well. Now we must work quickly." From an inside pocket, he produced a vial of a pasty substance and a handful of brittle white hairs. "Here, bend over and bring your face down here. This cream will make your skin look like aged parchment, like mine, and the hairs will stay pasted to it so that you will have a beard that resembles mine. Now some coal tar on your front teeth will make it seem that some are missing."

Gonzalo put a few final touches on Sebastian's face and then stepped back to survey his handiwork.

"Not bad," he said as he thrust his staff into Sebastian's hand. "Now bend yourself over as if you have the largest hunchback, scrunch up your face into the most contorted grimace you can manage and stamp on the ground with my staff."

Sebastian contorted his body and his face as Gonzalo had

instructed. He took the staff in his hand, pawed at the ground and produced a few gargling, gurgling grunts followed by a hacking cough.

Gonzalo clapped his hands. "Excellent! Now here are my final instructions. Do exactly as I say."

A short while later, the door to the passageway opened again, and the old friar emerged into the courtyard. He was obviously in a foul mood. He rampaged around the courtyard a few times, and then he banged on the gate with his staff. One of the guards came running to open it. The old friar bent his head, snarled and turned away. He mounted his donkey, rode out of the gate and turned once again toward the city. Moments later, he disappeared around the bend in the road.

"Hey, corporal," said the tall guard. "How many times is the old bat — oh, excuse me, I mean the old holy man — how many times is he going to pull this silliness? You think he's coming back?"

The corporal laughed. "Of course he's coming back. In fact, I think he's making headway with Dominguez. Did you notice that this time he didn't seem quite as agitated as before?"

The tall guard scratched his head. "He still ran around with his staff like a madman and made those crazy noises, didn't he?"

"That he did. But the fire of holy indignation wasn't raging like before. He seemed a little nervous but not screaming angry. I think he senses he's close to a breakthrough, so he's not so angry anymore. But he's nervous."

The tall guard shrugged. "We'll find out soon enough. If he stays on schedule, he should be coming back around now."

But five more minutes passed and then ten more, and still, there was no sign of the old friar. The corporal left the guards stationed at the door to the passageway and walked down the road until he turned the bend. The road and a patchwork of smaller byways stretched before him down the hillside. As far as the eye could see, there was no sign of the friar or his donkey.

The corporal spun around and ran back to the monastery.

"Something's wrong, *muchachos*," he shouted.

He dashed for the door to the passageway that led to the interrogation room, the two guards hard on his heels. They burst into the room, and for a moment, they thought it was empty. Then they heard a muffled moan coming from behind the table.

The old friar lay on the floor in his undergarments, his hands and arms tied behind him with a pair of shirtsleeves. His feet were tied together with strips of dirty cloth that might once have been part of a shirtfront. A towel was stuffed into his mouth and secured in place by another dirty strip of cloth. There was an angry red bruise on his forehead, and an angrier red fury in his eyes.

"Quick, untie him," shouted the corporal.

The tall guard produced a sharp dagger, slit the old friar's bonds and helped him to his feet. The old friar immediately grabbed the earthenware jug from the table and hurled it at the wall, where it shattered into a thousand pieces. A large stain of water ran down the wall. Screaming with fury, the old friar grabbed the edge of the table and flung it over.

"Calm yourself, good father," said the corporal. "He will not get far. We will capture him and give him back to you. But this time we will stay in the room. We could have avoided all this if you had let us stay in the room."

The old friar glared at the corporal and made a motion indicating that he wanted some clothes.

"We will get you some clothes," said the corporal, "as soon as we recapture the prisoner. There is not a single moment to waste. Just stay here, Father Miguel. We will be back shortly, and we will take care of you."

The corporal and the two guards mounted horses and set out in the direction of the city. There were hardly any people in the open because of the blazing heat, and the few that were outside had seen nothing. After a half-hour of fruitless search, they returned to the monastery to sound the alarm. The Inquisition would mount a nationwide search. The prisoner would not escape.

As they rode back to the monastery, the tall guard had a thought. "What do you think happened, corporal?" he said.

"It so simple that any fool can see," said the corporal. "Dominguez knocked down the good father, stole his cassock and his staff and rode away on his donkey. What is so hard to figure out?"

"I don't think it's so simple, corporal," said the tall guard. "Did you notice that Dominguez had sprouted a straggly white beard, just like Father Miguel's?"

"No, I didn't notice," said the corporal.

"How about you?" he said to the other guard, who responded with a blank stare and an indifferent shrug.

The corporal looked at him through narrowed eyes. "Are you sure?"

"I am," said the tall guard. "He was bent over and the cowl hung over his head, but I could see part of his chin. There were white hairs on it, just like Father Miguel's whiskers."

"How would Dominguez manage that on his own? I mean he could overpower the old friar and steal his cassock and staff, but where would he get a white beard? Do you think Father Miguel had a hand in this?"

"It looks like it," said the tall guard.

"Impossible! Why would he do such a thing?"

"Why don't we ask him?" said the tall guard.

"Fine," said the corporal. "You go check on him, while I go tell the warden what has happened."

"He's going to bite your head off."

"I know."

But when the tall guard returned to the interrogation room, the old friar was gone. Within minutes, the warden and the corporal arrived with a large contingent of guards.

."Mount a search," the warden shouted to the guard. "A few of you men go upstairs and see if the friars saw him. For Heaven's sake, how far could he have gotten in his undergarments?"

"With your permission, captain," said the corporal, "I would like to take a few men and search outside the monastery."

"Outside? In his undergarments?"

"The man is mad, captain. I wouldn't put anything past him."

"Very well, Diego," said the warden. "Ride around and see what you can find, but try not to be such a fool this time."

"Yes, captain," said the corporal. He signaled to the tall guard and to two others and they went to get the horses.

Once again, the corporal and his men scoured the mountainside, but there was no sign of the old friar. It was already late in the afternoon, and the worst of the heat had passed. More people had emerged from the shelter of their homes and were going about their business, but no one had seen a sign of the old friar.

As the corporal and his men headed back to the monastery, they encountered a tall cavalier trotting toward them on a fine steed. The cavalier wore a brocade doublet in the resplendent colors of the royal guard and a dashing hat adorned with ostrich plumes. He sat erect in the saddle, his broad shoulders thrown back in a proud military posture.

The corporal tipped his hat and said, "Good afternoon, *señor*. I am Corporal Diego Santiago. A thousand pardons for disturbing you, Your Excellency, but could we trouble you to answer a question or two? A prisoner and his accomplice have escaped, and we are searching for them. We won't take more than a moment of your time."

"Very well," said the cavalier. "What is it you wish to know?"

"The escaped prisoner was wearing a stolen brown friar's cassock. He was riding on a donkey. He has been gone for over an hour."

"I cannot help you, corporal. I have not seen this fellow. How did he steal a cassock in the first place?"

"It is a long story, *señor*."

"And embarrassing, I am sure," said the cavalier.

"I'm afraid it is, Your Excellency," said the corporal. "Perhaps you have seen his accomplice. An old man with a stringy white beard."

"An old man, you say? Was he running about in his undergarments?"

The corporal sat forward eagerly in the saddle. "Yes, that is the one! Did you see where he went?"

"Well, I didn't follow him, of course. But I saw him come hopping down the road from up there below the monastery. He turned into the second lane around that bend. I think he ran into the woods. It seemed to me that he was quite mad."

"Indeed, he is," said the corporal. "Thank you so much, Your Excellency. You have been ever so helpful."

The corporal and his men spurred their horses and galloped off in pursuit of the deranged old man in his undergarments. The cavalier watched them for a few moments. Then he turned west toward the abandoned cabin on the hillside.

A PLACE TO HIDE · 3

J AGGED BRANCHES, BRITTLE AND LEAFLESS, protruded from both sides of the dead oak by the roadside. In between, the tree was withered white and riven apart almost to the ground. A single green leaf clung to the cleft of the oak as if it alone had found a small vein of life in the midst of so much death. A narrow, almost invisible trail led into the forest behind the tree.

Gonzalo Sanchez dismounted and walked over to inspect the tree. If all had gone well, Sebastian should have left a sign that he had been there and gone on to the cabin. If there were no sign, Gonzalo would have to head back toward Avila with all due haste to search for the missing young prince.

From the distance, Gonzalo had seen no sign in or around the tree, but as he came closer, he noticed thousands of ants swarming over a small piece of bread in the cleft of the tree. The bread looked no more than a day old. Gonzalo smiled as he mounted his horse and turned into the trail. Sebastian had been too cautious to leave a piece of cloth. That was good. He would need all the caution he could muster if he hoped to escape with his life.

The long evening shadows fell over the trail as Gonzalo slowly wound his way up the hillside. Night had fallen by the time he reached a ramshackle cabin that stood in a puddle of moonlight about twenty paces from the trail. The encroaching forest had so completely surrounded the cabin that it was almost completely obscured.. The roof had collapsed on one side and the front door hung askew on its hinges. There was no indication that anyone was inside, but Gonzalo was not surprised. He was sure that Sebastian was watching the cabin from a safe vantage point.

Gonzalo dismounted, tethered his horse and sat down to wait. A few minutes later, Sebastian emerged silently from the forest behind Gonzalo.

"Did you have any problems, Don Sebastian?" asked Gonzalo without turning around.

Sebastian chuckled. "I always knew you had eyes in the back of your head, Gonzalo. I had no problems. Everything went exactly as you planned it. I owe you my life."

Gonzalo turned around and smiled. "Not quite yet, my friend. When I get you safely to France, that is when you will owe me your life. Right now, we are in the greatest of danger."

"But you have a plan."

"Of course I have a plan. I always have a plan. But we are in the hands of the Almighty. Sometimes, we can fool ourselves into thinking that we are the masters of our own destiny, but every once in a while, we have to admit that our fate is not in our hands."

"So what do we do now?"

"We rest and we eat. And then we get a good night's sleep. We will be safe here through the night. No one will come up here in the dark. Did you by any chance look inside the cabin?"

"Actually, I did. It is filthy and infested with insects and vermin."

"Is it worse," asked Gonzalo, "than your accommodations for the past year?"

"It is paradise compared to my cell."

"Will you have a problem sleeping with the insects?"

"None at all, but I would still prefer to sleep out in the open tonight, even though it is getting a little chilly."

"Then that is what we will do," said Gonzalo, "but we will build no fires. There is no sense taking unnecessary chances. Are you hungry?"

"A little. I have become accustomed to living with hardly any food."

"Well, tonight we will have a feast. I have two loaves of fresh bread, baked in Avila this morning, and I have a half dozen oranges. There's a stream nearby. If I remember correctly, the water is as delicious and bracing as the best red wine from Rioja."

The two men unsaddled their horses and fed and watered them. Then they spread their bedrolls on a bed of pine needles and sat down to feast together. They ate and drank in companionable silence. Then they lay down and looked up contentedly at the star-studded sky.

"You know, Gonzalo," said Sebastian, "right now I feel like a king. Look where we are, sitting in the forest near a shack on a hillside, afraid to light a small fire. Come daylight, half the country will be searching for me to drag me back to my cell in the dungeon. I sit here and I wonder if I'll live till nightfall tomorrow, and I don't even dare wonder if I will ever see my family again. And yet … and yet … I feel free as the wind. I feel like an eagle soaring high. I see the beautiful stars above me, and I feel the clean forest breeze on my face. My mouth tingles with the juice of the oranges, and my belly is full of bread. And I can sleep through this night without fear that I will be dragged out of my bed and shipped off to Madrid. Who knows what tomorrow will bring, but right now, I consider myself fortunate and free. Free as the wind."

"You are fortunate, Don Sebastian. And tomorrow will bring you even more good fortune. Have faith."

"Oh, I do. I have faith. But people who have faith can also perish. My father told me that true faith is to accept the will of the Almighty, even if what He wants is not exactly the same as what we want."

"Well, if He took you this far, I think He may want to take you all the way to safety. I really believe that you will get through this safely."

"I would like to believe it, too, Gonzalo. I wish I had your resourcefulness and confidence."

"You have my resourcefulness and confidence, Don Sebastian. They are at your service."

"I know, Gonzalo. I can never repay you."

"You can repay me by letting me go to sleep now. The sun rises early these days. Let's get as much rest as we can."

Gonzalo rolled over onto his side and closed his eyes.

"Can we talk for a few more minutes, Gonzalo? I haven't had a conversation with another human being for over a year. I was hungrier for human contact than for bread and oranges."

Gonzalo sat up and look at Sebastian.

"Of course," he said. "We can talk as much as you like. I had plenty of sleep last night. Enough to last me for a week."

Sebastian smiled. "I won't keep you too long. You know, with all your planning and execution, you really risked your life for me today. So many things could have gone wrong, and then we would both have been cooked. You more than me. Why did you do it?"

"That is a strange question for a Spanish gentleman to ask. I am forty-four years old, and I have been a loyal cavalier to your father ever since I was seventeen years old. My father before me was a loyal cavalier to your grandfather. My life and honor are pledged to your family. Don Pedro was my lord, my liege, and I would gladly lay down my life to protect any member of his family. And I would be proud to do it. To do anything else would be dishonorable, and it is better to be dead than to live without honor."

"I understand that, Gonzalo. Believe me, I understand the code of honor. I grew up with it, and I feel it in my bones. My father died because of it. We could have fled Spain years ago. We could have been safe, secure and free today in Amsterdam or Constantinople or some other place that welcomes our people. Instead, my father is dead, and my family is uprooted. And why? Because my father's sense of honor and loyalty to the royal family and to the motherland would not let him abandon his duties. So he paid for his loyalty with his life. But there is a difference between your readiness to die for my father and his readiness to accept death for Spain. My father honored and cherished you in equal measure. So if you had died for him, you would have felt good about it. As good as anyone can feel about dying. But my father suffered the bitterness of knowing that those to whom he was loyal were the very ones that sent him to his death."

"Yes, that is true. I didn't tell you yet about the last moments of his life, and now is not really the time for it. But they were glorious moments. He gave up his life for the honor of the Almighty and for his religious convictions, and that is certainly a death with honor. The great tragedy of his death is that he was undone by his own loyalty. If only he had been little less loyal to his enemies, he could have glorified the honor of the Almighty by living for it rather than dying for it."

He paused for moment and looked over at the Sebastian.

"So if you understand all this, Don Sebastian," he said, "what was your question? How could you ask me why I am doing this for you?"

"It is because we are Jews. Did you know all along that my father was a secret Jew?"

"No, I did not. He never told me."

"You must have been shocked when you found out."

"I was. Very."

"But that didn't affect your feelings of loyalty?"

"No, Don Sebastian. It did not."

"Are you a Christian, Gonzalo?"

"Absolutely."

"Then didn't you feel a conflict between your loyalty to my father and your loyalty to the Church?"

Gonzalo nodded. "So that was your question."

"Yes, that was my question."

"It is a good question."

Gonzalo stood up and began to pace back and forth in the moonlight as he gathered his thoughts. Sebastian rose to his feet as well.

"I consider myself a Christian," Gonzalo said at last. "I consider myself a very good Christian. I try to live by its highest principles and ideals, many of which are inherited from Judaism. But I do not accept a lot of what the Church does. The Church has become like a tyrannical regime. It wants to control people and to make sure that everyone that lives in its domain is under its power. So the Church behaves like a tyrant. It frightens people into submission by claiming that anyone who does not become a Christian will never have salvation and that his immortal soul is condemned to eternal damnation. And it destroys people who refuse to accept its teaching and its authority."

"And you don't agree with that?"

"I believe that the Almighty cherishes good people. I believe he loves people who are kind and generous to others, people who are devoted to their families and their communities, people who are true to their convictions and obligations and to their heritage. I do not believe that the immortal souls of such people are doomed to eternal damnation."

"Even Jews?"

"Especially Jews," said Gonzalo. "The Jewish people are descended from Abraham, Isaac, Jacob, Joseph, Moses and so many other people in the Bible whom we admire and revere. The Jewish people championed the honor of the Almighty for over a thousand years before Christianity came along. The Church claims that Christianity has replaced the Jews and is now the new Israel. I'm not sure about that, although I would like to believe it. But even so, the Jewish people are certainly the old Israel, and for that they deserve everlasting honor and respect. That is what I think. Your father was a great man, a good person. His loyalty to his religion only made him that much greater in my eyes."

Sebastian stepped forward and embraced Gonzalo. "I am honored to know you, my friend," he said. "The world would be a better place if there were more people like you in it."

"The honor is mine, Don Sebastian. Now I think we should go to sleep."

The next morning, they rose early and were ready to ride before the sun had climbed over the horizon, but the sound of hoofbeats gave them pause. Sebastian climbed to the top of a tall tree from which he could see the road to Saragossa. It was swarming with cavalry. When he had predicted that half the country would be looking for him by morning, he had been exaggerating somewhat. But now it seemed that he had not been so far from the truth.

Gonzalo had planned to make a run for Barcelona on the Mediterranean coast where a fisherman friend of his had promised to hide them in his boat and take them to Italy. But that plan no longer seemed feasible. People throughout the entire countryside would be looking for two fugitives, the escaped Sebastian Dominguez and the mad old friar who had been his accomplice. The searchers would have realized by now that the friar was in disguise and that they could not be sure of his description, but there was no question about Sebastian's description. The scrutiny of all unknown travelers would undoubtedly be intense, and two men traveling together would arouse all the more suspicion and questions.

Splitting up was not an option. Sebastian would never survive without Gonzalo at his side. Staying where they were was also not an option. With so much manpower invested in the search, all the byways and trails would almost certainly probably be investigated.

In the end, Gonzalo decided to do the opposite of what was expected of them. The fugitives would be expected to try to get as far away from the Inquisition as quickly as possible. They would be expected to seek avenues of escape from Spain by heading for one of the borders or for the coast. The searchers would not be expecting the fugitives to head toward Madrid, the seat of the Inquisition. Therefore, that was exactly what Gonzalo intended to do. But in the beginning they would have to avoid all roads.

They set out into the open country to the south of the road to Saragossa. After a hard day of riding across difficult terrain they camped for the night on a high ridge in the southwestern Guadarrama Mountains not far from the town of Las Navas. In the morning, they both dressed as royal cavaliers and descended to the road that ran from Avila to Madrid.

They rode at a steady pace eastward in the direction of the capital. Along the way, they passed more than one troop of cavalry riding hard toward Avila. No one paid them any attention. In the late afternoon, they rode into the mountain village of San Lorenzo to the northwest of Madrid.

"Where are we going, Gonzalo?" asked Sebastian.

"We need to disappear for a while. There is a man here in

San Lorenzo named Carmello Villablanca. We will hide out in his house. We should be safe there at least for a little while."

"Who is this man?"

"He is the constable of San Lorenzo."

"What are you saying, Gonzalo? That we should hide out in the home of a constable? I should think that's one of the last places we'd want to hide."

"Don't be concerned, Don Sebastian."

The constable's house was on a quiet stretch of road just outside the village. It was larger than most of the village homes, but other than in size, it was indistinguishable from the rest. A maid showed the two travelers into a central courtyard that was open to the sky. A small table and four chairs stood in the shade of a portico. The maid invited them to sit while she went off to fetch the mistress.

A heavyset middle-aged woman presently appeared. The two men stood up and removed their hats. She took one look at Gonzalo, and her face broke into a broad smile.

"Gonzalo!" she declared. "It is such a pleasure to see you. Carmello and I had given up on seeing you ever again."

"The pleasure is all mine, Graciela. You and Carmello have never been far from my mind."

She gave Sebastian a coy look. "And who is your young friend?"

"Where are my manners? I have forgotten to make the introductions. I am so sorry. Graciela, this is Luis Alvarez. He is my new aide. Luis, this is my sister-in-law Graciela Villablanca."

The name by which Gonzalo had introduced him, Luis Alvarez, caught Sebastian by surprise. They had neglected to discuss an alias, and on the spur of the moment, Gonzalo had used the alias that Sebastian had chosen for himself years earlier when he had joined a group of clandestine Jews in Toledo. The name brought back painful memories for Sebastian, but he recovered quickly. He swept his hat aside in a broad flourish and bowed deeply from the waist.

"*Encantado de conocerle*," he said. "I am pleased to meet you, *señora*."

She smiled at his gallantry. "*Mucho gusto*," she replied. "A pleasure. Are you married, Señor Alvarez?"

"No, I am not, *señora*." Sebastian laughed lightly and sought to change the subject before it became too personal. "I did not know that Señor Sanchez had a sister-in-law. He never mentioned you."

"If he would ever think about us," she said, "he might actually have thought of mentioning us."

"You judge me too harshly, *señora*," said Gonzalo. "I always think about you. You are just about my only family." He turned to Sebastian. "Her husband Carmello and I have the same mother. He is somewhat older than I am, but we are the best of friends and brothers."

"It's easy to be the best of brothers," snorted Graciela, "when you never see each other. We haven't seen you in almost three years. How's Pedro?"

"Pedro?" asked Gonzalo, suddenly on guard.

"Your son. Pedro."

"Oh, Pedro. Of course, Pedro. Yes, Pedro is just fine. He is with his regiment in Badajoz in Extremadura."

"Extremadura," she repeated. "That's brutal country. Hot and dry."

"Yes, but he gets into Cadiz on his furloughs. I spent a week with him there a few months ago. Cadiz is beautiful, and the sea breezes are heavenly. He's almost twenty-one."

"It's so sad about your wife, Gonzalo. You should remarry, you know."

"Who's getting married?" said a voice from the portico.

A moment later, the voice was followed by a large man with a florid face and small twinkling eyes. He caught sight of the visitors, and his mouth dropped open. Without another word, he ran to Gonzalo and grabbed him in a bear hug.

Over dinner, the conversation flowed as freely as the wine. Graciela spoke incessantly about the latest French fashions in dresses and the most popular new productions on the French stage, while Carmello kept reminding her that the French were killing Spanish soldiers in the Spanish Netherlands and the Rhineland. Sebastian contributed no more than a word or two here and there just to be polite, but otherwise, he thought it safer to remain silent.

"Did you hear the news from Avila?" said Graciela after the maid had cleared away the dinner dishes and served strong tea. "They're still trying to figure out how that young Dominguez managed to escape. I heard that a horrible hunchback got into the prison on a flying donkey. They say he used a magic formula to put the warden and all the prison guards to sleep and then he flew off with the prisoner and vanished."

Carmello cackled. "Oh, the things you believe, Graciela. I'm surprised there were no wizards and witches and goblins in the story. The only part you got right is that they vanished. No one can find a trace of them. What do you think, Gonzalo?"

Gonzalo shrugged. "No one vanishes. I expect they'll find them sooner or later."

"Wait a minute!" said Carmello. "Didn't you serve under Don Pedro Dominguez, the escaped prisoner's father?"

"That's right," added Graciela. "You named your own son in his honor. It must have come a great shock when you found out that all along he was a dirty Jew doing all kinds of horrible —"

She stopped in midsentence, and her hand flew to her mouth. Her eyes opened wide as saucers, and she stood up abruptly, spilling hot tea all over the tablecloth. Carmello looked from his wife to his brother and back, the light of comprehension dawning in his eyes.

"Gonzalo?" he said, pointing at Sebastian. "Is this who I think it is?"

Gonzalo laced the fingers of his two hands together, then put them behind his neck and leaned back. "I'm afraid it is, Carmello. And where should we turn for refuge if not to the safety of my brother's house?"

"Gonzalo, Gonzalo, what have you done?" said Carmello. He looked at Sebastian. "How could you let him do this, young fellow? How could you let him risk his life like this? How could you let him endanger the future of his son?"

"What has he done?" said Sebastian. "I knocked on his door and asked him to help me find shelter for the sake of my father's memory. He was honor bound to help me. What else could he do?"

"But didn't he help you escape from prison?"

"Who? Gonzalo? How would he do that? No, Gonzalo had nothing to do with it. The hunchback helped me escape. He just flew in and carried me off."

"The Devil's henchman," breathed Carmello.

At the mention of the hunchback, Graciela let out a piercing shriek. She crossed herself several times and put her hands over her ears. "I can't listen to this any more. Heaven have mercy on my soul. Carmello, you have to arrest them right now."

"My own brother, Graciela? Have you taken leave of your senses? I can't do something like that."

"Carmello," she wailed, "I don't want my soul to suffer eternal damnation. I want to go to Heaven. If you don't arrest them, I will turn them in first thing tomorrow morning."

"If you do that, Graciela, you will be in Heaven before tomorrow night, do you understand me? You will remain silent. You will not breathe one word of this to anyone. Not to anyone. Do you understand me?"

Graciela nodded grudgingly.

Carmello turned to Gonzalo. "How long do you intend to stay here?"

"Maybe a week or two," said Gonzalo. "Just until things quiet down."

"And then what will you do?"

"We will head for Saragossa and then on to Barcelona. From there we should be able to get to Italy without too much difficulty."

"Fine. Let's make that one week, and not a day more. Agreed?"

Gonzalo nodded. "Agreed."

Soon after the household was asleep, Gonzalo awakened Sebastian. He held his finger to his lips to ask for silence. "We are in mortal danger here," he whispered to Sebastian. "We have to leave right now, and we have to get as far away from here as we can."

Fifteen minutes later, they were on the road, riding by the light of the silvery moon. But they were not headed for Saragossa, as Gonzalo had told Carmello. Instead, they headed south, deeper into the heart of Spain. They rode through the night, going as fast as the horses could manage. They gave Toledo a wide berth, going instead through Aranjuez and Ocaña. Before dawn, they stopped in a secluded spot in a wooded area near the Cedrón River.

Just as they settled down to catch a few hours of badly needed sleep, a drama was playing itself out far to the north. An Inquisition wagon rolled up to the door of Carmello Villablanca's house. A priest in a black cassock and two men of the Hermandad in white robes and black cowl hoods emerged. The priest banged on the door several times before it was finally opened by the maid. Carmello appeared right behind her, rubbing his eyes.

"We have come for Dominguez, the escaped prisoner,"

said the priest in the black cassock. "While my men search the house, the two of you remain here."

Carmello was stunned. "B-b-but ... how? I mean ... who?'

"I told Father Jose in the church in the village," said the maid. "He ran to the Holy Office."

"B-but how did you know anything? Were you listening at the door?"

"I certainly was," she said, lifting her chin in defiance. "Suspicious things were going on, and someone had to report them if you and the *señora* didn't."

"According to your maid," said the priest, "you and your wife are innocent. If our investigation supports her testimony, you will not suffer any consequences for these fugitives appearing uninvited at your doorstep."

One of the men from the Hermandad appeared.

"The fugitives are gone," he reported. "They must have left in the night."

The priest turned to Carmello. "Did they say where they were going?"

"Yes. They mentioned Saragossa and then Barcelona."

The priest looked to the maid for confirmation. She nodded.

"Good, you are cooperating," he said. "If you hear from them you are to report to me immediately. And *señor*, there will be no retaliation whatsoever against your maid. Do you understand? If there is, she is to report to me, and I assure you, sir, it will not be pleasant for you."

"No, of course not," stammered Carmello. "She was doing her sacred duty."

"Why did they leave?" asked the priest. "Did they think you would report them?"

"I don't think so," said Carmello. "But my wife and I made it perfectly clear that they weren't welcome here. So

I think they just ... decided to look for someplace else to stay."

"Do you have any idea where they might have gone tonight?"

"None at all. Believe me, father. I have no idea."

An hour later, a large search party set off in the direction of Saragossa, while a number of smaller search parties searched in a fifty-mile radius around Madrid.

FLIGHT TO TANGIER · 4

M ANY MILES TO THE SOUTH, Gonzalo and Sebastian caught two hours of peaceful sleep, unaware of the closeness of their escape. They awoke while the sun was still climbing into the sky and breakfasted on a loaf of bread washed down with water from the river.

"Just about now," said Gonzalo, "they'll notice that the horses are gone, and they'll look in our room and see that we've left."

"Do you think they'll report us?"

"Carmello is a good man, and he's my brother. He won't want to report us. But Graciela will push him to do it for their protection. She'll argue that since we've gone anyway they might as well report us and stay in the good graces of the Inquisition. He'll give in to her, but he'll insist on waiting until later today or maybe tomorrow. He'll try to give us some time to get far away. By the way, Don Sebastian, thank you for saying that I wasn't involved in your escape. If they ever catch me, it will help me somewhat."

"They won't catch you, Gonzalo. You lead a charmed life."

Gonzalo laughed bitterly. "A charmed life? You call mine a charmed life? A wife that dies in childbirth. A son that I never see. My liege lord is burned at the stake, and I'm fleeing with his son, one step ahead of disaster every day."

"I am sorry, Gonzalo," said Sebastian. "What are we going to do now?"

"We go to Córdoba."

"What's in Córdoba?"

"Don Alejandro Quinones, Marqués de Murillo, a dear old friend of your father. You and your family will need money when you start your new lives in Amsterdam or Constantinople or wherever you decide to go. Your father once told me that if anything happened to him and if his family needed money, they could turn to Don Alejandro. I didn't understand what he meant at the time. Why would his family need to go to Don Alejandro for money? There is always money in the royal coffers for the kinsmen of the royal family. The truth of the matter did not occur to me. Anyway, you will need money, so we will visit your father's friend."

Sebastian looked at Gonzalo doubtfully. "Do you think it is safe?"

"Don't worry. Don Alejandro will not betray you. Come, let us go to Córdoba."

It took them several days to get to Córdoba, traveling mostly in the early mornings and the late afternoons. The heat during the middle of the day was so scorching that in many places the vegetation on the sides of the road caught fire and burned steadily.

The old walled city of Córdoba lay on a flat plain along the Segura River between the Sierra Morena and the Sierra Nevada mountains. The Marqués de Murillo had his baronial estates further up amid the wide open spaces and cool breezes of the mountains, but he kept an office in the walled city for the occasions when he had to perform his obligatory duties for the crown. Gonzalo decided to seek him out in the city, where they would draw less attention to themselves. They would go in the heat of the afternoon, when they were less likely to meet people.

They stabled their horses and walked though the fields toward the Almodovar Gate. The sun beat down on their heads, and they felt as if the door of a furnace had opened and the air had blasted out into their faces.

They entered the city and immediately plunged into the warren of tiny streets that branched off from the central square. It was like walking through a maze, but Gonzalo seemed to know where he was going. The streets were practically deserted. Most of the shops were closed.

"Where are we going?" asked Sebastian.

"I'm taking you to the old Judería, the Jewish quarter. There used to be a Jewish community here. I'll show you a synagogue. Would you like to see it?"

"Of course."

They continued through the labyrinthine streets until they came to a narrow street called the Calle des Judeos, the Jews' Street; it was more like an alleyway, ending at a building that blocked egress.

"That building was the synagogue," said Gonzalo. "You probably imagined a large impressive building. I am sorry to disappoint you."

"It's not what I expected," Sebastian admitted ruefully, "but it's still something. It is the most Jewish thing I've seen in public in my entire life. Thank you for bringing me here, Gonzalo."

"And you'll thank me for getting us away from here very quickly. If we linger in this street we will attract attention. Not a good idea. Come, let's see if we can find the Marqués."

They found the office of the Marqués deep in the interior of an immense stone building. An aide made a note of the names they gave and asked them to wait. The Marqués called for them nearly two hours later. He had obviously tried to ward off the heat with the help of a few bottles of wine.

"What can I do for you, *señores?*" he said.

Gonzalo looked around to make sure there was no one else in the room. "Your Excellency, this young man with me is Don Sebastian Dominguez, the son of your good friend Don Pedro Dominguez, Duke of Monteverde. Don Pedro once told me that if his family should ever be in need of funds they could turn to you for help. Don Sebastian is fleeing for his life. With the help of the Almighty, he will reach safety and rejoin his family in Paris. They will need money to start a new life. They need your help."

The face of the Marqués changed colors several times as Gonzalo was speaking. First, it was red from the wine, but as soon as Gonzalo revealed the identity of the visitor, the blood drained from his face and it turned white. Then as the enormity of what was happening dawned on him, his face once again became red, but this time with a towering anger.

"You are a madman," he hissed, his earlier stupor completely gone. "How dare you bring a fugitive from justice — an unrepentant heretic of all things — into my domain? How dare you put me in a position where I must decide if I should report you to the authorities or perhaps to the Inquisition? The Holy Office is not far from here, you know."

Gonzalo and Sebastian sat there in silence. They did not move.

"What an outrage!" fumed the Marqués. "Don Pedro was a good friend of mine, a very dear friend of mine, but he was not honest with me. He never told me that he was a secret Jew. What would he expect me to do? Jeopardize my position and my good standing for the sake of doing a favor for a dead man who does not deserve it? Absolutely not."

"I was under the impression, Your Excellency," said Gonzalo, "that the money he wanted you to provide to his family was his own property, and that you would know how to access it."

"You insolent dog. Are you insinuating that I want to steal money that doesn't belong to me?"

"Heaven forbid, Your Excellency. I just —"

"Be quiet! Not another word from you! Nor from you, young Sebastian. Don Pedro had no money of his own. He was not a merchant or a banker. Everything he possessed came from the crown and his princely estates. Everything he had was acquired under false pretenses. He was not entitled to any of it. If you ever make it out of this country alive, Sebastian, you will be penniless, as you should be. All I will do for you, for the sake of the friendship I thought I once had with your father, is let you leave here without reporting you. And don't think I'm doing it for his sake alone. I don't need to sully my good name by association with a heretic who was burned at the stake and his fugitive son." He stood up, trembling with rage. "Now, get out of here! And don't you ever show your faces here again, either of you."

The Marqués turned his back to them and placed his hands on his hips. Gonzalo and Sebastian bowed courteously and left.

"This was a disaster," said Sebastian after they had left the walls of the old city behind. "What do you think he'll do, Gonzalo?"

"I don't know. I think he meant what he said about not reporting us, but we are in serious danger. He may have someone else report us so that he will not be connected with us. Who knows? We have to get out of Spain, and as quickly as possible."

"Should we head for Cadiz?"

Gonzalo shook his head. "Too dangerous. They'll be watching for us in every port city."

"So how do we get out?"

"We swim. Are you a good swimmer, Don Sebastian?"

"This is not a time for jokes, Gonzalo."

"I'm not joking. Are you a good swimmer?"

"Fairly good."

"What does that mean? Can you swim for miles?"

"I'm a strong swimmer. But I can't swim all the way to Italy."

"We're not going to swim to Italy. We're going to swim to Morocco across the Straits of Gibraltar."

Sebastian stared at Gonzalo. "All right, I'm listening."

"We can't go to any of the ports, even to fishing villages. The danger is too great. So we go south and find a spot on the coast from which we can see across to Morocco. And then we cross."

"And then we cross," Sebastian repeated. "Just like that? We just cross?"

"Well, I'm sure it's not going to be so simple, but we'll figure it out when we get there. We may have to swim part of the way. The problem is how two men traveling together can get to the coast. Our descriptions have probably been circulated all over the country."

"You're the master of disguise, Gonzalo. Do you have any ideas?"

"Well, we could steal one of those Inquisition wagons, but that wouldn't give us much time. Its absence would be noticed quickly." Gonzalo stroked his chin. "So let's see … hmm … what can we do? … Aha! I have it, Don Sebastian. You and I must get married."

Sebastian gave Gonzalo an odd look. "Have you completely taken leave of your senses? What kind of drivel are you talking?"

"Look, Don Sebastian. They will be looking for two men. We will be a man and a woman, an old peasant couple. We'll travel most of the way south through the mountains on horseback, but when we get near to our destination we will make the transformation."

A few days later, while they were still more than twenty miles from the coast, they caught sight of the Rock of Gibraltar, a massive limestone rock jutting up against the sky from the flat coastal plain. It was time to assume new identities.

The next day, a small cart laden with vegetables rolled into the marketplace of the town of Gibraltar. An old peasant dressed in rags held the reins and cursed the recalcitrant mule to which the wagon was hitched. The peasant's wife, also shabbily dressed, with a black shawl draped over her head, sat beside him, chewing on an onion and berating the mule.

The old peasant made some inquiries and found a trustworthy local boy to stand in for him while he and his wife went to look at the famous rock, something they had dreamed about all their lives.

The rock was even larger up close than it had seemed from the distance, a veritable mountain where no mountain was to be expected. It took two long hours to climb to a high vantage point from which they could see across to Morocco. Before making any plans, however, they shared a loaf of bread.

Gonzalo finished his bread quickly, but Sebastian was distracted by the beauty of the panorama that lay before him. Behind him was Spain, to his right the Atlantic Ocean, to his left the Mediterranean Sea and directly in front of him, the continent of Africa. A large sailing ship was passing though the Straits of Gibraltar, and numerous fishing boats plied the coastal waters. He was nibbling at his bread and watching in fascination when suddenly he heard a shriek. He looked up and saw a miniature ape, with pale hair, pale eyes, and long gangly arms, shrieking and running straight at him. Startled, Sebastian jumped back and dropped his bread. The ape grabbed the fallen bread and ran off.

"What was that?" cried Sebastian in bewilderment.

Gonzalo laughed. "I should have warned you about the Barbary apes. They live here on the mountain. They're just monkeys, not very dangerous."

"It just gave me a fright for a moment."

"You can't allow that to happen," said Gonzalo, suddenly serious. "Who knows what may come at us before this is over. You cannot lose yourself. You have to be alert and prepared to deal with anything that happens. You cannot allow yourself to be startled. Expect the unexpected."

"Yes, of course, Gonzalo. I allowed my vigilance to lapse, and I deserve your reprimand. I gather you've been here before."

"Yes, I have. I was here with your father. The look on your face reminded me of his reaction the first time he was here. It is an awesome sight." He pointed across the straits. "That is our destination."

"It doesn't seem so far," said Sebastian. "Do you really want to swim across?"

"It is farther than it looks, my young friend. We will only swim as a last resort. So take a good look. From what point do you think we should leave?"

Sebastian pointed to the west. "That village across the bay. I think that would be a good spot."

"That's Tarifa. A good choice. I agree."

"So when do we go? Tonight?"

"No, not tonight. We have to wait a few days until the moon is gone. We need the cover of darkness."

Sebastian looked out over the waters where the land of Morocco stretched out toward the horizon.

"Do you think we'll be safe in Morocco, Gonzalo?"

"Safer than in Spain, that's for sure. We won't tell them that you're Jewish. The Moroccans aren't so friendly to the Jews these days. I hear that Moulay Ismail keeps threatening the Jews, and every time, it takes a big bribe to turn him away. They say there's no end to the man's greed. He's a really nasty fellow. I hear that when Moulay Ismail took over the city of Marrakech about twenty years ago he had the most prominent Jews burned in public."

Sebastian shuddered and didn't say anything.

"I am amazed at you Jews," said Gonzalo. "The world certainly doesn't make it easy for you. Exiles and expulsions and massacres and extortions. How do you people keep this up for so many hundreds of years? I mean, there's a limit to stubbornness, you know."

Sebastian smiled. "It's who we are. We have a covenant with the Almighty, and we are here in this world on a special mission. Our covenant and our mission are more precious to us than life itself."

"Yes, I suppose."

"You know, Gonzalo, I am very excited about going to Paris and then to Amsterdam. It's not only because I'll be reunited with my family. It's because I need to know more about this covenant and this mission. I need to know more about what it means to be Jewish. I'm risking my life to be a Jew, but I really know so little about it."

"So how do you know that it's worth the risk? I mean, hundreds of thousands of Jews here in Spain accepted Christianity rather than risk their lives. And no matter what the Inquisition says, we all know that most of the *conversos* did abandon their Judaism. So why are you so set on being Jewish?"

Sebastian was silent for a moment or two. "That's a hard question to answer, Gonzalo. The first answer that comes to mind is that my father died for his Jewishness, and if I were to abandon it I would be dishonoring his memory. But it is much more than that. While my father was away, when we thought he had perished at sea, he spent two years studying with a rabbi in Poland. He told me that discovering the holy Torah was the most incredible experience of his life. I saw it in his eyes whenever he talked about it. My father was a different person when he came back, a more exalted person. He was in touch with the Divine. That is what being Jewish meant to him, and he was willing to die for it. I want to make that discovery too. I want to touch the Divine. I want to transcend the ordinary human existence and live with unending inspiration, spirituality and … and … yes … honor. If I was once willing to die for the honor of the King of Spain, I am certainly willing to die for the honor of the Almighty, the King of the Universe."

"And I am willing to die for the honor of my liege lord Don Pedro, so I understand what you are saying. And I hope you find what you seek. But I have traveled to other lands, and I have seen many of the Jews that live there. It does not seem to me that all of them live with that kind of inspiration."

"I admit that I know very little, Gonzalo. But I think that those who spend a good part of their time learning the Torah, as my father did during those two years in Poland, those are people who live with inspiration. And I also believe that their inspiration carries over to the rest of the Jewish people."

"As I said, Don Sebastian, I hope you find what you seek. Anyway, getting back to what we were discussing before, Morocco is not the best place for us. If this greedy Moulay Ismail gets hold of you he just might decide to sell you back to Spain. No, I think our best hope is to go to Tangier. I understand that Moulay Ismail is trying to get his hands on the port, but for the time being, it's in the hands of the British. And I heard that there's a small Jewish community there. If we head a little west from Tarifa it should take us straight into Tangier. Unless we get swept out into the ocean, that is."

On a dark moonless night, two silent figures dressed in black from head to foot ran across the beach to the west of Tarifa. They pulled a skiff from its place of concealment in the underbrush and carried it to the water.

The skiff glided smoothly away from the shore as the two men paddled steadily. The weak silvery starlight reflecting off the water only underscored the immense darkness that surrounded them, just as the soft gurgling murmur of the sea underscored the vast silence of the night.

After about an hour, a few faint points of light appeared on the murky Moroccan coastline.

"Look to you right," whispered Gonzalo. "That's Tangier."

"What's that other light?"

"What light? Where?"

"Over there," said Sebastian pointing into the dark. "A little to the east of Tangier. There's a faint light and it's moving in this direction."

"It must be a Moroccan coastal patrol boat. The Moroccans are blockading Tangier, but what are they doing wide awake in the middle of the night?"

"Looking for people like us. What do we do?"

"We're not so far from the Moroccan coast. Let's make a run for it. We'll find a place to hide near the shore until the coast is clear, and then we'll get over to Tangier."

As the patrol boat drew closer, they paddled vigorously for the shoreline. It was a race against time. The shore was tantalizingly close. It seemed that there would be enough time to get there undetected.

All of a sudden, they felt themselves being pulled westward toward the patrol boat and the lights of Tangier beyond. They had run into an outward current, and all their paddling could not change the direction of their movement. Instead of going against the current, they decided to go with the flow and gradually edge past the current into calmer waters. After a desperate struggle against the sea, they finally managed to free themselves from the clutches of the current.

Once again, they turned toward the shore, but the patrol boat loomed ahead, and it was coming directly toward them. Someone must have spotted the skiff, and now the patrol boat was on its way to investigate.

"Don Sebastian," said Gonzalo, "the time has come to go for a swim. They can see the boat, but maybe they won't be able to spot us in the water. Try not to splash too much when you swim. If we get separated, we'll meet in Tangier."

The two men dove over the side of the skiff and struck out side by side toward the shore. They swam slowly with even strokes so as not to attract the attention of the looming patrol boat and also to preserve their strength. The dark outline of the coast seemed close, but they both knew that it was misleading.

After a while, they could see the running lights of the patrol boats turn away from the general location where they had abandoned their skiff. For the moment, they were safe. They turned onto their backs to float for a few minutes and catch their breaths.

The soft undulation of the waves rocked them back and forth gently. Far off to the east, a faint line of dusty light appeared on the horizon, the first harbinger of the morning sun.

"Gonzalo," called Sebastian in a hoarse whisper.

"What's the matter?"

"I think I saw something."

"What did you see?"

"I think I saw a dorsal fin pass by."

"A dorsal fin? Like the thing on the back of a shark?"

"Yes, that's what I mean," said Sebastian. "It's still quite dark, but I thought I saw a dorsal fin cutting through the water."

"Where?"

"Off to the west. About two hundred paces away."

"It could be a shark," said Gonzalo. "I heard there are sharks in these waters."

"So what do we do?"

"We don't panic. I heard that sharks bump you before

they attack and that if you hit them on the nose with your fist they go away."

"Hit the shark on the nose?" said Sebastian, fighting hard to keep back the panic. "Heaven help us. And what if there are a few of them?"

"Say a Jewish prayer, and let's swim for the shore as fast as we can. But only smooth strokes. I heard that thrashing and splashing attracts the sharks."

"Don't be funny, Gonzalo. This isn't a time for humor."

"I was being perfectly serious, Don Sebastian. Let's move."

They rolled over onto their stomachs and swam for the shore as quickly as stealth would allow. Soon, they could feel the undertow of water returning seaward from the shore. They were almost there. Minutes later, their feet scraped the rocky bottom. They ran the rest of the way to the shore as fast as their legs could carry them. Only then did they turn to scan the straits behind them. The horizon had brightened somewhat, and off in the distance, a single dorsal fin cut through the water moving toward the west.

The two men clambered up the rocky shore to the concealment of some scrub coastline vegetation where they could rest and take stock. The outlines of the buildings of Tangier loomed very close. Although they had swum straight for the shore, the edge of the current had apparently drawn them westward and put them ashore closer to the British colony.

"Do you have the money, Gonzalo?"

"The money is safe," said Gonzalo, tapping his waist. "The money belt really weighed me down out there in the water, but I couldn't very well drop it. We're going to need money in Tangier."

"Absolutely. How far do you think it is to Tangier?"

"If we walk fast, we should reach Tangier in less than an hour."

Sebastian stood up. "Fine. Let's go."

"We can rest here for a few more minutes if you wish."

"We can rest in Tangier."

"Spoken like a true soldier," said Gonzalo as he stood up. "Let's go."

As they neared the city, the sound of hoofbeats coming from behind them intruded on the stillness of the early morning. A cloud of dust signaled a group of horsemen approaching at a gallop. It could only be Moroccan soldiers, and they could not be expected to be friendly. The two men looked around desperately for a place to take cover, but there was none.

Sebastian pointed to where a few clumps of seaweed and some driftwood had washed up on the beach. The men had been out of the water for a half-hour, but their clothes were still soaking with seawater. They rolled around on the beach until they were covered head to toe with sand. Then they lay down behind the seaweed and the driftwood and hoped for the best.

The hoofbeats drew closer, and then they slowed down, as if the riders were searching for something or someone. Sebastian and Gonzalo remained where they were, thankful for the last remnants of darkness. They took only short shallow breaths to minimize the movement of their bodies. The riders dismounted and shouted to each other in Arabic. But after a few tense minutes, they lost interest in their search and rode off.

Sebastian and Gonzalo remained where they were for a few moments longer. Then they returned to the road and ran toward Tangier.

Suddenly, three men in red coats and cocked hats emerged from a roadside hut and blocked their way. They were armed with sabers and daggers, and they carried matchlock muskets in their arms. One of them stepped forward and held up his hand.

"Halt!" he shouted in English. "Who are you?"

"*Habla español?*" asked Gonzalo.

"Sorry, mate. We only speak the King's English."

"I speak a little English," said Sebastian. "Are you British soldiers?"

"That we are, mate. And who might you be?"

"My name is Sebastian Dominguez, and this is my friend Gonzalo Sanchez. We are fugitives from the Spanish, who are trying to kill us. We are also trying to avoid capture by the Moroccans. When their patrol passed, we were hiding on the beach. Now, we want to seek refuge in Tangier."

"Let me get this straight, mate," said the British soldier. "You two are enemies of the Spanish and the Moroccans? You're running for your lives?"

"*Si, señor.*"

"Well, as our friends the Arabs say, the enemy of my enemy is my friend. Welcome to Tangier, mates."

A GLIMMER OF HOPE · 5

NEARLY A YEAR PASSED before Sebastian and Gonzalo arrived in Paris. The French government had been reluctant to allow them entry into France. Repeated petitions by the Spanish government and by the Holy Office of the Inquisition for the return of the fugitives only reinforced the disinclination of the French to open their doors. In the meantime, Sebastian and Gonzalo remained marooned in Tangier, fighting boredom and flies. They survived on the money Gonzalo had brought with him and on whatever they could earn through their enterprise and ingenuity. In the end, an impassioned personal appeal by Doña Angelica to King Louis XIV finally secured the permission for her son's entry into France.

The reunion of family was bittersweet to say the least. Their idyllic life in Madrid was nothing more than a remote memory. Don Pedro was dead, and Sebastian had languished in prison for over a year and in Tangier for another. The family was broken and impoverished. Yet at the same time, it was an exceedingly joyous moment. The oldest son had returned to take his rightful place as the head of the family. Things would be better from now on. They couldn't very well get much worse.

Sebastian had visited Paris a number of times together with his family, and the city brought back many fond memories. A few generations earlier, one of Sebastian's grandmothers had intermarried with a member of the royal family, and this had made the family relatively close cousins with many of the kings and queens of Europe. As a princely family connected to the Hapsburg bloodlines, they always enjoyed the most luxurious accommodations in Paris. Expense was never an issue. Somehow, Sebastian had not imagined different circumstances for his mother who was living in Paris under the protection of the French King. Pampered child of the Spanish nobility, it had never occurred to him that it might be otherwise. But otherwise it was.

Doña Angelica lived with her daughter Carolina and her son Felipe in a small house on the Rue Parmentier, which was quite far from the royal palace at the Louvre and the glittering magnificence of the surrounding boulevards. The house had three small bedrooms, which meant that Sebastian would have to share a room with Felipe, and Gonzalo would have to find lodgings of his own. There was one tiny servant's room, occupied by a dour Norwegian woman who doubled as cook and housekeeper. There was also a small stipend for food and other basic expenses. In order to augment the meager family income, Carolina became a Spanish tutor for the children of a wealthy merchant, and Felipe found employment cataloguing the personal library of one of Don Pedro's kinsmen.

Sebastian found Angelica in a desperate state of mind. The family did not seem to be in mortal danger anymore, but they could not yet move on to a place like Amsterdam, with its large and flourishing community of Jews from Spain and Portugal and a government that granted them rights almost equal to those enjoyed by the gentiles. They still needed the protection of the King and his assistance in recovering any of their properties and possessions outside Spain. In the meantime, they were penniless, and daily living was an endless struggle with no relief in sight. Furthermore, she was worried about her children.

Carolina was already twenty-four years old. She needed to get married, and her prospects were limited. She had to marry someone of a similar background, someone from a family of *conversos* who had reverted to Judaism. Most of these originated in Portugal or in the Portuguese enclaves in Spain; there were hardly any secret Jews of Spanish descent remaining in Spain. The Portuguese communities were deeply involved in commerce. Most of their members were prosperous or even wealthy, and they would expect a sizable dowry. Where would she find a dowry for her glorious, effervescent Carolina?

And then there was Felipe. Twenty-one years old, bright, intelligent, articulate, charming, and with such beautiful manners. What kind of future awaited him? He could not find employment fitting his station, because after all, he was a Jew or at least a heretic. So he was reduced to being a librarian. How they had fallen.

The only bright spots in their lives, and especially in Felipe's life, were the periodic visits of Rabbi Menachem Mendel Strasbourg who lived in the city of Metz on the edge of the Duchy of Lorraine, some distance to the east. The Jews of Metz had been expelled in 1365, but when the French had taken possession of the city in 1567, they had allowed Jews to settle there once again. A large Jewish community had grown up in Metz during the century after their return. Rabbi Strasbourg studied with Felipe whenever he came to Paris. These sessions were the highlight of Felipe's life, and he had expressed a desire to seek employment in Metz and send money to his family. *Perhaps*, thought Doña Angelica with a deep sadness, *that would be for the best.*

A few days after Sebastian arrived in Paris, Rabbi Strasbourg arrived to make his acquaintance.

"My mother has told me about you, Rabbi Strasbourg," said Sebastian. "We are grateful for everything you have done for our family, especially for Felipe."

"You are very kind. I consider it an honor and a privilege to help your family. But before we go on, let's establish one thing. You can call me Mendel, if you will allow me to call you Sebastian."

Sebastian shook his head. "I can't call a rabbi by his first name."

"Then you can call me Reb Mendel. That is a customary honorary title among Ashkenazi Jews. And if you wish, I can call you Reb Sebastian."

"No, Sebastian will be fine ... Reb Mendel."

"Excellent," said Reb Mendel. "Has your mother also told you the nature of my connection to your family?"

"Not really. She said it has something to do with my father. She started telling me, but then she said that since you would be coming very soon she would let you tell me."

"All right. You know that your father spent two years in Poland when everyone thought he was dead."

"Yes, I do."

"Did he tell you anything about it?"

"He said that it was the most incredible experience of his life. He also told me some of the things he learned during those two years."

"Did he tell you where in Poland he had been?"

"No. I mean, he might have mentioned it, but it didn't stick in my mind. Do you know where he was?"

"Yes, I certainly do know," said Reb Mendel. "He was in a place called Pulichev. And the rabbi with whom he studied is Rabbi Shlomo Strasbourg. That rabbi is my father. Some people call him Rabbi Shlomo Pulichever, because that is where my family has served as rabbis for generations, but our family name is really Strasbourg, after the city in which we lived until its Jewish community was destroyed."

"Destroyed? What do you mean?"

"There was a terrible plague back then that killed half the

population of Europe, maybe more."

"Yes, I know," said Sebastian. "The Black Death of 1348."

"Yes, that's the one. People blamed the Jews. In Strasbourg, a few hundred Jews were herded onto a platform and burned alive. The rest were expelled. My family was fortunate to be among those who were expelled."

"That is very sad."

"It is truly sad, Sebastian. And it is the story of our people for over a thousand years. The world measures heroism by feats of valor on the battlefield and other acts of a similar nature. But I think there is nothing more heroic than the devotion of our people to the Almighty and His Torah despite all the persecution we have suffered. It would have been so easy to just give it all up and blend in with the rest of the world. We could have spared ourselves so much pain and suffering. But we remained loyal and steadfast. Even in Spain, where our people gave in outwardly rather then be killed or expelled, so many risked their lives by remaining faithful Jews in the privacy of their homes. You are a true hero. Your father was a true hero. Your mother is a true heroine. They had everything a person could desire in this world — rank, honor, wealth, a beautiful family. And they put it all in jeopardy for the sake of their faith."

Sebastian felt his eyes grow moist. "Thank you so much. You know, when my father first told us about who we really were, I was excited. It was such a romantic notion. Imagine, in addition to everything I already had, I now had a secret faith. It was very exciting, at least to me. I had a sister — Isabel, may she rest in peace — who was crushed by the revelation. I think her reaction was more in touch with reality than mine. But I have come to appreciate the harsh reality of who I am. I have suffered for my Jewish identity, and it has become all the more precious to me."

Reb Mendel stood up and walked to the window, allowing Sebastian a moment to compose himself.

"I never had the pleasure of meeting your father," said Reb Mendel as he returned to his seat. "I was married in Vienna and lived there for the first two years after my marriage. When the Jews were expelled in 1670, we all moved to Metz — that is, my wife and I and her family. I've only been back to Pulichev once since then, and it was after the two years that your father spent there. But my father spoke of him often. He considered him a really extraordinary person."

"I didn't recognize your name or your city," said Sebastian, "but I remember that my father considered himself very fortunate to have found a man like your father to teach him. He spoke a great deal about your father's qualities, both as a scholar and as a human being." Sebastian saw the question on Reb Mendel's face and smiled. "He really did speak about him often, but he always referred to him as his rabbi, so I didn't become familiar with his name."

"It doesn't matter," said Reb Mendel.

"Oh, but it does. I owe your father a debt of gratitude, which I would like to convey to him personally. I would like to meet him some day, only I don't see travel plans to Poland in my immediate future."

"Anything is possible, Sebastian. Poland is not so far away. Not more than a few weeks' journey. And besides, my father may come here one day. He's been here before."

"I look forward to that day."

"So do I. In the meantime, I am at your service. If you would like me to learn with you during my visits here, as I have been doing with your brother Felipe, it would be my greatest honor. And if there is anything else I can do for your family, please give me the opportunity to help. If my father were here he would extend himself to his utmost ability to assist you. I am ready to do the same on his behalf. And on my own."

The door opened and Carolina burst into the room. "Sebastian, Rabbi Strasbourg, dinner is ready. Oh, this is so thrilling. The whole family together — I mean, well, you know — and a guest at the table. It is almost like home."

Doña Angelica was waiting for them in the small dining room. She seated Sebastian at the head of the table with Reb Mendel to his right, and she herself took the seat at the opposite end with Carolina on her right and Felipe on her left. The table was set with fine china and cutlery. Two tapers in the center of the table provided candlelight, while oil lamps on the wall illuminated the room. A small vase of cut flowers stood near the tapers. The Norwegian housekeeper brought baskets of warm bread and platters of salads and laid them out on the table.

"This is a really a special occasion," said Doña Angelica when everyone was seated. "Sebastian is here, and we are having a formal dinner, with everything prepared kosher exactly according to the rabbi's instructions. Tonight I don't feel quite like the widow that I am. Tonight I feel joyous and elated. So let's have a wonderful evening. Let's talk only about happy things and not about things that will make us sad."

"That, dear Mother," said Felipe, "eliminates just about every topic of conversation we could have."

"Oh, shush, Felipe," said Carolina. "Don't be such a cynic. Let me tell you about the children I tutor. They are the most miserable group of troublemakers I have ever met, but I love them dearly."

The wine flowed freely as Carolina regaled everyone with story after story about the difficulty her students were having with the Spanish language. Her imitations of their butchered Spanish sentences delivered with a heavy French accent were so perfect that the dinner table erupted in laughter. Even Reb

Mendel, who spoke no Spanish, was amused and laughed politely.

The mood of the evening was mellowed by the wine, the food and the conversation, and everyone around the table contributed reminiscences and stories that amused, touched and sometimes brought tears to the eyes of the listeners. The last to speak was Sebastian who chose to retell the story of his escape from prison with the assistance of the holy hermit who would be transformed by legend into a hunchback with magical powers. There were many amusing parts to the story, but the graphic depiction of the mortal dangers he had faced brought a shudder to Doña Angelica's shoulders and a tremor to her lips.

"I am so sorry, Mother," he said quickly. "I should not have told this story."

"No, it's all right, Sebastian," she said, quickly composing herself.

But the mood was broken.

"Listen, I have some good news," she said with forced brightness. "At least, I think it is good news. I have been petitioning the King to help me recover our estates and properties in Alsace, Luxembourg, and Burgundy. My cousin Giscard Duvalier, Comte de Bonvilliers, came by this afternoon and told me that the King has decided to grant us an audience and hear what we have to say. It may not happen right away, but at least it has been put on the calendar."

"That is wonderful news, Mother," said Sebastian. "We have hope at last."

Carolina leaped from her chair and embraced her mother. "Oh, I will miss those little troublemakers and their absurd Spanish," she said, "but I will learn to live without them."

"Giscard also asked that you come around to his cottage, Sebastian," said Doña Angelica. "Giscard enjoys calling it a cottage, but it is at least forty times as large as this house. He says he may have something for you to do while we wait for the king to give us a hearing."

"That is good news, too, mother. I was wondering what I would do with myself here in Paris. Perhaps he can find something for Gonzalo as well, although I think that Gonzalo can take perfectly good care of himself."

"That he can, Sebastian. And thank Heaven for his resourcefulness and the protection of the Almighty that brought you back to us alive and well. Oh yes, and one more thing. Very, very important. What could it be?" She put her fingers to her forehead as if trying to recall some elusive piece of information. "Ah, yes. Now, I remember. Giscard said that when we come to our audience we should bring Rabbi Strasbourg along."

Reb Mendel recoiled in shock. "The King asked for me? How can that be? He doesn't even know who I am."

"My dear Rabbi Strasbourg," she said. "My family is a bone of contention between France and Spain. The King extends his protection to us, not out of chivalry to a widow in distress, but because it embarrasses the Spanish crown. The French government knows everything about us, everywhere we go, every *sou* we spend, everyone that comes to visit us. Believe me, Rabbi Strasbourg, they know everything about you."

"But what do I have to do with your petition? Why does he want to see me?"

Doña Angelica shrugged. "Who knows? We will find out."

"But I live in Metz," said Reb Mendel, his agitation unrelieved. "It takes me days to get to Paris. Will I have to remain here until the audience?"

"Royal palaces move slowly, Rabbi. We will be given notice many weeks in advance of the date of our audience.

And even then, we may have to wait in attendance for several days, if not more, until the King finally sees us. You will have plenty of time to get here, Rabbi."

The summer passed by without any word from the palace. Autumn came softly to Paris. Gentle rains fell almost daily from the middle of September into October. The traffic in the fashionable districts and in the government center grew heavier as the families of the aristocracy returned from their summer homes. The leafy planes turned russet and gold before they shed their foliage onto the boulevard to be turned to mulch under the wheels of the elegant carriages. October melted into November, and in the Rue Parmentier, the Dominguez family still waited for the call from the royal palace that failed to come.

Life continued in its tense and desultory fashion. Doña Angelica puttered and worried and read the latest French and German literary works. Carolina tutored, read and dreamed. Felipe worked at the library and studied with Reb Mendel at every opportunity. Sebastian was occupied with his duties at the chateau of Giscard Duvalier and sat in from time to time half-distractedly when Reb Mendel and Felipe studied together. And all of them lived on the edge of high anxiety.

Finally, when the icy winds toward the end of November heralded the approaching winter, Duvalier, a florid man in his late thirties, with fashionable long hair and a mustache, appeared on their doorstep with specific information about the audience. He informed the family that the audience would take place on the morning of 16 December. He also asked that the Rabbi from Metz be available in Paris a few days beforehand and that they all meet in the Rue Parmentier when the time of the audience drew closer.

Two nights before the appointed time, they gathered in

the Dominguez home. They all had a glass of white wine. Then Giscard Duvalier addressed them.

"With your permission, Madame Dominguez, my esteemed kinswoman, let me explain the political situation in Paris right now, and then we will see how we can take the best advantage of it. By the way, do we need to be concerned about your housekeeper who keeps puttering about?"

"Helga?" said Doña Angelica. "She is harmless. And besides, she only speaks Norwegian and a tiny bit of French. If we want to be absolutely sure she doesn't understand what we are saying, we can speak Spanish or German. She does not speak a word of either language. Oh yes, Rabbi Strasbourg doesn't speak Spanish, so I suggest we converse in German tonight."

"That is perfectly fine," said Duvalier. "Now, here is the situation. I do not need to describe to you the greatness of King Louis XIV. He has brought France to a level of power, prosperity and culture greater than perhaps at any time in our history. The whole world trembles before France. The whole world buys our products. The whole world reads our writers. The whole world even imitates our fashions. The whole world fears and hates us but at the same time adores us. All this is to the credit of our King."

"*Vive le Roi!*" said Sebastian. "Long live the King!" The others quickly followed suit.

"Yes, indeed," said Duvalier. "Long live the King. He is in his prime now, at the height of his powers. Did you know that people have taken to calling him the *Roi Soleil,* the Sun King? Just as the planets revolve around the sun, so does the French court and all of France revolve around him and, increasingly, so does all of Europe. This is what our king is accomplishing. This will be his legacy. But there can only be one sun among the planets, and the King is competing with another sun. Do you know who it is?"

There was a brief, somewhat uncomfortable silence.

"No doubt you mean the Pope," said Doña Angelica.

"Yes and no," said Duvalier. "It is not so much the Pope as a man, although Pope Innocent XI is certainly a formidable personality. It is even more so the ecclesiastical establishment of the Catholic Church in Rome. They project their power into France. They send in their Papal Legates at will, and this greatly displeases the King. Did any of you hear about what has been going on at the palace this last month?"

Doña Angelica shook her head. There was no other response.

"A year ago," continued Duvalier, "the King convened an Assemblé de Clergé, a conference of the most important churchmen in France. Under the guidance of the King, this group is on the verge of issuing a declaration that will severely limit the power of the Roman churchmen in France. Among a long list of other enactments, no Papal Legate will be allowed into France without the express consent of the King, and the King will now have the right to issue laws on ecclesiastical matters. It is a revolution, my friends. A veritable revolution."

"It is not surprising then," said Sebastian, "that we have not heard from the palace in such a long time."

"Yes and no," said Duvalier. "The King and his councilors have had many other things on their minds besides the Dominguez family, but the conference of churchmen has certainly been one of them. In any case, let me not mislead you. You should in no way underestimate the importance of your petition. The King will not want to give in to the demands of the Pope and the Catholic Church outside France at this time. On the contrary, I think he may be inclined to look with favor on your petition simply as another act of defiance to reinforce the independence of the French Church."

"Then that is good," said Doña Angelica. "There is hope for us."

"Well, yes and no," said Duvalier. "It would be much easier for the King if you were a good Christian widow being persecuted by the Spanish Church. But you are a Jew, and that presents a bit of a problem. Now, don't get me wrong. I am not one of those bloodthirsty hatemongers of a darker age. I consider myself an enlightened man, a student of science and philosophy. While I am a Christian, I do not follow it in the old superstitious ways. In fact, in a certain way, I admire the Jews. And I certainly admire you, my esteemed kinswoman." He bowed gallantly toward Doña Angelica. "Our blood connection means much more to me than a small matter like your connection to the tribe of Moses. But you have to understand, in the world at large a Christian is a Christian and a Jew is a Jew."

"So are we going to suffer once again because we are Jews?" said Sebastian. "Is it a serious problem?"

"Again I have to say, yes and no. The king has shown himself to be a friend of the Jews in his own way. He has signed letters patent several times confirming and even increasing the privileges of the Jews of Metz. You know, about ten years ago a Jewish peddler in Metz, a fellow named Raphael Levi — strange that I should remember the name — was accused of killing a Christian child for some silly reason. The man was arrested, condemned and tortured to death. Did anyone hear about this?"

"I did," said Reb Mendel quietly.

"Yes, of course. You would know about it, wouldn't you? In any case, an enlightened clergyman named Richard Simon brought the case to the King. The King ordered his council to investigate the records of the Metz Parliament, and based on this investigation, he concluded that judicial murder had been committed. He then decreed that any criminal charges against a Jew must be brought directly to the King."

"So it seems," said Doña Angelica, "that he is sympathetic to the Jewish people?"

"Well, *madame* ..."

"Yes and no?"

"Exactly. Yes and no. He seems personally sympathetic, but the Jewish people are still forbidden to settle in France, although the government turns a blind eye to many of them that live here unofficially. The Jews have a natural talent for making money, you know. They are the perfect bourgeois, and they contribute a lot to the economy. So we stuff our pockets with the money, and we make believe they don't exist. Now, if you will excuse me, my mouth is dry."

He poured himself another glass of wine and took a long sip.

"Where will we be going for the audience?" asked Doña Angelica.

"Ah, yes, of course. You need to know that, don't you? You will come to the Chateau de Versailles. The king and the queen will both receive you."

Carolina clapped her hands and squealed with delight. "I hear it is being made into the most spectacular palace ever built."

"It is all that and more, young lady," said Duvalier. "But don't get me started on Versailles and the importance of the place to the king's plans. Otherwise, we will be sitting here all night."

Carolina laughed. "Perhaps another time, *monsieur*."

"It will be my pleasure, *mademoiselle*," said Duvalier. "Unfortunately, you will not be coming to Versailles this time. Only your mother, your brother and the Rabbi are invited. I will come by in my carriage an hour after dawn and take you there. The King has asked that I accompany you to the audience."

"Do you have any idea, *monsieur*," said Reb Mendel, "why I have been summoned to this audience?"

"No, I do not, Rabbi. We will find out in due course, I am sure. In any case, I think we have covered all the important points about this audience. I hope I have made myself clear."

"So basically what are you saying, my dear Giscard?" said Doña Angelica. "What are we to expect?"

"Madame Dominguez, I haven't the faintest idea."

AN AUDIENCE
IN VERSAILLES · 6

O N THE MORNING OF THE APPOINTED DAY, Paris was covered with a blanket of snow that had fallen during the night. Giscard Duvalier's carriage was at the Dominguez home well before dawn to ensure that they would not be late for the audience with the King.

As the carriage pulled away, a black horse-drawn cab with black curtains drawn across its windows pulled around a corner and followed in its tracks. The black cab stayed well back as it followed the carriage. From time to time, the curtains would part ever so slightly, and a glint of watchful eyes would flash in the cab's interior shadows. The cab followed the carriage until the outskirts of Versailles. Then it pulled into a side street and disappeared from view.

The carriage entered the village of Versailles, its passengers unaware that they had been followed. The stately trees with their bare snow-laden branches and the snow-covered bed of leaves on the road created a muffled silence through which they rode. Presently, the silence was broken by ragged sounds of banging, hammering, and shouting that grew increasingly louder. Then the royal hunting lodge came into view. The building had been massive to begin with, but now that the King had chosen to make it his principal palace and the seat of the French government, it was being expanded to mammoth proportions. The skeletal outer wings, which stretched out almost as far as the eye could see, were covered with scaffolding and tarpaulins. Hundreds of laborers hurried back and forth bringing materials from the piles of bricks and planking that sat like a miniature mountain range on the endless front lawn. And the noise was ceaseless.

The Dominguez family was shown into a waiting room that smelled of new paint. After about two hours, they were led into a lavish sitting room. The King and Queen were sitting in richly upholstered armchairs. An unoccupied high-backed chair stood directly in front of them.

King Louis XIV was a man in his early forties with long dark hair, a long nose and imperious, intelligent eyes. Queen Marie Thérèse was the same age, a pale, dwarfish woman with the protruding upper lip of the Hapsburg family. To the right of the king stood his powerful minister of finance, Jean Baptiste Colbert, a cold-faced man in his low sixties. Three dwarfs stood beside the Queen, dressed respectively in outfits of red, green and blue. Their eyes danced with merry mischief.

The Dominguez party bowed deeply to the King and Queen.

"Madame Dominguez," said Colbert, "out of deference to you, a lady and a royal kinswoman, Their Majesties have granted you permission to sit in their presence. The chair is for you."

Doña Angelica curtsied and took her seat. Sebastian stood two steps back to her right, with Reb Mendel beside him, and Giscard Duvalier stood two steps back to her left.

"*Madame*, you understand that we are in a difficult position here," said the King. "We understand that you are living on a stipend from our government and that you want to recover the properties of your husband in the lands that are in our domain. We are sympathetic to your situation. We also understand that the Spanish Crown and the Spanish

Inquisition are demanding that we return you and your children to Spain.

"Your husband was our kinsman. His great-grandfather King Philip II of Spain was also our great-grandfather and Her Majesty's great-grandfather. Therefore, we feel obligated by blood and honor to come to your assistance. If you should agree to disabuse yourselves of this notion of following the Jewish religion, it would make matters much easier for us. Would you consider that?"

"Your Majesty, my husband lived and died for his faith," said Doña Angelica. "We would dishonor his memory if we even considered abandoning it."

"Yes, of course. We do not approve of your choices, but we admire your gallantry. Still, it is rather odd to be such a close relative to a Jewish family. We have been a good friend to the Jews who have settled in our domain. We have found their presence beneficial to the motherland, but they are an alien tribe. They are not our countrymen, and we have never felt any sort of kinship for them whatsoever. This is a strange and extraordinary situation. But we are inclined to help you and your family, *madame*."

"Thank you, Your Majesty," said Doña Angelica.

"We have not yet decided exactly how to help you," said the King. "Her Majesty wished to hear from you."

The Queen spoke in a high piping voice. "*Madame*, we are distressed that our kinswoman and her family should have turned their backs on the truths of Christianity. We are distressed that they should choose to jeopardize their immortal souls by clinging to heretical and blasphemous beliefs. At the same time, we are deeply grateful to your husband for his pure devotion to our brother, King Charles II of Spain. We believe he was the only one in the entire royal palace of Madrid who truly cared about our brother and considered his welfare and his happiness. Our brother loved your late husband. He was very upset that he had to witness the death of your husband in the Plaza Mayor, and we believe that he has never recovered from his grief."

The Queen dabbed at her eyes with a lace handkerchief.

"Because of our deep gratitude, we would advise His Majesty to help you and your family even if your late husband had not been our kinsman. We encourage him to do so even more because of the royal blood that flows in the veins of your children."

"Thank you, Your Majesty," said Doña Angelica. In a perverse way, it occurred to her at that moment that the Queen's French with her heavy Spanish accent was probably just as bad as the Spanish of Carolina's students with their heavy French accents. But she did not find the thought amusing.

"We asked that your Rabbi accompany you," said the Queen, "because we have a curiosity about a certain Jewish belief. It would be unseemly to invite a rabbi to the palace just for that purpose, but in this situation …."

The Queen leaned back and whispered to one of the dwarfs who stood beside her. The minister motioned to Reb Mendel to step forward.

"Your Majesty," he said to the queen, "this is Rabbi Menachem Mendel Strasbourg. He is a teacher of Jewish texts in Metz."

"That is precisely what we need," said the Queen. "Someone who knows something about the Jewish texts. Are you familiar with the Talmud?"

Reb Mendel opened his mouth to speak but no words came out. He tried again and finally managed a response. "Yes, Your Majesty. I have studied the Talmud for most of my life."

The Queen clapped her hands. "Good. You will answer our question." She pointed to the red-clad dwarf. "Hannibal, ask him the question. We will sit back and listen."

The dwarf bounded forward on his short legs until he stood almost face to face with Reb Mendel.

"The question," he said in an incongruously deep baritone, "is in regard to a woman's choice in choosing a mate. Someplace in the Talmud it states that a man may not marry a woman unless he sees her first because she may not find favor in his eyes and they will not have a happy marriage. But a woman may marry without ever seeing her prospective husband because of ..." The dwarf pulled a piece of paper from his pocket. "Because *tav lemeisav tandu milimeisav armelu*. I don't know if I got the pronunciation exactly right. The translation I was given is that it is better to live with someone else than to live alone. Is that right, Rabbi?"

"Yes, that is the phrase," said Reb Mendel. "Your pronunciation was good. And so is your translation."

"That seems to mean that a man is concerned about the qualities of the person he marries while a woman would be willing to marry anyone just so she shouldn't have to live alone. Her Majesty wishes to know why the Talmud holds women in such low esteem and why Madame Dominguez, after having experienced life as a royal princess, would want to live in a society where she and her daughter would be so demeaned?"

The dwarf glanced back at the Queen. She nodded, and he returned to his place. The King put his hand across his mouth to conceal his smile.

"That is our question, Rabbi," said the queen. "Do you have an answer?"

Reb Mendel cleared his throat to give himself a moment to collect his thoughts.

"Your Majesty, I am familiar with that passage in the Talmud," he said. "I have seen it many times. But I do not believe it is meant in the sense that Monsieur Hannibal suggests. There are undoubtedly some women who live in conditions of such distress and impoverishment that any marriage would be a welcome deliverance. But such women cannot be more than a tiny minority. None of the women in my family or in my wife's family would ever have agreed to marry anyone at all just so they could be married. They always insisted on men of the highest personal quality and the finest prospects for success, men that would bring them honor, respect, and wealth, men that would be good husbands and fathers. They would never settle for just anyone."

The Queen nodded vigorously. "That is as it should be. But how do you explain those words in the Talmud?"

"Your Majesty, the Talmud is discussing someone who sends an agent to stand in at his or her wedding. A man is forbidden to do so if he has never seen the bride, but a woman is permitted to get married by proxy even if she has never seen the groom."

"Aha!" said the Queen. "That is exactly our point. What is the difference?"

"Your Majesty, in both cases, a great deal of inquiry was made about the prospective bride or groom. Information was gathered about the lineage of the families, their financial standing, the character of the prospective bride or groom, their physical appearance, their personalities, everything."

The queen nodded. "Yes, of course."

"So let us talk first about the man," said Reb Mendel. "When he sends off the agent to marry his bride by proxy he knows he will be getting a woman who is perfectly suited to be a wife to him and a mother to his children. But even though, based on the information, the woman sounds exactly right for him, when he sees her in person it is possible that she will just not appeal to him. There are always intangibles. Logically, everything may seem right, but emotionally, he may just not care for her. And then what happens? He finds himself married to her, and his dislike turns into resentment and then into hate, and the home becomes a hotbed of discord. That is why the Sages forbade a man to marry a woman unless he had seen her first and found her appealing."

"We understand," said the Queen. "And what about the woman?"

"The woman we are discussing has also done her research very thoroughly. She has learned that the man she is considering is a good person, a kind and caring person. She has learned that he is from a respectable and prosperous family and that he has excellent prospects in commerce or as a scholar. She has learned that he is of a good appearance, that his manners are gentle, and that he is always clean and dresses elegantly. According to what she has learned from her reliable sources, this man is perfectly suited to her. He will be an excellent husband and father to her children. She has chosen well. But then she sees him, and he does not quite appeal to her."

"Exactly! So what does she do?" said the Queen.

"The woman is more practical than the man. If she has finally identified a man who meets all her requirements, she will make the marriage work, even if in the beginning she does not find him so appealing. She will work at the marriage with the knowledge that they will grow together and that in time, as they strive together toward their common goals, they will achieve the closeness that she cherishes so much."

"That is true," said the Queen. She looked at the king. "Women are the practical ones, Your Majesty. Isn't that true?"

"They certainly are," said the king fondly. "Without you, we would be lost."

"We certainly would be," said the Queen. She turned back to Reb Mendel. "So what is the meaning of that phrase Hannibal read to us before?"

"The Talmud is explaining," he replied, "why women are more practical than men when it comes to choosing a spouse.

A woman is a natural mother and homemaker. Her sense of self is based on having children and running a household. But a man, on the other hand, is a warrior, a merchant, a scholar. His sense of self is not so connected to his home. Therefore, a woman is more motivated to get married, and she will be more clearheaded about it than a man."

The King smiled broadly and turned to the Queen. "That seems quite an excellent explanation, Your Majesty."

"Indeed, it does, Your Majesty," said the Queen. "That is exactly how our royal marriages work. It is the women who are the practical ones, and the men have their heads in the sands and the stars."

The King laughed. "Precisely," he said.

The Queen smiled at him, and then she turned back to face Reb Mendel. "We appreciate your coming here today and responding to our question."

"It was one of the great honors of my life, Your Majesty," said Reb Mendel.

"Your words have the ring of truth. As we understood them before, they didn't really make much sense. We are aware that Jewish women have an important position in your community. Your explanation seems much more reasonable to us. In fact, it reflects a profound wisdom that we find enjoyable."

"Your Majesty," said the King, "should we invite the Rabbi to come regularly to the palace to tutor us in the Talmud?"

The dour Colbert allowed himself a tiny smile. Hannibal and the dwarfs began to titter, but a sharp look from the Queen silenced them.

"We will take the matter under consideration, Your Majesty," said the Queen. "We have heard what we wanted to hear."

Colbert bent down and murmured something to the King, who nodded and turned to Doña Angelica.

"We have given this some thought, *madame,* and this is what we are prepared to do. There are two issues before us: the personal safety of your family and the recovery of your properties. We will guarantee your safety, the safety of your family and the safety of your husband's cavalier who has accompanied your son from Spain for as long as all of you are in our domains. We cannot protect you if you leave to some Portuguese center such as Amsterdam or Hamburg. We also understand that it is not feasible for you to remain in Paris where there is no Jewish community. Therefore, we have decided that it would be best for you to settle in Metz. We will make the arrangements for you and provide you with assistance. We will also express our desire to the leaders of the Jewish community of Metz that you be given every courtesy and consideration."

"We are most grateful, Your Majesty," said Doña Angelica. "May the Almighty bless you with long life filled with glory and success."

"Do not think this is the first time we have received a Jewish blessing, *madame.* All prayers on our behalf are welcome, even the prayers of Jews. As for your claim to the properties of your husband, that will not be a simple matter. We understand that there are very substantial sums involved. It would be much easier if you embraced Christianity, but as you are not inclined to do so, it will be difficult. Still, your husband did hold personal title to these properties. They were not part of the hereditary ducal estate. It is a matter for the lawyers and the judges. We have asked Monsieur Colbert to look into the matter and to do everything he can to recover all or at least a large part of your fortune."

Doña Angelica burst into tears. "Thank you, Your Majesty," she managed to whisper. "Oh, thank you so much."

The carriage was ready and waiting for them when they emerged from the royal hunting lodge. By the time the car-

riage was rolling through the streets of Versailles, its passengers were absorbed in an excited review of the successful
audience with the king and queen. As they passed through
the outskirts of the village, they did not notice the black cab
with black curtains on its windows that emerged from a side
street and followed them into Paris.

The move to Metz took place soon after the winter passed.
In response to the King's request that every courtesy and consideration be given to the Dominguez family, the community
provided a handsome house near the synagogue. The house
was well furnished and considerably more spacious than the
house on the Rue Parmentier.

It was a time of great joy and hope for the family. For
nearly two years, they had been suspended between two
worlds, outsiders to the world of their birth without having achieved entry into the world of their faith and ancestry.
Their lives had been in danger and their future clouded. But
now at last, they were going home, not to a home they had
ever known, but to a home about which they had dreamed
and for which they had yearned for years, a home in which
they could live their lives as they chose, a home in which they
could be themselves.

Doña Angelica would once again become a lady with
social standing, a mother who could concentrate on finding suitable matches for her children. Carolina would find
good friends and, with the help of Heaven, a husband; her
free spirit would finally find expression in an environment
of safety and support. Felipe would pursue his Torah studies
and his intellectual development. As for Sebastian, he had
ambitions. He had trained in the conduct of commerce in
the employ of Giscard Duvalier, and he would now have the
opportunity to integrate himself into the network of Jewish
merchants and bankers. When he recovered his father's

properties, he would invest the proceeds and amass such a great fortune that the family would once again be able to live in princely style, only this time they would be Jewish princes.

They left on a Sunday morning so that, despite the uncertainties of the road, they would be reasonably assured of reaching Metz before the following Shabbos. Helga packed all the belongings of the family onto a cart and sat herself down among the packages to make sure they were not stolen while in transport. She snapped an order to the driver, and the cart rumbled off.

A short while later, Gonzalo came by to see them off. He seemed happy and content with his new life in France, but he would forever be bound heart and soul to the Dominguez family. He embraced Sebastian and Felipe and assured Doña Angelica that she could always call on him. And then it was time to go.

The family got into the carriage Giscard Duvalier had provided to take them to their new home in Metz. The driver cracked his whip over the heads of the horses, and the carriage rolled away.

EFFIGIES AND LAWSUITS · 7

THE FAMILY ARRIVED IN METZ on Friday afternoon. They rode through the busy streets of the Jewish quarter where Shabbos was approaching with frenetic activity. Matrons, followed by children or maids carrying baskets, examined the wide variety of produce on display. In front of the synagogue — a large stone structure with a broad elevated courtyard — peddlers were selling books and religious articles. Men in the colorful garb and plumed hats of the Portuguese Nation, as the former *conversos* from the Iberian Peninsula were known, gesticulated extravagantly as they conversed with German Jews of more modest attire and demeanor.

There was an excitement in the air, a sense of anticipation unfamiliar to the Dominguez family. In Spain, the observance of Shabbos had been an important and venerated ritual for the family, but they had not had any contact with other secret Jews. They had lit candles on Friday night in the privacy of their chambers and recited a few psalms. For the rest of the Shabbos, although they had tried to limit themselves to leisurely activities, they had behaved as if nothing was essentially different. In Paris, their observance had not been limited by fear but by ignorance, and by their isolation from the community of other Jews. In Metz, however, even before they had stepped out of the carriage for the first time, they were already encountering the singular experience of Shabbos.

The community had provided a house for the Dominguez family in the neighborhood where the Portuguese population of the city was concentrated; it was no more than a five-minute walk from the synagogue. The representation of the Portuguese Nation in Metz was relatively minor, certainly when compared to the Portuguese communities of Amsterdam and Hamburg, but it was just enough to make the Dominguez family comfortable during this period when they had to remain close to the royal palace in Paris. There was no Portuguese synagogue or rabbi, and all the Jews originating from the Iberian Peninsula prayed together with the German Jews; those who were more learned prayed on their own according to the Sephardic custom, while the others just followed the Ashkenazic custom of the rest of the congregation.

The family's belongings had arrived a day earlier, and Helga had managed to unpack before they arrived. As the exhausted travelers entered their new home in Metz, they were greeted by the blended aromas of Shabbos cooking. Miriam Strasbourg, Reb Mendel's wife, was bustling about the kitchen, making sure everything was exactly as it should be. The arrival of the Dominguez family was a sensation in Metz, and the kitchen table was covered from end to end with cakes, kugels and savory dishes, each with a little note attached identifying the person who had sent it.

The family just managed to wash off the dust of the road and change into fresh clothing when darkness began to fall. Doña Angelica lit the candles a little early. She covered her eyes and offered up silent prayers until her emotions overflowed and she had to stop before she broke down in tears. In the meantime, Reb Mendel came by and escorted the men to the synagogue.

Sebastian and Felipe were welcomed as celebrities. Everyone had heard about the fabulous Don Pedro and his heroic demise in Madrid and about Sebastian's hair-raising escape from the clutches of the Inquisition. The Portuguese Jews crowded around them and embraced them, and the German Jews solemnly shook their hands.

The Rabbi invited them to sit next to him on the East Wall. Felipe was already quite proficient in Hebrew, but Sebastian could hardly read.

"I'm not very good at Hebrew," he whispered to the Rabbi, "and I don't know my way around the prayer book. Maybe it would be better if I sat more toward the back."

The Rabbi smiled. "You are our honored guest, and you must sit here this Shabbos. Afterward, we will find you a suit-able place in the synagogue. For now, Rabbi Strasbourg will sit next to you and show you what is being said, when to stand and when to bow down. You can say what you like. You need not be embarrassed. Everyone knows your story, and besides, you will be far from the first secret Jew who has come here without being fluent in the holy tongue. Do not be con-cerned, my young friend. Just sit back, and enjoy yourself."

And enjoy himself he did. The synagogue was ablaze with light, and the walls reverberated with the grand liturgy and the songs welcoming the Shabbos Queen. Unlike the churches of his experience in which the responses had a mechanical and regimented decorum, the responses in the synagogue were bursting with passion and individuality yet united in an integrated, harmonious cry of love of the Almighty. Here the community highlighted the special qualities of the indi-vidual and helped him form a relationship with the Creator in the greater context of His covenant with the Jewish people. Sebastian felt confident that in this place he would find the expression of his personal Jewish identity.

During the next few months, the Dominguez family finally began to develop a Jewish life in an atmosphere of relative normalcy, a Jewish life that could then be transported with them to any community they chose as their permanent residence. One of the first things the Rabbi did for them was assign them Hebrew names. Angelica became Abigail and Carolina became Rachel, both according to the Sephardic pronunciation. Sebastian became Shimon and Felipe became Pinhas. He also assigned a name to Don Pedro posthumously: Akiva, after the great sage who gave his life to sanctify the Name of the Almighty. Except for the recitation of their names during the Torah reading, however, the family continued to use the old names, as did many of the Portuguese Jews.

As they acclimated themselves to Jewish life, much of the family's time was still occupied by meetings with Giscard Duvalier, visits to various government offices, and endless meetings with attorneys and financial agents. But at the same time, there were also community functions and social affairs. There was a thoroughly enjoyable Pesach spent in the home of the Rabbi with many members of the community coming to visit throughout the festival. There was genial company, stimulating conversation and camaraderie.

Above all, there was the pervasive presence of the Torah in every aspect of Jewish life, something the Dominguez family had never seen and could never have imagined. Every little step of daily life, from the first waking moment, was somehow connected to the performance of a mitzvah or the reinforcement of a Torah concept. Every milestone — be it a wedding, bar-mitzvah, *bris*, funeral, dedication of a building or any other family or community function — was commemorated by a Torah thought appropriate to the occasion or to the weekly Torah portion, usually both. The thought, which was almost always inspirational, was delivered by the Rabbi or by one of the laypeople. Often it was also entertaining and sometimes it was technical, but the Dominguez family did not mind. The very idea of having the entire community involved in a scholarly understanding of the Torah on one level or another was incredibly exhilarating.

In the meantime, life was progressing. Doña Angelica was gaining a wide circle of friends and admirers, and she was in her element. Her children were also doing well.

Carolina continued to tutor children in Spanish and French. She was already twenty-four years old, and most of the women her age were married. But this did not deter her from forming solid friendships with them and helping them with their young children. A few good matches were suggested despite her relatively advanced age, by which most young women were long married. Her radiant personal qualities, as well as the prospect of a generous dowry once Don Pedro's properties were recovered, provided ample motivation for the matchmakers of Metz and Hamburg. Carolina was taking her time to decide, even though she knew she did not have much time to spare before they would begin offering her widowers and divorced men.

As for Felipe, it was becoming increasingly clear that he was intent on becoming a rabbi, both for his own intellectual and spiritual edification and because of his desire to help other Jews who found themselves in similar predicaments. The Portuguese Nation was in desperate need of leaders, and he aspired to be one of them.

Sebastian was the only one who had not quite found his rhythm yet. He went for long walks along the Moselle River, which ran through the city of Metz, his hands thrust into his pockets, his gaze fixed on the ground in front of him. He did not notice the dark-clad figures that often followed him at a distance. When he visited the offices of some of the Portuguese merchants to explore potential business opportunities, he was not aware of the followers that blended into the jostling crowds.

Eventually, Sebastian decided to pursue a business adventure on a grand scale. He procured letters of introduction from Giscard Duvalier and presented them to M. Armand Giroux, the chief financial agent for Charles Léopold Nicolas de Vaudemont, Duke of Lorraine. The city of Metz was the capital of the region of Lorraine, which had been ruled since the end of the first millennium by a long line of hereditary dukes. When the French occupied Lorraine in 1670, the ruling family had fled. Charles Léopold assumed the title in 1675 while living in Austria under the protection of the Hapsburgs, to whom he was connected by marriage. Nonetheless, he retained extensive estates and other financial holdings in Lorraine, which were managed in absentia by Giroux, the former minister of finance. Sebastian offered to use his contacts in the Jewish community to arrange for some advantageous investments. Giroux promised to bring up the matter on one of his regular visits with the duke in Austria.

As he left Giroux's office, Sebastian hummed to himself and walked with a jaunty spring to his step. He did not notice the malevolent eyes staring at him from the shadows of a doorway across the street.

On a warm day in June 1682, Giscard Duvalier arrived unannounced on the doorstep of the Dominguez home in Metz. After they had shared a bottle of wine, he broke the news he had brought.

"*Mesdames et messieurs,*" he began, "I have heard that you are flourishing here in Metz, and I am very pleased. As you know, we have also been making some progress toward recovering your properties in the French domains. The government of Spain has opposed our claims, but we have made strong arguments to the courts in your favor. Our strongest argument, of course, has been that the King wishes that you recover your properties. That is a very persuasive argument. However, we have run into a snag."

"A snag, Giscard?" said Doña Angelica. "What kind of a snag? Is it a serious snag?"

"Well, yes and ... yes. It is a serious snag. There have been developments in Spain. The news has just arrived. I came here immediately."

"What news?" said Doña Angelica. "What can have happened in Spain?"

Duvalier cleared his throat. "Well, it seems that ...."

"Out with it, Giscard. Tell us. You poor dear, you cannot bear to be the bearer of bad news."

"Yes, of course. It is rather unpleasant for me, but as you say, I might as well tell you straight out."

"Straight out."

"Very well, straight out. You and your children, *madame*, have been put on trial by the Holy Office of the Inquisition in Spain. After having made numerous attempts to have you returned to Spain to stand trial in person, the Inquisition officially acknowledged that you would not be returning, especially since the King of France has extended his protection to you and guaranteed your safety. Therefore, the determination was made that you should all be tried in absentia."

"And what does that mean?" asked Sebastian. "What does it matter if we will not be returning to Spain?"

"It matters a great deal, Sebastian. You were all found guilty and condemned to be burned at the stake."

Doña Angelica shuddered and Carolina winced. Sebastian and Felipe sat stone-faced.

"Go on," said Doña Angelica.

"Six weeks ago, there was a small *auto-da-fé* in Burgos," said Duvalier. "You and your children, *madame*, were burned in effigy."

"I know what that means, Giscard, but can you be more specific?"

"They made dummies in your likenesses and tied them to stakes. Then they burned the dummies as if they had been real people."

Doña Angelica took a deep breath. She knew what was coming, but she wanted to hear it anyway. "Go on," she said, her voice barely above a whisper. "Go on, Giscard. Give us the news."

"According to the rules of the Inquisition," he said, "the properties of the condemned are confiscated by the Inquisition. That is how the Inquisition finances itself."

"And that is why so many of its victims are the rich," said Felipe bitterly.

"That is correct, Felipe," said Giscard. "If they don't burn, they don't eat. When they burned your father at the stake, they declared the confiscation of all his properties. But since you had escaped from Spain before his condemnation, our claim was that you had taken possession of the properties in France before the Inquisition could make any claim to them. It is a debatable point, but as I said before, the King is on our side. However, now that all of you have been burned in effigy the Inquisition has laid claim to everything you possess in Spain, France or anywhere else in the world."

Doña Angelica twisted the handkerchief in her hands and gritted her teeth.

"Just this month," she said, "the King's appointed Council of French Clergymen has issued a historic declaration. The French church has broken away from the control of Rome. It is now controlled by the King. Is he subject to the rules of the Spanish Inquisition?"

"No, he is not, *madame*. But it seems to me that the king will not take on the entire Catholic establishment on your behalf, *madame*, even though your husband was exceedingly kind to his brother-in-law, the king of Spain, and even though you are related to him by blood. It seems to me that he does not stand to gain enough for himself and for France by undertaking such a battle."

"So is this the end, Giscard?" she said. "Is there nothing we can do? Are you telling me that the battle is over and we are slain?"

"No, *madame*. We can argue in the courts that the rights of confiscation of the Spanish Inquisition do not extend beyond the borders of Spain."

"And would we succeed with such an argument?"

Duvalier shrugged and threw up his hands. "As they say in Spain, *quien sabe*, who knows. It is rather bleak, *madame*. I cannot tell you otherwise."

The lawsuits continued through the summer and into the autumn. The legal expenses were staggering, but for the time being, they were being borne by Giscard Duvalier who could well afford them. Sebastian managed to secure several good investments for the Duke of Lorraine and turned a handsome profit for himself as well. He saved and reinvested all his profits, denying himself even small extravagances, just in case Duvalier would stop paying their legal expenses and they would have to do it on their own.

The mood in the Dominguez home changed from optimism and even ebullience to gloom and doom. They were grasping at straws, and they knew it. But in the meantime, they had no other hope. If they failed, they would be destitute. They could not count on the King of France supporting them indefinitely. After all, it was quite amazing that he had done it for so long.

There was one bright spot in their gloom, but even this had an edge of darkness. A young man named Uriel Pereira, from an excellent Portuguese family in Hamburg, had been suggested for Carolina. He was twenty-eight years old and just recently returned from Istanbul, the capital of the Turkish Empire, where he had made some important contacts. The prospective couple had met one time and liked each other.

A subsequent meeting was being discussed, but first there would have to be a meeting of the minds regarding the dowry. The Pereira family was prepared to give ten thousand Reichsthalers, and they expected no less from the other side. The match had progressed on the assumption that the Dominguez family could provide such a dowry and even a much larger one once they recovered their properties in France. The people of Metz had gotten wind of this forthcoming match, and the rumor had reached all the way to Amsterdam.

The downturn in the Dominguez fortunes was not yet common knowledge, but Doña Angelica was beside herself, worrying whether she could achieve this advantageous match for her beloved daughter. If the match should fall through because of their destitution, the humiliation to the family would be unbearable.

In November, Sebastian was summoned to the palace in Versailles. His mother was expressly not invited. This was an ominous sign, but the family still refused to give up hope.

When he arrived at the royal palace, Sebastian was shown into an office in the Ministry of Finance. Jean Baptiste Colbert, the dour old minister, was waiting for him.

"Monsieur Dominguez, thank you for coming," said the minister.

Sebastian inclined his head slightly but said nothing.

"We will not burden the King," said the minister, "with being party to our discussions. I believe we can conclude our business without imposing on his time. We are talking, of course, about the disputed properties. There is a gentleman who will be here shortly who has much to contribute on the subject. In the meantime, can I offer you a glass of wine?"

"No, thank you," said Sebastian, "but a glass of water would be very welcome?"

The minister gave him a quizzical look. "Is our wine forbidden?" he said. "Or is it perhaps forbidden for a Jew to drink with a Christian?"

Sebastian flushed a bright red. "I cannot allow myself the luxury of a glass of wine, *monsieur*. I need to keep my wits about me."

"Indeed, you do." There was movement outside the door. "Ah, here comes our visitor."

The door opened, and a heavy man in Spanish attire entered the room. It was Don Alejandro Quinones, Marqués de Murillo.

"So we meet again, young Dominguez," said the Marqués. "You are a long way from Córdoba. I see that you have made it safely."

"Yes, thank you, Your Excellency," said Sebastian, subtly reminding the Marqués that he had failed to report him to the authorities. "I hope you are well."

The Marqués sneezed. "As well as one can be in Paris during the winter. Enough of this patter. Let's get down to business. I am representing the Spanish Crown on this matter. I have come to Paris to conclude it once and for all. Your family has dragged us through the courts, and our patience has run out."

"Your Excellency," said Sebastian, "we are only trying to recover what is rightfully ours."

"Yours? Yours?" sputtered the Marqués. "How dare you! Who worked for this money? Did your father sell perfumes or cattle for a profit? Did he engage in commerce of any sort? He got his wealth from the coffers of the Crown. He got whatever he had from the taxes and revenues that the Crown collected from the good people of Spain. And all the time he was a secret Jew, an impostor posing as a good Christian, a faithful child of the holy Church. Everything he ever had he acquired under false pretenses. Would he have received a single franc if it were know that he was a Jew? Answer that question, young Dominguez. Look me in the eye, and answer it. Would he have received a single franc?"

Sebastian sat in silence. He did not say a word.

"You are silent, because you have nothing to say," said the Marqués. "What can you say? Nothing! Your lawsuits are scandalous. Why should money taken from the royal coffers support a Jewish woman and her children, people who are renegades from Spanish justice and from the Holy Office of the Inquisition, the defenders of the purity of the holy Church? The King has been protecting you because he is a gallant French gentleman and your mother has gained his sympathy, but this outrage must come to an end. The Spanish government is prepared to bring this matter before every court in the land and in Christendom. We will do anything to ensure that your family does not succeed. We will not rest until the properties are recovered and returned to the Spanish Crown, the Spanish Church and the Spanish people, even if the expense of recovering the properties is greater than the value of the properties themselves. We will drive your kinsman Giscard Duvalier, the Comte de Bonvilliers, into ruin. We will drive you into such deep ruin that you will not recover for generations."

"What do you want, Your Excellency?" said Sebastian. "Why did you call me here? What is it that you want from me?"

"I want you to desist from this foolishness," said the Marqués. "It is humiliating for the Spanish Crown to be dragged through the courts by a family of renegade Jews. I know that the French King is enjoying it —"

"That is somewhat unkind, *monsieur*," interrupted the minister, who had remained silent throughout the tirade. There was a malicious twinkle in his eye that he did not try to conceal.

The Marqués grunted and turned back to Sebastian. "In any case, that is what I want from you, young Dominguez. Enough of this foolishness. Enough of these frivolous lawsuits. They are an embarrassment to the Spanish Crown, which your father would never have tolerated if he were alive, and they will bring you down to everlasting ruin."

"If he were alive," Sebastian repeated bitterly.

"We are not here to discuss whether or not your father deserved to die," said the Marqués. "But I will tell you one thing. Your father could have fled from Spain for years before he was arrested. And do you know why he didn't leave? Do you know, young Dominguez?"

Sebastian nodded.

"Say it," said the Marqués. "Why didn't he leave?"

"Because the Crown needed him," said Sebastian.

"So do you think he would countenance what you are doing?"

"Since he was so loyal to the crown," said Sebastian, "that he gave up his life, isn't he owed something in return?"

"Owed something? What was he owed? The queen offered him the opportunity to return to the Church and keep all his titles and estates. I think that was a very generous offer. The Crown owes him nothing beyond that. And it certainly owes you nothing at all."

"So this is a threat?" said Sebastian.

"Call it what you wish," said the Marqués. "I call it a fair warning for the sake of your father, whom I once considered among my good friends."

"I would like to add something," said the minister. "This lawsuit is certainly an embarrassment for the Spanish Crown, but it is also becoming somewhat unpleasant for the French Crown as well. The King, therefore, has asked me to inform you that you may pursue this lawsuit to the fullest extent, but that the Crown will no longer explicitly or implicitly support your claims. The royal support you and your family have enjoyed in this matter is not canceled but it is suspended for the foreseeable future. The royal protection for your personal safety, of course, remains in place."

"I see," said Sebastian. "So that is it. We have lost."

"I believe you have, *monsieur*," said the minister.

THE EVIL EYE · 8

THE EFFECT OF THE DISCONTINUATION OF THE LAWSUITS was immediate. Within a few weeks, all the proper-ties were liquidated, and the proceeds were transferred to the Inquisition. The Dominguez family was effectively destitute, but it did not come as a total shock. Their prospects had been in steep decline ever since they had been burned in effigy.

In a strange way, it was somewhat of a relief. It liber-ated them from the past and allowed them to face the future and make a completely fresh start. They were talented and resourceful people, and they felt confident that somehow they would survive and even prosper. They had sacrificed everything for the Almighty, and in turn, He had shielded and protected them thus far. They trusted in Him that He would continue to do so. The support of the Almighty, they told themselves, was more important than the support of the king of France.

Doña Angelica was concerned about one thing above all. The match between Carolina and Uriel Pereira was becom-ing very serious. They had met again, and it had gone very well. The Pereira family had indicated to the matchmaker that they were just about ready to finalize the match. But what would happen when the Pereiras discovered that the Dominguez family could not provide the couple with even one hundred Reichsthalers, let alone ten thousand? Their interest would quickly evaporate. The glamour of the

Dominguez name and legend would not provide Uriel with the capital to enter international trade markets in a serious manner. The match would never take place, and Carolina would be humiliated and heartbroken. But no matter how much she racked her brain, Doña Angelica could think of nothing to do. She understood full well that according to the customs of the middle and upper classes in both Jewish and gentile society of the times, both families were expected to provide substantial dowries to the new couple. But there was no way in the world she could secure the sum of ten thousand Reichsthalers or even a significant fraction of it.

One day, she decided to pay the matchmaker a visit.

"Frau Klinger, I have to be forthright with you," she said.

"Ah, that is wonderful," said the matchmaker. "I wish all my clients were forthright with me. You would not believe some of the stories I could tell you."

"Oh, I'm sure I would believe them."

"Yes, I suppose you would. And you really should. People tell me so many things, and then they turn out to be so far from the truth that you cannot even see it in the distance. One mother told me that her daughter was so talented that she could sew a wedding dress in a single day."

"And she couldn't?" said Doña Angelica.

The matchmaker grabbed her head from both sides. "A wedding dress in a single day! It would take five angels to do it. I don't know how I could have been so foolish as to believe such a thing. Well, it turns out that the girl was able to take out the seams and adjust the dress for a heavier person. And it took her a whole day to do it!"

"That is an amazing story. Why, I can hardly believe it. In any case, getting back to what we were discussing, I have to tell you that our financial situation has deteriorated. We thought we would be able to recover our holdings in Alsace,

Luxembourg, and Burgundy, but it appears it will be impossible."

"Because of the effigies?" asked the matchmaker.

"You know about that?"

"Of course, Señora Dominguez. Everyone does. The Portuguese Jews know all about these things, and they told the rest of us. No one mentioned anything to you, because no one wanted to cause you pain, but we are all aware of your predicament. Everyone in Metz holds you and your family in the highest esteem, and we all pray for you. The Almighty will help you. You will see."

Doña Angelica felt her eyes mist over. "I am so grateful. I really am. You have all become my family. Your sympathy and support means so much to me, but there are some things that you simply can't … I mean … I don't see how the match can go through. I mean, ten thousand Reichsthalers! I would be hard-pressed to raise a hundred. I don't want to pretend that we can do what we said we would. I don't want to mislead them. We will have to let this match go. The Pereira family will find a better prospect."

"A better prospect? Is there a better prospect than your lovely daughter? I've come to know that young woman well, and she is a rare catch, so intelligent, so full of life and joy. Every moment of her life is a celebration, isn't that so?"

Doña Angelica smiled though her tears. "Yes, that's my Carolina. I don't know where she gets it. Her father was such a serious person, and so am I."

"Well, it doesn't matter," said the matchmaker with a wave of her hand. "She has it, and that's what counts. She will bring her husband many long years of happiness. I think that's more precious than a few Reichsthalers."

"So do I, but will the Pereiras be willing to forgo the considerable dowry they were expecting?"

The matchmaker leaned forward and placed a hand on

Doña Angelica's arm. "There has been a development," she said, lowering her voice for dramatic effect. "I have received a letter from Uriel Pereira's father. He has heard about your troubles, and he is still prepared to go forward with the match. Apparently, arrangements have been made, and the sum expected from your family had been secured elsewhere. The children will not be lacking for capital when they start out their new life together."

"What are you saying?" said Doña Angelica. "What do you mean by arrangements? I don't understand."

"Well, to tell you the truth, I don't understand either. I'm just repeating what I read in the letter. But one thing I've learned in my long career as a matchmaker. When there are no problems, you don't look for problems. If the Pereira family is happy with the so-called arrangements, then so am I. And so should you be. Now is not the time to probe. Do you know what I'm saying?"

Doña Angelica took a deep breath and let it out slowly. "Yes, I think I do. But just for my own curiosity, do you have any idea whatsoever about the nature of these arrangements?"

"None whatsoever. And I don't want to think about them anymore. There are other matters to discuss. This match is going to happen. I feel it in my bones."

And happen it did. In the beginning of January 1683, two weeks after Chanukah, Uriel Pereira, his parents and one younger sister sailed from Hamburg to Rotterdam in Holland at the mouth of the Rhine. From there they sailed upriver in a small coastal vessel until they reached Bonn. From that point, the river climbed toward Basel in Switzerland, and sailing was no longer possible. They transferred to a light barge which was pulled upriver by horses following a riverside path. The men on the barge also used long poles to push the barge along. The barge brought them all the way to Strasbourg, from where they traveled overland to Metz.

The Pereira family was allowed a day to recover from the rigors of their winter journey. The nuptial agreement was signed the following day. Considering that the Pereira family had a much broader circle of family and friends than did the Dominguez family, the wedding was set to take place in Hamburg in the spring on Lag Ba'Omer, the thirty-third day of the Omer, about a month after Pesach. There would be plenty of time for guests to arrive from near and far.

Three days after the Pereira family left for Hamburg, Carolina went out to the market to buy some vegetables. The sun was shining brightly. The snow on the ground was white and crisp, and it crunched deliciously under her feet. Her heart sang with joy as she hummed a merry tune under her breath. In the marketplace, she strolled from stall to stall, examining the produce and exchanging pleasantries with the peddlers and some of the other customers.

Suddenly, there was an ominous rumble, and a large slab of ice came loose from alongside the chimney of one of the houses on the market square. The ice gathered speed as it slid down the roof and launched itself into the air. It struck a horse on the rump. Frightened more than injured, the horse reared up on its hind legs and whinnied wildly. Then it hurtled through the marketplace, turning over several carts that blocked its path. One of the carts struck Carolina in the back and sent her sprawling. As she fell, Carolina hit her head and lost consciousness.

People came running immediately, and a doctor was summoned. When the doctor arrived, Carolina had already regained consciousness. She had no idea what had caused her to lose consciousness other than a vague recollection of a horse making panicky noises. She plied the bystanders with questions while she remained sitting on the ground in the snow.

The doctor wanted to examine her, but she protested that she was just fine. She only needed a minute or two to recover from the shock and catch her breath. When she tried to stand up, however, her leg buckled under her, and she fell back to the ground. The doctor determined that thankfully nothing was broken but her ankle was swollen and discolored. She had suffered a nasty sprain, and the doctor recommended cold compresses and bed rest until the swelling went down.

Carolina's appointments with the dressmakers had to be postponed until she could walk or at least stand in one place while she was being fitted. After a few days in bed, the swelling went down, and Carolina was able to walk gingerly on the ankle for short distances. The ankle continued to improve, and in a few more days, she was almost back to normal.

When she was ready to resume her fittings, Doña Angelica made it easier for her and arranged to have the dressmaker come to the house. That same day, Frau Klinger came by to check on Carolina and reassure herself that there would be no impediments to a timely wedding. She had a substantial fee coming, and she was prepared to do whatever necessary to prevent any hindrance or delay.

Carolina came down the stairs with the slightest of limps.

"Good morning, my dear," said Frau Klinger. "How are you feeling?"

"I'm just fine, Frau Klinger. Thank you for asking."

"How is your ankle?" said Frau Klinger. "Can you walk around?"

"She's just fine," said Doña Angelica. "In a day or two, she'll be as good as new. Isn't that so, Carolina?"

"Even better than new, mother."

"Can I look at your ankle, child?" said Frau Klinger.

Carolina looked at her mother, who shrugged in response.

"Of course," said Carolina.

The swelling had indeed gone down considerably, but Carolina still winced when the matchmaker probed with her finger.

"Not too bad," said Frau Klinger. "Stay off it for a few more days, just to make sure it heals properly. I know about these things. You're not the first bride that sprained her ankle, you know. I could tell you stories —"

"Frau Klinger, if I may," interrupted the dressmaker. "I always love to hear your stories, but I have two other appointments today, so I must get started. Señorita Dominguez, are you ready to work with me?"

"Here I am," Carolina declared. "What should I do?"

"First, we will choose some fabrics," said the dressmaker. "Here, how do you like this chartreuse taffeta?"

As Carolina took the bolt of cloth in her hand, it began to swim before her eyes. A moment later, she swooned and fainted away.

"Carolina!" cried Doña Angelica.

The dressmaker reached into her satchel and pulled out a bottle of smelling salts. She held it under Carolina's nose, and the young woman stirred and opened her eyes.

"Have I fainted again?" she said. "I'm so embarrassed."

"It is all right," said the dressmaker. "It is perfectly normal for brides to faint during their fittings. They are nervous, and it is a little warm in this house, you know. There is no cause for concern."

"Well, I'm concerned anyway," declared Doña Angelica. She summoned Helga and sent her off to fetch the doctor.

When the doctor arrived, he instantly noticed a slight rash on Carolina's neck. After a brief examination, he determined that her fainting spell was not connected to the incident in the marketplace. It was triggered by a fairly common skin ailment that caused inflammations and chills. He gave Carolina a vial of powder and told her to spend the rest of the day in bed. There was no cause for concern. She would be fine. But there would be no more fittings that day.

After the doctor and the dressmaker were gone and Carolina had gone to bed, Frau Klinger lingered to speak with Doña Angelica.

"Señora Dominguez, I am worried," she said.

"Why?" asked Doña Angelica. "It seems a fairly harmless affliction. The doctor did not seem the least bit concerned. I was watching him carefully."

"He may not have been concerned, but I am. Oh yes, I am."

"But why?"

"Because I think Carolina has fallen victim to an *ayin hara*, an evil eye."

"An evil eye? What are you saying?"

Frau Klinger leaned forward. "Have you never heard about the evil eye?"

"I have. But I've never taken it seriously."

"Well, you should. The evil eye is a real thing. When people are jealous of what other people have, when people hate or resent other people, they can give them the evil eye. I don't know exactly how it works, but it's an established fact. You can ask anyone. It's in the Torah and the Talmud."

"Really? And what happens when someone falls victim to the evil eye?"

"Oh, terrible things can happen. They can get hurt or suffer a loss."

"And you think Carolina has fallen victim to the evil eye?"

"Absolutely. Oh yes, absolutely. She is so happy and so radiant that people might look at her with jealousy and give her the evil eye. Look at it. A few days after she is engaged to a wonderful young man from an excellent family, a horse goes wild and knocks her down so that she sprains her ankle. Thank Heaven, it was nothing worse. And then, a few days later, she faints again, this time because of a skin rash. Something is going on, I tell you. Something is going on, and I don't like it. This is not the first time I've come face to face with an evil eye."

Doña Angelica was becoming agitated. "So what do we do?" she asked. "Should we go see the rabbi?"

"We could," said the matchmaker. "But what would he do? He would give you a blessing. Well, I can do better."

"You? What can you do?"

"A lot," said the matchmaker, and she opened her eyes wide. "I have been trained in the art of removing the evil eye. Carolina must be saved from the forces of evil, and it is your good fortune that I am here to do it. Nothing will stand in the way of this match, I tell you. Not even the evil eye!'

"So what are we supposed to do?" said Doña Angelica in a tentative voice. "I mean, how are you going to remove the evil eye?"

"Listen, we need your kitchen. I have to go home and get a few things, and then we need to use your kitchen. Can you send your Helga away for the rest of the day?"

"Where am I supposed to send her? No, I can't do that. It's impossible."

"I understand," said the matchmaker. "We'll have to do it tonight then. Are your sons here?"

"No, they are in Strasbourg."

"Good. I prefer privacy. I'll come back here maybe ten or eleven o'clock. We'll have the kitchen to ourselves then."

"Yes, I suppose we will. Are you … I mean, will you … need Carolina for whatever it is that you intend to do in the kitchen?"

"Absolutely. We can do nothing without her. The evil eye has attached itself to her, so she must be there. No, nothing can happen without her. Tell her to take a good nap during the afternoon. And perhaps you should take one, too."

The matchmaker returned in the dead of night. She was carrying a mysterious wooden box. She knocked on the door, and when it opened, she looked about surreptitiously before entering the house.

"My things," she whispered conspiratorially. "Come quickly."

She headed for the kitchen with Doña Angelica and Carolina close behind.

The matchmaker lit a fire on the stove. She took two containers from her box, filled one of them halfway with water and placed both of them on the table. Then she took out a saucepan and placed it on the fire.

Carolina stared at her in disbelief. "What are you doing?" she asked.

"I'm going to do something called *bleigiessen*, which means pouring the lead. Have you ever heard about it?"

"I don't think I have," said Doña Angelica.

"Well you are about to find out," said the matchmaker. "Let's begin. But first light two candles and turn down the lamps."

The kitchen was soon plunged into murky darkness, the flickering candlelight casting bizarre shadows on the bare walls.

The matchmaker's face glowed orange whenever she bent over near the candles to arrange her instruments on the kitchen table. She chanted under her breath as she worked, but every once in a while, she interrupted her chanting to mutter some comments to herself. Carolina shuddered and hugged herself.

"Will this hurt, Frau Klinger?" she asked.

"Of course not, young lady," said the matchmaker. "It will only make you feel better. Here, sit in this chair."

She took a few bars of lead from her box and tossed them into the saucepan on the fire. Then she took out a large green cloth.

Carolina shrank back. "What's that?"

"Sit still, young lady," she said. "I'm going to cover you. Don't move."

She spread open the cloth and draped it over Carolina. She took a quick look into the saucepan on the fire and saw that the lead had melted. With a murmur of satisfaction, she took the water container in one hand and the saucepan with the molten lead in the other. She held the water container in the air over Carolina's head and whispered an incantation, and then she carefully poured the molten lead into the water.

The hot lead made a hissing sound as it struck the water. The matchmaker put the saucepan back on the stove but not directly on the fire. Then she took the water container and drained off the water into the empty container. A number of pieces of lead remained in the bottom of the water container. The matchmaker touched them gingerly to make sure they were cool enough to handle. Then she lifted out one of the pieces.

"We're ready," she declared. "You can take off the cloth and take a look."

Carolina removed the cloth, and she and Doña Angelica both craned their necks to see what the matchmaker was holding. It was a curiously shaped piece of metal that resembled a bulbous flower on a long stem.

"Here, you see the eye?" said the matchmaker. She pointed to the bulbous mass. "This is the eye itself, and this part here is the nerves and the blood vessels that attach the eye to the body. Do you see it? It is clear as day. There it is. That's the *ayin hara*, the evil eye."

She reached into the container with the pieces of solidified lead. They made a rattling sound as she rummaged among them.

"Here, look at these," she said as she held up three more pieces of lead that had formed themselves into similar shapes.

"You see the eyes? You have quite a few of them on you. They are watching you with malice."

She looked into the container and pulled out a long, serpentine piece with a row of ridges along its spine.

"And look at this one," she said. "Do you see the snake? Here, look at the front. You see that gap? That's the mouth. The snake is talking about you. It's talking, talking, talking. That's not healthy. It's not good."

She looked into the container again and rummaged among the pieces.

"Look at those things!" she exclaimed with exasperation. "There are so many of them. It's no wonder you had your accidents."

"So what do we do?" breathed Doña Angelica.

"We say more prayers to dispel the evil eye and we continue to check the lead pieces to see how successful we are."

"But I don't know the prayers, Frau Klinger," protested Doña Angelica.

"You don't need to know them," said the matchmaker. "I know them. Here, let's do it again. Would you like to pour the lead, Señora Dominguez, while I say the prayers against the evil eye?"

"Do you think I could do it? Is there a special way?"

"There's no special way to do it," said the matchmaker. "When I give you the signal, just pour the lead into the water slowly and steadily."

She tossed all the pieces of lead into the saucepan on the stove and moved the saucepan onto the fire. The lead began to melt.

"All right, young lady," she said. "Time to cover up. Put the cloth over your head."

She started rocking back and forth, her lips moving almost without sound as she repeated her formulas and incantations. Halfway through, she lifted the water container over Carolina's head and nodded to Doña Angelica.

Doña Angelica's hand trembled as she lifted the saucepan from the stove and poured the molten lead into the water container over her daughter's head. She shuddered at the hissing sound and replaced the saucepan on the stove.

The matchmaker drained the water into the empty container and peered at the new lead formations. She reached in and pulled out a few of them.

"Better, much better," she declared. She held up a piece of lead formed of two attached strands. "Here, look at this one. You see the two pieces? That's you and your future husband. You're going to have a happy marriage. I can tell. I know about these things. But we're not finished yet. Look, there are still a few eyes and a snake. Here, look at these eyes. They're smaller, weaker, almost broken. Do you see it? It's clear as the day. And the snake, it's more like a worm now than a snake. Come, let's do it again. Cover up, young lady."

She tossed the pieces of lead into the saucepan and waited for them to start melting. She lifted the water container, began her incantations and nodded to Doña Angelica, who lifted the saucepan and, with more assurance this time, poured the molten lead into the water. After another hiss, the matchmaker drained off the water and inspected the residue. She reached in and pulled out a smallish flower-shaped formation.

"Here, there's still one evil eye left," she said. "It's a stubborn one, but we will get rid of it. Take a good look at it, look how weak and fragile it is. One more push, and it will fall apart."

"Is that the only one?" asked Carolina. "Is there anything else in there?"

"Look for yourself, young lady. Nothing but scraps and sticks. We're doing well here. Now, let's do it one more time. Let's hope it will be the last."

Once again, Carolina sat in the chair with a green cloth draped over her head, the matchmaker said her incantations, and Doña Angelica poured the lead. Once again, there was a hissing sound. Once again, the matchmaker drained off the water, leaving the residue in the container. She lifted out one large chunk of misshapen lead and held it up for all to see.

"Aha!" she cried out. "It's finished. There's nothing left of the evil eye."

"Are you sure?" said Carolina as she removed the green cloth from here head.

"Absolutely. Here, look for yourself. There's nothing here but a clump of harmless lead. You're safe, my child. All the evil eyes are gone."

THE HERRING STAIN · 9

THE BOAT TRAFFIC ON THE MOSELLE RIVER was returning to normal levels. People strolled through the streets and along the embankments of the river, listening to the raucous noises of a city awakening from months of winter slumber. In the Jewish quarter, Reb Mendel and Sebastian sat on a bench in the sunshine and watched the last traces of the Purim celebrations being swept away.

"It was very kind of you and your wife," said Sebastian, "to invite our family for Pesach. My mother and sister are completely preoccupied with the wedding preparations, and it would have been a real burden to prepare Pesach, especially since we've never really done it properly. Last year, the rabbi invited us, but we weren't expecting him to invite us again. So your invitation was really a lifesaver. I hope it's not too much trouble for your wife."

"Don't be concerned," said Reb Mendel. "We will have plenty of help in the house. We can well afford it. There will be no hardship. Having your family as our guests for Pesach will be our greatest pleasure and honor."

Sebastian inclined his head. "The pleasure and honor will be ours."

"You said you wanted to talk to me about something. We have time now. There is something I have to tell you as well. But first, tell me what is on your mind. You seem troubled lately."

"I am troubled," said Sebastian. "I feel I've completely lost my bearings. I don't know who I am or what I want to do. I don't understand my relationship to my people, to my religion. Somehow, I am neither here nor there." He stood up and looked off into the distance. "I have never talked about it, Reb Mendel, but I carry a heavy burden of guilt."

"Do you want to talk to me about it now?"

"Yes, I suppose I do. But my guilt is only part of it."

Reb Mendel remained silent, letting him take his time.

Sebastian sighed. "My parents were always extremely discreet abut their Jewishness," he began. "They never went to secret assemblies, and they never told anyone about their Jewish identity. We were like a tiny Jewish island, a speck, in a vast Christian ocean. We had a sort of private faith with no connection to any religious community. A strange way to be religious, wasn't it?"

"They did what they could," said Reb Mendel, "under the circumstances. They did not prefer it that way."

"Of course not, but that's the way it was. Anyway, while my father was away — when we thought he was dead — I went to a few secret assemblies in Toledo. I even took Carolina with me one time. I was a fool. I told them my name was Luis Alvarez, and I thought it would make me safe. But it was just the tiny chink in our armor that the Inquisition needed, and it brought about our downfall. My father was very upset when he returned and found out what I had done, but it was too late. They tracked us down. My family was uprooted, and my father was killed. And it was entirely my fault. I was responsible. I am responsible."

He buried his head in his hands, and when he lifted it, his eyes glistened.

"How old were you then, Sebastian?"

"Nineteen."

"You were little more than a child," said Reb Mendel, "a

young and impetuous child, without the guidance of his father. You made a mistake, but you cannot carry it around with you for the rest of your life. I'm sure your father forgave you."

"He said he did, and I know that he meant it. But his forgiveness doesn't change what I did."

"You made a mistake, and you've regretted it deeply for so many years. Your father forgave you, the Almighty has forgiven you, and now you must forgive yourself. According to your man Gonzalo, your father's last question when he was tied to the stake was about you, and when he thought you were safe he died happy. You must live and flourish for your father's sake. He will continue to live through you but only if you can lay aside this burden of guilt and become what he would have wanted you to be."

"I know that what you say is true," said Sebastian. "I've said this to myself many times. And I've tried hard to be the inspired Jew my father was for the last years of his life, but it isn't working for me. I'm ignorant of Jewish learning, and I'm confused about where I'm heading. Back in Spain, when I went to those secret Jewish assemblies in Toledo disguised as Luis Alvarez, I felt so alive, so exhilarated, so inspired. I felt close to the Almighty, and I loved my people although I didn't know them and they didn't know me. But now, I can't recapture that excitement. I yearn to feel that bolt of lightning going through my body, but it doesn't happen."

"I understand," said Reb Mendel.

"Do you really? In Spain, I was a prince, a warrior. I lived with danger and the specter of death every day. I thrived on it. And the danger of being a secret Jew, that was the ultimate thrill for me. My father was a deeply committed Jew, but I think that my own attachment is only superficial."

"You've sacrificed so much for your Jewishness, Sebastian. It can't be just a superficial attachment. Are you happy in Metz?"

"No, I'm miserable. My life seems to be drifting along aimlessly. I've trained for commerce, but I really don't like it. I grew up as a nobleman and a soldier in the king's army. I am a cavalier, a warrior. Business doesn't satisfy my soul. I have to be honest. When I thought we'd be recovering my father's properties, I dreamed of making investments that would bring us fabulous profits." He chuckled dryly. "The prospect of great wealth can make a warrior into a businessman. But there are no properties and no prospects, so all that lies before me is a lifetime of struggle to make enough money to survive. It's not a pleasant thought."

"Sebastian, it is as you say, you're neither here nor there. You're here in Metz just temporarily until you find a permanent place, perhaps Amsterdam, perhaps somewhere else. So that makes you unsettled right away. Then you don't know what you want to do with your life. That doesn't help. You're ashamed of your lack of knowledge about Jewishness, even though you were prepared to give your life to it. That will certainly make a person unsettled. And finally, you carry a heavy burden of guilt that you cannot relinquish. There's no easy answer to your dilemma. It may be beyond me, but let me think about it."

"I'm glad you said that," said Sebastian. "If you had given me an answer right away, it just wouldn't seem genuine to me. I feel that my problem is really vast. You know, my mother is adjusting nicely, Carolina is on a cloud, and Felipe is doing just fine. His head is always buried in a Jewish book, and he is absorbed. I sense that he's found some of the feeling that keeps eluding me. I'm the one that's lost. I'm the ignorant horseless cavalier."

"Don't berate yourself, Sebastian," said Reb Mendel. "There is an answer for you. In the meantime, prayer always helps. Do you find prayer difficult?"

"Actually, I don't. I unburden my soul to the Almighty

every day, and it makes me feel a little better. But I'm still waiting for the answer to my prayers. But that's enough about me." He forced himself to smile. "You mentioned that you wanted to tell me about something."

"Yes, I do," said Reb Mendel. He took a deep breath. "I wanted to tell you that we will be leaving Metz. I've already mentioned it to Felipe, but I told him that I would like to tell you myself."

Sebastian was stunned. "I don't understand. You're leaving Metz? You mean for good?"

"Yes, I'm afraid so. My wife's parents have returned to Vienna. The expulsion thirteen years ago is a thing of the past. More and more Jews are moving back and doing extremely well there. There are many opportunities in the imperial capital, as you can well imagine. Anyway, my father-in-law has not been well lately, and my mother-in-law is not getting any younger either. My wife feels we should be living closer to her parents, and I agree. Seeing them once every few years is no longer enough. And living in Vienna, we'll be much closer to my parents in Poland. We'll be able to see them more often."

"I understand. Do your wife's parents actually live in Vienna?"

"Not really. They live in a town about two miles away called Eggenschlag, but my father-in-law goes into the city to do business just about every day ... that is, when he's feeling well enough. The imperial government has come to the realization that the empire needs the help of its Jews, and they're turning a blind eye to all the Jews coming into the city every day. Some Jews are even living inside the city walls, although they don't have official rights of residence. My wife's parents wouldn't live in the city proper unless they had an official right of residence, but they're hoping that day will also come soon. I guess when I said we are moving to Vienna it would have been more accurate to say that we are moving to Eggenschlag."

"Eggenschlag, Vienna, it's all the same. And what will you be doing there? Do you intend to go into business as well?"

"There's talk of establishing a new Jewish school in one of the towns near Eggenschlag, and I've been assured there will be a useful role for me. My wife and I will really be sorry to leave Metz; we've been treated well here. But we're definitely looking forward to Vienna. There's a new spirit of enlightenment and tolerance abroad in the gentile world, and somehow, I think expulsions are a thing of the past. If that's really true, if the Jewish community will be secure in Vienna, it can become one of the most important in all of Europe."

"But isn't it dangerous to go to Vienna these days? I hear that the Turkish army is moving north through Hungary. Three hundred thousand men! They say it's the biggest army to cross into Europe since the Persians invaded Greece almost two thousand years ago. Instead of you going to Vienna, perhaps you should be getting your wife's parents to leave."

"We've suggested it, but they refuse," said Reb Mendel. "Actually, I don't think my father-in-law is strong enough to travel any great distance. They have decided to stay, and they are hoping for the best. They believe the Turks will not advance on Vienna. According to my father-in-law — and I am sure this is not his own opinion — the Christian nations of Europe may allow Hungary to fall to the Turks, and even Poland, but they will not allow Vienna to fall to the Turks. Vienna is the gateway to Europe, and if it falls to a Muslim army, all of Europe could fall next, and that would be the end of Christianity. The Christian powers will fight to the death to prevent that from happening."

"So you are saying that the Turks understand this," said Sebastian, "and that they will not advance on Vienna."

"That is what the people of Vienna and all of Lower Austria are hoping. And besides, the Jews probably have the least to fear from the Turks. Jews are treated very well in the Turkish Empire."

"But even so, if Vienna becomes a war zone, it's not where you want to be."

Reb Mendel nodded gravely. "It's true. But the same can be said of just about every place in Europe. There has been no shortage of wars and bloodshed recently right here in France, Alsace, Lorraine, Franche Comté, Luxembourg, Flanders, the Spanish Netherlands and the United Provinces. The French, the Austrians, the Spanish, the Germans, the English, they all fight and kill one another all the time. Everyone is struggling for the upper hand; sometimes this one aligns with that one, sometimes with the other one. That is Europe. It is a land of incessant wars. No one is safe anywhere in Europe. My wife's parents are placing their trust in the Almighty and taking their chances in Vienna. And so are we."

"I understand," said Sebastian. "Life is never without risks. I wish you all the best, and my prayers will always be with you. When will you be leaving?"

"Right after Pesach."

"I see. And does that mean you won't be coming to Carolina's wedding?"

"I'm afraid it will be impossible. It would be a difficult journey in any case, what with having to leave the children behind for weeks or else taking them along, which would be even more difficult. The move to Vienna makes it impossible. But my thoughts will be with you and my blessings, for whatever they're worth. This wedding celebration will complete the integration of your family into the broader Jewish community after so many generations of isolation. Perhaps this will pave the way for your marriage as well."

Sebastian smiled. "Since when have you become a matchmaker, Reb Mendel? But you're right. I am thirty years old, and it's time I should think seriously about starting my own family. But I'm not quite ready yet. Before I can find a wife, I have to find myself."

Pesach came to the Dominguez and Strasbourg households with a flurry of last-minute rushes quite apart from the regular preparations for the festival. The Dominguez family would be leaving for Hamburg and the Strasbourg family for Vienna within days after Pesach, and there were endless tasks that had to be done beforehand. But somehow or other, everything was accomplished in time, and when the setting sun ushered in the honored festival, it was welcomed with relief, calm and eager anticipation.

After the men came home from the synagogue, the two families sat down around the Seder table. Reb Mendel sat at one end of the table, with his two sons, twelve-year-old Gedaliah and seven-year-old Moshe, on either side of him. His wife Miriam sat at the other end of the table with nine-year-old Sarah beside her. Two younger children had died in infancy. The Dominguez family sat on either side.

Before the Maggid part of the Seder began, Reb Mendel asked for the indulgence of his guests while he said a few words of introduction. "This part is the heart of the Seder," he said. "It tells the story of our deliverance from bondage in Egypt three thousand years ago. This story is the foundation of our *emunah*, our belief in the Almighty, and it is the affirmation of our eternal covenant with Him, a covenant and a mission more precious to us than life itself. We've never forgotten it. We tell the story year after year. We pass it down from generation to generation, from fathers and mothers to sons and daughters. We recall it every single day in our observances and every Shabbos and every festival, but on Pesach, that is when we spend the whole night telling it to the children."

He picked up the Haggadah.

"Not everyone here understands Hebrew or Aramaic so perfectly, so I will translate for you. There is a little paragraph here that we say before we begin the Maggid section of the Haggadah. It is in Aramaic. Why Aramaic? Because the spoken language of Eretz Yisrael in ancient times was Aramaic, and that was the language that people understood best. So that tells us something about this paragraph. The whole Maggid is in Hebrew, but this opening paragraph is in Aramaic. It must be very important. Let's listen to the words."

Reb Mendel paused and looked around. He had clearly piqued their interest. All eyes were riveted on his face. Sebastian especially was watching him intently.

"Listen to these words," he repeated. "We hold aloft a piece of matzah and we say these words. '*Ha lachma anya* … This is the bread of affliction that our ancestors ate in the land of Egypt. Whoever is hungry may come in and eat. Whoever is needy may come in and share our meal. Now we are here, but next year we will be in the land of Israel. Now we are in bondage, but next year we will be free.' These are the words. There are many questions. Does anyone want to make a comment?"

"It's a strange passage," said Sebastian. "I think it would have been more appropriate to invite the hungry and the needy when we were still in the synagogue. To do it now seems a little late. To whom are we talking?"

"Good point," said Reb Mendel. "Many commentators ask this question. Does anyone else have a comment?"

"I don't understand something else," said Sebastian. "Which matzah are we talking about here? Is this the matzah they carried on their shoulders when they were leaving Egypt?"

"No, it is not," said Reb Mendel. "According to many commentators, this matzah represents their meager meals when they were working as slaves."

"So why do we mention it now?" said Sebastian. "Why is it so important?"

"Good question. Very good question. We'll get to it soon."

"I also have a question," said 9-year-old Sarah. "Can I ask it?"

"Absolutely," said Reb Mendel. "This Seder is all about you."

"Well, I don't understand," she said. "After Yom Kippur is over, we say, '*Leshanah habaah b'Yerushalayim.* Next year in Jerusalem.' And the same thing after the Seder. We have a song for it that we sing in school all the time. So why did you just now say, 'Next year in the land of Israel'? Why didn't you say it the regular way?"

Reb Mendel looked at her with genuine amazement. "What a superb question. And from such a young girl. Sarah, I'm impressed."

The little girl flushed with pleasure, and her mother beamed at her with undisguised pride.

"If I may," said Reb Mendel, "I would like to tell you how my father explained this paragraph. I believe it will answer all your questions. One of my ancestors who lived almost two hundred years ago was a famous sage and scholar named Rabbi Gedaliah Strasbourg. My son Gedaliah here carries that holy name. Now if I were to tell you a story that happened with my ancestor, it would be hard to relate to it in a concrete way. The story would have an abstract quality, because it happened so deep in the mists of the past. It is much easier to relate to a story about someone we actually know. When we know the people and we hear the story about them, it feels as if we are actually there. Isn't that true?"

Everyone nodded, even the children.

"Now what if I told you that this white *kittel* I'm wearing is an heirloom inherited from Rabbi Gedaliah Strasbourg, would that make him more real? I mean, his arms were in these sleeves, and these buttons closed over his beating heart. Wouldn't that make him seem more like a life-and-blood person to you?"

Everyone nodded again.

"And what if I told you," continued Reb Mendel, "that this herring stain on my lapel came from a piece of herring he was eating at his Seder?"

Miriam Strasbourg suddenly sat bolt upright. "What! How can there be a stain on your *kittel*? I checked it myself."

Reb Mendel chuckled. "Don't worry. There's no stain here. I was just trying to make a point. This *kittel* was not inherited from my ancestor. But what if it had been? And what if there had been a stain on it that dated back to his Seder? Wouldn't that make him very real for us?"

"Yes, it would," said Sebastian softly, sensing the direction Reb Mendel was taking. "It would make me feel that he is someone I know."

"Exactly," said Reb Mendel. "And then when I tell you the story about my ancestor, it's not just something that happened a long time ago. It's something as real and immediate as if it had happened just yesterday."

"Yes, I see that," said Sebastian.

"Well, it is the same when we tell the story of what happened to our ancestors in Egypt three thousand years ago. It is very important that this story should be real to us, that we should feel as if it happened to people we know. But what do we know about our ancestors that will make them concrete people? What can we do to put faces on them? We don't have their *kittels* and their herring stains, but we do have something else. We know the food they used to eat when they took a break from their backbreaking work.

"We say to the people at the Seder table, 'Look at this piece of matzah. This is the food they used to eat when they were miserable and suffering.' And we also know something else. We know that they shared this meager meal with anyone who was hungry. The rest of the paragraph I read before is what they used to say when they sat down to eat their bread of affliction. They said, 'Whoever is hungry can come share this piece of matzah.' They said, 'Whoever is needy can come share our meal.' They said, 'Now we are here, but next year we will be in the land of Israel.' There was no Jerusalem yet at that time. They said, 'Now we are in bondage, but next year we will be free.'

"Now we have an image of our ancestors that makes them real. Now we can relate to them as real people. We know them. We can almost reach out and touch them. We see the humble bread that they used to take into their mouths when they came in exhausted from work and sat down to eat. We see their kindness and generosity, as they were prepared to share their morsels with the hungry and the needy. We see their nobility of spirit because even in the darkness of their oppression they never lost hope that they would one day return home and be free. We know these people. We care about them. They are our beloved grandparents, and now when we tell their story, it will penetrate into our hearts."

TRAVEL ARRANGEMENTS · 10

D ESPITE ALL OPTIMISTIC HOPES, Europe girded itself for a cataclysmic war that would determine the future and the very nature of European society. A vast Turkish army was moving northward and westward across the Balkans, headed for Vienna like a dagger at the European heart. Nonetheless, European politics were not set aside in the face of the Muslim invasion. Austria stood to suffer the most at the hands of the Turks, and its sworn enemy France refused to come to its rescue.

The key to the defense of Vienna, therefore, was King Jan Sobieski of Poland, a brilliant military commander who had defeated the Turks at Podhajce in 1667 and Chocim in 1673 while he was still a general in the Polish Army and again at Zurawno in 1676 after he had been crowned king. But Sobieski owed his allegiance to France, whose influence had placed him on the Polish throne, and his willingness to come to the aid of Austria was highly questionable.

Back in January 1683, while the Turks were occupying and subduing Hungary, the pope had sent a papal legate named Cardinal Pentucci to Warsaw with an urgent appeal for Sobieski's help. Pentucci warned Sobieski that if the Turks took Vienna, Krakow would be next and then Warsaw. The Turks would avenge their humiliation on the battlefield at the hands of Sobieski. They would crush Poland until nothing remained of it but a memory. Only then would they turn their attention to Germany, France and the rest of Europe. Pentucci also appealed to Sobieski as a blessed child of the Church to rise to the occasion and save Christendom from the infidel. If he would come to its aid, the Church would be forever grateful to him.

Sobieski turned to the Imperial military men who had accompanied Pentucci to Warsaw and asked them for their detailed assessment. They informed him that Sultan Mohammed IV had not wanted to attack Vienna and rouse the Christian world against him, but Kara Mustafa, his Grand Vizier, insisted on a campaign against Austria. With an enormous army of three hundred thousand men, about half of whom were fighters, he was confident he could overwhelm the defenses of the imperial capital and burst through into the heart of Europe.

Although he remained skeptical, the Sultan deferred to his Vizier's judgment. But he expressed his lingering skepticism by handing Kara Mustafa a length of green cord and saying, "If you fail to capture Vienna, you must hang yourself with this cord." Ever since, Kara Mustafa always wore the cord around his neck in public to demonstrate his determination to achieve a glorious victory.

The Turks were dangerous and deadly, the Imperial military men concluded, and their leader was desperate. France had the most powerful army in Europe, but King Louis XIV was content to sit back and watch the Turks destroy his enemy Austria, thinking perhaps that he could defeat the Turks later, a rather arrogant assumption. It was clear that the only reasonable hope of thwarting the Turks was a coalition led by Poland and its brilliant king. The Austrians, commanded by the Duke of Lorraine, would number about twenty-three thousand men. The Germans, commanded by Prince Waldek, would number about twenty-eight thousand men. Another thirty-five thousand fighters from Poland would complete a coalition with a fighting chance, especially with Sobieski in command. If Sobieski failed to join the coalition, however, Vienna would fall, and all of Europe would lie exposed before the Turkish juggernaut.

Sobieski laced his fingers across his expansive paunch and let his large, egg-shaped head fall onto his chest. The rest of the room fell silent so as not to disturb the Polish king's contemplation. Finally, Sobieski lifted his head.

"It takes time to assemble an army and march," he said. "I cannot arrive at Vienna before September. Can the city hold out until then?"

"It will have to," said Cardinal Pentucci. "Heaven help us if it doesn't."

"Then I will rescue Vienna," said Sobieski. "Victory will be ours."

The war clouds gathering over Vienna were far from the minds of the Dominguez family as they arrived in Hamburg for Carolina's wedding almost two weeks before the event. The Pereira family received them as royalty, and the entire Portuguese community, which had followed the fortunes and misfortunes of the family with keen interest, received them as celebrities.

The evening after their arrival, the Pereiras gave a lavish reception in honor of the bride and her family. Just about everyone in both of Hamburg's Jewish communities, Portuguese and Ashkenazic, put in an appearance at some time or another during the evening. The people congratulated both families on the forthcoming union and wished the prospective couple good fortune and many blessings. Many people expressed their condolences to the Dominguez family over the tragic demise of the illustrious Don Pedro, royal councilor and minister to the Spanish king, and also their admiration for the heroic manner in which he had faced his end.

Sebastian, tall and dark-haired, with chiseled features and the noble bearing of a former prince, was a center of attention in his own right. The story of his hair-raising escape from Spain was widely known, and more than a few people gave him sidelong glances and speculated among themselves about his matrimonial eligibility.

Gonzalo Sanchez had also made the trip to Hamburg, and he stood near a window with a glass of cognac in his hand and a contented smile on his face. *Don Pedro*, he thought, *would have been pleased*. His family had gone through a lot, but it seemed that better times lay ahead.

Once the evening was well under way and most of the guests had been greeted and made welcome, Señor Pereira pulled Sebastian aside.

"There is someone I would like you to meet," he said. He lowered his voice. "You know that we did not insist on your family delivering the promised dowry."

"Yes, I do," said Sebastian. "That was very kind of you."

"Not really. You see, someone else provided the dowry. Not quite the full amount, but enough to satisfy our needs."

Sebastian was baffled. "Someone else! But who? Why weren't we told?"

"Well, at first, I thought there'd be no point in telling you, since you weren't likely to meet him. He's an elderly gentleman, and he lives far from Hamburg. But as it turns out, he did make the journey to attend the wedding, so I think it is only fair that I tell you about him and that you thank him personally."

"Believe me, *señor*, I am profoundly grateful to this man, whoever he is. But I don't understand. Who is this man, and why did he do this?"

"I'll let him answer the question. Here, let me introduce you to him."

Señor Pereira led Sebastian to a corner of the room where a tiny man was regaling his listeners with amusing and amazing stories about his travels. The man stood out in the crowd because of his diminutive size and vivacious personality. He had a short grizzled beard, a deeply lined face and eyes that never stopped dancing. His dark waistcoat and tall dark hat identified him as an Ashkenazic Jew.

Señor Pereira waited until there was a pause in the laughter, then he tapped the tiny man on the shoulder to gain his attention.

"Herr Ringel," he said, "this is Señor Sebastian Dominguez, the son of Don Pedro, may he rest in peace. Señor Dominguez, this is Herr Elisha Ringel of Poznan, Poland. He was a friend of your father."

Sebastian extended his hand. Elisha Ringel grasped it in both of his hands and shook it vigorously.

"I will leave you two together," said Señor Pereira. "I must go see to my other guests."

"We will manage, Señor Pereira," said Elisha. "Thank you."

Señor Pereira bowed courteously and walked away.

"Herr Ringel," said Sebastian, "on behalf of my mother, my sister and my entire family, I want to express —"

"Just wait a minute, young man. Two things. First of all, I was going to tell you to call me Elisha, but then I changed my mind. I'm almost seventy years old, and I don't think it would be appropriate. But Herr Ringel sounds like someone else. So why don't you call me Reb Elisha? It's —"

"I know that one," said Sebastian. "That what I call Rabbi Strasbourg."

"Reb Mendel?"

"That's right. Anyway, Reb Elisha, as I was saying —"

"That's the other thing I was going to say to you. Thank-you speeches make me uncomfortable. So you're welcome, and let's move on. Señor Pereira told me he was going to tell you, and I didn't object. After all, the Talmud says that if you do someone a good turn you should let him know about it. So now you know about it, and we can move on."

Sebastian nodded. "Fine. A simple thank-you, and all the rest is understood. And now, can you tell me who you are and why you did this wonderful thing?"

"I found your father on a beach in France after he had been wounded in a sea battle with pirates. He was close to death, but I nursed him back to health. Then I brought him to the home of my good friend Rabbi Shlomo Strasbourg in the city of Pulichev in Poland. Your father and I spent a lot of time together, and we became good friends. He was a great man, a truly extraordinary man. He also spoke of you often. I could see that he was really proud of you … may I call you Sebastian?"

"Please do."

"When your father died, I felt a terrible sorrow, and I determined to do something for his family in his holy memory. I have made and lost fortunes in my life, but I have made many more than I have lost. My children are grown and are successful in business. My money will eventually go to them, and I'm sure they will put it to good use, but as long as I am alive, I intend to enjoy it. So I made inquiries and found out what your family needed most at that time. And I have to tell you that very few things I've done with my money have given me as much pleasure as this that I've done for your family. It is I that should be thanking you profusely. But I don't believe in long thank-you speeches."

"Thanks accepted," said Sebastian with a smile. "You're welcome. And speaking of thanks, there's something else for which I'm grateful to you. My father felt that those two years he spent with the elder Rabbi Strasbourg in Poland were the best time of his life. Those years transformed him, and although he didn't live too long afterward, they were a very precious gift. Thank you. I only wish I could thank Rabbi Strasbourg in person as well."

"Yes, he would have enjoyed meeting you. He actually considered coming to Hamburg for the wedding, but he is even older than I am, can you imagine such a thing? It would have been too difficult a journey considering that he and his wife are also going to Vienna to see their son and his family. They've just moved to Vienna, as you surely know."

"Yes."

"But me, I'm still spry enough to travel about," said Elisha. "I've been doing it all my life, so I guess it's easier for me than for other people. I can fall asleep in an oxcart riding over a rutted track. Not many people can do that. Anyway, as I was saying, I can still travel, and I'm going on to Vienna from here. I can convey your thank-you to Rabbi Strasbourg. Since it will undoubtedly be a short thank-you, it won't weigh me down on the road."

Sebastian gave Elisha a speculative look. "Wait a minute. You say you're going to meet Rabbi Shlomo Strasbourg in Vienna?"

"That's what I said."

"Would you mind if I traveled along with you?"

"I don't think that's a good idea, Sebastian. You are under the protection of the French king, and you should stay in his domains. There's a small risk even in a quick trip to Hamburg, but for your sister's wedding, I suppose it may be justified. But Vienna? In the heart of the Austrian Empire? If you're recognized, you'll be arrested and sent back to Spain."

"Why should anyone recognize me? I'll grow a beard, put on a tall hat and dress as an Ashkenazic merchant. I can even walk with a cane, as if I'm lame. No one will give me a second look."

"But why? Just to say thank-you to Rabbi Strasbourg? It's really very nice of you to want to thank him personally, but I can do it for you. And if you want me to make a long thank-you speech, just tell me what you want me to say, and I'll say it. All of it. But listen to me, Sebastian. Don't go to Vienna. It's too dangerous. Why would you want to go there?"

"It more than just to say thank-you," said Sebastian. "I'm hoping that if I spend a little time with Rabbi Strasbourg I will … I don't know how to … I'm not sure … I mean … My father was inspired by Rabbi Strasbourg. He changed his life. So I guess what I'm saying is that my life also needs changing right now, and I'm hoping that Rabbi Strasbourg can help me find what I'm seeking."

Elisha gave Sebastian a long, hard look. "I'm still against it," he said.

"But …?"

"But I understand what you're saying, and the decision is yours. If you wish to travel with us, it will be my pleasure."

Elisha looked around and motioned to a man in Ashkenazic garb to come join them. The man was about twenty-five years old, a veritable mountain of flesh and bone, with massive arms and legs and a neck like the trunk of a tree. His broad face was ringed by a sparse blond beard, and his small blue eyes were the gentlest that Sebastian had ever seen.

"Sebastian," said Elisha, "I would like you to meet Tanchum Ringel, my youngest son. Tanchum, this is Sebastian Dominguez."

Sebastian looked from the diminutive Elisha to the mammoth Tanchum and back again. "This is your son?"

"That's right," said Elisha. "He takes after his mother."

"Oh," said Sebastian, not quite sure what else to say. He

stuck out his hand, and Tanchum grabbed it in his own so that it completely disappeared.

"Nice to meet you, Sebastian," said Tanchum in a thin, high-pitched voice.

Elisha looked at Sebastian and shrugged. "Who can figure out the ways of the Almighty?" he said.

"What's going on?" said Tanchum.

"Sebastian may be coming with us to Vienna," said Elisha.

"Terrific. I enjoy good company."

Later that evening, when the Dominguez family returned to the lodgings provided for them, Sebastian waited until his mother was alone in the parlor before he mentioned that he had something important to tell her. Doña Angelica had Helga bring in tea for both of them, then she dismissed her for the night. She looked at Sebastian, her shoulders hunched forward and braced herself.

"All right," she said. "I'm ready."

"Relax, Mother. I'm not bringing you bad news."

"But I sense something ominous coming. What is it? Don't break it to me slowly. Just go straight to the point and tell it to me."

"Very well, Mother. Tonight, I met a gentleman named Elisha Ringel. Does the name sound familiar?"

"Vaguely. I seem to recall hearing such a name, but I cannot place it. Is he one of the Ashkenazic merchants in Metz?"

"No. He is from Poznan in Poland. He found Father wounded on the beach in France, nursed him back to health and helped him make the connection with Rabbi Shlomo Strasbourg."

Doña Angelica brightened. "Yes, yes," she said excitedly. "Now I remember. Your father spoke of him often, but usually as the spice merchant from Poland rather than by his name. I should like to meet this man and thank him."

"I will arrange it," said Sebastian. "There is something else for which you should thank him. He provided our part of Carolina's dowry."

Doña Angelica's eyes opened wide, but she was too flabbergasted to speak.

"He was Father's good friend," said Sebastian, "and he did it in his memory. He claims he is very wealthy and that it was not a hardship for him to do it. And he gets very uncomfortable with long thank-you speeches, long meaning more than three or four words. Just say thank-you and go on."

"We will have to repay him someday, of course. I will tell him that we will repay every farthing."

"I think that would offend him, Mother. It wasn't charity or a loan. It was a gift to a friend who had perished to sanctify the Name of the Almighty. It helped relieve his grief and his sorrow. He says it made him feel much better, and I could see that he was speaking the truth. Just a thank-you will be more than enough."

"All right. I'll do as you say, Sebastian. Is that all you wanted to tell me?"

"Not quite. Herr Ringel is going to Vienna to meet Rabbi Shlomo Strasbourg. I have asked him for permission to accompany him. I want your blessing."

Doña Angelica caught her breath. She put her hand to her throat and closed her eyes for a moment.

"You asked me for my blessing," she said at last, "not my permission. That means that you're determined to go, even though it is dangerous. It is important to you. You want to meet Rabbi Shlomo Strasbourg."

"Yes, Mother. He inspired Father, and I'm hoping he will inspire me."

She shook her head. "It is more than that, Sebastian, even if you don't realize it yourself. You miss your father and feel guilty about what happened. Meeting his Rabbi and talking about him will bring him back to life in a certain way, and you are hoping that in this experience you will somehow find salvation."

Sebastian's face darkened, and he lowered his head.

"I don't know, Mother," he said. "You may very well be right, especially about my not understanding my own motives. I don't really know what is in my own heart, and that is what I find most troubling of all."

"Then I give you my blessing, my son. Go to Vienna after the wedding, and may the Almighty watch over you and bring you back to me safe and unharmed."

A KNOCK AT THE DOOR · 11

T HE JOURNEY TO VIENNA WAS UNEVENTFUL. There were four people in the traveling party: Elisha Ringel, his son Tanchum, Sebastian and Gonzalo, who had insisted on coming along. Sebastian, who called himself Moshe Metzger, was dressed in traditional Ashkenazic garb and his face was covered by a short beard. Gonzalo went as Juan Gomez, a bodyguard-for-hire from the island of Ibiza.

Most of the distance from Hamburg was covered by riverboat on the Elbe River across the great flat expanses of the German Plain. They spent Shabbos in Prague. From there, they hired a fast carriage that would bring them to Vienna by the middle of the week, a few days before Shavuos.

The days spent on the riverboat were truly placid. The river was calm and languid, the weather was warm, and the breezes coming off the water were soft and gentle. The last flocks of geese returning from their winter migrations glided high overhead in perfect formation. While Gonzalo and Tanchum fished, played dominoes or napped, Sebastian and Elisha spent most of the day in conversation.

Elisha had brought along a Chumash, and every morning, after they put on their tefillin and prayed, he suggested to Sebastian that they learn from it together. Sebastian was familiar with the stories of the Chumash, having read them in the Old Testament section of the Christian Bible, which was the primary source of Jewish knowledge for all secret Jews in Spain. In Metz, he had learned from a real Chumash with Reb Mendel on several occasions, but he found that his difficulty with the language caused him to tire quickly. With much time on their hands on the riverboat, Sebastian tried again with Elisha, but he could only manage short stretches at a time. Instead, he preferred to have Elisha convey to him orally the explanations of the Midrash and the commentators, after which they engaged in lengthy and lively discussions.

The last leg of their journey was more of an adventure. There was only room for four people on the two facing seats in the carriage Elisha hired in Prague. Sebastian sat with Gonzalo on one bench. Elisha and Tanchum shared the other seat, but because of their vast discrepancy in size and weight, the carriage listed to one side. This presented serious handling problems for the driver when he was trying to negotiate the narrow mountain roads. On more than one occasion, he asked Tanchum to sit in the center with Elisha on his lap, while Sebastian and Gonzalo squeezed themselves into the corners.

Once they reached the Danube River near the Austrian city of Linz, they sped along the Imperial Highway that followed the river eastward for one hundred miles until they arrived in Eggenschlag on the outskirts of Vienna.

Sebastian had not conjured up an image of Rabbi Shlomo Strasbourg in his mind. At most, he had imagined an older version of Reb Mendel. But he was nothing of the sort. The man who came out of the house to greet the new arrivals was tall and austere, with a long white beard, sharp blue eyes and shoulders held erect with a visible effort despite the invisible burden of advancing old age. He embraced Elisha, patted Tanchum on the cheek and shook hands solemnly with Sebastian and courteously with Gonzalo.

Later that night, after the rest of the weary travelers were snoring peacefully on their cots in the attic, Sebastian still tossed and turned from side to side, waiting for the sweet oblivion that refused to come. Frustrated, he got dressed and crept down the steps so as not to disturb the sleeping household. He let himself out the front door and stood in a puddle of moonlight breathing in the cool night air and trying to clear his head.

A sudden squeak startled him, and he spun around in a defensive crouch, ready to fight off an assailant. But there was no one there. Heart pounding and fists clenched, he advanced toward the shadowy shrubbery on the right side of the house. As he moved closer, he could see the outlines of a small porch partially concealed by bushes. Then there was another squeak.

"I'm right here," said Rabbi Shlomo Strasbourg. "Would you like to join me? There is a second rocking chair here."

Sebastian relaxed and came forward. "Yes, I would."

"What are you doing up so late, young man? I would think that after such a long journey, you would be exhausted."

"Actually, I'm very tired. But my mind is racing so fast that I simply can't fall asleep. You know that I came here to meet you, don't you?"

"Yes, I do."

"Is it possible that we can talk now for a little while? Unless you want to go to sleep, that is."

"I don't sleep much these days. Sleep is another of the pleasures old age has taken from me. But old age also has its compensations, as you will find out some day. Yes, we can talk now. People are asleep inside. But the walls of the house are thick, and if we don't raise our voices, no one will hear us."

"First of all, Rabbi Strasbourg, if it's not too much of an imposition, I would like to hear about my father, particularly about the relationship you had with him., Other than the time spent in prison toward the end, my father was always part of my life, except for those two years he spent with you when we all thought he had died. He did speak to me about that time in his life, but he was always so reserved about personal matters; he didn't make me feel as if I had shared the experience with him, if you know what I mean. I was hoping I'd get a more personal picture from you. What was he like with you? How did he change? Was he excited? Was he frustrated by the language? What was Shabbos like for him? Did he speak about himself? About his family? What were his thoughts? His feelings? You know, those are the kind of things I was hoping to hear from you."

The old Rabbi nodded. "You want me to help bring your father back to life for a while by showing you new sides of him that you had never seen."

"Yes, I suppose I do. Actually, that's exactly what my mother said to me before I left Hamburg."

"Then let's do it."

For the next hour, while Sebastian listened without uttering a word, the Rabbi spoke about Don Pedro's years in Poland. He described his sense of wonder at each new discovery, his deep spirituality, his unquenchable thirst for knowledge, his curiosity about everything Jewish, even the mystical secrets of the Kabbalah, his transformation into a passionate scholar and his integration of his Jewishness into all aspects of his personality so that it became his very identity.

The Rabbi also described Don Pedro's behavior during the lighter moments. In Pulichev, he had been a free man, with no duties or pressures other than the demands of his own personal growth, and he was able to relax as never before. A new side of him emerged after a few weeks. He began to display a devastating sense of humor. He went for long leisurely walks in the forest and along the river. And when he was alone, he almost always hummed to himself. He was happy.

When the Rabbi finished, Sebastian took a deep breath and let it out slowly. "This is exactly what I wanted to hear from you, Rabbi. I can't tell you how grateful I am. I never knew my father in this way. I did see some of his new sense of Jewish identity when he came back. But I never saw him in a state of carefree happiness, never in my entire life. He was always harried and burdened by responsibilities and duties. It was always something. If it wasn't one thing, it was another. I never heard him hum. I never heard him laugh out loud. But as you describe it, I can imagine it in my mind, and — this may sound strange — all this will become part of my memory of him."

"It is not strange at all."

"Rabbi, my journey here was worthwhile just to meet you and to spend this hour with you. It's a precious gift, and I would gladly have gone to the ends of the world to receive it. But if I can beg your indulgence, I'd like to bring up one more subject. Or perhaps you would prefer that it wait until tomorrow."

"No, now is better. Tomorrow, there will be many people about. Now they're all asleep. What is on your mind?"

"It's about inspiration," said Sebastian. "When I was in Spain, I was excited about being Jewish. It was important to me. I was ready to give my life for it, and I almost did. But now, two years after my escape to freedom, I feel … so … lost … so … so …. ordinary. Yes, that's the word. Ordinary. I don't know what I'm doing or where I'm going. And I thought that … perhaps … somehow … you could … you know …"

The Rabbi smiled. "You think I can give you some magic formula, a powder you can swallow, and your problems will be solved."

"Naïve, I admit. But I suppose that's what I thought."

"Well, let me see," said the Rabbi. "You spoke about your escape to freedom. That is such an enigmatic word. Freedom. Everyone wants freedom, but what exactly is freedom? Life, even under the best of circumstances, confines and restricts us on all sides. True freedom is achieved only when the spirit is liberated and rises above the trivial pursuits of the world, and we believe that this can only be achieved through Torah. Only someone involved with the Torah, say our Sages, can be considered a free person. The yoke of Torah liberates. You may not understand it now, but someday you will."

"I hope."

"You will, Sebastian. If you want to understand it, you will. Our Sages say that if you seek you will find." He paused for a moment. "Many years ago, there was a Jewish king named Rechavam. Have you ever heard of him?"

"Yes. I think he was the son of Shlomo. He was a sinful man."

"It would seem so at first glance. The prophet says that he did evil in the eyes of the Almighty. But what exactly does that mean? In Divrei Hayamim — the Book of Chronicles — it says that when he finished building the fortifications of the country he abandoned the Almighty, and all of Israel followed him. Seems awful, doesn't it?"

"It does."

"But if you look into the Midrash in Parashas Bo you will see that Rechavam was a good king, that his reign was an occasion for rejoicing. And there are many proofs from the text to support this view. So what did he do wrong? The answer is in Divrei Hayamim. We are told that 'he did not prepare his heart to seek the Almighty.' Inspiration, my dear Sebastian, comes from a relationship with the Almighty, a relationship that must be the single most important factor in your life. It doesn't matter how much time you have to spend plowing your fields or standing in the market. If your life is focused on your relationship with the Almighty, you will be inspired."

"But —"

The Rabbi held up his hand. "Listen. When King Rechavam was building fortifications, he was absorbed with the defense of the Torah, and he was inspired. He lived with the Almighty every day from morning to night. But when he finished the fortifications and returned to everyday life, his thoughts were no longer absorbed with the Almighty. Of course, he prayed and studied and performed all the mitzvos required of him, but he did not prepare his heart to seek the Almighty. That was the evil thing he did."

"So why was he considered a good king and his reign an occasion for rejoicing?"

"Because he did a lot of good, and his shortcomings were not his fault. But that's a discussion for a different time. The point I am making is that you are very much like Rechavam."

"Me? How?"

"When you were in Spain and being Jewish meant danger and risks, you were inspired. Just as Rechavam was inspired when he was building his fortifications to protect the Torah and the Holy Temple in Jerusalem. But it was an artificial inspiration. And when life returned to normal, it evaporated. Your inspiration was also artificial. It was a response to persecution and a desire to preserve old and treasured traditions. It did not come from an intimate relationship with the Torah. And when your life as a Jew was normalized, you lost your inspiration. But that is not your fault, just as it wasn't Rechavam's fault."

"So what can I do?"

"You have to find inspiration in living as a Jew, not only in risking your life to be Jewish. Your father did it, and you can, too. But it may not necessarily be in the same way."

"So what would you suggest?"

"I would suggest we go to sleep. I don't know about you, but I'm tired already. There will be time to continue our discussion tomorrow. And you will be our guest for Shavuos. We will have plenty of time to talk."

The next day, however, a long stream of people passed through the house, some waiting to ask Rabbi Strasbourg's advice and others seeking his blessings. After nightfall, when all the people had gone, the Rabbi was too exhausted to get into long and serious discussions, but he invited Sebastian to join Elisha Ringel and him for a cup of tea and reminiscences of old times. Tanchum and Gonzalo were away making arrangements for the return journey, and Reb Mendel was in the synagogue, learning with a group of men.

As the three men sat together in companionable conversation, there was a loud banging at the door. They looked at each other, puzzled by who would knock on the door like that. Perhaps there was an emergency of some sort.

After a moment's pause, the banging resumed, even louder and more insistent than before. The clatter in the kitchen stopped, and Miriam Strasbourg came running to the door. But she stopped at the last moment.

"Should I open it?" she asked her father-in-law in a frightened voice.

The banging resumed again, louder and harder than before, and the door trembled in its frame.

"Open it," said the Rabbi.

Miriam slid back the latch and opened the door slightly. A meaty hand pushed it open all the way, and three Imperial dragoons burst into the house. A fourth dragoon remained in the street, holding the reins of their horses. Two dragoons positioned themselves at the sides of the door, their muskets at the ready, while the officer in command inspected the front rooms.

"Are these all the men in the house?" he demanded.

"What is the problem, officer?" said Elisha.

"Just answer my question, little man."

"Yes, we are the only men here."

"Fine," said the officer. He pointed at Sebastian. "You! Who are you and what is your name?"

"Moshe Metzger, sir," said Sebastian in impeccable German. "I am a merchant just arrived from Hamburg."

"You will come with us," said the officer. "We have information that there is a Spanish fugitive in this house, and you are the only one who fits the description. This one is too short, and that one is too old."

"But this is a mistake, officer," protested Sebastian. "I am no Spanish fugitive. These men will vouch for me. The fugitive you seek must be hiding in one of the other houses in the town."

"Enough talk," said the officer. "You Jews think you're smarter than everyone else. You're under arrest. If you don't come this minute, we'll drag you out and arrest your friends for harboring a fugitive."

Sebastian was about to say something, but he thought better of it. He clamped his jaw and stepped forward.

"Hold out your hands," said the officer.

Sebastian did as instructed, and the officer signaled to one of his men to tie Sebastian's hands. Then the two dragoons grabbed Sebastian by the arms. Just as they were about to march him out, Brachah Strasbourg, the Rabbi's wife, came running out of the kitchen with a small sack.

"Here's some food for our Moshe," she said. "The holiday is coming, and if this misunderstanding isn't cleared up right away, he may not be back in time. Please make sure he gets this."

The officer took the sack and surveyed the room again. Then he held up the sack and tipped his helmet to Brachah.

"Good evening," he said, and he closed the door behind him.

There were five horses outside. One of the dragoons mounted his horse. Sebastian was thrust onto another of the mounts. A second rope, much longer than the first, was tied around his waist, and the other end of the rope was handed to the mounted dragoon, who tied it to his saddle. Then the officer and the other two dragoons mounted their horses.

"Listen to me," the officer said to Sebastian. "If you try to escape, we will shoot you down like a dog, and then we'll come back for your friends. Do you understand?"

Sebastian nodded.

"And by the way," said the officer, "the lady in the house gave us some food for you, but you really want to share it with us, don't you?"

Sebastian nodded again.

The officer laughed in his face. He handed the reins of Sebastian's horse to one of his men, and they set off at a brisk trot.

Soon, the massive moonlit walls of the Imperial City loomed in front of them. The gates to the city were still open. They rode in without being stopped or questioned and went directly to the municipal prison, a sinister stone building that protruded inward from the city wall.

Sebastian was placed in chains and deposited in an underground dungeon. The door slammed shut behind him, and he heard or saw nothing more for the rest of the night.

The following afternoon, he was brought before a magistrate in the Imperial Palace. Shackled hand and foot, and with two armed guards beside him, there was no chance of escape. He would have to bluff his way out of this.

"What is your name?" asked the magistrate.

"Moshe Metzger."

"According to our information, you are Sebastian Dominguez, the son of Don Pedro Dominguez, a kinsman of his Imperial Majesty."

"Your honor, do I look like a kinsman of the Emperor? Would I be dressed like this and living among the Jews if I were a kinsman of the Emperor? This is clearly a case of mistaken identity. I am Moshe Metzger, a simple Jew looking to do a little business in Vienna."

"Hmmph! Well, we'll see about that. Fortunately, there are people here in Vienna who can identify you, Señor Dominguez."

"I beg your pardon, your honor, but I am Moshe Metzger. I am so sorry that this error is causing you inconvenience."

"I don't believe you," said the magistrate, "but we'll soon find out."

The door opened, and the bailiff came in and whispered in the ear of the magistrate. The magistrate nodded, and the bailiff hurried out. A moment later, he ushered in a stout gentleman in flamboyant Spanish attire. It was Don Alejandro Quinones, Marqués de Murillo, the man who had literally turned his back on Sebastian and Gonzalo when they had visited him in Córdoba, the same man who had sat with him in Paris and threatened to destroy him if he did not abandon his attempts to recover his father's estates.

"Good afternoon, Your Excellency," said the magistrate. "I'm glad you could spare a few minutes from your diplomatic duties to help us out here."

"What do you need?" asked the Marqués.

"We need you to identify this fellow here," said the magistrate, pointing to Sebastian.

The Marqués had not noticed Sebastian when he first came into the chamber. All he had seen was a bearded man in Ashkenazic garb. Now he looked at him more closely.

"Do you recognize this man, Your Excellency?"

"Why should I recognize him?" said the Marqués. "He looks just like any other of your German Jews. How would I know him?"

"Please look closely, Your Excellency."

"I have looked closely," said the Marqués. "If you've nothing else to ask me, I shall bid you a good day."

"This is Sebastian Dominguez," said the magistrate. "He is the son of your friend Don Pedro Dominguez, formerly Duke of Monteverde. Do you recognize him now?"

The Marqués stared at Sebastian. Then he turned on the magistrate.

"Are you some kind of an imbecile?" he snapped. "Are you playing games with me? I've told you that I've never seen this man. Do you doubt my word? Do you think that if you tell me his name my memory will suddenly return? This is a disgrace. I've never seen this man. And if he really is the son of Pedro Dominguez, ship him right back to Spain. They're waiting for him there."

"A thousand pardons if I've offended you, Your Excellency," said the magistrate. "I just thought —"

"That's the problem. You just thought. Who asked you to think? Who asked you to waste my time? I mean, just because I knew Pedro Dominguez years ago, does that give you the right to drag me away from my duties for the Spanish Crown and waste my time here? Outrageous!"

Without waiting for the magistrate to reply, the Marqués turned on his heel and left the chamber. Sebastian breathed a sigh of relief. The Marqués could have said that he'd met Sebastian in Paris, but he clearly wanted no connection with him whatsoever.

The magistrate and the bailiff exchanged looks, and the magistrate shrugged. Sebastian looked from one to the other and saw doubt on their faces. He felt a spot of hope grow within his heart. Perhaps there was still a way out of this dreadful situation.

The magistrate peered at Sebastian with disdain and shook his head.

"If you're Sebastian Dominguez," he said, "you defile this place. And if you are a German Jew named Moshe Metzger, as you claim to be, you also defile this place." He made a dismissive sign to the bailiff. "Bailiff! Go see if the other gentleman is available. In the meantime, remove this prisoner from my sight, and bring in the next prisoner."

Sebastian was left to cool his heels in a room no larger than a closet while his guards sat outside the door and played cards. After two hours, he was brought back into the magistrate's chamber. A well-dressed man was standing off to the side with his back to him. He was giving instruction to a young page.

The magistrate coughed deferentially. "M. Giroux, the prisoner is here. Can you identify him for us?"

The man turned around, and Sebastian felt a chill grip his heart. It was M. Armand Giroux, the chief financial agent for the Duke of Lorraine. Sebastian had met with him in Metz and offered to use his contacts in the Jewish community to arrange profitable business ventures on behalf of the Duke. Giroux had promised to convey the offer to the Duke on one of his frequent visits to Vienna, but nothing had ever come of the meeting. Until now.

"Do you know this man, *monsieur*?" the magistrate repeated.

"Actually, I do," said Giroux, "although I've never seen him looking like this. This man is Sebastian Dominguez."

"Are you sure?"

"Without a doubt."

"Thank you," said the magistrate. "We need trouble you no further."

Giroux nodded curtly to the magistrate. He cast a parting, cold-eyed glance at Sebastian, and followed closely by his page, he left.

"Let the record indicate," said the magistrate once the door had closed, "that M. Armand Giroux has made a positive identification of the prisoner as the Spanish fugitive Sebastian Dominguez. Let the record also indicate that this aforementioned Sebastian Dominguez is a Christian guilty of heresy and blasphemy who, although a fugitive from Spanish justice, has been condemned in absentia and burned in effigy by the Holy Office of the Inquisition. Let the record also indicate that the prisoner is hereby remanded to confinement in the Imperial Prison until such time as notification of his capture is sent to Madrid through official channels and proper arrangements are made to transfer him with security to the lawful Spanish authorities."

The magistrate pushed back his chair.

"Get him out of my sight," he said.

THE TUNNEL RAT · 12

S EBASTIAN LANGUISHED IN HIS CELL for weeks before he heard anything at all about what was happening with his case. He had not expected it to be otherwise. Just to send a message to Madrid and receive a response would take weeks, and then the wheels of the hidebound governments of Spain and Austria would begin to grind slowly and deliberately.

There would be no urgent demands to send him back to Spain with all possible haste. Sebastian was no longer in a backwater prison in Avila run by illiterate soldiers. He was now incarcerated under heavy guard in an Austrian prison in the Imperial City, and there would no longer be any daring escapes orchestrated by holy hermits. As long as the prisoner was securely confined, the Holy Office of the Inquisition would wait patiently for his return. Patience was a trait that the Inquisition possessed in abundance.

Sebastian went back to the prison routines he had developed to keep himself in good condition physically and mentally. This time, as he marched back and forth across his cell, he reviewed many of the new prayers that had lodged themselves in his memory during the previous three years. He also reviewed to the best of his ability some of the Torah he had learned: verses from the Chumash as explained by the commentaries and a few passages from the Talmud.

Most of all, he struggled against despair. During his year in the prison of Avila, he had resigned himself to his fate. In a way, the prospect of dying as a martyr to sanctify the Name of the Almighty did not lead him to despair. On the contrary, it filled him with pride. But this time, it was somehow different. After that midnight conversation with the Rabbi, the prospect of living rather than dying for the sake of the Almighty had become so tantalizingly real. He had hungered for the experience, and now, just when it was almost in his grasp, it was about to be snatched away from him. The thought of returning to Spain and dying at the stake no longer filled him with pride. It filled him with a dreadful regret.

On a hot day in early July, Sebastian had his first visitor. Sebastian heard the key turn in the lock, a sound he had not heard since the magistrate had sent him back to prison. He braced himself for the worst.

A guard opened the door, and a middle-aged priest in a white cassock and a shock of thick white hair entered the cell. A second guard stood behind him, holding a chair in his hands.

The priest sniffed delicately and held a handkerchief to his nose as a barrier against the stench of sweat and excrement. Then he shuddered.

"I cannot sit in this place," he said to the guard. "I need a clean and decent room. Put the prisoner in irons and bring him to me. And for Heaven's sake, pour some water over him before you let him come near me."

The guards took the priest literally. They poured several buckets of water over Sebastian's head. He was still soaking when they brought him to the priest, and in his mind, he thanked the Almighty for the pleasure of the cool water on his sweat-encrusted skin.

"Sit down, Dominguez," said the priest. "I am Leopold Karl von Kollonitsch, Bishop of Wiener Neustadt not too far to the south of the city. I am adviser to His Imperial Majesty Leopold I, Holy Roman Emperor. Have you ever heard of me?"

Sebastian shook his head. "I'm afraid I haven't."

"That's quite all right. I knew your father. He was in Vienna in 1668 and again in 1670 when we expelled the Jews." Kollonitsch chuckled. "At the time, I thought he was on our side, but one never knows, does one? I was shocked to find out that he was a …"

"A secret Jew?" prompted Sebastian.

"No, no. He wasn't a Jew. Nor are you. He was a duly baptized Christian, and you cannot just resign from membership in the Christian community. The Church is not a club that you join or leave at will. No, my friend. Your father was a Christian, but he was also a heretic. And the same goes for you."

He paused to give Sebastian the opportunity to respond, but Sebastian remained silent.

"I want to make you an offer," said Kollonitsch. "You've been condemned and burned in effigy in Spain. If you go back there, you haven't a chance. The best you can expect is to be strangled before you are burned at the stake so that you won't suffer the agonies of being burnt alive. It is very painful, I hear. Do you know that?"

"Do I know what, that it is painful or that I haven't a chance?"

Kollonitsch smiled. "You've spent too much time with your Jewish friends. You're beginning to sound like one of them. Anyway, here's my offer. If you repent and ask to be taken back into the loving embrace of the Church, you will be set free and some of your titles and privileges will be restored. I will have this offer guaranteed by the Pope. I don't know if you will be welcomed back in Spain, but I can assure you that the Inquisition will never be able to touch you again."

Sebastian gave the bishop a speculative look. "Why are you making me this offer? Why don't you just ship me back to Spain to face my sorry fate?"

"Aha! You think I am trying to trick you. But I'm not. When we expelled the Jews from Vienna thirteen years ago, I was younger and much more hot-blooded. But I'm older now, and I see things more clearly. Harsh measures don't work. Just look at our own city. We expelled the Jews, and now they're back in full force. Mark my words, soon they'll be buying houses inside the walls. I'm convinced that we'd do much better with them if we smothered them with love. And that certainly goes for our unfortunate Christian brothers and sisters who have stumbled into heresy. We shouldn't burn them at the stake. We should treat them with love and compassion."

"A very commendable point of view," said Sebastian.

"Ah, you are being ironic, but you are correct. It is a commendable point of view. I want to demonstrate the folly of the methods of the Inquisition, and I want you to help me do it. I'm not threatening you. I just want to tell you that my heart is full of love for you, and that if you repent, not only will you save your immortal soul from eternal damnation, you will also make me a very happy man. So what do you say?"

"I must decline your kind offer," said Sebastian.

"Oh, so fast? You didn't even give it two minutes of thought." Kollonitsch stood up. "I certainly don't expect a quick answer from you, Dominguez. I'll be back in about a week or so. That should give you enough time to really give some serious thought to my offer."

"Nothing will change," said Sebastian. "I decline your offer."

"I understand. But don't be so obstinate. I'm not asking you for commitments or promises. Just say you will think about it. That's all."

"If I said I would think about it," said Sebastian, "it would be an affront to the Almighty. I am a Jew, and that's all there is to it."

Kollonitsch walked to the door and opened it.

"Just think about it anyway," he said, and he left.

Kollonitsch's offer seemed genuine to Sebastian, and for a few days, he gave some thought to how he could exploit it to his advantage. Nothing, however, came easily to mind. But then a new development captured his thoughts.

The atmosphere was changing in Vienna. There was a new energy flowing through the city. He could feel it even in the depths of the dungeon. His meager meals were being tossed in impatiently, and sometimes, they were even forgotten altogether, as was his chamber pot. Guards were running back and forth, shouting to one another. Doors were clanging. Something was happening, and there could be only one explanation.

Yes, he was sure of it. The Turkish army had arrived at the gates of the city. Vienna was under siege. But what did this mean for him? Would a Turkish conquest of the city be his salvation? Would the Austrians execute their prisoners if the city was on the verge of falling to the enemy?

The next day, Sebastian's suspicions were confirmed as the bombardment of the city began. Even from his cell, he could hear the explosions, and in his mind, he imagined blocks of buildings collapsing under a barrage of cannonballs. One explosion sounded like a thunderclap, and he was certain that a munitions arsenal had been struck. From time to time, he also felt slight tremors in the dungeon as cannonballs struck the outer walls of the city.

Exactly a week after his first visit, Sebastian was once again taken from his cell in irons and brought to Kollonitsch.

"So, young man," said the Bishop, "have you given some thought to my generous offer?"

"There's no doubt that it is a generous offer, but I can't even consider it, as I told you last time."

"You know, of course, that our beautiful city is under siege by the infidel."

"It would be impossible not to know."

"Yes, no doubt," said Kollonitsch. "Our Emperor has removed his family from the city and taken them to Linz, further up the Danube. But before he left, I told him of my offer, and he was in favor of it. He is ready to reinstate you, if only you repent and return to the holy Church."

"As I said, I must decline."

"Even if it costs you your life?"

"Yes."

"Perhaps you think that if the Turks capture the city you will be set free. Do not deceive yourself. Your only hope for salvation is my offer."

"I understand."

"Think about it some more," said Kollonitsch. Then he stood up and left.

Another month went by without any relief from the bombardment. Kara Mustafa, the Turkish grand vizier who wore the green cord around his neck, had originally intended to storm the walls of the city. His army of three hundred thousand over one hundred thousand of whom were fighters, vastly outnumbered the eleven thousand defenders inside the city. An immediate direct assault on the city would most likely overwhelm its defenses. But the Austrians had cleared all structures from a half-mile killing field all the way around the city, depriving an attacking force of any cover. This meant that a direct attack would result in extremely heavy casualties. Instead, Kara Mustafa chose to mount a siege and wear the city down.

He spread the vast Turkish army across the plain along one side of the city. Hundreds of cannons were emplaced in the front lines, and in the back of the Turkish encampment, there were thousands of luxurious tents, filled with fine furniture, bejeweled ornamentation, barrels of figs and all sorts of delicacies, which the pampered pashas and officers had brought along to ease the hardships of the separation from home.

In the city, on the other hand, food supplies were dwindling rapidly, and the defenders faced the specter of starvation. Moreover, the need for constant vigilance drove the soldiers on the walls beyond exhaustion. Bishop Kollonitsch walked among them at all hours of the day and night offering solace and encouragement, while Count Reudiger, commanding officer of the defenders, ordered that any soldier caught sleeping at his post should be shot on the spot. Despite the hardships, the city held on, hoping against hope that Sobieski, the king of Poland, would arrive with his armies in time to lift the Turkish siege before the city fell.

Feeling the pressure of time, Kara Mustafa set his sappers to work. These engineers from France, Poland and elsewhere in Europe directed teams of laborers who burrowed into the ground and dug tunnels that ran safely under the killing field. The tunnels advanced daily aiming for the walls and the city beyond. Once the tunnels undermined the city, they would be filled with explosives and the walls would be blown up, leaving the city exposed and defenseless.

The sappers were a hardy group, who worked in shifts around the clock in the subterranean shafts by the illumination of lanterns. They dressed in light shirts and heavy shoes and came up for air several times a day, their faces red from the heat and dirt caked into every crease and crevice.

On a cool evening in late August, a new sapper appeared at the entrance to the tunnels. He joined a group of sappers eating mutton and drinking beer around a low campfire and speaking in German, the language common to all of them. One of the sappers gave him a tankard of beer.

As he sat among them sipping his beer, he studied the faces of the sappers and listened to their conversation, trying to find the proper candidate for his scheme. Finally, he settled on a pudgy sapper with a huge mustache and a French accent. He called the man aside.

"I'm Juan Gomez," he said. It was the name under which Gonzalo had traveled to Vienna. "I'm an experienced engineer from the island of Ibiza off the coast of Spain."

"And I'm Pierre," said the Frenchman. He did not offer a last name.

Gonzalo dangled a bag of coins in front of the Frenchman's bulbous nose.

"Are you interested?" he said.

"What will it cost me?" asked Pierre.

"A little work," said Gonzalo. He spread out a crudely drawn map of the city inside the walls and pointed to a spot alongside the wall. "This place here, this is the city prison. I have a friend in there, and I want to get him out."

Pierre shrugged. "It's your money. I have no problem with a breakout. Where did you get the map?"

"I have my ways," said Gonzalo.

Pierre looked it over carefully. "Doesn't look like much, but it's a good piece of work. Must have cost you a pretty penny."

"It wasn't cheap."

"I'll bet good old Kara Mustafa would love to get a look at this thing. It might loosen up that green cord around his neck."

"He'll have to get his own," said Gonzalo. "All right, down to business. Do any of the tunnels pass the prison?"

"Not too far. But if you want to get into the prison, we'll have to dig a short side tunnel."

"How long will that take?"

"A couple of days. Maybe three. It's going to be a lot of work, and I'll have to divert some of my tunnel rats from the main shaft in this sector."

Gonzalo held up the bag again. "There's more where this came from."

"When do you want to start?" asked Pierre.

"Right now."

An hour later, a team of tunnel rats headed by Pierre and Gonzalo were crawling on hands and knees deep underground. They carried their tools with them and a supply of water. The tunnels were framed in sturdy wooden boards and illuminated by dim lanterns spaced far apart. They were wide enough for two or three men, and several times, they passed men returning with heavy sacks of excavated dirt.

The air circulation in the tunnels was very poor, and Gonzalo found it difficult to breathe, although the tunnel rats seemed accustomed to the stale air. Every once in a while, they passed a pipe that had been driven through the roof of the tunnel all the way to the surface to let in a little fresh air. Gonzalo stopped at each of these pipes to draw a few long breaths before moving on.

As they went deeper into the tunnel, the sweat poured from Gonzalo's face and shoulders, and he found himself gasping for breath. He felt a wave of panic coming over him, and he realized that the close underground confinement had given him an attack of claustrophobia. He dropped to the ground and closed his eyes, willing himself to remain calm.

"Hey you, Juan," said Pierre. "Are you all right? I thought you were an experienced sapper."

Gonzalo took a deep breath and looked up. "I've never been in a tunnel so far from the surface. But I'm all right. I just needed a moment to recover. I'm fine."

"All right. Let's move."

Gonzalo got back onto his hand and knees, and the team of tunnel rats moved forward. Fifteen minutes later, Pierre called for them to halt.

"This is the spot," he said after consulting the map for a full minute. "We dig to the right."

The digging proceeded for two days. The diggers scooped out the soil, the framers worked behind them to support the roof and prevent it from collapsing, and the rest of the team filled sacks with the loose soil and dragged them back to the tunnel opening far from the city walls.

By the second day, Gonzalo was a seasoned tunnel rat. He moved easily through the near darkness and breathed without a trace of panic. He dug and filled sacks tirelessly and exhorted the other tunnel rats to work at top speed.

At the end of the second day, Pierre pointed to the blank space at which the side tunnel ended. The soil had been removed, and they faced a stone wall.

"That's the wall of the dungeon," he said. "I'll have my men loosen up these stones so that you can slide them out and crawl through. But I don't know how you plan to find your friend once you get inside, let alone get him out and away."

"To tell you the truth," said Gonzalo, "I'm not sure either. But I'll find a way. This is a small dungeon. Most prisoners get sent to a real prison. Once I get inside, I'll figure it out."

Pierre shrugged. "It's your party. As long as you pay me tonight, you can do whatever you like tomorrow."

The next morning, Gonzalo returned to the tunnel by himself. He carried two pistols and a dagger in his belt. He reached the wall of the dungeon and gently removed one of the stones. The breeze of dungeon air that bathed his face seemed cool and sweet compared with the air in the tunnel. Through the opening, he could hear the whistle of cannonballs overhead and the explosions as they wreaked havoc in the city.

He removed another two stones and peered into the dimly lit dungeon. There was a row of cells far to his right. A ring of keys hung on the wall. A single massive door led into the dungeon, and it was closed. There were no guards inside the dungeon itself. *They're probably on the other side of the door,* thought Gonzalo. If he worked quickly, he could climb into the dungeon, grab the keys and open Sebastian's cell door. Then they could be through the opening and into the tunnel before the guards noticed that their prisoner was missing.

Gonzalo reached out to remove more stones when he heard a key turn in the lock. He quickly replaced the two stones he had already removed, leaving a slight crack through which he could at least see the guard's shoes.

The door creaked open, and the guard came in. Gonzalo heard him more than saw him. There was no jangle of keys, which told Gonzalo that the guard had not taken the ring off the wall. He heard the heavy footsteps of the guard recede toward the cells. He heard a single panel open and then slam shut. Then the heavy footsteps returned. He had obviously delivered food to one of the cells.

One of the cells! This meant that there was only one prisoner in the dungeon. He would not have to search through cell after cell to find Sebastian. But wait. Maybe there were others. Maybe the guard would soon return with food for the others. He would have to wait and see.

Gonzalo waited for a half-hour, but all he heard were the whoosh of hundreds of cannonballs and the thunderous explosions that followed. The door to the dungeon did not open.

Slowly and carefully, Gonzalo removed several lines of stones from the bottom of the wall and crawled through on his belly. He was just about to reach for the keys when he heard a very loud whoosh, and then the cannonball struck the weakened wall at the rear of the dungeon. The entire dungeon shook, and the wall through which Gonzalo had just crawled, weakened by the removal of the lower stones, collapsed right onto Gonzalo and sent him sprawling.

The door flew open, and a guard came running in. Gonzalo tried to struggle free from the pile of stones under which his legs were pinned, but he could not budge them. He tried to reach for his pistols, but it was futile. There was no way out. He was trapped.

The guard took one look and sounded the alarm. Three guards with muskets at the ready immediately appeared, followed by the captain of the guard.

"Well, look what we have here," said the captain. "An unexpected visitor. It's a good thing that we have a few empty luxury suites. Lock him up!"

THE BATTLE OF VIENNA · 13

SEPTEMBER FOLLOWED AUGUST with no relief in sight for the beleaguered city of Vienna. The hundreds of Turkish cannons belched with fire almost incessantly. There were ragged holes in the walls where the repeated cannon fire had blasted through the thick stones. The sappers had undermined several bastions and blown them apart with explosive charges, leaving glaring gaps in the fortifications. The defenders threw up barricades across the gaps and prepared themselves to fight in the streets of the city.

Kara Mustafa could taste the victory that was almost within his grasp. His army was arrayed to defend itself against the Austrian forces of the Duke of Lorraine and the German forces of Prince Waldek, while at the same time maintaining its pressure on the collapsing defenses of the city. His sappers prepared to set their final explosive charges and seal off the tunnels so that the detonation would achieve maximum effect. In a few days, Vienna would lie exposed before his army. The only eventuality that could affect his strategy was the Polish forces, but they had departed from Krakow on 15 August. They would never get to Vienna on time.

The Turkish Vizier, however, had not counted on the military brilliance of Jan Sobieski, the Polish king. He took his army in a forced march straight over the mountains, heading for Vienna almost as the crow flies. The Polish infantry and heavy cavalry, thirty-five thousand strong, arrived on the outskirts of

Vienna on 10 September and joined up with the Austrians and the Germans. Sobieski was reaffirmed as commander-in-chief, as had been agreed in Warsaw months earlier.

Kara Mustafa was dismayed to learn that the Polish forces had arrived on the scene before he had finished subduing the city. He fingered the green cord around his neck nervously and improvised a new strategy that would take the new threat into account. He arrayed his army in a broader arc but refused to withdraw the soldiers engaged in the direct attack upon the city. He was determined to strike the death blow to the city even as he fought off the armies that had come to its rescue.

The day before the battle, Sobieski inspected the bivouac of the infantry and spoke to his troops about the importance of their mission. They knew that many of them would die, but they were soldiers, and it was expected of them that they give their lives for their King, their country and their faith. Afterward, Sobieski inspected his hussars, the heavy cavalry that were his most potent weapon. The spirit among the hussars was strong; they were eager for battle and confident that their King would lead them to victory.

After his tour of inspection, Sobieski returned to his tent. While he was reviewing the battle plans with his commanders over a few tankards of ale, an aide entered the tent and spoke into the ear of the King.

"Your Majesty, I apologize for the interruption," he said in a low voice. "A man has showed up in camp who claims to be the King's old friend. I tried to send him away, but he said the King would be upset if he were not brought in."

"Who is this man?" said Sobieski. "Did he give you his name?"

"He's an old Jewish rabbi. He said his name is Strasbourg."

"Shlomo Strasbourg?"

"I'm not sure, Your Majesty. I'm not familiar with Jewish names."

"Bring him to me."

The aide hurried off. Five minutes later, he returned with the Rabbi. The king stood up and embraced the Rabbi in a hearty bear hug.

"Rabbi! It's so good to see you. Come outside where we can talk privately." He took the Rabbi by the elbow and led him out of the tent. "What are you doing here in Vienna, Rabbi?"

"I'm visiting my son and his family. He lives in Eggenschlag."

"Ah, yes, I've seen Eggenschlag on the maps. They should be fine. The battle will not reach Eggenschlag."

"I know, Your Majesty."

"So what's on your mind? It must be something very important to bring you here on the eve of a great battle."

"Yes, Your Majesty. It is."

"Well, I haven't forgotten that you saved my life ... when was it ... sixteen years ago? By all the saints in Heaven, doesn't life fly by in a flash? Sixteen years! No, I haven't forgotten that I owe you my life. What can I do for you, Rabbi? What can you possibly need from me tonight?"

"I am here on behalf of a friend, a young man named Sebastian Dominguez. He is being held in prison in Vienna."

"Dominguez? Any relation to the Spanish duke that was burned at the stake?"

"His son."

"Ah! And now he has been captured in Vienna, and they want to send him back to Spain."

"Yes. Your Majesty only needs to be told one word to grasp the entire picture. The Dominguez family escaped from Spain, but they have been harried and persecuted. And now, this young man came here incognito to speak with me, but he was betrayed and arrested."

"I see. And when I enter the city in triumph after the battle is won and the siege is lifted, you want me to set him free."

"Yes, Your Majesty. The young man and his aide, a Spanish cavalier named Gonzalo Sanchez. They are both in prison."

Sobieski stroked his ample chin. "Rabbi, I will do you one better," he said. "Cardinal Pentucci, the papal legate, has promised me that the Church will be forever grateful to me if I come to the defense of Vienna. I will ask him to have all claims and charges against the Dominguez family rescinded and that they be allowed to live as Jews wherever they please without any interference from the Church or any government. I cannot promise you any influence with France, however."

"France is not our problem. The King of France has extended his protection to the Dominguez family."

"Then consider it done. The Pope will not refuse me any request. Believe me, I also have a list of other requests. He will not get off cheaply, I assure you."

"Thank you, Your Majesty. I cannot begin to tell you how grateful I am."

"Not as grateful as I am to you for saving my life. What would I do without my life? Where would I be?"

The Rabbi smiled, and the King, amused by his own witticism, burst into jolly laughter. Then he turned suddenly serious.

"There is something I want from you in return, Rabbi."

"Anything, Your Majesty."

The king led the Rabbi to a high knoll overlooking the Turkish encampment and the walled city beyond. He lifted his hand and pointed an emphatic finger in the direction of the city.

"That is the prize, Rabbi," he said. "That is the reason I have brought tens of thousands of men over the mountains.

Tomorrow, we do battle. I want a glorious victory as much as I've ever wanted anything in my life. I want to go down in history as one of the great warrior kings. And do you know what I want from you, Rabbi?"

The rabbi remained silent.

"I want your blessing," said the king. "Last time we met, you gave me your blessings for success at Podhajce, and I had a smashing victory. You also told me I would have many more victories and a glorious future. That also came true. Now, when I'm facing the biggest and most important battle of my life, the Almighty has sent you to me again. There is no doubt in my mind that He is sending me His blessing through you, so please give it to me, Rabbi."

The Rabbi nodded. "Your wish is my command, Your Majesty," he said. "May you prosper by the force of your sword. May your enemies fall before you like stalks of wheat before the harvester's scythe. May the Almighty bless you and protect you. May He give you a glorious victory and bring you through it unharmed. And may the world recognize your greatness and the nobility of your spirit and remember them for generation after generation. May the Almighty reward your goodness with a good and long life."

Sobieski was quiet for a few moments. "Thank you, Rabbi," he said in a grave voice. "Before, I was confident that we would win. Now, I am sure of it."

Before dawn on the morning of 12 September, the Turks launched an attack against the Allied Forces, and the historic battle began. The Austrians led by the Duke of Lorraine counterattacked and drove the Turks back, while the Germans and the Poles pushed forward in the center and on the right flank. The battle of the infantries raged all day, while the heavy cavalries were kept in reserve. By five in the afternoon, both sides had taken heavy casualties; they were exhausted. The Allied

Forces had gained some of the high ground, and now, all the armies prepared to withdraw for the night and resume the battle on the following day.

Sobieski sat astride his horse on a rise overlooking the battlefield. He watched the fighting winding down as the battles slowly drew apart. But something piqued his interest. As the armies were disengaging, he saw that the light cavalrymen were breaking through the Turkish lines sporadically, and it occurred to him that this might be the moment of greatest Turkish vulnerability.

There were still a few short hours before nightfall. There was time for a full-scale cavalry attack. Wheeling around, he gave the order for the elite hussars to come to the front, followed by the rest of the heavy cavalry and every other fighter who could ride a horse. He also sent messages for the Austrian and German cavalries to come forward to the front. "Begin the charge when my cannon fires. We will ride all the way to the walls of Vienna."

When the signal was given, twenty thousand horsemen charged over the hillsides onto the battlefield, with Sobieski himself leading the charge. The charge smashed through the Turkish lines and scattered the Turks in disarray. At the sight of the breakthrough, the defenders of the city came pouring out onto the battlefield and attacked the Turks from the rear. The rout was complete. The battle was over in one glorious burst of effort. The Turks retreated to the south and west of the city, and Sobieski rode into Vienna at the head of a victory procession. Two months later, with the Turkish army in full retreat in the Balkans, Kara Mustafa would be strangled with the green cord in the Serbian city of Belgrade, and Jan Sobieski would be hailed as the greatest hero in Europe.

FREE AS THE WIND · 14

THE DAY AFTER THE SIEGE of Vienna was lifted, Sebastian and Gonzalo were taken from the dungeon, under guard but unshackled, and brought to the Imperial Place. They were given a room in which to bathe and don clean clothing. There was also food for them on the table. They were given no explanation for the change in their treatment.

When Sebastian was sufficiently refreshed, a page took him to the office of Bishop Kollonitsch. Gonzalo remained behind in the room.

"Good morning," said the Bishop, "and a glorious morning it is, isn't it?"

"Actually, it is … I think."

"I assure you that it is, Dominguez. For all of Vienna. For all of Christendom. And also for you. Today, you are free as the wind."

"Free? You mean … I'm free to go?"

"Yes, you are. This morning, the King of Poland gave me a message to convey to the Pope. He asked that all claims and charges against your family be rescinded and that you be allowed to live as Jews wherever you wish without any interference. Oh, and a full pardon and amnesty for your friend Gonzalo as well. I have instructions from Cardinal Pentucci, the Papal Legate, that all the King's wishes will be granted if he saves Vienna from the Turks. Well, he's done that, so his wish is our command. You are free to go."

Sebastian stood up and turned to go.

"But ..." said the Bishop.

Sebastian stopped and turned around.

"Now that you are free," said the Bishop, "and under no coercion of any kind, I beg of you to give some thought to your immortal soul. Why should you be condemned to eternal damnation? Come back to the Church, and you will be as great a hero as Jan Sobieski."

Sebastian looked at the Bishop. "I am a Jew. I would rather die than do what you ask of me. I hope you can understand that."

The Bishop leaned back. "I actually do, Dominguez. I actually do. Anyway, before you go, you have one more stop to make. The page will take you there."

The page led Sebastian through a series of halls bedecked with huge portraits of emperors, queens and generals to a different part of the palace. He led him through a waiting room to an inner office and opened the door. He stuck in his head, then motioned to Sebastian to enter.

"Come in, Sebastian," said Don Alejandro Quinones, Marqués de Murillo. "I hear that you have been set free on Sobieski's instructions."

"Yes, Your Excellency."

"Good. I'm happy to hear that. You know, we have met each other three times. Once in Córdoba, when I was furious with you for coming to see me and jeopardizing my position and perhaps even my life. Then we met in Paris together with Colbert, the French minister, when I had to represent the official Spanish position regarding your father's estates in the French domain. Then we met again in front of the magistrate, when I denied ever having seen you. That was again for my protection and also for yours. Unfortunately, Giroux was in Vienna at the time, and he identified you. This is the fourth time we are meeting. It is the first time, at least for me, that we are free to speak what is in our minds and in our hearts."

Sebastian stared at the Marqués. He had nothing to say.

"Your father and I were very good friends," continued the Marqués. "He confided his secret to me, and he charged me with certain responsibilities to his family in case he should ever be exposed and condemned."

"Certain responsibilities?"

"Mostly financial. But he also asked me to look out for the safety and welfare of his family. I am sorry to say that I wasn't able to do anything to get you out of prison. But I can help you financially. Your father entrusted me with certain funds that were unknown to anyone and beyond the reach of the Inquisition. He amassed these funds in secret for just such a contingency. When you return to Metz, letters of credit in the sum of one hundred thousand Reichsthalers will be delivered to you. These instruments are as good as cash. It is a princely sum. You can use it to start a new life in Amsterdam or anywhere else you choose."

Sebastian stared at him. "I don't know what to say."

"You don't have to say anything. Your father expected you to take on the responsibility of being the head of the family if something happened to him. With that in mind, he said that the hundred thousand Reichsthalers should be apportioned as follows. Ten thousand each to Carolina and Felipe. Twenty thousand to your mother to ensure that she is comfortable and independent for the rest of her life. The rest to you, with the understanding that you are responsible for the others if they should turn to you. Do you accept that responsibility?"

"Yes, I do," said Sebastian. "I would accept it even if I were penniless."

"Of course."

"Your Excellency, do you —?"

"You can call me Don Alejandro. Your father and I were

very good friends. And I would be honored if you would look on me as your friend as well."

"The honor would be mine."

"You began to ask me something?"

"Yes, Don Alejandro. Do you know who betrayed me here in Vienna? How did they know I was here and how were they able to find me?"

"I regret that I have no information for you on that, Sebastian. I sincerely hope that those ill-disposed toward you will leave you alone now that you'll be receiving immunity from the Pope. I hope you'll be perfectly safe from now on."

"Yes. If only I could be sure."

"It is good to be sure, but there are so few things in life of which we can be sure. Anyway, you can be sure that the money will be delivered to you in Metz. There is one thing I must tell you. You must leave this country immediately. The brave Emperor will be returning from Linz very soon, now that the battle is over, and you must make sure he does not find you here. He is unpredictable. If you are gone, he will not give you another thought."

"I will leave immediately, Don Alejandro. Thank you for the warning, and of course, thank you for your loyalty to my father. You are a good friend."

"That I am," said the Marqués. "That I am."

He stood up and put his hand on Sebastian's shoulder.

"There is another reason that you must go back to Metz immediately," he said slowly and deliberately. "It is because of your mother."

"My mother! Has something happened to my mother?"

"Listen to me, Sebastian. I have just received the information. Your mother's housekeeper came down one night and saw something strange going on in the kitchen. Your sister was sitting with a green cloth draped over her head. Your mother and another Jewish woman were saying incantations and pouring molten lead from pot to pot over your sister's head. The housekeeper was very disturbed about this, and finally, she told her priest about it during confession."

Sebastian held his breath. "And?"

"Your mother has been accused of witchcraft."

To be continued …

Optimism

Optimism

Bob
Brown

Reflections on a life of action

hardie grant books
MELBOURNE · LONDON

Published in 2014 by Hardie Grant Books
Hardie Grant Books (Australia)
Ground Floor, Building 1
658 Church Street
Richmond, Victoria 3121
www.hardiegrant.com.au

Hardie Grant Books (UK)
Dudley House, North Suite
34–35 Southampton Street
London WC2E 7HF
www.hardiegrant.co.uk

Cataloguing in publications data available from the National Library of Australia
Optimism: Reflections on a life of action
978 1 7427 0766 2

Publisher: Pam Brewster
Cover and text design by Philip Campbell
Cover image courtesy of Newspix
Illustration by Michelle Mackintosh
Typesetting by Kirby Jones
Typeset in Adobe Garamond Pro 12/15.5pt
Printed and bound in Australia by Griffin Press

To Rosario Godoy and Ben Oquist

Contents

Introduction

OPTIMISM, LIKE PESSIMISM, feeds on itself. In my earlier years I spent a decade or more deeply pessimistic and depressed. Even though it was a reasonable reaction to the way the human world malfunctions, it wasn't an enjoyable way to live.

These days I am an optimist and I like it. It is also a reasonable option because optimism is a key ingredient for any successful human endeavour – and isn't keeping Earth viable the greatest endeavour we can ever undertake?

There's a hitch, though. The twentieth-century philosopher Bertrand Russell, much reviled by the British establishment, put it in a nutshell: 'The trouble with the world is that the stupid are cocksure and the intelligent are full of doubt'!

We don't know what the future holds but we can be sure that leaving it to stupidity – which is almost always manifested in the inability to see beyond one's self and one's own times – is a recipe for disaster.

Yet the intelligent are unsure. They weigh things up. They look beyond the here and now. They worry about legacy and about grandchildren and using finite resources wisely. They even consider themselves no more valuable than anyone else.

I have some simple advice for heavy thinkers: get over it. Mulling things over while the stupid and greedy ravage the planet is, after all, not very intelligent. Worse, it is a certain road to depression.

Get active rather than depressed. It worked for me.

In this book are some anecdotes from a life set for downfall that found its salvation in action. We have a choice and it is empirical: pessimism or optimism, stupor or action. Suit yourself.

I've been lucky enough to meet remarkable people who are challenging the greed and small-mindedness of our age at risk to themselves, but with an unswerving and intelligent mission: that our global society should not be left to fail under this rampaging age of Materialism.

The contradictions of human society must be challenged: not least the fact that climbing the ladder of political power is easiest for those who care least about treading on other people's fingers and faces. To put Russell's dictum another way: the trouble with the global political arrangement is that the power falls most readily into the hands of the selfish, cruel and cocksure.

But it is no good feeling hopeless.

The challenge to intelligent, sensitive folk is to take over. To do that, the people must be won over. For that to happen, the megaphone message delivered by the captains of Materialism has to be contested and outdone.

Who knows the future of the biosphere? None of us.

But everywhere I go I run into people with the ambition and nous to create a future when the current pillaging of Earth's living resources will be ancient history.

It is exciting to be with them taking up the challenge to bring on an era of a truly sustaining relationship with the one planet that hosted us into life and that, if we get it right, will host our kind into a magnificent future.

I am writing this at Boolcoomatta, in the arid lands of South Australia, west of Broken Hill. Here are 65,000 hectares of Earth in recovery. The sheep (up to 85,000 were shorn each year in the woolshed a stone's throw from my desk) have gone, the saltbush and mulga are returning, and kangaroos and emus once again dominate the plains.

Yesterday Paul and I watched eagles taking off from and soaring above the rocky pinnacles to the west of this homestead: safe, sure and forevermore out of danger from the guns and traps of the last century.

This is Bush Heritage Australia country dedicated to its own ancient natural ecosystem, funded by intelligent, caring people and corporations who find uplift in the idea of restorative ecology, and a new action-oriented reverence for the living planet.

Two nights back we sat on a hilltop far from here, awaiting the end of a total eclipse of the Moon by Earth. We watched Earth's shadow move very slowly off the Moon, from right to left, in a place where Aboriginal Australians have celebrated this interconnectedness between the Sun, Earth and Moon for thousands of years. Below us was a large round boulder: the Moon on the hillside. Near the boulder, on creekbed red rock, were multiple circular etchings of the Moon.

We will not, short of the complete destruction of society as we know it, return to such reverent depictions of the solar system. But we cannot go forward without appreciating Earth's unique place in that system that affords us all we are and have. That appreciation, asserted and enacted, despite the sneering and perhaps violent opposition of the current moguls, will be the world's salvation.

In the Senate I had the following words printed on the back of my business card:

Caring

Optimistic

Defiant

We strive for peace democracy

and a fair go for everyone.

We champion

future generations

and life on Earth

in all its brilliance.

The future is Green.

Here are some stories from my journey to this simple philosophy for happiness.

BOB BROWN

BOOLCOOMATTA, 19 APRIL 2014

Optimism

1
Rhapsody of Oura Oura

I SET OFF one Saturday afternoon in November 1973 to drive from Launceston to the Liffey Falls, at the top of the 'remote upper Liffey Valley' (as a contemporary Launceston *Examiner* story about a drug bust described it). While up there, I saw an old-fashioned white cottage tucked in under the towering dolerite cliffs of Drys Bluff.

A year earlier, having crossed from the mainland to Tasmania by ferry for a three-month job in a Launceston medical practice, I had sent a postcard to my parents back in New South Wales: 'I am home.' They seemed happy that their son had settled down, at least geographically.

Now, as I drove back from the falls, old Frank Page was putting his cows over the gravel road. I stopped, wound down the window and asked if there were any properties for sale in the area. Frank, his weather-beaten face the picture of country kindness, said, 'Well, no.' He added, 'Though the white house up the road was for sale. I think it was sold this week.'

I had that feeling you get when the person you have suddenly fallen in love with turns and stares you gently in the eye and says, 'I'm seeing someone else.'

Repressing waves of disappointment, I turned the car around and drove back up the valley. I walked across the rustic bridge over the swirling Liffey River and up the long-grass paddock to the white cottage. The owners, John and Stephanie Dean, also showing the essence of country kindness, confirmed the sale but added, 'The buyer's wife is coming up from Hobart to see the house on Tuesday.' Late on Tuesday John phoned me with the news that the buyer's wife had taken one look and said, 'I'm not going to live in a dump like that.'

Someone else's dump was my delight. The cottage, along with 10 hectares of vibrant forest and meadow and nearly a kilometre of riverbank, cost me $8000. The barred bandicoots, rare sweet-faced bettongs, ruby-eyed white goshawks and boobook owls were included, gratis. I called it Oura Oura (pronounced 'Oo-ra Oo-ra'), after the Aboriginal girl who, it is said, took a red feather from a young French sailor on Tasmania's southern shore two centuries ago. 'Oura Oura' is also Palawa (Tasmanian Aboriginal) for black cockatoo.

With Fran Newman, a good friend from Sydney University medical school days, I spent the 13th and 14th of December 1973 at Oura Oura in a mood infused with euphoria. Here was a warm cocoon, an envelope of intense contentment. At Liffey, the windows on the wider world became opaque.

A month later I climbed Drys Bluff. In the highest rock gully, with its waterfall and remnant alpine rainforest, I came across the ropes used by the Deans to ascend the cliffs to the top. I was enraptured. From Bass Strait in the north to the southern ranges near Hobart, a vista of Tasmania's wild heartland lay beneath. A wedge-tailed eagle flew across the treetops below me and the sun cast my shadow from this cliff-top lookout onto the 200-metre-high cliff due west.

I raised my camera to snap the scene, lost my balance and nearly fell. I was saved by drop-squatting and crab-crawling backwards over the rock plateau.

On getting back down to Oura Oura I sat a while on the old wooden bridge and, out of nowhere, a platypus surfaced beneath my feet.

This little valley produced an endless flow of natural surprises, diluting my dismay at what British philosopher Bertrand Russell had called his deepest impression on life: the needless cruelty of human affairs.

As I settled into sleep that evening my body 'jumped' – I was back on the cliff-edge and about to fall. But I woke with a smile, infused again with that contentment. A couple of winters later the same waking smile led me to write a poem called 'Winter's Night at Liffey':

> *When sleep shuts off*
> *the winter gale*
> *with its freezing rain*
> *and hail that clatters*
> *on the iron*
> *then silence wakes me*
> *to a still*
> *a softest quiet*
> *I smile to myself*
> *knowing through the night*
> *it's snowing.*

So, for four decades, my locality, my geographical certainty and my hedge against the impossibility of the Universe has been this little white cottage at Liffey.

Settling in at Liffey had its challenges.

A lot happened. There were practical problems: the occasional shooters hell-bent on culling my possums and wallabies; the pipe that burst one frosty weekend in my absence, flooding the house and pitting the ceiling; the snake that took up residence in the rock wall at my back door; the thieves who swept through while I was off bushwalking.

Once, a couple of escaped prisoners took up residence in the back shed while I was away in Hobart. A few weeks later, under the shed bed, I found a sawn-off shotgun that they'd apparently left when they fled, hunted by the police.

And, of course, there was much happiness. I took up daytime residence on the front verandah to write philosophy, even when winter afternoon temperatures lingered in single-digit figures. I cooked on the open fire, saving the cooled vegetable juices for the next day's lunch. On Fridays I cycled the 50 kilometres to Launceston, keeping watch over the doctors' patients until Monday morning and then, backpack full of groceries, I would happily ride back home for a week in Liffey's enfolding comfort.

The Liffey Valley is sensationally beautiful. I've walked along the river and up the mountainside hundreds of times. I've felt the crunch underfoot of a midnight frost on the moonlit meadows, slept in the woods, strolled over frozen tarns on the bluff, watched snow falling across the host of springtime daffodils, and seen platypuses foraging together in the pool beneath the bridge. Nature, which cradled *Homo sapiens*, also created an inseparable bond between itself and us. We love nature. I love Liffey.

The walnut tree near the house has shaded Greens' fundraising picnics; Wilderness Society dam blockade meetings; the birth of Bush Heritage Australia, helped by my lifelong friend from Bellingen, Judy Henderson, as a national land-purchase organisation for saving ecologically valuable places; a marriage or two, and the commitment ceremony for my partner Paul and me in 2009; children whooping on my father's cartwheel swing; and possums fighting over the autumn walnut crop (whatever's left over, that is, after Paul's Christmas raid for pickling). These events were all lit by Liffey's beauty: its sheer loveliness, its turbulent weather and its ever-changing mood.

One night as I walked with friends to the theatre in Hobart, I had an inexplicable urge to go home; I left them there and drove through the night to Liffey, where I found a storm had torn sheets of iron off the roof. I spent the rest of the night hammering them back on to the old rafters.

And now Oura Oura is in the safe hands of Bush Heritage Australia itself. Deans Track up Drys Bluff is open to all comers, and so are those meadows by the Liffey River. I hope they give others – as many as may be for as long as may be – the joy they have so freely given me.

2

The best doctor in town

In 1972 I went to Tasmania to replace one of three doctors in a Launceston practice. The following year I bought Oura Oura.

For a while I worked weekends at the practice. While there I slept on an examination couch in the back room. It was high, narrow and hard, but I had a good pillow and blanket.

Near midnight one Saturday, just as I was getting to sleep, the practice phone rang. A worried mother told me that her 18-year-old son had stomach pains and she thought it was appendicitis.

'When did the pain start?' I asked.

'This morning,' she replied.

I chided her for not calling me earlier, dressed, secured my doctor's bag on the bike rack and rode up the hill to the housing estate at Mayfield.

My patient's street was in darkness because the streetlights had been shot out. Helpfully, halfway along the second block, light beamed from an open doorway in which a man slouched, holding his midriff. I grabbed my bag and jumped the fence.

'How are you going?' I asked the fellow in the doorway, who seemed older than 18.

'Not so bloody good, Doc! The pain's been going all day,' he groaned. I could smell alcohol. His mother had gone to bed.

The house entrance was untidy. I asked him to lie on the carpet in the bedless room just inside the door and did a quick examination. Two things stood out: his pain was in his chest rather than his abdomen, and he told me that his father had fallen dead of a heart attack just a few months earlier.

There was no arrhythmia or heart murmur, no raised temperature or pulse rate, and no abdominal tenderness. This man was more anxious than ill. He was also more than a little drunk.

'Well, your heart's healthy and you'll be okay,' I reassured him, not making obvious my pique at being called out so needlessly.

'You know, Doc,' said my clearly relieved patient, holding out a small wad of banknotes, 'you're the besht bloody doctor in Launcheshton. I called all the other doctorsh and they didn't come, but I didn't call you and you did come!'

The penny dropped. I was at the wrong house.

So, turning down the money, I jumped the fence again and crossed the street to the right house.

After calling an ambulance for the 18-year-old who did have appendicitis, I had a settling cup of tea with his mum and then coasted back down the hill to catch up with my sleep on the practice couch.

3
Rescuing Strawberry

FARMER RON HAD heard that a young doctor had moved into the Liffey Valley. So he drove down from high up near the rocky tops of the Cluan Tiers to ask that I make a home call.

'It's Strawberry!' he told me with an anguished look when we met on my bridge over the Liffey. 'She's got a piece of wire cutting into her ankle and I can't get it off.'

Strawberry was Ron's black-and-white Friesian milking cow. The fencing wire had tangled around her back leg. Ron's tentative attempts to untangle it had caused Strawberry to kick with pain.

I went back to the house to fetch my doctor's bag and then to the shed for a fine-nosed pair of wire-cutters, and joined Ron in his truck for the bumpy ride up to see this unusual patient.

Strawberry was standing on a small rise from the track, strapped to a strong wooden fence as if bailed for milking. She was not struggling or making any sound. She was refusing to eat the nice pile of hay that Ron had given her, but it seemed that she was less apprehensive about her predicament than her owner.

Strawberry's near back leg was a mess. The wire could not be seen because the leg had been engorged by inflammation and the blocked blood flow from her hoof. Beneath the hair her lower leg looked like a blue football.

I got down on my knees and cautiously moved rearwards under the cow's belly, beside her udder, using a fine probe to locate the metal embedded in her trussed-back limb. With my head between her legs, my next task was to manoeuvre the wire-cutters in through the swollen tissue. That's when she flinched.

As I closed the cutters around the wire Strawberry let out a roar and kicked her leg against the restraining straps. The straps held but she lifted her tail and let go with a flood of liquid manure – all over my head and shoulders.

I backed out and stood up, dripping, wiping the warm faeces from my hair, face and clothes. Ron looked thunderstruck, as if I might retaliate.

'Poor Strawberry, she's nervous!' he exclaimed.

I broke out laughing at his heartfelt defence of his bovine milk factory. At that, Ron laughed too.

Shitty as my circumstances were, Strawberry's suddenly took a turn for the better. The wire snapped. The cut ends jutted out from her wound and the wire was easily removed.

Soon untethered, though hobbling, Strawberry was back on track.

Ron was delighted and happily drove me back down the valley. My own pleasure at the successful operation was not complete until I had taken a refreshing swim in the river.

4

The love of John's life

Dairy farmer James Malley and I parked at the end of a logging road in the Milkshake Hills in the north of the Tarkine wilderness. We put our packs on our backs and headed south into the rainforest in search of the Tasmanian tiger.

It was November 1973, at the end of a wet spring in one of the wettest places in Australia. The next two days in the depths of the Tarkine forest set my mind on fire, even as the rain tumbled down in big drops from the green forest canopy above. We found no trace of a tiger, not even a footprint, but the nights were alive with the calls of boobook owls and the scurrying of marsupials.

In places we found ourselves bashing a slow path through dense bauera scrub, cutting grass and Tasmania's infamous horizontal thickets. Horizontal is a thin, hardy tree that falls and throws up branches, which fall again until, with the resulting entanglement, you can find yourself negotiating a wicked wickerwork 5 or 10 metres above a gully or creek. As you bend forward to deal with this predicament, the unyielding horizontal repeatedly snags your backpack and hauls you to a stop until you bend back and wriggle enough to disentangle. (In the hands of furniture makers, horizontal provides unbreakable legs for stools and sturdy backs for chairs.)

I had more than horizontal and Tasmanian tigers tormenting my mind. A week earlier I had offered $7500 for Oura Oura, the little cottage by the Liffey River that was to become my home. The asking price was $8000. 'You poor, stupid wretch!' I kept accusing myself as I lay awake, tossing and turning in my sleeping bag, wondering how many other buyers were offering the full price while I was stuck out in the wilderness. I decided that I would offer $8000 as soon as we got back.

After two nights in the rainforest we headed home but were halted by a flood in the Little Rapid River. We had crossed the river in knee-deep water two days earlier, but the rain had raised it to a torrent. James couldn't swim, and there was more rain in the offing. It looked like we might have to camp for days before making the crossing safely.

However, James had an even greater urgency to get to the other side of the river. He needed to get back to Trowutta for that night's milking, so he insisted we cross.

The fast-flowing current was above my waist. I got to the far bank, secured a line and returned. Packs on backs, we slowly crossed the slippery pebbled riverbed through the surging current. I knew that if James slipped and fell there would be little I could do to help him, but he was as strong as an ox and soon made the far bank.

At the first phone box I sealed the purchase of the Liffey cottage. The next morning James dropped me off at the Ulverstone bus shed for the trip back to Launceston.

An elderly man was already there, his bicycle propped up against the wall. His name was John and we waited together for the bus, which was late. He enjoyed hearing about my walk in the Tarkine and how happy I was with purchasing the house at Liffey.

I have never forgotten this kindly man's own story. He told me how, just the year before, he had ridden his bicycle north along the back roads of Australia's Great Dividing Range. He knew how to live on nothing. When he developed saddle sores he found a deserted hay barn near Cooma and rested there until the wounds on his backside healed. In southern Queensland he got homesick, and so he rode south and caught the ferry back to Tasmania.

But there had been more to his mainland melancholy than Tasmania being on the other side of Bass Strait. He carried with him wounds from a terrible childhood event.

John's grandfather, a convict, had been transported in chains in the hull of a sailing ship from London to Tasmania. The convict's son, John's father, had been a tyrant who eked out a meagre living on a bush block at the frontier of rainforest clearance near the Tarkine in north-west Tasmania.

The Bible says that the sins of the father will be visited upon the sons and then the son's sons, even to the fifth generation. When I was told this as a boy, at St Paul's Presbyterian Sunday School in Armidale, it struck me as a particularly frightening example of God's failure to intervene. Maybe it was John's mother who stopped the onflow of nastiness from overtaking him. Whatever did, I was enthralled by the white-haired stranger's story as we waited for the Launceston bus.

Gentleman John, then in his seventies, lived his life alone.

When he was 15, he had run barefoot through the forest to a secret rendezvous by the river. On that sunny summer's morning, ten minutes from his family's rough bush hut and trembling with a new and astonishing excitement, John met up with the girl next door.

I saw in my imagination the two bush waifs coming together, embracing, disrobing and taking the sweetest plunge of their lives into the clear, cool waters of the river.

But their ecstasy was cut short by horror. John's father, with a club of four-by-two wood in his fist, had followed him.

My imagination was not spared what happened next. His father mercilessly bashed the boy unconscious with the sharp-angled club and left him for dead on the bank. Blood and serum from inside his fractured skull trickled out of an ear.

His mother eventually found him and carried her broken boy home.

Three days later, with his mother doing all she could to nurse and protect him in their hut, John regained consciousness. After a few more days, when he had recovered some strength, he climbed out the window and bolted as best he could into the forest.

John's busted bones mended as he lived out under the trees and stars. He snared bandicoots and potoroos to eat raw or, after he found some matches, roast on an open fire. He stole bread and other items of food and clothing from remote farmhouses and sheds. He avoided everyone and met no-one. While he had no human company, he communed with the living wilds – the birds, the flowers and the creatures that called in the forest at night. And all the while he dreamed of the girl who had lived next door.

John could never let her out of his mind. After some years passed he moved warily back into civilisation and got a job in the west-coast mines. He knew where his father was and made sure their paths never crossed.

More importantly, he found out where the girl was and kept the best track of her that he could, from a respectful distance. A shy, illiterate bush kid, he never had the confidence to contact her. Once, at a country fair, he actually saw her, though she did not see him.

She was the one love of his life. No-one ever replaced her.

He knew when she married and accepted that her life had to go on without him. He saw a picture of her with her family in a newspaper, which he kept. He never stopped loving her.

At the Ulverstone bus shed, his bicycle by the wall, his trousers tucked into his socks, he told me her name, where she was living now that she was a grandmother, and how content he was that her life had turned out well.

He was headed to the Launceston General Hospital for medical treatment and, from the sound of it, was not much longer for the world.

The bus arrived and, after some chitchat on the journey to Launceston, John and I parted. He had no address and I never saw him again.

Here was a man with good reason to be bitter. Instead he had kept his darkness at bay with the light of an enduring love. Before he died John shared his story with a young stranger at the Ulverstone bus shed. Forty years later I am glad to be passing it on in the hope that it lights up at least four more generations.

5

Jimi on a bier

JIMI HENDRIX INVITED us all along:

> When I'm playing, man, I go up in a rocket ship. Don't know
> where I'm going to go, but you can all come with me, every one
> of you if you want. Join me on my ship.

There was nothing to be done when Hendrix's body was wheeled
on an ambulance trolley up the little rise to the casualty department
of St Mary Abbots Hospital, in London, on 18 September 1970. As
the evening papers so mercilessly described it Hendrix, aged 27, had
died in his sleep – he choked on vomit after taking a cocktail of red
wine and sleeping pills. I saw the anguish in the faces of the people
accompanying his bier, not least that of the tall young blonde woman
who was keeping as close as she could, tripping along behind, helpless
as the rest of us.

On duty in my white doctor's coat, stethoscope around my neck,
I watched the sad procession. I thought I had almost nothing in
common with the dead man. Little did I know.

Hendrix described the world as 'mud'. Besides the Vietnam
War, we were in the middle of the Cold War. The Union of Socialist
Soviet Republics and the North Atlantic Treaty Organization were
manufacturing and deploying intercontinental ballistic missiles

(ICBMs) capable of lobbing thousands of nuclear bombs onto each other's cities. Safety resided in the theory of mutually assured destruction: MAD. The idea was that if one side attacked the other, both would be destroyed – and so neither would try it.

One morning I stood next to the statue of Eros in Piccadilly Circus. Black taxis and red double-decker buses were circling around. A year earlier, as a Canberra Hospital doctor, I had seen a movie based on a nuclear attack on Britain – the public had been banned from seeing it. The official advice to Londoners in such an event was to first pull the blinds down! I imagined a hydrogen bomb – the height of human ingenuity – exploding overhead. Like Hendrix, I thought I was going mad.

Brilliant young Russians were standing ready in the missile silos near Tashkent, Kazakhstan, to fire nuclear bomb–laden ICBMs at cities like London, Paris, Tokyo, New York and Chicago. Near Grand Forks, North Dakota, an equally brilliant roster of young Americans, with short back and sides, awaited the spiflicating moment when their trigger fingers would send off ICBMs to destroy Moscow, Leningrad, Kiev and, for good measure, Beijing. Whether the communist rockets could reach Sydney and Melbourne was a moot point and, in those cities, not much was thought about it. Nor is it now.

Post-mortem, the radio played and replayed Hendrix's gobsmacking version of 'The Star-Spangled Banner' and I understood.

'We're gonna play OUR American anthem.' He saw that 'there are some evil folks around and they want you to be passive and weak and peaceful so they can overtake you like jelly on bread'.

At St Mary Abbots a more senior Australian doctor took charge and signed the Hendrix death certificate. I went off to do what I could for a man who had fallen under a train.

That was more than 40 years ago and St Mary Abbots Hospital has now gone too. But Hendrix lives on. In *Starting at Zero: His Own*

Story, Alan Douglas and Peter Neal have collected the words of this electric guitarist and poet extraordinaire.

There is a dimension of the human soul, heaped in Hendrix, which, if we could tap it, would dismantle all the bombs.

While I was to become an environmentalist dealing with homophobia, Hendrix was a guitarist dealing with racism. His perky optimism was a winner. He said of the racism he had experienced:

> I used to have a childhood ambition to stand on my own feet, without being afraid to get hit in the face if I went into a 'white' restaurant and ordered a 'white' steak. But normally I just didn't think along these lines. I had more important things to do – like playing guitar.

His response, when accused of being obscene and vulgar, was:

> I am electric religion … I play and move as I feel … If they think our show is sexy, that's nice, and if the show gives them other feelings, that's just as good. If my music makes them feel free to do what they think best for themselves, that is a step ahead. As long as they're not passive!
>
> In New York the Daughters of the American Revolution tried to stop our show because they said we were too sexy. Imagine how these old ladies must have been turned on.

His thoughts on negativity were wise beyond his years:

> If you start thinking negative it switches to bitterness, aggression, hatred. All those are things we have to wipe away from the face of the Earth before we can live in harmony.

He spoke with an eloquent planetary awareness:

> There's a great need for harmony between [people] and Earth …
> [my] home isn't America, it's the Earth. My goal is to erase all
> boundaries from the world!

Yet the contradictions of the world proved too tough for this 27-year-old citizen of Earth. At the time I shared his chagrin but had none of the public pressures that brought Hendrix down.

Hendrix could see that we are all part of a human continuum: that the next generation should inherit the Earth in at least as good condition as we have. In considering those who will come after us, is there any better feeling than knowing that the world is the better for us having lived?

After all, as Hendrix put it, 'in the long run we shall be our own children.'

6
Drumnadrochit

THERE IS A huddle of cottages towards the northern end of Loch Ness called Drumnadrochit.

I reached that hamlet tired and soggy after the trudge up from Glasgow in November 1970. I had been planning a grand coach, rail and walking tour of Scotland but, after my pocket was picked in a camping goods store in London's Strand, I resorted to a cheap tent and sleeping bag and a rail ticket to Glasgow. From Glasgow I walked north into the Scottish winter.

A few nights before Drumnadrochit I had been refused accommodation at the almost-empty hotel at the Kyle of Lochalsh where the ferry crossed the narrow sound between the Scottish mainland and the Isle of Skye. That night I had erected my tent on a nearby shingle beach in driving rain, in the dark, and went to bed wet through.

By Drumnadrochit I was scraggier. The pack on my back was heavy with wet gear. My beard needed a trim, and long locks of curly hair fell in disorder about my face.

I spoke to the sole Drumnadrochit resident to be seen: he looked at me doubtfully and reckoned that my only chance of a bed for the night would be at 'old Peggy McKenzie's – she's the second-last house on the right'.

When I got to the white cottage gate, I saw an old woman crouched down and polishing the brass knob on her front door. She was talking to herself and her voice, besides the Scottish brogue, had a sad lilt to it.

'Excuse me, Miss McKenzie, I was told you might still be open. Do you have a room for the night?' I asked her from behind, hoping against hope. A cold drizzle was falling as the night closed in.

The old woman stood slowly up, turned around, and stared at me for a long, long time – though maybe only a minute or two by the clock. Eventually she asked me where I was from and what I was doing there.

I told her I was walking from Glasgow to Inverness.

'Well, all right, Laddie!' she replied, her voice edged with reluctance. 'First you can load the coal …' She indicated a place for my pack outside the door. I retrieved sacks of coal from the shed in the alley beside the house and loaded up the fuel box by her fire. Boots off and on at the door. Other chores followed.

Two hours later, as rain pattered against the windowpanes, I had my first hot shower in a week. I came down to find my washed socks on the clothes horse and my boots, on a newspaper, drying by the fire.

More amazingly, as I sat down ready for a three-course dinner, old Peggy bustled happily around her kitchen. God, it turned out, had come to my (and her) rescue.

'Robert!' she explained while peeling potatoes at the sink,

Yesterday I closed for the season and so today I was feeling melancholy. As I was polishing the doorknob, I was praying to the Good Lord not to leave me alone through winter. No sooner had I put up my wish than your voice was over my shoulder asking for a roof over your head. So what was I to do?

The Lord moves in mysterious ways, His (or Her) wonders to perform. For her part, old Peggy had been astonished to find out, after the shuttling of the coal and other chores were done, that her dishevelled guest was a family doctor, fresh up from London and shortly to be working his way home to Australia as an assistant ship's surgeon on a passenger liner. I plied her with none of my troubles.

She gave me a warm room, a double bed with satin sheets and my best night's sleep since Glasgow. Next morning, before heading north to Inverness, I enjoyed a full Scottish breakfast, fried black pudding aside. Old Peggy refused any payment.

A few weeks later, from London, which was having its first white Christmas in seven years, and with a blizzard blasting northern Scotland, I sent old Peggy a dish decorated with flowers and bluebirds and a letter expressing the hope that she would have more company before the winter was through. Anyway, I wrote, she could always be sure that I was thinking of her kindness as the SS *Northern Star* lifted anchor in Southhampton and carried me home to sunny Australia. I wished she could come too.

Back in Sydney Peggy's reply caught up with me, and her admonishment ('Robert, you should not have spent all that money on an old woman like me.') could not hide her pleasure, nor her ongoing melancholy.

My later letters went without reply.

In the south of Tasmania, so much like Scotland, where the Channel Highway skirts the scenic D'Entrecasteaux Channel, there is a huddle of farm buildings. At the gate is a wooden sign: 'Drumnadrochit'. I intend to call there one day and ask about any link with Peggy McKenzie.

Whether there is or not, I will recount the story of that November evening in 1970 when I walked up to Miss McKenzie's cottage gate and she was talking to herself and I was hoping against hope.

7
Fasting on Mount Wellington

THE SCOTTISH BOTANIST Robert Brown climbed Mount Wellington, the lofty backdrop to Hobart, in 1804. One hundred and seventy-two years later, his namesake was about to follow.

I was in my Liffey kitchen getting ready for dinner in the spring of 1976 when the radio brought news of excitement in Hobart's CBD. The nuclear-powered aircraft carrier USS *Enterprise* and its approximately 1800-strong crew were coming to town. The chamber of commerce estimated that $2 million would flow through the cash registers as a result, not least at the casino. 'Party girls' were flying in from Sydney's Kings Cross.

Whereas a decade earlier I had joined a throng of 250,000 Sydneysiders crammed dangerously onto a dock to see the USS *Coral Sea*, by then I was aware that this visitor to Hobart would bring with it eight nuclear reactors, scores of nuclear bombs and enough delivery aircraft to destroy dozens of cities. A nuclear accident would have awesome environmental consequences – this ship was not allowed into New York or Boston for this reason – and I was immediately concerned for Hobart's Derwent River.

So I packed a tent and some warm clothes and went down through Hobart to fast on Mount Wellington in protest. There were icicles hanging from the television towers above my campsite near the Pinnacle. Norm Sanders (later to become the Australian Democrats

Senate spokesman on nuclear issues) came up to report for ABC TV. He gave me the line that the nearest nuclear reactor we needed was the Sun, 93 million miles away. He interviewed me as the Sun set red in the west, and his segment showed film of the *Enterprise*, surrounded by a flotilla of welcoming craft, securing its anchorage in the Derwent River near the casino far below. The background music was the Beatles song 'The Fool on the Hill'. I explained that I would have protested just the same if the ship had been the Russian aircraft carrier *Kiev*.

I drank water but ate no food until the ship departed a week later (when friends Bob Graham and Helen Gee baked me a dinner in their wood-fired stove in Hobart's Lower Jordan Hill Road). Along with the large slice of cheesecake it went down extra well.

It was fine and cold on the mountain. Some nights people supported the protest by camping nearby. The engine block of one of their cars cracked when it froze.

My father's sister, Irene, arrived one sunny morning with a brown paper bag containing two cheese sandwiches: she slipped them into my tent to give me some sustenance. Unbeknown to me she had gone on a sympathy fast and was to end up in a Hobart hospital as a consequence. (She recovered and is now living remarkably well into her nineties!) I didn't eat Aunt Irene's sandwiches but will never forget her empathy: her visit, with my Uncle Frank, while I was out of contact with my closer family and friends on the mainland, was more sustaining than a loaf's worth of sandwiches.

However, not all was friendly. At night men would arrive to yell abuse – 'You fucking commie!' was popular – or throw beer bottles that smashed among the dolerite boulders sheltering my tent. These were boozy locals who didn't know much and were afraid to come closer in the dark. I thought about what would happen if someone arrived with a searchlight and a gun.

The sailors who came up the mountain to see me knew a lot and had much worse prospects to think about. 'Well, Buddy,' one lanky African-American told me, 'when we practise a scramble' (to get the planes up off the ship within minutes of the start of a war with Russia) 'I think of the day it will be for real and know I'll never see my wife and kids in Chicago again. I support what you are doing.'

The United States government, backed by Canberra, had perfected the fudge of refusing 'to confirm or deny' that there were nuclear weapons on such ships. 'Those nuclear bombs are just through the bulkhead from where I sleep,' another sailor told me.

A young man, a little overweight and with a straw hat and pleasant Southern drawl, came puffing up the mountain track to question me about who was behind the protest. He was a bit obvious. His job, though he didn't say so, was to get intelligence on my connections with the communists. He went away with nothing to report. There was a flow of thoughtful visitors and kindred souls. Some, including friends in the United Tasmania Group – the nascent Greens Party – came down from Launceston.

I had early-morning visits from a lovely man called Larry who would sit on the rocks and talk with me about how the world could be fairer: for example, if the money going into nuclear bombs and ships were to be spent on global poverty. He was a union worker, and his socialism sounded closer to Christ's teachings than much I had heard from the pulpit. He brought thermos flasks of hot water so I wouldn't use body energy warming it up.

Halfway through my fast he stopped coming. Larry's only son had been on his way to an end-of-year school celebration with friends when he was killed by a car running a red light to escape pursuing police. Larry endured three devastating days at the teenage boy's bedside before the life-support machines were turned off.

That smash was so indiscriminate and cruel. It defied the search for justification. So how could anyone get their mind around what the nuclear weapons stockpilers in Washington, Moscow, London and Paris were readying themselves to unleash? Down in Hobart the *Enterprise*'s officers and crew were living it up and the bars were doing a roaring trade. Up on the mountain, as I lay under the Milky Way through those frosty October nights, I had a lot to ponder.

8

1976

1976 WAS MY year of reformation. After a January walk with friends Paul Smith, Peter Thompson and Tony Booth to the remote Western Arthurs Range in south-west Tasmania, in February Paul Smith and I rafted down the Franklin River to the Gordon River. That adventure altered my life. It drew me into the Franklin River's turbulent history until the threat of four dams being built in its gorges was finally removed seven years later. The campaign to save the Franklin, in turn, put me into the Tasmanian Parliament in 1983, and led me to the Australian Senate in 1996.

After Paul Smith and I returned from the Franklin journey, we thought about how to raise public awareness of both the wild rivers and those proposed dams. Besides getting a double-page spread in the Launceston *Examiner*, Paul had the idea of filming a second rafting expedition in early 1977. In a happy confluence of events, another group of Tasmanian adventurers had canoed down the Gordon River through its spectacular Gordon Splits chasms while we were on the Franklin. Yet another group had floated on li-los (small inflatable mattresses) down the Franklin's major tributary river, the Jane.

The combination of these Tasmanian river trippers' experiences sent out a ripple of excitement about the sheer beauty of the threatened riverine wilderness. Like the inundation of the Lake Pedder National Park by the Middle Gordon dams just four years earlier, the Franklin,

Gordon, Jane and an array of smaller wild rivers were to be obliterated by a Tasmanian Hydro-Electric Commission (HEC) dam-building spree within the next decade.

We were hopelessly aware that, further north, the HEC's bulldozers were already gouging into the wilderness for a suite of dams that would rob Tasmania of the nation's best tourism rafting river, the Pieman, along with its Huon pine forests and spectacular scenery like the Heemskirk Falls. These were obliterated with no commotion.

Kevin Kiernan and Geoff Holloway were, I was warned by more sedate environmentalists, two young 'hotheads' running the remnant Lake Pedder Action Committee that had morphed, after the Lake Pedder campaign was lost, into the South-West (wilderness) Action Committee. I liked their style. As Liffey was in central Tasmania and a convenient meeting place for the disparate Tasmanians opposing the HEC's next rash of dams, I hosted a meeting at Oura Oura over the last weekend in June 1976. Sixteen greenies in beanies turned up for this midwinter get-together and Kevin, who had set up support groups in mainland capital cities, suggested the committee's name be changed to the Tasmanian Wilderness Society. The society's first formal meeting was held in Hobart in August and the membership fee was set at two dollars. From there the campaign to save the last wild rivers surged.

However, the wilderness society's first campaign, in our first year, was to stop construction of a concrete loggers' bridge across the Picton River, the major tributary of the Huon River in southern Tasmania. We failed and the Picton Valley forests have since been blitzed.

A young person is as prone to be asexual as a butterfly is to keep its wings folded. The problem for me, now aged 31, was to keep my wings folded while flying in the world of environmental activism. Something had to give.

Before setting off down the Franklin River I had told Paul Smith I was homosexual. He laughed. He was a keen trout fisherman. 'Bob, I'm definitely not. But I can tell a good-looking man like I can tell a good-looking trout!' he said. I laughed too and through what became several rafting and bushwalking trips we became and remain good friends. When we returned from rafting the river in 1976, and while respecting my confidence, Paul, a rational thinker, urged me to go public about my sexuality.

As a little boy holidaying in Sydney I had found myself up the ladder and on the high diving board at the Manly harbour-side baths. There was a queue of older kids coming up the ladder and I had no parachute. It was terrifying but I walked out and jumped.

This jump was of an inexplicably greater magnitude, but I jumped – into an ABC TV current affairs interview. Through this raged fear for my family, friends, neighbours and workplace. I walked to neighbouring farms at Liffey and knocked on their doors and said, 'I've come to tell you I am a homosexual.' They were good Baptist folk but, though clearly taken aback, took it very well. 'We think we've got an uncle like that, don't we?' one woman said to her nodding husband.

The next day I flew to the mainland to tell my family. They were solicitous and loving and relieved that the air was cleared at last.

Meanwhile the Launceston *Examiner* had driven out to Liffey and insisted on an interview. It took a pretty unflattering photo (I refused to line up and smile) that, next morning, was front page under the headline 'DOCTOR SAYS HE'S GAY'. I had never used the word but was going to have to get used to it. That article was to be reprinted or copied and distributed repeatedly, with punishing effect, by anti-green campaigners in the decades ahead.

But the genie was out of the bottle.

Scores of letters arrived in my roadside letterbox, which was vandalised almost as often as I was away. Censorious citizens from near and far quoted St Paul and advised I change my ways or burn in Hell. Even more men and women wrote thanking me for this breakthrough news and telling me of their troubles – or the risk they were taking by writing to me. I replied to all of them. Their letters were unexpected and reassuring: my 'coming-out' was helping unknown soulmates.

In much of the world it is no longer possible to feel and comprehend the cruel and all-pervading bigotry against homosexuals that prevailed before the great and ongoing changes in public opinion that make it a much happier place for everyone.

Yet there is a long way to go before Australians can feel easy that every non-heterosexual child feels special and good about her or his emergent sexuality. There is much further still to go before the benighted children of homophobic nations like Iran, Uganda and Russia are free of the threat of shame, public humiliation, imprisonment or death just for being as their god made them.

As for me, the angry homophobic tirades from wound-down car windows, the subtle innuendos from political opponents, the cowardly sniggers from people passing on the street, have almost dried up. Instead, from time to time, I get stopped in the street or shop or airport by men, women and couples who thank me just for being gay. Or say what it means for their daughter or son or sister or brother.

I couldn't know in 1976 that I'd be alive 40 years later to see homophobia vaporising and the discriminatory laws being abolished – much less that I'd be getting ready to celebrate 20 years with my companion, Paul Thomas, and feeling happier than ever before in my seven decades on the planet.

As that year of taking risks, including my fast on Mount Wellington, drew to a close, I had opened up new dangers for the future, but the first I had to face was very welcome. In January 1977 Paul Smith and I set off with friends to make a film about rafting down the Franklin. I was back on the river that had set me free.

9

The Irenabyss

IN THE SUNNY January of 1977 Paul Smith and I returned to the Collingwood Bridge in central Tasmania with Peter Thompson, Amanda (Sam) Stark and Rick Rolls for our second rafting trip down the Franklin River.

Three days later we entered Descension Gorge north of Frenchmans Cap and steadied ourselves, ready to negotiate its long set of rapids. The weather was perfect. The ride was exhilarating. We shouted to each other, bounced off the rocks, went down sluices backwards and, after dropping through the final noisy cascade, spun out onto the suddenly calm and quiet waters of the Irenabyss.

Paul had gone first, stopped halfway down, tethered his inflatable raft and got out onto a boulder to film the rest of us going by – no doubt hoping for a spill! He had a hand-wound Bolex 16mm movie camera I had bought for him, second hand, at a camera shop in West Ryde in Sydney. Paul had the idea of a half-hour television documentary to show Tasmanians the Franklin River most would never get to see: its remote gorges, rapids and wildlife as it winds in an arc from north to south and westwards around Australia's most majestic mountain, Frenchmans Cap, and then south through rainforested lowlands to the Gordon.

Once we were camped on the bank in the forest beyond the Irenabyss, we paddled back up through this smooth-walled canyon and Paul took shots of us floating and gently turning with the swirls of the current back down to camp. We lay back looking up at the narrow slit of sky above us and listening to the 'plink, plink, plink!' of water dripping from the mossy overhanging cliffs.

I dropped a stone tied with twine and it found the bottom 63 feet (20 metres) deep. The Franklin had cut this chasm through solid rock over countless millennia before us. While it must be a foaming, roaring spectacle in flood, we were experiencing its summer calm and I called it the Irenabyss (pronounced 'Irennerbis') from the Greek words for 'peace' and 'chasm'. The rapids above churn out natural detergent from these wilderness waters to produce fine white arabesques swirling slowly down the dark surface of the Irenabyss in endlessly fascinating patterns.

We secured our tents above the flood line, tethered the rafts, jumped in for a swim and then enjoyed a communal dinner around the campfire while gazing back into the chasm. I slept well through the warm night, listening to the whistling chatter of ringtail possums in the nearby tea-tree thicket and the distant choir of the downstream rapids.

Rick and I, who were sharing a tent, planned to climb Frenchmans Cap the next day. In the pre-dawn hours I woke from a nightmare. Though we had a zippered, mosquito-proof tent, I dreamed a large snake had come inside the tent between Rick and I. This seemed so real that, half-awake, I sat up and unzipped the tent to let the reptile out. Waking up a little more I realised I was dreaming, so I pulled the zipper down and went uneasily back to sleep.

We got up just after dawn to be heartened by the glow of a magnificent morning. Mist swirled down through the Irenabyss. Slowly, as the Sun came up, the mist lifted from the river and the forests and then the hills high above us. Rick and I set off. After a short scramble up the creek, which tumbles down to the Franklin at its exit from the Irenabyss, we soon emerged at the start of the long ridge leading south-east up to the Cap.

This is Palawa country: for thousands of years Frenchmans Cap has been called 'Mebelek'.

I knew that in 1822 convict Alexander Pearce had crossed the Franklin and passed south of the Cap in his horrific escape from the Macquarie Harbour prison: he ate his five companions and then attacked Aboriginal people to steal more food.

However I was not aware then that the famed West Coast adventurer Thomas Moore and his three companions had crossed the Franklin further downstream and walked up this same ridge 90 years before us, on 24 February 1887, to reach Frenchmans Cap's summit where their 'eyes feasted in the glories of nature'. Moore noted, 'No traces exist of anyone having climbed the heights from the westward and I may confidently assert that we are the first party from that quarter.'

This walk of unfolding panoramic charm is rewarded near the top of Frenchmans Cap (at 1446 metres it is 1200 metres, or three Empire State Buildings, above the Irenabyss), with views over glacial lakes, gorges and forested valleys to Macquarie Harbour, the Southern Ocean, Cradle Mountain and, far to the south, Mount Wellington.

It was a brilliant day and when Rick and I stopped for a breather, overlooking Lake Nancy, he said to me, 'I had this scary dream about snakes last night, Bob – it woke me up!' So I told him about my similar nightmare and we wondered what had been put in our stew.

The final climb onto the white quartz Cap was easier than expected. We were greeted on top by a cornice of snow from the previous winter and a field of rare purple six-petalled Hewardia (*Isophysis tasmanica*) flowers. From the summit it is a skip and jump to the brink of what mountaineer David Neilson described in 1972 as 'the most impressive rock face in Australia'. I found it terrifying. However the insouciant Neilson had woken to 'a sunrise without equal' after he and a companion had 'bivouacked' – that is, roped on to – the middle of the sheer 500 metre-high cliff face to sleep overnight.

Ten years earlier, another pioneer of this incredible climb, Peter Sands, also went to sleep roped on halfway up after writing in his diary:

> We are now high up on the edge of the east face ... the full moon rose and the wall just glowed ... it was an awesome experience ... there are occasions in a young man's life when it is better his mother does not know what he is doing!

Rick and I had lunch, soaking in the 360-degree panorama of western Tasmania from this remote citadel that, if all the proposed Franklin dams were built, was to be left surrounded by a vast gutter of drowned and decaying forests.

We came down a lot faster than we went up. At the Irenabyss camp our companions were still basking in the late-afternoon sunshine. Sam was reading a book and just below her a huge black tiger snake, lying in a rock hollow, was also soaking up the sun.

'We've watched that come out of its hole a couple of times today,' she said, holding aside her book. 'Come and see where it goes!' She pointed to a large hole disappearing underground at the top end of our tent – only a few centimetres from where our heads, inside the tent, had rested the previous night. That explained our dreams: our brains had been clicked into gear by this big reptile slithering in and out of its den, only inches away from our ears, in the dead of night.

After another dip, a hearty meal and an exchange of the day's events around the campfire, we nodded off in the same place and slept soundly, oblivious to the snake's nocturnal progress.

A couple of days later Sam, a teacher, left us and walked out over the hills to the nearest road to get back for the start of the school year. The rest of us continued rafting down the Franklin through the Great Ravine to the Gordon River and then caught a lift on Reg Morrison's cruise boat, *Denison Star*, to Strahan. As we crossed Macquarie Harbour we could see the great white half-dome of Frenchmans Cap on the skyline far to the north.

Paul cut the film, Peter Thompson did the narration, and we paid $800 to have it shown on Saturday night television (in those days there was only one commercial channel) right across Tasmania, with the TattsLotto draw in the half-time break. So the Franklin flowed into the living rooms of most Tasmanian homes. Subsequent polls showed that a majority of Tasmanians wanted the river saved from the proposed dams.

Yet there would be another six years of campaigning, $70 million spent on preliminary dam works by the Hydro-Electric Commission, a swing back in Tasmanian majority sentiment behind the dams, World Heritage listing for the wilderness, a national furore as hundreds of protesters were arrested in the rainforests, tens of thousands joining 'No Dams' street rallies, and a change of national government, before the waters of the Franklin were finally assured of being left to flow untrammeled through the Irenabyss, on around Frenchmans Cap, down through the rainforests, and free to the sea.

10

Impossibility and certainty are together on Earth

THE SHEER IMMENSITY of the Universe, with its billions of stars like our Sun, is beyond the comprehension of our humble human brains. Yet, evolved in the fertile little valleys of this tiny life-covered planet, we draw certainty from our own locality and our own upbringing.

In 1973 I helplessly looked upon the Cold War, in which some of the world's brightest young humans sat in missile silos ready to press the buttons of nuclear Armageddon; upon a Presbyterian upbringing at odds with my own homosexuality; and upon the plainly unnecessary injustice of global poverty.

The little house at Liffey – Oura Oura – gave me an anchor in this anxious existence. In the comfort of Liffey was the hope of certainty. None of the world's worries went away, but Liffey soothed my soul.

However, this comfort eventually proved too thin to keep the real world out. The penalty clause for ordinary intelligence is reflection and conscience and the urge to make things better. My denial mechanisms failed.

So in 1978 I patted the verandah post twice and left home, accepting that Liffey would be a refuge. The rest of my life would be out there where forests are smashed down, more A-bombs are built, human rights are exchanged for oil, and resources are thieved from people who have never needed to read or write. I went to Hobart to help the Tasmanian Wilderness Society's campaign against the damming of the wild and wondrous Franklin River.

Curiously, in this Australia where Christianity claims moral authority, it had become clear to me that the human propensity for denial is never so great as in the accumulation of riches, despite the biblical warning that a rich man has no better chance of getting to paradise than a camel does of climbing through the eye of a needle. I know some exceptionally humane and wonderful millionaires. But read a *Business Review Weekly* and you'll see what I mean. Don't expect to find in those pages a dissertation on equality, frugality, compassion or even plain common sense.

The denial of the unsustainability of our current gluttony is a perverse byproduct of our need to deny our mortality. Zest for life cannot flower if one's mind concentrates on the ineluctable reality of personal extinguishment.

We don't like to think that a hundred or so years from now we will all be dead and replaced; it's hard to honour the rights of our great-grandchildren. The enjoyment of riches is inversely proportional to our understanding of the humiliation and suffering of other people's poverty. Our capacity for denial is built-in. We all have it. But it collides with our intellect. This sets tensions in train – as the mind-blocks evaporate, so does our comfort. It's not easy being Green.

Liffey has been my respite and, though I've been away most of these last 30 years, it has been with me everywhere. For years I have carried a cameo reproduction of Val Whatley's painting of Oura Oura in my wallet.

Oura Oura turned my anxious soul into an organised force joining and helping coordinate the many other enlivened people striving to make our common human tenure on Earth longer, safer, fairer and happier.

11
The old man in the shed

My father, Jack Henry Brown, was born in 1909 at 9 Belmore Street, St Peters, in Sydney. The home that was his birthplace, along with its peach tree, was demolished for the suburban rail that these days rushes commuters from the city via Tempe to suburbs like Rockdale, Hurstville and Cronulla.

He remembered the single-carriage horse-drawn trams in Sydney, with their drivers holding whips as long as the carriage. 'Whip behind, boss! Whip behind!' boys on the street would shout to get a driver to flick his whip over the carriage at passengers 'scaling' a free ride on the back.

But horse power was coming to an end.

'Gertrude!' his visiting grandmother, with black bonnet and long black dress, exclaimed to his mother when he was ten, 'I've just seen the most disgusting spectacle!'

'And what was that, Mother?'

'I was walking down the Broadway and was passed by a motorised hearse! They were rushing a man to his grave in a motorised hearse!'

How my great-grandmother would have coped with today's preference for cremations, let alone, if you are very rich, having your body rocketed into space, I don't know.

When he was 12, Jack, hotly pursued by a police officer, swam the Cooks River. I forget the alleged misdemeanour that led to the chase, but he lit a fire on the other side of the river and dried off his suit before going home to face his mother, Gertrude Brown, who was raising nine children.

My grandfather George was a policeman and my father, in turn, was to become a police constable. Aged 17 Jack crossed the Pacific to San Francisco as a saxophonist in a ship's dance band. That sax also got him into the New South Wales Police Band and he met my mother, Marjorie, at a dance in the Inverell Town Hall. He treasured photos from a camping trip the two took to secluded Patonga Beach after rowing across the Hawkesbury River north of Sydney. It is a blissful scene!

I have a brother from my mother's previous marriage – she had divorced in the days when that was shocking – together with two more brothers and my twin sister. We twins were born two days after Christmas in 1944 at Oberon Hospital west of Sydney. Oberon is famously snow country, but our births coincided with a local bushfire.

When we were two, our father, Jack, was transferred to Trunkey Creek on the old gravel coach road from Bathurst south to Goulburn. Trunkey had one rough-as-guts hotel, three very basic churches and the long-closed Golden Hind Inn. Its sturdy brick police station and residence was set in a five-acre police paddock, with adjoining woodlands, on a hillside overlooking the village.

Trunkey had a population of 150 and no electricity or light switches. There was tank water and long-drop toilets and no sign of bitumen, washing machines, television or margarine. Swaggies sometimes turned up and the picture-show man, circus or gypsies were rare and thrilling visitors to the township.

Marjorie May hailed from a dairy farm near Glen Innes in New England, New South Wales, so she knew how to milk a cow and make butter. She also made us clothes on a pedalled sewing machine. Marjorie had a cow and Jack had a pig, a lot of chooks and a large organic vegetable patch including spinach. My first jailing was for refusing to eat that spinach.

Aged six, I made a stand against the repugnant stuff. It was in a wet green pile beneath some gravy on the side of my mother's otherwise excellent Sunday roast dinner. I had my eye on the lime jelly, which had cooled and set on the windowsill, but it wasn't long before I was on my way, in my father's custody, to the single wooden jail cell up behind the police station. The iron bolt shot home as he locked the door and I was left to consider my defiant refusal to eat the spinach.

By the time I settled in Liffey I had developed a much greater respect for my policeman father and the firm but devoted guidance he and my mother gave us. In 1969 my parents retired to Coffs Harbour, halfway between Sydney and Brisbane, and Jack realised his dream of becoming a licensed handline fisherman.

In 1983, just after the Franklin River was saved, Marjorie came to spend her last few months at Liffey before she died of cancer. Afterwards 'Old Jack', as the Coffs Harbour fishermen now called him, would drive down to Tasmania to spend the summer months away from the tourists jamming his adopted city.

We spent many a pleasant evening with a beer as his chooks went to roost and his vegetable patch grew, watching the shadows fall across the Liffey Valley with dinner cooking on the open fire up behind the house. He took up residence in the shed, also behind the house, which a friend from the Franklin blockade had insulated and lined with pink, yellow and blue pastel–coloured masonite.

A sign emblazoned 'Jacob' appeared over Old Jack's shed door. A few days later he suddenly exclaimed: 'I'm a silly old coot! It was Joseph who had the coat of many colours, not Jacob!' (But the sign has stayed there.)

He grew a long white beard. I was making tea for visitors one afternoon when their little boy, who had gone out to explore, came back looking amazed. 'Mr Brown,' he demanded to know, 'why are you keeping that old man up in the shed?'

My father had been having his afternoon nap in his pyjamas when he heard a tap on the door and opened it to see the boy looking up, his mouth wide open in astonishment. The boy bolted back to the house.

Jack had a good sense of humour as well as a strong sense of fairness. He did not like bigwigs and loudmouths. As a police officer he would sort out minor infractions of the law with a warning rather than an indictment where he could. But he believed in capital punishment and said 'I have lived just in time' as he saw populations exploding, factory ships marauding the world's fisheries and well-to-do people whingeing about not having enough.

One evening by the fire we returned to Trunkey Creek. I recalled my refusal to eat Dad's homegrown spinach and the consequent spell in the jailhouse. It had turned out to be excellent preparation for my jailing in environmental protests decades later.

'But, you know,' I complained with feigned indignation, 'treating a six-year-old like that was cruel and unusual punishment.'

'How's that?' he asked with a twinkle in his eye.

'Well,' I reminded him, 'after half an hour you let me out but then you made me eat the spinach, which was still there, cold, on my plate!'

I also got Mum's jelly, with preserved apricots, custard and a sprinkle of coconut: there could not have been a sweeter ending to the saga.

12
Jack Spooner

TWIN SISTER JAN and I arrived on Earth two days after Christmas in 1944 in the Oberon Hospital in the Central Tablelands of New South Wales, her half an hour before me. I was given my father's name, Jack. We were called Jack and Jill until our proper names were settled a few weeks later. Jack was crossed off the birth certificate and replaced with Robert, a very popular name in the war years.

At 15, I finally convinced my reluctant mother to drop 'Robert' and call me Bob. She accommodated, along with everyone else (my father had always called me Bob), except for my fond old Aunt Lillian.

My father's father had grown up in Lancashire in England as George Spooner but joined the New South Wales Police Force after his arrival in Sydney at the turn of the nineteenth century as George Brown. Was he dodging the draft for the Boer War in South Africa? If so, good on him.

So, while Jack Spooner was where I was headed, Bob Brown is where I ended up.

There was an even bigger identity problem to sort out. By the age of 12 I realised I was homosexual. (It wasn't until years later that I heard the word 'gay' used for the same thing. Homosexuality was sticks and stones. In fact the homophobic word 'faggot' comes from the name for the sticks used to burn homosexuals at the stake in the purest age of European scriptural piety.)

Before I knew anything much about sex – in our 1950s Australia there was no such thing as sex education – a teacher at my public school in Armidale put his hand in my trousers a number of times and became so blatant about it that, much to my confusion and consternation, I was taken from school to make the necessary statements to detectives prior to his arrest. It was the last year of primary school and I had been a good speller, mathematician and athlete. Three months later, in first term at Armidale High School, I was bottom of the class and had withdrawn from everything. The other kids had a whiff of the scandal.

My parents were extremely concerned and did all they could to fix up this predicament. They moved to coastal Bellingen and from there a mob of us caught the daily school bus and train to Coffs Harbour High School. My schoolwork and sports improved. I even became the sergeant-major in the school army cadets corps (aaaatenSHUN!!!!!! shoulderrrHARMS!!!!!!). I won the .303 rifle-shooting contest at the annual cadet camp at Singleton Army Base. But I was gay and that was taboo.

What's more I was a Presbyterian Christian who had attended St Paul's Presbyterian Sunday School in Armidale and now St Andrew's Presbyterian Fellowship in Bellingen. I knew that in St Paul's New Testament letter to the Romans, written perhaps 100 years after the death of Jesus Christ (who never mentioned homosexuality), he warned that men 'who have burned in their lusts one toward another … are deserving of death'. St Paul, who also reviled wisdom, was certain about killing homosexuals. So was the Church's Grand Inquisitor who later set the faggots burning. So was Hitler.

In his letter, which is little more than a nonsensical stream of consciousness, St Paul, the twisted pillar of ancient morality, condemned countless thousands of men, who were designed by God to love one another, to public humiliation, torture and appalling deaths. Countless more have suffered a living hell of self-hate, denial and deceit, which has often, in turn, wrought havoc on others around them.

By the time I was a teenager the death penalty for male homosexual acts had been abolished in Australia, but long jail sentences and lifelong humiliation were the order of the day.

There was a very large sign over the stage in Armidale's St Paul's church hall saying 'GOD IS LOVE'. It added to my consternation. How could someone who had created the whole Universe, was all powerful, all knowing and a solid block of love, also want me burnt to death? As if that conundrum wasn't enough, how could the all-powerful, all-good God permit the legion of cruelties occurring every day on Earth?

In the following years I tried prayers to Jesus and self-help in order to transform into a legal heterosexual but failed in both pursuits. I left the Presbyterian fellowship, though I regretted no longer meeting the kindly young women and men who, in diminishing numbers, still attended.

We moved from Bellingen to Windsor, on the Hawkesbury River west of Sydney, and I caught the rail motor to Blacktown Boys High School, which, with the Blacktown Girls High School next door, was the largest high school in New South Wales. I fitted in pretty quickly and was soon in the athletics, baseball and basketball teams. When a local champion fell ill, I snatched a rare victory in the senior 120-metre hurdles in the regional high schools' athletic carnival at Penrith. Just ask me about it.

Then came the first election campaign I ever organised. It was for my new friend Kevin Stephenson to be high school captain – and he won. But almost immediately things went pear shaped. The school principal sacked Kevin for bopping another boy who had bullied Kevin's sister. In the manner of many a dictator overriding democracy, the principal installed me instead. My references from Coffs Harbour High School were glowing and, still new to the school, I became a victim of those kind words.

I was acutely aware of the scandalous consequences for the school if I were to be accused or somehow found out as being homosexual. I was so distraught by this predicament that I worked up the courage to go to the formidable headmaster's office to tell him I would not accept. He said I had no choice and rejected my resignation.

Triage. My best friend dethroned. My personal plea rejected. A school yet again agog at a scandal, with me in the middle of it. And my poor mother nonplussed by such good news plunging her son back into an inexplicable torpor.

I scraped into medical school at the University of Sydney. Happily my friend from Bellingen, Judy Henderson, was there too. I joined the Uni Athletics Club but, besides running a slow third leg in the men's 4 by 100–metre relay, I was an introverted failure.

My physics was worse. In the midyear practical exam I was the last in the hall of 600 students, left pondering hopelessly over how to connect up a diagram of electrical circuitry. My brain was blank. An angel came to the rescue.

There were two women watching over the examinations and, with everyone gone except me and them, the older one went to the toilet. The younger woman walked quietly down from the dais and along the aisle and stood beside me: she carefully guided her finger to the appropriate missing link on the circuit board and motioned how to fix it: without a word she then walked back to the dais and was having a drink of water when her co-overseer returned. I pencilled in the circuit solution and left, unable to thank her – and passed the exam.

In a second-year science subject my professor was more proper. After I scored minus 8 in a multi-choice questionnaire he called me to his office. 'Brown, you have two choices. Either you keep wasting your parents' hard-earned money or you leave now!' (A few years later a distraught student from overseas lifted a beaker of cyanide to his lips in that same office and drank it.)

By sheer rote learning and some luck I passed each subsequent year. Correctly identifying a dissected clitoris on a plate, I even got through the anatomy exams. And, while a loner, each year at university I was fortunate to be with an undemanding, lovely group of other students who were mostly from the country. They, unlike me, were having a great time: after the staid 1950s were rocked by Elvis (the Pelvis) Presley in his pink-and-purple shirts, Australia, like the rest of the Western world, was emerging from the Victorian era 60 years after the empress had died. This was the Permissive Society and the university was rocking.

'Hambones', a new ritual in which students would strip naked to the chants of the refectory crowd, were testing the laws of the day and had everyone talking. There was a sensation when a lecturer from the Blue Mountains advised students that masturbation was fine! The Sydney press went into paroxysms. The uni paper, *Honi Soit*, had paroxysms of a different sort: it ran irreverent and uproarious news, ribald pictures and breathtaking opinion pieces.

Most of the time, besides the lectures, I was back in the boarding house room with my usual crisis: what to do about my homosexuality. Unable to sleep, I would put on the greatcoat I kept from school cadets and walk the streets of Earlwood or, later, Bondi, weeping in the night and seeing no way out.

It was a joy to catch the electric train to Blacktown and then the rail motor home to Windsor on weekends. Besides family, the woods and paddocks along South Creek, a backwater of the Hawkesbury, gave me hours of unpressured pleasure. Holidays on the sheep farm of my mother's oldest brother, Bill, and my indulgent Aunt Lillian at Shannon Vale, 10 km east of Glen Innes atop the Great Dividing Range in northern New South Wales, were like heaven's rescue remedy. The woodlands, granite boulders, kangaroos, snakes, possums, lorikeets, foxes and a secluded swimming hole in the creek where, half a century earlier, my mother had planted a willow, were my solace.

One day back in town, as I walked up Parramatta Road to Sydney University from Broadway, I promised myself and every other homosexual that might be – for I knew none – that if ever I got out of this impossibly repressed mess, I would do what I could for them.

Although this was a decade after the Wolfenden report to the UK Parliament had recommended the decriminalisation of homosexuality, the newspapers continued to report the arrest and ruin of young men found loitering in parks or seen kissing other men by a passing police officer. In response to someone else's diatribe I wrote to the Sydney *Daily Mirror* to outline the trials of being homosexual but I didn't sign the letter and the paper didn't print it.

In 1966 I passed all the exams except for 'practical medicine' in which, at the Royal North Shore Hospital, I went before a notoriously stern examiner. I correctly diagnosed a woman's thyrotoxicosis after spotting her fine hand tremor. However the examiner pointed out my own even greater tremor – I was shaking with nervousness – and failed me. I passed the supplementary exam and, in 1968, became a Junior Resident Medical Officer assigned to the Canberra Community Hospital. Once again I was among a bunch of lovely and exuberant people in the Resident Medical Officers' Quarters, and began a lifelong friendship with fellow graduate doctor from the country, Frances Newman.

Two attempts to be 'cured' of my homosexuality failed. The first was with a Macquarie Street psychiatrist who gave me injections of testosterone in the buttocks, but nothing happened – not even more hair on my chest! – aside from emptying my bank account.

Later I went to the Prince Henry Hospital for aversion therapy: this required sitting in a chair with a screen set up to show pictures of naked women and men. A condom was affixed and attached to a volume-measuring device to detect any reaction. When a naked woman was shown it was safe but when a naked man came up I received an electric shock through electrodes strapped to my fingers.

This trial was run by doctors earnestly trying to save young men from a life of criminal shame, and I was a volunteer and I have always thought well of them. For the first time other men knew that I was gay and they were easygoing about it. Of itself, that was a crucial comfort. However this shocking therapy did not work.

At the end of 1969, after being in hospital with a potentially lethal bout of fulminant colitis (bowel inflammation) due to anxiety, and a night beside Lake Burley Griffin in Canberra considering suicide, I bought a one-way air ticket to London. That broke the circuit.

Throughout 1970 I did casual work as a doctor at a series of small London hospitals. The second psychologist I consulted was a handsome young heterosexual man on the south side of the Thames and he sat me back in my chair. 'Bob, why don't you accept who you are and be proud of it? You are homosexual so accept it and build your life around being who you are, not what other people think you should be.' This wasn't psychotherapy, it was psychosanity, and it was a bolt from the blue.

For the first time I shared time with other gay men and found out that the world was home to many of us. What good people these men were – well, a mixed bunch like society at large – and what harrowing stories we shared. However the world was still hostile, homosexuals were being routinely rounded up and arrested, and years in very unfriendly jails awaited those who were discovered.

Yet better times were on the way.

13

Her Majesty's Prison, 1982

THE CAMPAIGN TO save the Franklin River culminated in the 'Franklin blockade', which attracted thousands of Australians to sit in front of the Hydro-Electric Commission's bulldozers that were invading the wilderness to build the Gordon-below-Franklin Dam. Thirteen hundred people were arrested and 500 were jailed, including me. The following is a letter to my parents, beginning with the 'instructions' on the mandated prison writing paper.

INSTRUCTIONS

CORRESPONDENCE

No article or message of any description may be conveyed to or from a prisoner except through the officer-in-charge of a prison.

Letters must be written plainly in English and must not contain comments on prison management or the administration of justice. Any letter not complying with the conditions will be withheld.

Newspapers may not be sent to a prisoner but approved newspapers may be supplied to him through the prison office on payment of subscriptions in advance. Undesirable publications will not be accepted.

Should friends and relatives be desirous of sending money to the credit of any prisoner, it is desirable that they send it by registered post, rather than handing it in at the prison.

Tobacco and toilet requisites are issued in the prison and none may be received for a prisoner.

VISITING

Sentenced prisoners

A prisoner at the Risdon Prison may be visited twice each month in the presence of a prison official. The maximum number of visitors permitted at a visit is three. Ex-prisoners will not be admitted without special permission. Visits will be terminated immediately in the event of any improper conversation or conduct. Visits will not be allowed on Christmas Day or Good Friday.

Remand prisoners

Prisoners on Remand and Appellants may be visited twice per week in the presence of a prison official.

— — — — — — — — — — — —

From: Bob Brown

To: Mr & Mrs J H Brown
31 Bonville St, Coffs Harbour
18.12.1982

Dear Mum & Dad,
All my love to you both.

Please disregard the above address as it is only temporary. But I wouldn't mind staying longer: the food is extra good (chops and vegetables for tea tonight, corn silverside etc. for lunch). So is the company – there are 48 in the yard where my cell is, all arrested on the river and all fine people from all walks of life. I am one of the older ones. My cell looks over to Peter Storey's: he is a retired businessman (in his forties) and an old friend; his wife is still down at our Strahan office. For once, I am getting some exercise. We are not supposed to comment on the administration (see over) but I don't suppose they'll censor me for saying that the staff are very good and fair, which is the case. A couple of the youngest men here have had some tears, especially because their families oppose them and favour the dam and so they are being brave getting jailed for their beliefs – but they are getting a lot of support from their friends in here (and from me). Everyone is in good spirits. After all my months in the office, planes and meetings of this campaign recently, it was very pleasant to be back in the Gordon River rainforests – even if only for a day. I was copped on the opposite side of the river to where they expected: the young policemen found me sitting with two others near a waterfall, enjoying the view. He was very surprised and nervous – in fact if I hadn't grabbed his hand he would have fallen into the river. He read me the HEC riot act and then arrested us. Then I had a good talk to him as we walked to the police launch about his bushwalking experiences – (the police radio then announced that 'No. 1' – me – had been taken at St John Falls). I am, of course, extra pleased that no-one has been hurt. In fact, I don't know of tempers being raised.

Before being nabbed, I thought about you both as I sat in the forest. It must be very hard to understand me at times. But I believe in what I am doing and so do the others I mix with.

It was good to hear Prince Charles's comments tonight. All in all, it is amazing that the federal government made the wrong decision as it did. I have had plenty of visitors, and a pile of letters already.

Love, Bob

PS Merry Christmas! – My case comes up for a further hearing on Dec 24, so it looks like I won't make it home after all. Never mind: I'll see you soon. Bob

PS Monday – all is going well (we had a three-course Sunday dinner). Bob

14
The new religion

MODERN MATERIALISM HAS sanctified using 120 per cent of Earth's renewable living resources. That's why most of the world's fisheries are collapsing, there are fewer forests every day and the rate of extinction of life on Earth is the fastest since an asteroid struck the planet and the dinosaurs were eliminated 65 million years ago.

Worse is coming. Materialism, the prevailing religion of the world, the motivator of nations, adores greater consumption. (I am capitalising 'Materialism' just as Christianity, Buddhism and Islam are capitalised.) Materialism worships the god Growth and, as with most cults, thrives on fear. The high priests of Materialism warn that nothing so dreadful awaits us as the anti-Growth of an economic downturn, bringing with it the punishment of unemployment, poverty and social upheaval. This is compelling. If this century's inaugural Global Financial Crisis isn't enough to bolster the virtues of Materialism and drive the masses into the arms of Growth, last century's Great Depression provides a stark reminder of the dreadful consequences of turning away from this new god.

Materialism is a marvelous religion of limitless wellbeing. Its supreme god, Growth, is kept docile by the people's hard work and increased productivity. Growth is the one door to happiness and a good life and Materialism's high priests monitor its pulse with announcements in appropriately upbeat or sombre tones. Materialism accepts and happily incorporates earlier religions – as long as they reject frightful ideas like wealth being sinful, and stories like the one of Jesus upturning the businessmen's tables outside the Temple in Jerusalem. Growth incorporates the old gods by rewriting their scriptures. The Golden Rule is out.

However, like those old-time religions, Materialism singles out its most ardent proponents for special treatment. It is worshipped most avidly by, and cossets most ardently, the wealthiest people. They are the chosen ones. The richest people who on Earth do dwell sing to their god from the citadels of the stock markets, with joyful voice. And, paralleling earlier belief systems, the high priests of Materialism excoriate those with the least wealth for their obvious personal failure to uphold Growth. Their god's retribution is their destitution.

Just as earthquakes, typhoons and massacres presented a problem for those promoting the earlier almighty god of love, so belief in the supreme saving grace of Growth requires faith over logic. The core problem of faith over fact is Earth itself. It is a Growth-stopper simply because it is finite.

Earth's resources, living or not, are all it will ever have. So how do the priests and scribes of Materialism think they'll get ever more consumption from a finite storehouse? The new faith demands belief in the holy trinity of techno-fix, extraterrestrial stores and permanency (the spirit that lingers in every heart and tells us that the Universe cannot be without us). Human society cannot collapse. Earth cannot fail to fulfill our Materialistic god's promises. And, even when apostates point to the bleeding obvious facts of collapsing fisheries, diminishing forests and the extinction of species, Materialism's high priests can bolster their own sense of security by remembering that scarcity itself brings them Growth in prices.

Earlier religions promised more life after this one. Whatever logic there was in this came with the bonus of being impossible to disprove. But Materialism's promise of ever more wealth for ever more people on a finite planet is plainly bunk.

Common sense requires that *Homo sapiens* live within Earth's means. We have to tighten our belts, treat and empower everyone as equal, and respect the people, and our fellow creatures, who will breathe Earth's air in the future, as we respect ourselves. Humanity will govern a long-term and sustainable relationship with its unique planet or not govern at all. That's logical, but is not how Earth is being managed at the start of the twenty-first century. Getting there will take a collective decision to take back the extraordinary power of Materialism's priests and scribes. Moving on to a new celebration of our Earth, ourselves and those who will follow us requires a revolution in global culture. That is, an exit from the worship of Materialism.

The post-Materialism poet Drew Dellinger puts it to those priests and scribes, and all of us, in this part of his poem 'Hieroglyphic Stairway':

> it's 3.23 in the morning
> and I'm awake
> because my great great grandchildren
> won't let me sleep
> my great great grandchildren
> ask me in dreams
> what did you do while the planet was plundered?
> what did you do when the earth was unraveling?
> surely you did something
> when the seasons started failing?
> as the mammals, reptiles, and birds were all dying?
> did you fill the streets with protest
> when democracy was stolen?
> what did you do
> once
> you
> knew?

15
Flying with Di

IN MY THREE terms in the Senate I boarded 2000 flights. One of the last involved an attempt to land from the south at Hobart Airport with gales topping 130 kilometres per hour blowing from the west. As we circled to make the final approach I watched the jet below us abort its landing and head straight back up into the sky. Now it was our turn.

We descended over the ocean and then the sand dunes and then the verge of the runway, rocking and rolling, to within a few metres of the tarmac where the pilot gunned the engines and went up again. Passengers squealed and white-knuckled the armrests. Over the intercom the pilot assured us that he was not going to try that again and we all flew gratefully back to Melbourne.

Back in the early 1980s the Franklin River campaign helped me overcome the reasonable anguish I had about getting into planes. Young Melbourne pilot Doug Hooley offered to fly me about to Save-the-Franklin events and I adjusted to single-engine flights at comparatively low altitudes where the air seems more turbulent and storm clouds look more forbidding. He was diligent and calming and those flights proved very helpful and recuperative in the boisterous final year of the campaign.

One stormy Friday night, the eve of the VFL grand final, I was in a jet liner heading back to Hobart from a Franklin campaign meeting in Melbourne. We flew into thunderheads of cloud over Port Phillip and started to pitch, with a series of sudden drops. Out the window, in the light cast by the plane's headlights, I watched as the rain turned to hail. Soon there were hailstones the size of eggs flashing past. Three blue lightning flashes were accompanied by cannon-like booms of thunder. I thought of the tendency of some severe storms to aggregate hailstones into blocks bigger than footballs – enough to smash a wing.

We emerged from the thunderheads ten minutes later and, at Hobart, 150 passengers gratefully walked into the terminal to tell their kith and kin about the ordeal.

It had intimidated me. So when I caught a flight back to Melbourne a few days later I took a back seat and, although it was a cloudless day with the beautiful scenery of Tasmania below, I concentrated on reading the newspaper. Before the tea trolley arrived, the back of the plane was suddenly lit up by a blinding flash. I threw my newspaper into the air only to see a lady with a flash camera standing in the aisle exclaiming, 'Oh, Dr Brown, I do hope you don't mind me taking your photo.' She got a bigger fright than I did.

However neither of us were as startled as the passengers on a TAA Airbus flight from Perth to Melbourne at the height of the campaign to save Tasmania's Franklin River in 1983. A mysterious young man, holding a black box that he said contained a bomb, hijacked the plane and ordered the pilot to divert to the Franklin River. Pleading the need to refuel, the pilot landed instead at Melbourne Airport and the passengers found themselves exiting via emergency slides while the police once again came to the rescue.

My most memorable flight was from King Island to Wynyard near Burnie on the Bass Strait coast of Tasmania. In 1989 Dianne Hollister was elected as the first Greens member for the north-west seat of Braddon in the Tasmanian House of Assembly. Her friend Christine Milne had recommended that I ask Di to stand because she had also been outspoken in the campaign to protect the farmlands of Wesley Vale from the proposed polluting pulp mill. Di was living proof of the dictum that often the best political candidates are the ones who least want to stand.

She agreed to my invitation because the fate of the farmlands rested on the outcome of the election. In a very close count she won the last of the seven seats in Braddon. This deprived Robin Gray's pro-mill government of its majority, so it was vital to the farmlands. Di became one of the most popular parliamentarians in Tasmania.

So when she asked me to go with her on a visit to her Braddon electorate outlier of King Island I agreed. We had a delightful couple of days visiting the famous dairy farms, tourist resorts, seal colonies and the beautiful coastline that, sadly, is also the scene of Australia's worst maritime disaster. In the blackness of 4.30 am on 4 August 1845 the Canadian-built barque *Cataraqui,* carrying migrants from Liverpool, was blasted ashore and 405 of the 414 people aboard perished.

That dreadful event was still on my mind as our car pulled up at the tiny King Island Airport waiting-shed for our early afternoon flight back to mainland Tasmania. Di and I had joined half a dozen other passengers on the benches when an awesome storm blew in from the Southern Ocean and enveloped the airport with roaring wind, lightning flashes and horizontal rain and hail.

In a brief lull in the storm the inbound flight arrived and the plane was parked against the gale, with the pilots tethering its wings to the ground.

A very young couple from the twin-engine plane came into the waiting-shed and, with their backs to the wall and faces sickly white, slid slowly down to the floor and declared to us waiting passengers, 'Never again!' Their eyes rolled around and they repeated it: 'You'll never get us on that plane again!'

Nevertheless the booking clerk, who had curly ginger hair, arrived at the counter and announced above the ongoing roar of the gale that the flight was leaving as scheduled: 'Please check in now.'

Di and I had a quick talk about waiting for another flight but decided we had to get back to the mainland of Tasmania for other community engagements. The young police officer ahead of us in the queue showed better sense: he asked the clerk to change his ticket to the next day's flight. As an especially strong blast of wind rocked the shed the clerk complied – while mocking the officer with a chicken-like 'paark-puck-puck-puck-puck', which was very funny – although no-one broke out laughing.

We clambered into the plane as it swayed against the tethers. I was last aboard, and shouted 'good-bye' to the clerk, who shouted back, 'Yes and good luck!' as he slammed and locked the door behind us. Untethered, the little plane took off in another break in the tempest and we headed up and south-east, straight back into the heart of it.

This was frightening. As the plane gained height the cabin got gloomier. We experienced a series of sudden jolts and could see the two pilots hanging on to the joystick or fiddling anxiously with the dials. The windscreen in front of them looked and sounded like it was being hit by a torrent of nails. Di, mindful of her fellow passengers' terror, turned around and called to the cabin reassuringly, 'This isn't so bad – Bob has been in a plane that was struck with lightning!'

Instantly there was a blinding blue flash and thunderclap as the plane suffered the first of a series of lightning strikes. People hugged each other as well as their seats and the little aircraft flew into the most violent and terrifying tumbler I had ever experienced.

We survived and when we finally landed at Wynyard Airport the storm had passed. I heard the pilots on the tarmac agreeing ruefully that it was the worst weather they had flown through. They would never fly into a storm like that again.

As we drove the 70 kilometres back to Di's home in Devonport, emergency vehicles with flashing orange, red and blue lights were hurrying to-and-fro on the highway. Creeks were flooding, countless trees were down in the paddocks and roofs were missing from sheds. At Di's house, workers were tying a blue tarpaulin over her bedrooms where the roof had blown off. A large gum tree was lying over her crumpled car in the street. Distant rolls of thunder told of the storm's damaging progress to the east.

The hero of that day was the young policeman back on King Island. I don't know who he was or whether he had children (though I suspect he did) or whether he was leaving or returning home. But, in the maelstrom, he made the most sensible decision of all – and he was prepared to put up with some humiliation to carry it through. That man would be a sure and sane head in any emergency: let's hope he has been promoted.

16
Banning lesbians

THE WORST MOMENT of my political career came early.

I was the Green Independent for Denison (central Hobart) in the Tasmanian House of Assembly when, in 1987, Attorney-General John Bennett of the Liberal government introduced the Sexual Offence Bill, which included amendments to the Criminal Code to make it 'gender neutral'. The word 'person' would replace the words 'male' or 'female' in the code. Previously, for example, rape was a crime that could only be committed by men against women.

However Bennett deliberately excepted Section 123, which made 'indecent practice between male persons' an offence punishable by up to 20 years in prison. This law had destroyed men's lives.

To quote one young victim from Launceston:

> If there had been reform in 1958 I would have been saved from the worst period of my life. I was 21 and living with another man of the same age. The police came to the house and asked who lived there. When we said we did, they asked where we slept and we pointed to the only bed in the house. We were taken to the police station, interviewed and charged with gross indecency. In the Supreme Court I pleaded guilty. I had no legal representation. I got three years [in prison] …

Section 123 was to remain for men only. There was some speculation that the Labor Opposition would move to delete Section 123, which had caused this poor man's ordeal, from the code. In South Australia the modernising premier Don Dunstan had got rid of the law criminalising homosexuality a decade before, but this was not for Tasmania. When the time arrived, Labor did nothing. So I moved to abolish Section 123 but got neither Labor nor Liberal support.

I was desperate not to let the rare opportunity to remove discrimination against homosexuals go by with no change. I moved impulsively to have Section 123 brought into line with the rest of the Criminal Code by making it gender neutral as well. I was surprised when the government and opposition said 'aye!' without demur and the debate moved on to the rest of the bill. That left me more time than I needed to think through the ramifications of my rare legislative success. I went home with the horrors.

Libby Lester, political reporter for the *Launceston Examiner*, had also worked out what I had done. Her front-page headline on Saturday 11 July 1987 said it all: 'LESBIAN BAN LOOMS'.

Here's how Lester's story began:

Tasmania is likely by next week to be the only Australian state where homosexual acts between consenting females are illegal. Homosexual acts between males are already illegal in Tasmania, but previously female homosexuality was not mentioned in the law. An amendment by Dr Brown MHA (Ind., Denison) to include lesbians in legislation which previously only outlawed male homosexuality was passed by the House of Assembly this week and is unlikely to be touched when it is debated by the conservative Legislative Council.

After denying I had made an oversight, I lamely told Lester, 'What the amendment does is replace a discriminatory non-operative clause with a non-discriminatory inoperable clause. The law has no right in consenting adults' bedrooms.'

The calls from distressed lesbians and many other citizens started coming in as the story went national. What had I done?!

Too late I had learned an axiom of good parliamentary practice: never legislate on the run.

Attorney-General 'Bullbars' Bennett made it clear he had no intention of reversing my amendment in the Legislative Council, which had a well-earned reputation as the most hidebound and reactionary upper house in the western world. It was my mess and I alone would have to try to fix the unfixable.

I went through the list of 25 councillors – all male except one – and picked out the least conservative among them. I called him to explain my absurd mistake and made a heartfelt plea that he move to reverse it. But he told me he thought banning lesbians wasn't a bad idea at all.

I had snookered myself. I feared history would record my defining career outcome as a stupid if not spiteful act against the thousands of women in Tasmania who loved other women. Overnight I had made myself the global wowser for banning lesbian rights.

I was imploding.

But then, as so often happens in out-of-control adversity, something fell unexpectedly from the sky. It was Joh Bjelke-Petersen.

In Brisbane the notoriously conservative premier of Queensland, a staunch advocate of jailing homosexual men, was asked if he would ban lesbian activities in Queensland. 'Oh goodness! No, no, no ...'

Premier Joh's disfavour opened a possible door for me.

I knew better than to make a personal plea to the Legislative Council. It loathed 'Greenies', let alone homosexuals. In 1982 it had voted to dam the Franklin. A few years earlier it had blocked a bill to set up an ombudsman in Tasmania: the councillors themselves were the rightful watchdog for the people of Tasmania. Way back in 1856 the council had been empowered by Governor Denison, representing

Queen Victoria (whose 1834 portrait has dominated the chamber to this day), to put a stopper on 'the excesses of democracy' that were liable to erupt from the House of Assembly.

So I sent all 25 councillors the news clip giving Premier Joh Bjelke-Petersen's opinion. I added an anonymous note pointing out that the amendment to the government's bill in the House of Assembly had been made by none other than Dr Bob Brown.

Fortunately, in her 'Lesbian Ban Looms' article, Libby Lester had repeated the apocryphal story that Queen Victoria:

> would not allow the [British] legislators to mention indecent acts against females because she refused to believe that it could happen. As a result the female gender was not mentioned in Tasmanian law.

The test became clear: would the councillors side with Queen Victoria looking down over them from her Huon pine and gilt–framed portrait, and with Premier Joh Bjelke-Petersen, or would they side with the homosexual Dr Bob Brown?

The Legislative Council rescinded my amendment and the lesbians of Tasmania were saved.

17
Waiting for catastrophe

My next foray into legislative reform was also in 1987 but this time I was much better prepared. Hobart solicitor Roland Browne and his friend Paul Chatterton drafted a bill to prohibit semiautomatic machine guns and I took it up. These guns have magazines that carry a bundle of bullets, enabling multiple shots to be fired without reloading. They had been used with deadly effect in recent massacres in the US and, infamously, in the Hoddle Street massacre in Melbourne in which 26 innocent people were gunned down in the street.

Instead of no debate and unanimous 'ayes' in the House of Assembly, this bill, when it finally came up for debate several years later, was met with a wave of disapproval. I was howled down by the Liberals in particular as I explained the need to restrict the use of semiautomatic machine guns to use by the police and farmers with a proven need.

The gun lobby advertised against me: 'Bob Brown is coming to take your guns!' However, the public feedback was positive and an opinion poll showed that even gun owners thought there was room for better controls.

As a boy in the 1950s I had shot rabbits, foxes and snakes and a white cockatoo. The latter episode took place on my uncle's property outside Glen Innes in northern New South Wales and is seared into my brain. The mortally wounded bird fell to the ground screeching and crying while I stood beneath the tree feeling guilty, useless and shocked at what I had just done. I'd expected the bird's flock to take off in a clamour and fly away. It didn't. Instead its whole marvelous community began screeching and flying up and down around their stricken mate, which I was then obliged to put out of its dying misery in front of them.

Many years later, after I began work as a doctor in Tasmania, a woman rang one Saturday to whisper to me that her husband had a gun and she was frightened he was going to shoot her and their children. She lived out in the country. I did my best to reassure her and called the police, aware of the predicament in which this also placed those police officers. I didn't hear any more about the matter until I read in the paper some months later that she had been shot dead. Should I have done more? Absolutely.

So in the State Parliament a decade later, the jeers of other parliamentarians as I presented my bill had no effect on me – the bill was in honour of a dead mother.

It was voted down.

In 1996, 35 men, women and children were slaughtered by one man armed with high-powered semiautomatic rifles at Port Arthur. The massacre shocked Tasmania, Australia and the world.

I had left the Tasmanian Parliament. However the new Greens leader, Christine Milne, immediately took my 1987 legislation to the state and federal governments. The newly elected prime minister, John Howard, called an urgent meeting of the Police Ministers and the National Firearms Agreement was born. The Commonwealth's role was to fund a buyback of prohibited weapons and to ban their import into Australia. Howard quickly legislated, with the backing of both the Coalition and Labor in both houses of the national parliament, to increase the Medicare levy to fund the buyback of prohibited semiautomatic rifles. Bans were brought in by the states and territories, with Tasmania the first to move – just as my 1987 bill had sought to do.

Since the Port Arthur massacre these laws have saved hundreds of lives in Australia.

I met Roland when he was one of the hundreds of Franklin Dam blockaders arrested in 1982–1983. Roland went on to be a notable advocate for the environment, social justice and gun control. He is still campaigning for better limits on the availability in Australia of automatic hand guns (there are perhaps 300,000) – pistols with magazines from which a killer can fire multiple shots without reloading. However it seems that, short of a catastrophe like that at Dunblane in Scotland where a killer shot many small schoolchildren at their kindergarten, Greens attempts to control these multiple-shot handguns will continue to be howled down or, at best, ignored.

This story raises the question of whether catastrophe has to overtake our community before we use our God-given intelligence to save ourselves. I'm not one for waiting to find out.

18

A good gully, a good damper

IN 1991 IT was emerging that Labor Premier Michael Field, with whom we had signed the Green–ALP Accord ensuring government after the May 1989 Tasmanian election, was about to renege. I warned Field that if he bowed to the powerful logging industry and broke the accord he would lose office.

The accord had been innovative and highly successful. With Tasmania entering the economic downturn Federal Treasurer Paul Keating famously described as the recession Australia 'had to have', we Greens backed Field's economic reforms – which later gained him the Order of Australia. My fellow Greens were Dr Gerry Bates, first elected in 1986, and Christine Milne, Di Hollister and Reverend Lance Armstrong, all newly elected in 1989.

The accord's innovations included the *Freedom of Information Act*, the Parliamentary Legislative Research Service, the addition of 650,000 hectares of mountain, river, forest and coastal wilderness to the Tasmanian Wilderness World Heritage Area, and the abandonment of former Liberal premier Robin Gray's offer of $20 million to North Broken Hill and Noranda Canada to build the Wesley Vale pulp mill on farmlands near Devonport. (Gray's contentious proposal had brought farmers and the fishing industry into the popular campaign led by a local farmer's daughter, Christine Milne, to protect the Wesley Vale farmlands and Bass

Strait fisheries from the mill's toxic pollution. It cost him the 1989 election.)

While Section 8 of the accord confirmed that 'there will be no new pulp mill at Wesley Vale', Section 7 also ditched a proposed woodchip mill in the Huon Valley: 'The Huon Forest Products venture will not be allowed to proceed.'

And Section 9 was unequivocal: 'The State export woodchip quota will not exceed 2.889 million tonnes per annum.' Section 9 was a major concession by the Greens because it allowed Tasmania's three export woodchip mills, processing native forests and wildlife habitat, to continue operations while putting a lid on their future expansion. Yet less than two years later Field was yielding to the industry's demands to lift that lid. He brought in the accord-busting legislation to take the cap off the export woodchip quota and was immediately backed by Gray, who was now leader of the Opposition.

Premier Field was forced to withdraw his bill when I moved a motion of 'no confidence' in his government – a move Gray couldn't wait to back. When Field withdrew the bill I withdrew the motion.

A week later, bowing to the howls of rage from the industry and, in particular, the Launceston *Examiner*, Field reneged again and re-introduced the same bill under a different name. In the consequent election in 1992 Field lost office to the Liberals but we Greens held all five seats.

This was tough going. In the middle of the turmoil in 1991, I went home to Liffey and took a walk in the woods and, by the fire that night, wrote about the walk with only a hint of the political storm brewing in Hobart:

> I've got a damper on the go. It's something to relish after tea, when there's been a lot of effort clambering over hillsides between sunup and sundown.
>
> The Cluan Tiers are like a lot of Australian hills – little thought of by the neighbours except as a place to get wood or

a nice bit of scenery behind the farms where cattle shelter and forage in winter.

So when I set out down across the bridge to walk up the gulley on the other side of the valley I expected nothing special. The Liffey Valley is made up of Drys Bluff on the southern side where my house is, the Cluan Tiers on the northern side, and the Liffey River running in between.

There is a row of minor cliffs across the lower gulley on that Cluan Tiers side. These are where the paddocks stop and the steeper wooded hillside begins. The map says there is a geological fault or 'slip' here. What slipped when I do not know, but I was hardly into the creek before I found myself slipping in all directions. It is a mossy, wet, loose-rocked little gully, most of which never sees the winter sun.

An unnamed creek pours down over the continual rise of sandstone. Right at the paddock's edge, but hidden in a copse of blackwoods and tree ferns surrounded by blackberry brambles, is the first waterfall. Also hidden nearby is a great wombat hole: many years ago, on a moonlit night, I saw three wombats grazing on this verge and wondered how they had survived the midwinter nights when the possum shooters come roaring up with searchlights, guns blazing and androgens flowing. But have you ever seen a wombat run?

The next two or three hours, ascending the gully, were of immense charm – and not another bramble. In one spot a cascade over the edge of a dripping ledge; in another the creek pouring 2 metres into the largest plunge-pool in the gully; time and again the water disappearing among the boulders and then rumbling through the cauldron below.

Whereas the hills above are gum tree country (that's why the loggers want them) the gully is rainforest. Over the continuous array of tree ferns (one I measured at 30 handspans high without counting the fronds) is a mixture of broad-leafed musks, aromatic green sassafrases, blackwoods and Antarctic beech or myrtles. One or two of the myrtles higher up are mighty old survivors with trunks nearly 2 metres in diameter carrying an assortment of limpet mosses, lichens, vines and ferns.

The gully has a moss bed. Even the boulders are covered. A mattress of thick sphagnum moss smothers the rocks except where the creek has washed them bare. Fallen sassafras flowers dot this carpet. Fungi flourish in the moistness: mauve, brown, yellow and red and superb clusters of white parasols. Fungi are such a curious worldwide family of deadwood rotters.

Although I saw no animals the soft, slippery soil of the gulley's sides was marked with their tracks. Near the creek in sandy soil opening on to one of these tracks was a fresh burrow as wide as my forearm.

Eventually blocked by the plunge-pool I left the creek and walked up the western side of the gully until I saw above me a sandstone overhang. Under the overhang were the scats of Tasmanian devils. The overhang is 30 or 40 metres long and dry, with its back to the west. Its northern end was decorated with icicles where the water, dripping from above, froze as it fell through the winter air. Some of the tree fern fronds were also festooned with icicles.

After rain in summer a cloud of mist sometimes lifts out of the gully. Now I know why. It's very cool in there and the warmer air condenses above it like breath on a windowpane.

In last night's windstorm a huge tree trunk from above the overhang had crashed down, coming to a halt against other trees in the gully below. I wondered if this overhang had been lived under by people and what terror would have filled their heads when such a tree fell crashing, shuddering and wrenching its swathe through the darkness.

Such great trees falling make the ground tremble and the thunder is heard for miles around. Nevertheless, modern society, its senses numb to the enormity of the destruction, drags down whole mountainsides of forests and thinks nothing of it.

I returned home via the western ridge with a scratch on my forehead, a wet left sock and the call of clinking currawongs tinkling in my ears.

Next time the mist rises above the gulley or a flock of yellow-tailed black cockatoos disappears into its shadows or the summer sun catches the yellow-brown of its sandstone overhang above the forest, I'll be watching from this side of the valley with a new sense of togetherness.

Dampers are not for choosers. Especially if you've had the flour a bit long and have had to sift out the grubs. But some butter and honey makes anything taste good at the end of such a good day in such a good gully.

With that I put out the kerosene lamp, went to bed and slept soundly.

Liffey was my solace from the political testiness of the Tasmanian House of Assembly. But by 1993 I had had enough of politics. I called my Greens colleagues to Oura Oura for morning tea and told them I was resigning. We were a diverse but thoughtful bunch and they understood. They elected Christine as the new leader and, soon after, Peg Putt replaced me in the seat of Denison.

I spent the next three years out of politics but agreed to stand as the Australian Greens Senate candidate for Tasmania when the 1996 elections got near. This time I was to spend 16 years in federal politics.

Meanwhile, southern farmer Paul Thomas had called at Liffey with our mutual friend Greg Middleton. Some weeks later I went to a Greens' fundraiser at Paul's farm near Cygnet. A bonfire ensued, and for me a special spark had been lit.

I had been happy with damper. However, one morning after the 1996 election, but before I took up my seat, Paul knocked on my Hobart door with a bag of hot croissants. I was now happier than a clinking currawong.

19
The Nelson Falls

THE UPPER NELSON River valley, a wondrous little universe tucked away in the mountains of western Tasmania, was included in the Tasmanian Wilderness World Heritage Area in 2013. It deserved to be. I advise visitors driving from Hobart to Queenstown not to miss the half-hour return walk to the lower Nelson Falls from the Lyell Highway.

Give or take the larger Barron, Wollomombi, Fitzroy and one or two other spectacular falls dropping east off the Great Dividing Range, the Nelson Falls are among the most pleasant and accessible in Australia.

Unlike the Forth and Heemskirk falls, which were drowned in the Tasmanian Hydro-Electric Commission's dam-building heyday, the Nelson River's triple drop remains beautifully intact above the dammed waters of the King River into which the Nelson flows.

After the Franklin was saved in 1983, Bob Burton and I scrub-bashed into the falls from the highway. Back in the State Parliament, I suggested that a proper track be opened to the falls and to the nearby lookout over the Franklin River and Frenchmans Cap at Donaghys Hill. Unusually, the government complied and, these days, the car parks for these walks are rarely empty.

I nurtured the idea of exploring further up the gorge with the prospect of finding more falls and, on Easter Saturday 1993, finally set off. Like Italy, the Nelson Gorge is L-shaped with the heel of the L pointing to the south-west. From the toes of the lower falls I clambered up the south side, high over the dripping limestone cliffs where red heartberries bob on their slender branches and white snowberries glisten in the morning sun.

I slid back down to the river upstream of the falls and walked cautiously to their brink. Four kilometres to the east I could see back to the sunlit tower of Bubs Hill, framed by the rainforest trees on either side of me.

By April the Nelson Falls are mainly sunless. I walked upriver and, as I rounded its bend (heel) to head north, with the growing boom of falling waters in my ears, the sun shone through the forest canopy above and lit up a patch of ferns on the southern bank.

A sassafras tree was leaning from the bend. Mist billowed up through its shiny green leaves into the morning sunshine. The middle Nelson Falls cascaded down over the cliff ahead. I had reached a marvelous precinct full of noise, moisture, mist and movement. Here was a hidden engine room of nature where the relentless force of water is wearing the gorge deeper and the falls are being moved upstream with imperceptible slowness as the water pounds down the cliff.

Having pondered this for half an hour I began to look for a way up out of the engine room. Both sides of the gorge are very steep and the west side is impassable. So I began a scramble up the east side 50 metres from the falls. Except for coming back down a few hours later, this proved the hardest part of the outing. This scramble-up is best tackled if you are two metres tall, can hang on to thin smooth trunks while rocks tumble away from under your boots, and are happy to use your knees to help grip and lever a way up the unstable 70-degree slope.

I climbed high up the gorge wall, came back to the river upstream of the middle falls, and walked carefully to their lip with the river swirling round my boots. The sun danced where the water shot out over the precipice and, below, the brilliant greens of the Nelson fernery combined with the flume of sunlit mist to lift the abysmal scene to softest splendour.

As I walked further up the river a yabbie appeared. This shiny little brown-shelled crustacean was almost vertical, on the rocks half a metre up from the water. I stooped for a closer look. It suddenly flung its long, clawed arms up and back and bared its blue-mottled chest at me while back-pedalling down towards the safety of the torrent.

I don't know what such a ferocious display does to a shag or a snake but I backed off and wished this ancient armoured acrobat well as she performed a half-tuck dive back into the deeps.

The upper Nelson Falls are the best. Twenty metres wide and some 60 metres high, they buck and bounce down a set of steps with a final twist to the west and sluice at the bottom.

They are also the easiest to ascend provided the river is running low. In the eastern corner are enough handholds in the ledges to make the climb a cinch. Just as well: the gorge walls here become sheer and well beyond scaling by a boltless and ropeless traveller. With higher water this section of the gorge would be impassable.

I walked a couple more miles up the Nelson River's 'shin'. It is a sedate little stream up there, much as it is below the falls. The Nelson Gorge and its triple falls are an abrupt and turbulent interlude in the river's otherwise restful life. Many a human being might relate to that.

Back in 1993 this showy little river had been kept off the World Heritage listing that protected the Tasmanian wilderness to its east and south, although no miner, dam-builder or logger – and no other politician – alive had been into or seen its gorge and falls. In 2011, when I walked into a room full of maps and planners working on the nomination to add the world's tallest flowering forests to the eastern side of the Tasmanian Wilderness World Heritage Area, I remembered my April day 18 years earlier in the lovely precinct of the upper Nelson and recommended it be added, and so it was.

Maybe it doesn't matter what is on the modern maps, where every square metre is allocated status according to its use or potential misuse. After countless winters making its gorge and falls, the Nelson is certain to keep tumbling down regardless of human intrusions.

That night in 1993 I lay alone in the rainforest beneath the stars. A ringtail possum whistled. A shooting star flashed across the Milky Way. I was out and free, having just resigned after ten years in the Tasmanian Parliament. The Moon climbed slowly through the branches. The roar of the falls echoed in my mind and, in the quiet of the wilderness evening, I went happily to sleep on Earth.

20
2.40 am

I WROTE THE following note in a fit of despair, knowing that putting problems down on paper can sometimes help resolve them. It worked and I slept for three hours before Canberra's cockatoos woke me to a promising day in politics.

Tuesday. 2.40 am. Canberra. 10 September 1996.
Well, today is my first Senate speech.

I should be asleep. But I'm wide awake, and aware that (when the time comes) I will be in real trouble: tired, brain-fused, anxious.

I need to relax. I think of how many young men have lain forlornly awake in trenches, how many young women have strained, harrowingly, in childbirth, at this hour.

This evening, however badly I do it, I am privileged to speak for the world we Greens aspire to, for a more humane, caring future.

This morning my good companion, Paul, now asleep, will come up from Tasmania. He will help me.

So too will the people at Parliament – Marg Blakers, Geoff Law, Ben Oquist, Steven Chaffer, Dee Margetts, Alan Carter and all.

Forests, equality, love, oceans, eternity, happiness, boundless horizons. If I don't sleep at all how can I complain?
The day will pass.

(My first Senate speech can be found at www.australianpolitics. com/ 1996/09/10/senator-bob-brown-maiden-speech.)

21
Turmoil in Timor-Leste

IN 2003 I was suspended from the Senate for 24 hours for refusing to retract my call that Prime Minister John Howard had used blackmail against Timor-Leste (East Timor). Australia, the wealthiest per capita country in the world, was and is abusing East Timor, one of the poorest countries in the world, through compromising its rights to oil and gas in the Timor Sea.

East Timor suffered reprisals – thousands of people died – while hiding and assisting Australian diggers during the Japanese invasion in the Second World War. In 1974 the little island colony was granted independence after three centuries of Portuguese rule. However Indonesia, having also freed itself from colonial (Dutch) rule after the Second World War, invaded East Timor on 7 December 1995, a day after US President Gerald Ford visited Jakarta and gave the 'green light' for the invasion. Australia's prime minister, Gough Whitlam, acquiesced and East Timor became the twenty-seventh province of Indonesia.

This followed the Kennedy and Menzies agreement with Indonesia's invasion and colonisation of West Papua in 1962. West Papua became its twenty-sixth province in 1962, a year after West Papuans had elected their own first parliament, which was promptly abolished.

Successive Australian governments backed the ruthless occupation of East Timor. In 1989 Labor Attorney-General Gareth Evans famously clinked champagne glasses with his Indonesian counterpart, Ali Alatas, as they flew over the Timor Sea to celebrate their treaty divvying up the oil and gas deposits below. Six years later Alatas, who was to describe his country's domination of East Timor as 'all pain, no gain', was appointed an Honorary Officer of the Order of Australia.

Through 24 years of turmoil and bloodshed the East Timorese fought back. More than one quarter of the people died. Australians maintained a popular community campaign to free East Timor and the Greens, like the Democrats, backed it.

After two of the independence movement's leaders were awarded the Nobel Peace Prize in 1996, I moved a motion in the Senate:

That the Senate:
(a) congratulates Bishop Carlos Belo and Mr José Ramos-Horta on their unremitting work in support of independence for East Timor and the recognition of their contribution by the award of the Nobel Peace Prize.
(b) notes that a report by the Indonesian Commission on Human Rights accuses the Indonesian Government and security forces of deliberately provoking violence in Jakarta in July 1996, following the ousting of the Leader of the Indonesian Democratic Party, Mrs Megawati Sukarnoputri; and
(c) calls on the Australian Government:
   (i)   to support self-determination for East Timor; and
   (ii) to represent forcefully to the Indonesian Government Australia's support for democracy and the rule of law in Indonesia.

The Senate, which had had 24 hours to consider the motion, agreed without dissent. It seems this was a rare case of the Howard government being asleep at the wheel. I held a press conference to publicise this as the first motion ever to pass in the Australian

Parliament supporting self-determination for East Timor. The Howard government promptly disowned it. Howard's leader of the government in the Senate, Robert Hill, who had supported the motion, now called it 'a little half trick' and Minister for Foreign Affairs Alexander Downer issued a statement that, while re-endorsing the other parts of the motion, included these toe-curling sentiments:

> Successive Australian governments have recognised Indonesia's sovereignty over East Timor since 1979.
>
> This government believes – as has its predecessors over the last 17 years
> - that the best means of bringing about positive change in East Timor and encouraging peace is by recognising the reality of Indonesian sovereignty
> - that in no way indicates approval of the way Indonesia incorporated East Timor into Indonesia
> - nor does it derogate from the government's recognition of the valiant efforts of Timorese who fought alongside Australian soldiers during World War II.

That is, abandoning the East Timorese to brutal occupation by the Indonesian military sat reasonably alongside the valiant efforts of the East Timorese to protect our soldiers from the earlier brutal occupation of their island by the Japanese. Disdain for the powerless is a hallmark of Downerian politics.

As if to shoot home to President Suharto the government's backing for Indonesia's annexation of East Timor, the Parliament House authorities then refused my request for permission to exhibit photos of the torture of East Timorese political prisoners. The harrowing photos were put up in the New South Wales Parliament and the Australian Capital Territory's Legislative Assembly instead.

There was turmoil in Indonesia leading to and following the downfall of President Suharto in 1998 but his successor, the more democratic President Habibie, offered East Timor a referendum on self-determination. The date was set for Saturday 30 August 1999. Meanwhile José Ramos-Horta had warned, 'Before [Indonesia] withdraws it wants to wreak major havoc and destabilisation, as it has always promised.' Indonesian-trained pro-integration East Timorese paramilitary groups were warning of 'a sea of fire'.

I went to see Downer at his ministerial offices in Parliament House, on the Thursday before the referendum, to talk about the repression of Tibet.

Two things are burnt into my mind from that meeting. The first was Downer's disdain for supporters of the 7 million Tibetans who also wanted an act of self-determination. He began his jibe at how I and the Greens were ostensibly backing the return of the old theocratic Tibet with, 'You lefties amaze me ...' I responded by saying how amazing it was that he and the Howard Government toadied up to the anti-democratic Communist bosses in Beijing. This did not strike him as perverse, although he had no response.

The second thing was his gratuitous assertion that worldwide speculation about violence in East Timor if the voters backed independence was wrong: there would be no such bloodshed. Our minister for foreign affairs, with more access to political information and intelligence than anyone else in Australia, could not have been more dangerously or irresponsibly out of touch.

The referendum on the following Saturday, with a stunning 98 per cent turnout of voters, saw the people of East Timor choose independence by 78.5 to 21.5 per cent.

In the wake of this result some 1400 civilians were shot, hacked, burnt or otherwise put to death by the militias with the help of the Indonesian Army, which was still ensconced in East Timor. The capital, Dili, and other towns were put to the torch. Islamic gangs ransacked Dili's Catholic Diocesan building and more than 20 people were murdered. In Suai nearly 100 innocent people were butchered. This bloodshed led President Habibie, who was unable to control his army, to seek United Nations help. On 20 September 1999 an international peacekeeping force led by Australian Major General Peter Cosgrove (later Governor-General) was moved in to restore order, and within five weeks the Indonesian troops had finally withdrawn.

The Greens were the first party to call for this military intervention. Nearly two years later I flew to Dili with Greens Chief of Staff Ben Oquist for East Timor's Independence Day on 20 May 2002. The great ceremony was held on a field miles out of Dili and I will never forget the tens of thousands of people of the newest nation in the world at the time walking happily, and mostly barefoot, along the dusty road to celebrate their freedom.

While there were more than 5000 Australians in East Timor to ensure the people's safety, Alexander Downer was pulling the rug from under the best hope for economic prosperity in East Timor.

Two months before independence, Downer had announced that Australia had withdrawn from the jurisdiction of the international courts on the issue of maritime boundaries. This was to ensure the East Timorese would never get arbitration of their very strong challenge to the unfair agreements on sea boundaries and oil resources that Australia had struck with Indonesia while East Timor was suppressed.

A year later the Senate was debating the Petroleum (Timor Sea Treaty) Bill 2003 and I told the chamber,

> last night, as the newspaper reports tell us, the prime minister phoned his opposite number in East Timor to deliver blackmail. What the prime minister effectively did was to coerce a poor and weak neighbour, through blackmail, into accepting an agreement to develop the fossil fuel resources.

Eric Abetz took exception and I was expelled because I would not withdraw the word 'blackmail'.

The press had reported that Prime Minister Howard phoned Prime Minister Alkatiri to insist the treaty (which gave East Timor a raw deal) be signed the next morning or else the Australian Parliament would delay the bill and so threaten East Timor with getting no revenues at all because its contracts with the petroleum companies were about to run out. Alkatiri had been holding out for a fairer deal.

After I was ousted from the Senate, the prime minister made a special statement to the House of Representatives denying that he had tried to 'strongarm or intimidate' the East Timorese leadership.

The deal meant that Australia would get 80 per cent of the revenues from the huge Greater Sunrise deposits under the Timor Sea, and East Timor 20 per cent – whereas East Timor would have gotten 100 per cent if the international court was to judge, as experts predicted it would, that the boundary between the two countries should be midway and not over on East Timor's side.

Alexander Downer put it this way: 'To call us a big bully is a grotesque simplification of Australia. We had a cozy economic agreement with Indonesia, we bailed East Timor out with no economic benefit.'

So why would this barefoot country think we were there for them rather than the money?

I felt ashamed to be an Australian legislator and, locked out, was not in the chamber when the unjust Petroleum (Timor Sea Treaty) Bill passed with 'bipartisan' support, but opposed by my fellow Greens senator, Kerry Nettle.

More than a decade later East Timor is still fighting for a fair go while Australia has permanently jettisoned the world courts on maritime boundaries, because governments know those courts would deliver justice to East Timor – and a fairer boundary with Indonesia.

In 2014 Australia was unable to suppress worldwide speculation that it deliberately bugged the new ministerial offices it built for the East Timorese government as a gift of 'friendship', so that it could illegally tap into discussions about such things as East Timor's strategy to get a better deal for its oil and gas resources.

You can judge a nation by how it treats its neighbours, and judge it best by how it treats the least of them.

22

Oh Tibet!

I WAS STANDING in the Barkhor square in front of the Jokhang Temple in Lhasa in 1998 when a Tibetan girl walked up, looked into my eyes, put a roll of paper into my hand and, saying nothing, disappeared back into the afternoon crowd.

She was brave. While the Jokhang is one of Buddhist Tibet's most iconic places of worship, the small square in front of the temple is surrounded by spy cameras. There is a commanding uniformed police presence in the square and plain-clothes police mingle with the crowd outside and inside the Jokhang. These Beijing-implanted police keep a special watch on westerners.

I put the bit of paper in my pocket and walked back to the hotel where I was to catch up with Stephenie Cahalan, who had volunteered to come with me on this fraught trip to see how things were in Tibet. She had a camera and we were accompanied by another young Australian woman who had spent a year in Tibet and was our unofficial guide.

En route to Tibet via Hong Kong, Xi'an and Xining, we had been pleasantly surprised that there were no delays or special questions asked. As a Greens senator and long-term campaigner for Tibet's right to self-determination, I assumed this was because my passport and tickets were in the name of Robert Brown, while my Beijing police file was in the name of Bob Brown. Whatever the case, there are lots of Browns and the computers didn't twig.

I was getting to sleep in our modest hotel in Xi'an after a very good street-stall meal with Stephenie when a phone started ringing two or three doors down the passageway. Then it rang in a closer room and then closer still and, finally and very loudly, at my own bedside. I thought, 'This is it! They're on to me!'

However the lady on the line asked instead, in very good English, if I was lonely because she wanted to come to my room to keep me warm and comfortable. I thanked her and declined the kind offer.

We met our Australian guide in Xining, which is midway between Beijing and Lhasa, and spent three frustrating days filling out forms for the all-important permit to enter Tibet. A US$100 'fee' paid for each of us to the police authorities finally did the trick. Meanwhile Stephenie and I took an arduous bus trip on gravel roads west towards Golmud on the edge of the Gobi Desert, where the spread of irrigated Chinese croplands was severing the ancient nomadic routes of the Tibetan yak-herders.

The array of MiG jet fighters beside the runway at Lhasa Airport was as telling as the convoys of military trucks and gauntlet of police-check stations on the way into town. We had arrived in the wake of a military crackdown on peaceful Tibetan demonstrations for freedom and democracy. Calling out 'freedom for Tibet' or 'we want our Dalai Lama back' was enough to get the locals a beating, a jail term, torture and months in 're-education' classes. When we booked into the luxurious Chinese-owned hotel in Lhasa we knew that, nearby, hundreds of Tibetan nuns and monks were in the dreaded Chinese-run Drapchi Prison.

We avoided Tibetan-owned hotels because, following an earlier visit to Lhasa by US Republican Senator Frank Wolf, who described Tibet as being 'under boot-heel subjugation', the Tibetan establishments he had stayed in were shut down.

We visited local Buddhist monasteries. At one remote mountain nunnery a maroon-cloaked nun called for us to come in but we declined. These ancient Tibetan cloisters – 6000 were ransacked in

Mao's 1960s Cultural Revolution and only a handful survived – have resident agents who report to the Chinese authorities.

But I was determined to take up one invitation. I had read of the remarkable endurance of a Buddhist nun in her twenties, one of many who had been released from Drapchi after years of torture and degrading treatment. Our guide, who had met the nun's younger sister, arranged a meeting. At the agreed hour I sat in a tiny backstreet Tibetan cafe growing increasingly concerned as time passed and she did not show up. I was going pink around the gills from so many refills of my mug of sweet yak-butter tea. When two hours had passed I paid up and left.

We learned later that the young woman had been walking to our rendezvous point but she noticed she was being followed by two men, so she walked off in a different direction. Poor woman: besides having gone through the horrors of Drapchi, she had been banned from her life's vocation as a nun and from any other form of employment, and was now under the occupying thugs' constant surveillance.

But this was of little concern to Australia's ambassador to China, Richard Smith. After a press conference back in Beijing a week later to talk about Tibet, I met him in the salubrious Australian Embassy. I talked to him about what we had seen and experienced in Tibet. He was blithely dismissive. He had taken tea in the prison garden with the governor of Drapchi just a few months earlier and told me that he had found it most pleasant there under the apricot tree. He had heard no cries.

I asked His Excellency to arrange a meeting for me with the appropriate minister in Beijing so that I could give my views to the Chinese government.

Immediately after I arrived back at our hotel in Beijing there was a knock on the door. In a corridor otherwise serviced almost entirely by females, a burly, nervous young man had arrived to say he was now looking after my room and would check to see that everything was okay. In the following minutes he went through a routine that made me think of *Fawlty Towers*: he flushed the toilet, plumped the lounge pillows, ran his hands through all of the floor-length drapes, checked the fruit bowl and disappeared briefly into the bedroom. I expected that was where he placed the main microphone. This nervous intelligence officer came back to 'inspect the room' every hour or so,

With not the slightest indication that my embassy had tried to get the meeting I had asked for, we left China. At the hotel departure I offered my ever-attentive hotel attendant a generous tip, which he rejected in a comical state of fluster.

At home in Australia the media was running the very angry reaction of the acting Chinese ambassador. He said that Senator Bob Brown should have minded his own business and attended instead to human rights abuses in Tasmania!

As the years have gone by I have gotten to know Tibet's exiled Dalai Lama who, in 1988, was awarded the Nobel Peace Prize. He is a remarkably good human being. While there are almost daily reports out of Tibet about atrocities against his people, he continues to seek dialogue with China and to share with the world his philosophy of peace and compassion. When the undemocratic brutes in Beijing who refer to the Dalai Lama as 'a splittist' and 'a criminal' are long gone, he will be remembered as a global leader who never gave in to their tyranny.

I had the Tibetans' plight in mind at the end of 2010 when, hearing that the Dalai Lama would be visiting Australia in June 2011, I asked Prime Minister Julia Gillard if she would meet him if he came to Parliament House. She said she would. However I did not count on the Mandarin-speaking minister for foreign affairs, Kevin Rudd. As the visit neared he declared that neither he nor the prime minister would be meeting the Dalai Lama. Consequently Gillard told me she had to withdraw from her commitment to avoid a stoush with her foreign minister. I told her what I thought of this reversal; but, care of Rudd, kowtowing to Beijing was the order of the day yet again.

Ten minutes after the girl who had handed me the note disappeared back into the throng outside the Jokhang in 1998 I returned to my hotel room in Lhasa. I took the piece of paper out of my pocket and read it. She had written, in pencil, in English:

Beloved Mr, I would like to express warmest welcome to you and hope you an enjoyable trip in Tibet, by the way, on behalf of six million Tibetans.

We warmly thank you for helping our freedom, and we hope you'll continue to help us. We have full confidence that His Holiness the Dalai Lama will come back to his own country soon and hope Tibet will become peaceful soon.

We are very proud that many great people like you help us. And we have His Holiness's great compassion.

An ancient Chinese proverb warns that 'dead ashes flare up again'. In Tibet this awaits the oxygen of global concern and the courage of the world's people, who talk so much about freedom, to confront the Beijing jackboot trampling over Lhasa.

I am banned from re-entering China, let alone Tibet. However I have never forgotten the Tibetan girl outside the Jokhang, or her call for help from the 'many great people' who live so easily in freedom outside Tibet.

23
Starry, starry nights

IT IS SAID that the young Lord Byron swooned when he met Lady Wilmot Horton at a ball in 1814. The next morning he wrote 'She Walks in Beauty':

> *She walks in Beauty, like the night*
> *Of cloudless climes and starry skies;*
> *And all that's best of dark and bright*
> *Meet in her aspect and her eyes:*
> *Thus mellowed to that tender light*
> *Which Heaven to gaudy day denies.*

At Trunkey Creek on the highlands west of Sydney, when I was four, my eyes latched on to the Milky Way, the Southern Cross and, one especially splendid evening, a glowing orange Moon rising from beneath the forested horizon of the eastern hills.

At Bellingen, on a cool dark night in 1957, our family went out to peer up as *Sputnik 1* passed silently across the sky. With it went the shock that communist Russia had jumped ahead of the capitalist US in the space race. A human-made satellite was orbiting Earth barely half a century after the US's Wright brothers had taken the first aeroplane aloft in 1903. I was 12 and Byron's poem was already in my mind.

In July 1969 the wealthy world watched black-and-white television as human beings landed on the Moon. Now aged 24, I saw this amazing event between shifts at Canberra's Community Hospital where the National Museum of Australia now stands. My Aunt Lillian had warned that God would end the world if scientists kept interfering with the heavens. I was on the side of the scientists but understood the solace and mystery that she wanted left in the heavens above.

In all of human existence people have gone to sleep while looking at the night sky full of moving stars, planets, Earth's satellite moon and the streaking amazements of 'falling stars' and portentous meteors and asteroids. Most cultures have located our origins or those of the gods in this vast celestial firmament. Since history began, people have been discussing its effect on their fortunes, not least their love lives.

Yet suddenly the world is giving up the night sky. An uncoordinated and growing hotchpotch of moving and flashing lights is compromising its natural beauty. Before long, people on Earth, never consulted about it, will be unable to see or remember what that tender light was like.

In the Senate, in the final week of sittings in 2000 (by then I was 55) I asked the highest authority in Australia about this loss. Here's the Hansard record of his answer. The interjections – salvos of derision – that drowned out much of our short exchange speak for themselves.

Tuesday, 5 December 2000:

Senator BROWN (2.26 PM) – As it is close to Christmas, I want to ask a question of the Minister for the Environment and Heritage about stars. Is he aware that the space station *Endeavour* will be brighter than the brightest star in the sky, Sirius, when it is in full play, after sunset and before sunrise? I ask the minister: are we the last generation ever to see a natural night sky? Who has consulted the people, not least the poets and lovers, about this loss of the starry commons? Does the government regret that we will be the last generation ever to see the starry climes at night?

Honourable senators interjecting

Senator HILL (Minister for the Environment and Heritage) – I do not understand the mirth; this is obviously a very serious matter. The best I could suggest is that we conduct some form of global plebiscite over the next 10 years, funded no doubt by AusAID. Perhaps the ALP would be prepared to make a contribution – trouble is, the ALP supplies in brown paper bags, as we know! The only stars I see in this chamber are on our side. I look at Senator Herron, Senator Minchin and Senator Vanstone – real stars within the Australian parliamentary process.

Honourable senators interjecting

Senator HILL – I have to apologise to Senator Brown that they are not taking his question seriously. I take it seriously, but I regret to say that it is just the product of progress.

The space station is brighter and moves much faster than any of the stars: when it is crossing the sky it does relegate Sirius to insignificance. Future installations will be brighter than Venus and, why not, the Moon.

But will an artificial moon cause the dingos to howl?

And what will this melange of superimposed ego-lights do for those, like Australian poet Christopher Brennan (1870–1932) in his poem 'I said, This misery must end', who find solace in the Cosmos?

I said, This misery must end

...

and stept into the mother-night

... and rais'd my eyes

erect, that they might drink of space,

and took the night upon my face,

till time and trouble fell away

and all my soul sprang up to feel

as one among the stars that reel

in rhyme on their rejoicing way,

...

24
Wielangta

IN 1990 I was leader of the Tasmanian Greens, in the balance of power, supporting the Labor government of Premier Michael Field. Early one morning, just as the Sun was rising, I answered a phone call from a resident of Wielangta, the forested outpost near Tasmania's east coast.

'They've brought in a bulldozer!' the caller told me. 'They' were logging contractors working under the direction of Forestry Tasmania. Their job was to force a road up the hill through the Wielangta Forest Reserve so the logging companies could cut down the forest on the mountainside behind the reserve. Most of the wood would go to the nearby Triabunna woodchip mill for export to Japanese paper mills.

The Hobart media had also been alerted. I set off to join the locals' stand against the bulldozers.

Wielangta, said to be an Aboriginal word for 'tall forest', is an hour or so from Hobart. By the time I arrived the Wielangta people were barricading the road and had already won the day. The threat of political tension and bad publicity from the planned invasion of the reserve, which harboured rare ground orchids, birds, marsupials and insects, not only halted the works for that morning but the road through the reserve has never been built.

The Wielangta Forest Reserve protected only a fraction of the 10,000-hectare Wielangta State Forest and the loggers wanted all the rest, so they built their road around the northern edge of the reserve. In 2004 I drove back out to Wielangta and had a homegrown organic lunch with Mark Agnew and Sally Meredith (who had made that phone call more than a decade before). After lunch we climbed Forestry Tasmania's locked gate to walk up the mountain and see the expanding logging operations. Blue ribbons on trees marked out the next death zone.

I was now a senator and was amazed by Prime Minister John Howard's sanctioning of logging that was destroying the habitat of nationally listed endangered species across Tasmania. He was not only the sanctioner, he was the grand architect. In fact, in 1997 he had made a special and highly publicised trip to Tasmania to sign the Regional Forest Agreement (RFA) at Forestry Tasmania's showplace at Perth, south of Launceston. The RFA exempted loggers from Howard's own *Environment Protection and Biodiversity Conservation Act*, which was supposed to protect Australia's environment and save its creatures from going extinct.

On his way to sign the agreement Howard's car had to drive through the peaceful but powerful citizens' protest at Perth, fronted by an Aboriginal man with a chain around his neck. As the car drove relentlessly through the crowd I came eye-to-eye with the ashen-faced prime minister sitting in the front passenger seat. I was knocked down backwards with a security man falling over me. A pistol fell out of his coat and spun around on the asphalt between our heads. 'You better hang on to that, mate!' I said as he grabbed it back.

The Wilderness Society's Geoff Law had been bounced off the car bonnet, leaving Howard's very cranky Tasmanian senator, Eric Abetz, to complain about the cost of fixing the resultant ding. I'm not sure what Geoff's own ding cost, but the RFA was Howard's dollar-free death warrant for thousands of creatures of the wilds.

The RFA licensed the obliteration of thousands of square kilometres of ancient life–filled ecosystems through the legalised lie that it was environmental good practice. By 2009 this farce was so bleedingly evident that thousands of people were protesting in the streets and forests of Tasmania.

In my office, Margaret Blakers, working with Hobart solicitor Roland Browne, selected Wielangta as the test forest for a challenge to the RFA in the Federal Court of Australia.

(In 1998 I had also taken Margaret's advice to go with her to Victoria's Goolengook Forest protest camp and stay overnight. I dallied too long in the forest, taking in the beautiful morning ambience, and was arrested for getting in the way of the logging. After a bumpy trip in a paddy wagon with three other forest defenders, I ended up in Orbost Jail. Fortunately Margaret discovered a vital map in the government's locker showing that the logging was in the wrong place and therefore illegal: so, after the great advocacy of Melbourne barrister Brian Walters, all of us forest defenders had to be set free. Of course, no-one in the logging industry was charged for their contempt of the law. Instead Premier of Victoria Jeff Kennett whizzed legislation through the State Parliament to make the illegal logging legal retrospectively.)

In the Federal Court in Hobart, Roland Browne instructed barrister Debbie Mortimer (now a Federal Court judge) to challenge Forestry Tasmania's logging of the Wielangta Forest causing loss of habitat for the Tasmanian wedge-tailed eagle, the swift parrot and the Wielangta stag beetle, all of which are on the national list of endangered species. After two weeks of hearings, we won. Judge Shane Marshall ruled that the logging breached the *Environment Protection and Biodiversity Conservation Act* and should stop. Outside the court building, where children were colourfully costumed as swift parrots, the crowd erupted into clapping, whistling and cheering. Wielangta was saved.

But it wasn't. In response to this finding, Prime Minister Howard and Labor Premier Paul Lennon rushed to sign a new regulation making the illegal logging legal. To boot, after I failed in an appeal to the High Court, I was left with a $240,000 bill for Forestry Tasmania's legal costs. This threatened me with bankruptcy which, under the Australian Constitution, meant I would lose my seat in the Senate. I appealed for public donations to help pay the bill and was inundated. This heartwarming generosity for the forests' cause left my Hobart office manager Michelle O'Toole counting a large surplus which we then used to fund campaigns for other Australian forests.

Despite the political treachery, a collapse in the global market for wood meant that the Wielangta Forest remained free of logging after the legal challenge. However, in March 2014 Tasmanians elected a Liberal state government committed to Wielangta's future piecemeal destruction.

The swift parrot is the fastest parrot on Earth. Whereas the ferry *Spirit of Tasmania* takes all night to cross Bass Strait, this little migrant crosses in three hours. It spends winter on mainland Australia and summer in Tasmania where it nests in trees that, because they are a century or more old, have hollows in their branches and trunks. Wielangta Forest is their nesting stronghold.

Once in great flocks, the swift parrot population these days may be 1000 pairs, and recent counts indicate its numbers are falling. That is why it is on the list of threatened species at state, national and international levels.

The biggest threat to its future was the export woodchip industry, which fed swift parrot nesting trees, including those in Wielangta, to the woodchip mill at the nearby port of Triabunna. The free market has come to their aid. Environmental philanthropists Graeme Wood and Jan Cameron bought the mill in 2011 and Wood has announced plans to turn it into a centre for ecological study, education and celebration. That brings closer the happy day when the biggest threat to the swift parrot in Tasmania will be all the visitors with binoculars wanting to glimpse their scintillating green, blue and red colours as they rocket through the forest.

25
Blackwater

IN THE RUN-UP to the 2007 election I was interviewed by Fran Kelly on ABC Radio National and knew I had crossed the line.

I told her that during the next term (three years) of government Australia should develop plans to phase out the export of coal. I explained, 'We are exporting to the rest of the world what is effectively a deadly threat to the whole planet and our children.'

The Murdoch media pounced. The Brisbane *Courier-Mail*'s headline was 'KILL COAL OFF, SAYS BOB' and the proposal to take three years to come up with a plan to phase out exports was reported as 'Greens Senator Bob Brown is calling for the death of Queensland's $24 billion coal industry and thousands of jobs, demanding an end to all coal exports within 3 years'. Apparently the editor couldn't find a journalist willing to risk his or her reputation with such a fabrication, so there was no byline.

Murdoch's Sydney *Telegraph* took a day longer to wind up. It had a reporter who wasn't fazed by what I hadn't said. Under the headline 'SACK 50,000 AUSTRALIANS', senior writer Malcolm Farr lit up with my 'demand that Australia's entire coal industry be shut down'. This luminary of the media was slavering at the thought that 'the plan also has the potential to cost the Greens votes at the next federal election'. (As it turned out, the Greens got their highest vote in history.)

This hubbub led the mayor of Blackwater, a thriving coal town in central Queensland, to publicly dare me to come up there and 'repeat' my threat. He had a town hall that would be packed with 600 people, including miners, if I dared to show up.

So I phoned him and took up the offer.

Blackwater, population 3000, is 300 kilometres west of Rockhampton. I flew to 'Rocky', on the Tropic of Capricorn, with my chief of staff, Prue Cameron, economist Richard Denniss and adviser Ebony Bennett. We picked up a hire car, stopped to buy a few groceries, and headed for the showdown at Blackwater. As we passed through the village of Dingo there were lightning flashes from a thunderstorm on the forward horizon.

This region had suddenly become one of the richest coal-mining centres on the planet and Blackwater's real estate prices had boomed. It was also in the grip of the great drought, which was made worse by global warming, which was made worse by coal mining.

Queensland Police had dispatched a special squad to the town to do what they could to protect Senator Brown from a possible lynch mob. We obligingly made the police station our first point of call in Blackwater.

As we arrived from the east the huge black-and-green storm cloud was rolling in from the west. Its menacing advance was marked by the incessant flashing of lightning and roar of thunder. There was worse to come.

The police asked us to follow their car down to the Blackwater Town Hall and showed Richard how to park the car with its rear to the back wall of the hall next to the back door. When the crowd in the hall surged forward during my speech, I was to run backwards off the stage through this escape door and Richard would be ready for a hasty escape. The good officers had a layout of the building and made sure my staff would also be near the stage to get away as fast as they could.

Before the public meeting the mayor, a good civic representative, had asked the mayors of nearby towns and the City of Rockhampton (the Beef Capital of Australia) to a one-hour preliminary meeting. This turned out to be a very proper and cordial affair and, over tea and nibbles in the anteroom, I took the opportunity to explain the Australian Greens policies for replacing fossil fuels with renewable energy and energy efficiency (reducing waste), which are highly promising industries for the 'Sunshine State' of Queensland.

While there did not seem to be much human commotion building up outside, the storm struck. Within minutes the streets of Blackwater were awash and our meeting was repeatedly interrupted by thunderclaps and the roar of the torrential downpour on the roof, accompanied by a power blackout. During that hour-long meeting, Blackwater received 75 millimetres, or 3 inches, of rain: at least the graziers would be happy.

The fateful hour arrived and, with the lights back on, I was led through a stage side-door to the microphone to take on the angry mob. However, it wasn't there: two-thirds of the seats were empty. The other third was occupied by a good-looking cross section of locals, remarkably like audiences I had spoken to in many other Australian halls.

My introduction drew no booing or hissing. Instead, as I outlined the global scientific alarm about our heating planet, and the core role of burning coal in creating this hazard, the people listened politely. I explained that the nearby Great Barrier Reef, which generated business worth $6 billion each year while sustaining 63,000 jobs – many more than the whole of Australia's coal mining industry – was already half damaged or destroyed due to human impacts, the worst being from the carbon dioxide from coal combustion entering Earth's atmosphere.

I talked about boom and bust. This got some heads nodding. Mining inevitably ends, and our Greens strategy was to look at options like base-load solar power stations, wind energy and geothermal power which, while assumed to be more expensive, were becoming cheaper than coal and oil if you took into fair account both the massive taxpayer subsidies the polluting fuels are given and the future cost of mitigating the global warming they are causing.

I discussed how this century would see huge damage to the productivity of the Murray–Darling Basin, Australia's premier food bowl, if the warming is not curbed. The British economist Sir Nicholas Stern, who had recently visited Canberra, held that by diverting 2 per cent of our wealth to tackle greenhouse gas emissions now we could save our grandchildren from a 6 to 20 per cent reduction in their wealth that adapting to global warming may cost them later this century.

I brought up a recent Commonwealth Scientific and Industrial Research Organisation (CSIRO) study that had revealed a promising alternative source of coke to the coking coal from Queensland used to make steel in Japan and China: Australian mulga trees, which would be grown in semi-arid areas like those to the west of Blackwater.

Instead of the anticipated shouting session, the question time was informed and even supportive. An impressive teacher stood up in front of her town peers and stressed the need for a good education, including in the dynamics of climate change, if the children of Blackwater, like those of all other towns, were to be prepared for a very different future world.

Instead of hurrying out the back door after the event, I went down with my good companions to chat with the audience over another cup of tea.

We left in calm order, although the storm had turned the Blackwater Town Hall grounds into mud and the car nearly bogged as we set off. It was fortunate we weren't really fleeing! However, deciding not to press this good fortune, we forwent dinner and headed back along the highway towards Rockhampton as the clock headed for 10 pm.

Everyone was hungry, so when we spotted a roadside picnic ground with a streetlight over the table we stopped to open our little bag of groceries: bread, cheese and tomatoes.

The headlights had picked up a few boulders on the lawn around the picnic table. As we walked towards the table one of these boulders jumped. I heard a shriek and turned to find Ebony up on the table. The large shapes, it turned out, were cane toads. They were out, about, and ready to procreate in the warm, wet wake of the storm. So great was the terror induced by these beasts, which appeared more than ready to surge forward, that we quickly packed up and drove off again.

And so, with everyone settled down, we enjoyed a light late-evening meal in the car while Richard drove us, in very good humour, back to the comforts of Rockhampton.

26

'You must hate the world …'

THE ELECT VESSEL, Bruce Hales, lives in suburban Sydney near former prime minister John Howard. He is the global leader of the Exclusive Brethren flock of an estimated 50,000, including 15,000 members in Australia. Besides being the spiritual descendant of St Paul, he is a multimillionaire. He advises his flock to hate the world and every feature in it.

Elect Vessel Hales flies in an executive jet, employs bodyguards and enjoyed entree to the office of Prime Minister Howard. However, like other members of the Brethren, he will not eat at the same table as 'worldlies' like you and me. According to a preceding Elect Vessel, James Taylor Jr, 'invariably we are contaminated when we go [and eat with outsiders], for the uncleanness comes out over the table'.

'Worldlies' are the 7.5 billion people on Earth other than this tiny sect, and we are all going to Hell.

Hales teaches sect members that when 'you come in touch with worldly people, you'll have some sense of defilement … and you're in control, you're superior, I mean morally'. At a meeting in Sydney in 2006 he echoed his hero St Paul:

the whole principles of the world have to be scorned and disdained and just hated, really hated. Unless you've come to a hatred of the world you're likely to be sucked in by it, and seduced by it. You must hate the world, every feature of the world.

My attention was caught by the Brethren when, as a Tasmanian senator, I met several former members who told harrowing stories of being 'withdrawn from' by the sect. This meant total excommunication from their spouses, children, siblings, parents and grandparents. Excommunication also meant eternity in Hell.

The Exclusive Brethren indoctrinate their children with a terror of Hell through excommunication. To be saved from it, Brethren children must not watch television, listen to radio, access the internet or go to university where so many wicked ideas abound. Public schools are avoided because, according to Melbourne journalist Michael Bachelard's book *Behind the Exclusive Brethren*, they are considered to be places of 'contamination and defilement'.

Women should be seen but not heard. As St Paul insisted, 'I suffer not a woman to teach, nor to usurp authority over the man, but to be in silence.' Women are 'the weaker vessel' and must submit to their men 'in every thing'. Hales refers to the men of his 200-year-old sect as saints.

These saints poison the minds of infants against parents who have left the sect. One Australian court-appointed psychologist described such actions as 'psychologically cruel, unacceptable and abusive behaviour'. Former chief justice of the Family Court Alastair Nicholson said that the sect's brainwashing was 'psychologically very damaging to the child'.

In *Behind the Exclusive Brethren*, which I highly recommend for readers seeking an insight into how such a contrived and cruel religious dogma can thrive in modern democracies, Bachelard relates the story of a 16-year-old girl, 'Sophie', who had kissed and 'indulged in a little fondling' with a boy. Both were subject to intimate interrogation by the saints. As Sophie related to Bachelard:

I was taken under the house to a dark kind of room with no windows, and these priests interrogated me: 'Did he put his hand here? Did he do that? Did he do this?' A whole lot of things I hadn't even realised people did, because I was pretty innocent.

The girl was interrogated daily by the same 'priests', going over the same lurid questions. Food was left outside her door and she was escorted to the toilet three times a day past a line-up of her horrified sisters. A younger sister who later broke out of the sect's grip remembers:

I was disgusted. They were all pervs, all those Brethren men ... my feeling is the energy more than anything else: this dark, dark, energy, and my sister's devastation. She was devastated. The tears! She was desperate. Absolutely desperate.

Bachelard notes that Howard had been meeting with Hales as far back as 1989. In September 2006, the prime minister met the Elect Vessel again and then wrote to him saying, 'I too enjoyed our recent discussions,' and reiterating that he was 'aware of the campaign against you by Senator Brown and others' (referring to the Senate inquiry I proposed that year). Meanwhile the Reverend Dr Dean Drayton, who represented the National Council of Churches in Australia and its four million members, failed in his several attempts to see Prime Minister Howard.

Sophie eventually left the sect and, amongst other things, went on to work with refugees. She explained, 'I can identify with people who are struggling, who have lost everything, because I've been there.'

She did not let Howard avoid her. Bachelard records that in Sydney in 2007 she confronted the prime minister:

I grabbed his hand in both of mine and said, 'Mr Howard, I'm [Sophie], and I'm an ex-Exclusive Brethren, and I feel utterly and totally betrayed by you. There are thousands of us who have lost our families.'

And he kept saying, 'I'm sorry, I'm sorry,' and was shaking his head like Noddy. He heard though. I just felt he heard. At least I got the message through.

* * *

IN 2004 SECT members, who are forbidden to vote, were revealed to be orchestrating campaigns against the Greens in Australia and New Zealand. The motivation for this foray into worldly politics was their homophobia at a time when the Greens alone advocated equal marriage laws. They campaigned to re-elect Prime Minister Howard, who legislated a ban on same-sex marriage. Conversely, in New Zealand, it was discovered that the Brethren was hiring private detectives to shadow Labour Prime Minister Helen Clark and her husband.

Former Howard staffer Damien Mantach, having moved south to become the Tasmanian Liberal Party's director, admitted advising the Exclusive Brethren in their virulent campaign against the Greens in the 2004 Tasmanian elections.

The Brethren, receiving millions of dollars in public money for its schools, was also alarmed by the Greens' policy of giving poorer schools more of the funding pie.

In 2006, Michael Bachelard, writing for *The Age*, and Channel Seven's James Thomas both ran a series of pieces raising public concern about the Brethren, bringing matters to a head. Supported by ex-Brethren, I moved for a Senate inquiry. My terms of reference for the proposed Senate inquiry were:

that the following matters be referred to the Community Affairs References Committee for inquiry and report by 8 August 2006.

The role of the religious organisation Exclusive Brethren in:

(a) family breakdown and psychological and emotional effects related to the practice of excommunication or other practices;

(b) Australian politics and political activities, including donations to political parties or other political entities and funding specific advertising campaigns;

(c) the receipt of funding from the Federal Government or other political entities;

(d) taxation and other special arrangements or exemptions from Australian law that relate to Exclusive Brethren businesses;

(e) special arrangements and exemptions from Australian law that relate to Exclusive Brethren schools, military service and voting; and

(f) any related matters.

This sent shock waves through the Brethren and there was an uproar in the Senate. Bachelard recounts that Howard's Senate leader, Eric Abetz, likened me to a Nazi: 'When the leader of a political party starts scapegoating religious minorities, the alarm bells of history should be sounding loud and clear.'

Senior Brethren asked to meet me. Mindful that these saints were risking defilement, I agreed.

On 6 June 2006, three Exclusive Brethren flew from Melbourne to meet me in my office in Parliament House in Canberra. They asked me to call off the inquiry. They were David Thomas (DT), David McAlpin (DM) and Richard Garrett (RG). My senior advisers, Prue Cameron and Richard Denniss, sat in on the meeting. I asked if the Brethren would mind me taping the conversation. One then brought a tape recorder out of his coat pocket, already turned on, and placed it on the table next to mine.

I started the meeting with an explanation of why I moved for the Senate inquiry: my concern regarding the Exclusive Brethren's entry into politics, spending tens of thousands of dollars advertising against the Greens in Tasmanian and New Zealand elections, and the mental trauma caused by the break-up of families as a result of the Brethren's beliefs. Here are some brief and edited extracts from the meeting, which went more than an hour.

BB: The Exclusive Brethren as a Christian church has become involved in campaigning against the Greens.

DT: That's not the truth.

BB: It is the truth, sir.

DM: No, it's not the truth.

BB: So ...

DM: No, it's not the truth.

BB: So ...

DM: Please, it's not the truth.

DT: The Church has never discussed, it never enters into discussion in the Church about politics.

BB: Well, what do you say ...

RG: That is exactly right. I didn't even know when those advertisements were placed in Tasmania. I mean I wasn't aware of what was going on until after it had happened. It's got nothing to do with the Church. It is concerned [with] individuals. I mean they are exercising their democratic right.

* * *

BB: [Holding up brochure.] Let me point you to advertising in Tasmania at the recent state election with my picture on the front ... authorised by Trevor Christian of Scottsdale who's a member of your church.

Now this has 'environmental veneer, question mark – vote against this deception'. One of the assertions is that the Greens want to introduce the regulated use of cannabis. Actually the policy is the regulated use of cannabis for medical purposes. That is, to alleviate people who might be dying of cancer, for example, from pain that is not alleviated by other drugs.

DT: Wasn't that taken direct off the net?

BB: 'Introduce the regulated use of cannabis' was taken off the net and the 'for medical purposes' was removed. So it was a lie that was put to the Tasmanian electorate by Trevor Christian from the Exclusive Brethren. It is important in politics that voters are not misled. The Scriptures say you must not bear false witness against your neighbour.

DT: Well that's Trevor Christian. The charge you made in Parliament is against the Exclusive Brethren, it's not against Trevor Christian. The Exclusive Brethren have nothing whatever to do with that as a church.

BB: Let me cite the brochure which was used against my fellow senator Christine Milne at her election two years ago, authorised by a member of the Exclusive Brethren and printed in a printery in Launceston owned by a member of the Exclusive Brethren. The exact same template was used in the campaign against the Greens in New Zealand. So it's not individual members of the Exclusive Brethren. There's an interconnection going on here which is much more organised than you would have me believe.

DT: Okay, take all that aside, take all that aboard. If you could lay a charge with what you've put into Parliament that it was the Exclusive Brethren, yes. But there's no attachment of the Exclusive Brethren to advertising politically. If Mr Howard suddenly came up with policies that are exactly what you've got, we would do, we would be no question, as far as I am concerned personally, I would do anything to alert people publicly. We want, we pray for government. We pray for the office of the Senate and everyone. Now I feel that Richard could explain it better than me as to our recognition of government.

RG: Yes. I mean I haven't had anything to do with government for nearly 20 years. Labor ministers, Democrats, Liberal. And I have the opportunity to speak to you today. Personally I am very, very concerned with the Greens' policies. The last couple of days I've got nine pages off the internet: the gay and lesbian policy and the support of same-sex marriage. Now I was honestly shocked. That will destroy society. That's against God.

BB: I have to tell you, as you probably know, that I'm gay and I have a same-sex partner and that it's a loving relationship.

DT: But that's against, that's against ... We repel it because it's against God's word!

BB: Well ...

DT: Sorry. It is!

BB: God is love you know.

DT: We don't want to debate it. I'm just saying my reaction to it is when you read Romans 1, I mean it's what happens. People get themselves so perverted and they just can't think morally.

BB: My thinking may have been like that many, many years ago. But I've realised that God has created a very diverse world in which love is a big key and hate is a very big foe. We get ourselves into trouble when we think we can define where love should be cut short.

RG: We've got to discern. We're mixing up love and lust. Now you referred to yourself personally. It certainly wasn't my ... I mean I didn't intend to bring it up at all. You're happy to. I appreciate that. My concern is when policies like that, same-sex marriages, are being put forward as becoming law. Government making provision for same-sex marriages. Now that is completely and utterly wrong. It's against God.

BB: But, you see ...

RG: It's against God!

BB: ... my view is that it is completely and utterly right and it's part of God's creation.

RG: It's not. It's not.

DM: God's judgement comes in on that in Romans 1. God hates that.

(St Paul's bitter and twisted first letter to the Romans in about 50 AD is a broadside against pagans. His self-deifying rant includes this:

> For the wrath of God is revealed from heaven against all ungodliness and wickedness of those men ... God has given them up to shameful lusts; for their women have exchanged the natural use for that which is against nature, and in like manner the men also having abandoned the natural use of the woman, have burned in their lusts one toward another, men with men doing shameless things ... being filled with all iniquity, malice, immorality, avarice, wickedness, being full of envy, murder, contention, deceit, malignity ... those who practise such things are deserving of death.

In his next paragraph this ancient sociopath wrote, without a hint of insight into his own malignity and hypocrisy, that judging others is inexcusable: 'for wherein thou judgest another, thou does condemn thyself'. In a further message, which got to the Romans but apparently didn't make it down to the Exclusive Brethren, Paul added the stricture that 'it is good not to eat meat and not to drink wine'.)

* * *

MAKING SURE CHILDREN will never again see or hear from a parent who leaves the Brethren mind-prison is advocated by the Brethren saints as being good for those children. Having the children believe their parent is evil is better still. Our conversation was getting to an end.

RG: Mr Brown, it's sin that breaks up families. That's what breaks families up.

BB: Is it not a sin to exclude families from seeing each other as the Exclusive Brethren does? You say that sin separates families. But when somebody steps outside the Brethren and is excommunicated, that breach of communication between father and children, father and mother, husband and wife, is of human creation.

DT: The history of fellowship is that something has been violated in the Scriptures. There's various Scriptures we could go over. Corinthians, 1 through 5. There's acts where persons are excommunicated but the intention always is to get them back. And even though they've had to be broken, the immediate intent is to get them restored …. there's been allegations made that Brethren are the only ones that can be saved: that's far from the truth …. when the Lord comes … I just hope you'll be there Mr Brown. But I don't know whether you would.

(St Paul advised the people of Corinth to:

expel the wicked man from your midst … if he is immoral, or covetous, or an idolator, or evil-tongued, or a drunkard, or greedy; with such a one do not even take food.

But giving such advice and living it can be two different things – as with the behaviour of James Taylor Jr, who reigned as the Elect Vessel from 1959. At a meeting of the Brethren in the Scottish city of Aberdeen in 1970, besides getting drunk, Taylor was found in bed with the naked wife of a 'brother'. He was later accused of raping a boy. It was this misfit who, in 1960, had ordered the Brethren to henceforth take St Paul's letter to the Corinthians literally and stop eating with non-Brethren. Taylor's edict forced the anguished separation of many spouses and families who had lived happily together for decades.)

BB: What's your feeling about women and children being locked up for years behind razor wire in the Australian desert by the Howard government? How does that fit with the Scriptures?

RG: Well I don't think we've, I don't think it's got anything to do with the discussion.

BB: Of course it has. Your elders and senior members have been advocates for the Howard government.

RG: Well we support, I personally support good government.

BB: Is that good government?

RG: And I don't, you know … I am very thankful for the current government we have in Australia. I mean, in my lifetime we haven't had a better government economically. Whatever way you look at it, we have an excellent government in Australia.

* * *

RG: We've got nothing to hide. We've got nothing to hide and nothing to parade. This notice of motion [for a Senate inquiry into the Brethren] I find extraordinary. No other Christian groups have been subject to this.

BB: No other Christian group has campaigned like the Exclusive Brethren in recent elections. Nor have I come across a group of any persuasion that's got such a harrowing series of stories about family break-ups.

RG: The Exclusive Brethren involvement you say. I mean we can only say it again, and I can't say it any more: it is individuals. It is not the Exclusive Brethren as a body or church. It is concerned individuals who have taken the initiative. Yes.

BB: I think that's a feint. And I think you know very well, just from talking to you gentlemen today, that there's an embedded disagreement with the policies of the Greens. You'll find disagreement with the policies of the other parties as well.

After some debate about the Brethren's selective disagreement with policies that are 'against Scripture', Richard Garrett offered me three gospel tracts he'd brought along. The tracts reiterated that homosexuals will burn in Hell

Finally the saints zeroed in on my age (61 at the time) to warn me that, as a life span is 70 years, I'd better hurry up and stoop to their dogma or, after God's 'day of vengeance', I will cook for eternity. It brought home to me the reign of mental terror that such embittered bigots have over children unlucky enough to be born into their hateful sect.

'Read those tracts!' Richard Garrett directed as he got up to leave. 'And we're glad of the opportunity to say that to you.' His overbearing injunction echoed the Inquisition in which the terror of Hell worked its worst on so many innocent human beings.

Due to the Liberal and Labor terror of tackling these religious zealots, the Senate inquiry did not go ahead. However, in 2009, with the support of the Labor government and senators Fielding and Xenophon, the Greens succeeding in removing the Exclusive Brethren's legislated right to refuse union entry to their businesses. A large contingent of upset Brethren saints left the Senate gallery after the vote.

That advance was possible because the Elect Vessel's entreaties to God to re-elect John Howard in 2007 had failed so badly that Howard lost his own seat. I cannot help wondering whether that electoral disaster might have been avoided if all the Brethren in Bennelong had voted for Howard, rather than prayed to God for him.

Common sense is the better road to salvation.

27
Afghanistan

AUSTRALIA'S CONSTITUTION is from the 1890s and looks it.

It assumes there will be no female ministers, let alone female prime ministers. It discriminates against First Australians. It bans millions of citizens, including soldiers, pensioners and public servants, from standing for Parliament simply because their income is paid by the state. Perhaps even more troublingly, Sections 62, 63 and 68 of the Constitution together mean that the prime minister decides when Australia should go to war. The Constitution sidelines Parliament.

On 11 September 2001 al-Qaeda terrorists killed 3000 people when they attacked the Twin Towers in New York, and other targets in Pennsylvania and Washington DC. The subsequent invasion of Afghanistan, on 7 October 2001, by the United States, the UK and Australia was justified. Mullah Omar's Taliban regime had been sheltering the al-Qaeda supremo Osama bin Laden in Afghanistan. When both Omar and bin Laden escaped into Pakistan, Afghanistan was free of the Taliban.

Seventeen months later Prime Minister John Howard made a major strategic blunder. Along with UK Prime Minister Tony Blair, he backed US President George W. Bush's attack on Iraq and, in the process, diverted the bulk of the occupying forces from Afghanistan. In this vacuum Mullah Omar launched the Taliban insurgency back into Afghanistan.

Howard gave the order for the Australian Defence Force (ADF) to join the invasion of Iraq on 20 March 2003 and the ADF remained there until 2009, two years after Howard was voted out of office. Three Australians died in Iraq, though not in combat. Many more were traumatised.

As most Australians forget the war, the Iraqis live on in deadly pandemonium. The Iraq Body Count website quotes US General Tommy Franks saying, 'We don't do body counts.' But by IBC's count 200,000 Iraqis have died in the post-invasion violence, and most of them were civilians. Since the withdrawal of foreign forces in 2009 the death toll has continued to mount and nearly 10,000 Iraqis died in the violence in 2013.

Though there had been comparatively little global protest against the invasion of Afghanistan in 2001, the 15 February 2003 global day of protest against the impending invasion of Iraq saw tens of millions of people turn out in cities around the world including an extraordinary three million in Rome. An estimated 200,000 people thronged the streets of both Melbourne and Sydney. Rallies were held in other cities and towns across Australia with, for example, 20,000 people protesting in Newcastle, 5000 in Armidale and 3000 in the coastal town of Bellingen.

Australia's Labor Opposition, like the Greens and Democrats, opposed sending our troops to Iraq but Howard, Bush and the UK's Tony Blair were not to be swayed by the public opposition. They predicated the bombing of Baghdad on the 'fact' that tyrant Saddam Hussein had weapons of mass destruction. Too late they found that he had none.

Iraq's lack of friends and weapons of mass destruction, together with its vast oil reserves, was its undoing. Communist North Korea had a tyrant in charge and it had obvious weapons of mass destruction, but Beijing was its friend and it had no oil. The right-wing trio bombed Baghdad rather than Pyongyang.

At least the US Congress and UK Parliament had a dedicated debate about going to war. In Canberra the Howard government, shepherded by the Constitution, offered none even though there had been a recent precedent.

In 1991 the Australian Democrats, led by Janet Powell, had succeeded in getting the Hawke government to recall Parliament to debate Australia's involvement in the first invasion of Iraq, after Saddam Hussein annexed neighbouring Kuwait.

The 2010 election result – by then Howard had gone and the ADF had come home from Iraq – left Labor needing the Greens to form government. The war in Afghanistan, which would have been over had Iraq not been invaded, was claiming ADF personnel's lives. I secured Julia Gillard's concurrence that, nine years after it began, there would be 'a full parliamentary debate on the war in Afghanistan'.

True to her word, Gillard called on the debate in both houses of Parliament late in 2010. This did not alter Labor's or the Coalition's insistence that Australian servicemen and -women stay in Afghanistan, nor the Greens' insistence that they be brought home. However it put the onus on every Member of Parliament to justify her or his stance on Australia's involvement in the war.

In October 2013, newly elected Prime Minister Tony Abbott confirmed Gillard's earlier announcement of the ADF's withdrawal from Afghanistan at the ADF headquarters in Tarin Kowt. He made the best he could of the mess John Howard had committed Australia to a decade earlier: 'Australia's longest war is ending, not with victory, not with defeat, but with, we hope, an Afghanistan that is better for our presence here.' Most of our troops were home for Christmas.

Forty Australians died in Afghanistan. Another 261 were injured. Hundreds more bear enduring psychological injuries. At last look, most of the projects that had been built under the ADF's $34 million development fund were abandoned or were in the hands of the Taliban or were simply off the radar. In Chora district in 2012 only one of the 32 schools built by the ADF had students attending it.

Some Australians will forget this war that their votes backed. I cannot forget one mother of a young ADF soldier in Afghanistan.

She came up to me at Melbourne Airport in 2011. She told me of her anguish and made a plea for me to justify what he was doing there. I couldn't: opinion polls were showing that more and more Afghanis wanted all foreign troops off their soil. The best I could do was honour her son's devotion to our country.

That mother's agony was the futile result of a prime minister's futile acquiescence to an inept president. She, her son and Australia deserved better. So did the Afghanis who, like the Iraqis, are now left to deal with the bloody post-invasion legacy.

Back in October 2003 President George W. Bush addressed a joint sitting of the two houses of the Australian Parliament, hosted by Prime Minister Howard. He began by referring to his friend John as 'fair dinkum'. Bush inanely explained that this meant 'man of steel'. When the president moved on to justify the war in Iraq I interrupted his speech by suggesting he respect the laws of the world if he wanted the world to respect him and that he should return the two Australians in Guantanamo Bay prison to Australia as he had returned the two American prisoners to the US. There was pandemonium. The Speaker tried to order me out but had no power to do so.

Political, media and public abuse followed this exercise of 'free speech'. One fellow MP threatened to punch my lights out. Several commentators favoured other forms of corporal punishment. Then followed the death threats so favoured by right-wing extremists.

Years later John Howard told an interviewer that he had met Bush overseas before the president's visit to Canberra and had warned him that I might interrupt his speech. This is possible, as Bush's response to the interjection was uncharacteristically good: 'I believe in free speech.'

However, Bush did not risk it again: he refused all further invitations to address foreign parliaments, including those in Ottawa and London.

There should be a rider to the Constitution's prime ministerial prerogative to send Australian citizens to war. That prerogative is required for an instant response in emergencies, for example if Australia is attacked. However it should also trigger the recall of Parliament to debate and, if needs be, alter the prime minister's decision.

Future prime ministers should know that besides advising the governor-general, she or he will need the approval of Parliament for sending Australian citizens to war.

28
Shackled in Mogadishu

In 2009 I had a cup of coffee at the Retro cafe with Jonathan Ledgard, a correspondent for *The Economist* in Africa. He was in Hobart to write a novel and phoned to catch up. He asked me why the Australian photojournalist Nigel Brennan, being held prisoner in Somalia, seemed to be getting no Australian government help. I said I would find out.

After this chance introduction to Nigel's plight and telephone inquiries to Nairobi, I phoned his brother, Ham (Hamilton), who was in Grafton in northern New South Wales. The story unfolded of a determined and loving family doing all they could to rescue their son and brother who had been kidnapped by a Somalian criminal gang, but being frustrated rather than helped by Canberra.

Nigel, 36, had gone to Mogadishu, the capital of the turbulent and failed state of Somalia, with Canadian reporter Amanda Lindhout, 27. They hired escorts to go to the world's biggest refugee camp at Afgooye outside the city, but on 23 August 2008 the party was overwhelmed by violent criminals and Nigel and Amanda were kidnapped. Their capture was followed by a demand for $1.5 million dollars each. The families could not raise such a sum.

The Australian and Canadian governments' unofficial policy was a lid of a single $250,000 payment for 'costs' for both the captives for fear more kidnappings would be encouraged.

The Brennans did all the Department of Foreign Affairs and Trade (DFAT) asked of them but as the months went by they became increasingly alarmed that Nigel would die in captivity. It was vital to keep in touch with him and phone conversations could only be arranged through the criminals. Yet the government took over the Brennans' phone number and let calls from Nigel and his captors go unanswered. For a few months, the government officials broke off all communications with the very risky idea that this might somehow lead the kidnappers to let the captives go.

Nine months after the kidnapping, on 27 May 2009, AFP reporter Mustafa Haji Abdinur in Mogadishu got through to the prisoners by telephone. Their pleas, with their captors standing over them, were distressing.

Amanda told him:

I have been sick for months. Unless my government, the people of Canada, all my family and friends can get one million dollars, I will die here. Okay. That is certain. The situation here is very dire and very serious. I have been a hostage for nine months. The conditions are very bad. I don't drink clean water. I am fed at most once a day. I'm being kept … in a dark, windowless room, completely alone. I love my country and I want to return so I beg my government to come to my aid …

Nigel said:

I've been shackled for the last four months … My health is extremely poor and deteriorating rapidly due to extreme fever. I implore that my government help me as a citizen of Australia … I ask for the help of my family in every way possible so that the ransom can be paid for my release. I love my country very much. I love my family, my girlfriend …

In Canberra a DFAT spokesman said, 'We are doing all we can to help the families and media coverage will not help negotiations.'

The Brennans, who lived near Bundaberg, north of Brisbane, had been warned that a publicity campaign might frighten the criminals into rash action and, if it was known they had raised a big sum of money, the ransom might simply be increased. Their dilemma seemed crushing. Nigel's sister, Nicola, and sister-in-law, Kellie, flew to Vancouver to meet Amanda's parents.

Meanwhile Prime Minister Kevin Rudd made a visit to Bundaberg to open the Hinkler Hall of Aviation. Nigel's mother Heather bravely made an 'unexpected approach' to him and he agreed to talk with her for 20 minutes – but this led nowhere.

Within the rules, the Brennans had done all they could. However they had also discovered an option that sidelined the government: the hire of a private contractor experienced in international kidnappings to negotiate the lowest possible ransom. Thanks to ABC TV's Kristine Taylor they had tracked down John Chase in London. He had helped set a number of kidnapped Britons free. But enough ransom money still had to be found.

While walking in Paul's paddock near the lookout over the ocean one wintry afternoon, I called Heather. She sounded strong but told me how she would sit up at night crocheting and wondering what was happening to her son. I had a yarn with Nigel's affable father, Geoffrey, as well. By now their son had been in captivity for a year and, despite efforts to raise money through barbeques and small community gatherings, the Brennans were not in the big-money league and couldn't see how to get there.

I had been thinking this over while sitting in the Senate and, back home, while helping with the washing-up, put to Paul that I should put in $100,000. We had a sizeable mortgage but, without missing a plate, he agreed. I told the Brennans, who had got together a few hundred thousand dollars themselves. The total was still way short of the mark, so I put my mind to who else might help and, because the victims were a Canadian reporter and Australian photographer taking the courageous risk of shining a light into one of the darkest corners of the world, reckoned that the first place to go would be Australia's media barons.

My initial approach was to the Murdoch empire. I got through to the News Limited CEO in Sydney, John Hartigan, and outlined the case while being clear that there could be no publicity before the Mogadishu pair was released. He was pleasant and not dismissive but made no commitment. A day or two later I rang back and pushed harder. The reaction was swift. 'What do you want me to do, pirouette on a sixpence?' he snapped – and that was that.

I then called James Packer. He was gentler but offered little encouragement. He would talk to Channel Nine's *60 Minutes* program about the case. I had drawn another blank.

Kerry Stokes was in England for the filming of *Robin Hood*, his office said, and my call was never returned.

I was feeling a little of the frustration the Brennans had borne for so long. They had mentioned Dick Smith on a list of people to approach but I held back because he was always the first to be buttonholed simply because he was a great Aussie philanthropist. A good heart is like a dinner bell.

Nevertheless, with the frustration rising, I called him. He listened to the story and said he would talk it over with Pip. Dick and Pip Smith had saved the historic peninsular forest at Tasmania's Recherche Bay in 2006. Now here I was asking him to consider helping out again with a similarly huge sum. I felt bad about it but kept thinking how much tougher things were for Nigel and Amanda.

Dick did some homework and spoke to the Brennans himself. When he found out about Chase he prudently checked him out too – and decided to help out by guaranteeing the ransom payment.

On 3 November 2009 Geoffrey Brennan called me to say that he, Heather and daughter Nicola were headed to Nairobi. They were very excited. I was assured that my $100,000 had been banked.

In Mogadishu there was a frightening hitch when the first attempt to pay the ransom, set at US$600,000, failed. Mercifully the money was not lost.

At 6.50 am on Thursday 26 November 2009, my Parliament House office manager Peter Stahel sent me the SMS: 'Nigel released!!!'

After 460 days in captivity, Nigel and Amanda were on their way home.

As Dick Smith commented in the *Bundaberg NewsMail*:

> After 11 months of the government's failure, in three months the family got them out. Bundaberg should be very proud that you've got such a competent family that could negotiate the release, when the Australian and Canadian governments couldn't.

Nigel and Amanda boarded a light plane and flew to Nairobi where Nigel's parents and sister gave him a teary, hugging welcome. The news went global.

In 2010 I moved for a Senate inquiry into the handling of kidnapped Australian citizens. This exposed senators from across politics to the excruciating dilemma of the Brennans and the loved ones of other Australians (such as John Martinkus and Douglas Wood who were kidnapped in Iraq in 2004 and 2005 respectively) who have experienced the horror of kidnapping.

The major recommendation from the inquiry to the Senate was that

- DFAT ensures that the next of kin of any future kidnap victim are made aware of the option of engaging a private kidnap and ransom consultant; and
- if the next of kin decide to proceed with a private consultant, DFAT ensures that any advice or information it then provides to the family is given in a non-judgemental way; that it is willing to co-operate and to share relevant information …

Straight after receiving Peter Stahel's SMS, I had called Dick and Pip Smith with the good news. They were jubilant too, though Dick declared, in his jocular way, that he might not be picking up any more phone calls from me!

29
Picturing Recherche Bay

RECHERCHE BAY IS as far south as you can drive in Australia. It was named after the *Recherché*, one of Rear Admiral Bruni d'Entrecasteaux's two battered ships (the other was the *Espérance*) that entered the bay and anchored on 24 April 1792.

D'Entrecasteaux's scientific expedition was also searching for the lost French naval hero La Pérouse. It established a tent village inside the north-east peninsula of the bay just four years after the British village of Sydney Town, which also began with tents, had been established in Port Jackson.

Sydney was populated by soldiers, convicts and a few free land– takers as part of the expanding British Empire, and its own expansion provoked inevitable conflict with the Australians already living there.

However, the French settlement at Recherche Bay was made up of scientists and sailors, a few soldiers and no settlers: it was to be temporary and the expedition had clear instructions from Paris to get to know the Indigenous peoples and leave.

On arrival, the botanist Jacques-Julien Labillardière was entranced:

> It is difficult to express the sensations we felt at finding ourselves
> at length sheltered in this solitary harbour at the extremity of
> the globe after having been so long driven to and fro in the

[Indian and Southern] ocean by the violence of the storms …
we were filled with admiration at the sight of these ancient
forests in which the sound of an axe had never been heard.

The camp at Recherche Bay had a bakery, a blacksmith's forge,
a mess hall, a garden, ship repair yards and a scientific observatory
centre. Measurements made at this camp in the southern hemisphere
provided a breakthrough in geomagnetism, which was a boon for the
future of global navigation. And the ships returned to Le Havre laden
with thousands of plant, animal, bird and geological specimens, which
fostered the first book on Australian botany, published in Paris in 1800.

In their rambles across the peninsula, d'Entrecasteaux's men saw
the framed bark homes of the local people who had decamped as the
ships with billowing sails arrived.

Repaired and reprovisioned, the expedition sailed away via
the northern tip of New Zealand and, after circumnavigating the
Australian continent, returned to Recherche Bay on 22 January 1793.

On 8 February the botanists, Labillardière and Félix Delahaye
(who later became Empress Josephine's head gardener back in Paris),
accompanied by two sailors, walked overland to Southport Lagoon.
That night 'the piercing cold we felt soon obliged us to kindle a large
fire'. It was a pitch-black starry night and one of the nervous sailors
heard a stick breaking.

At dawn Labillardière and Delahaye walked towards the lagoon's
southern beach. They heard voices and, peeking through the tea trees,
could see 42 Tasmanians of the Lyluequonny clan on the beach and
fishing in the shallows. The two hurried back to fetch the sailors.
Feeling safer, they returned to the beach to reveal themselves. As
Labillardière wrote in his diary, the sailors put their muskets on the
ground.

We had gone only a few steps before we met them. The men
and youths were ranged in front, nearly in a semi-circle; the

women, children and girls were a few paces distant behind. As their manner did not appear to indicate any hostile design I did not hesitate to go up to the oldest who accepted, with a very good grace, a piece of biscuit I offered him of which he had seen me eat. I then held out my hand to him as a sign of friendship and had the pleasure to perceive that he comprehended my meaning very well; he gave me his, inclining himself a little and raising at the same time the left foot which he carried backward in proportion as he bent his body forward. These motions were accompanied by a pleasing smile.

The French learned that the Lyluequonny knew their every move. A warrior had watched them sleeping in the night. Another insisted on going with Delahaye to the garden Delahaye had planted on the hill overlooking Recherche Bay a year earlier and pointed out which plants were Tasmanian and which – potatoes, cabbages and radishes – belonged to the French. The day ended with the French rowing back to their ship and the Tasmanians walking along the seaside 'looking towards us from time to time and uttering cries of joy'.

On the white sands of the Little Lagoon Beach at the seaward side of the north-east peninsula the French met up with the Lyluequonny repeatedly in subsequent days and enjoyed seafood feasts, interludes of music and an athletics contest. The Tasmanians sang in beautiful harmony: 'Several times two of them sung the same tune at once but always one a third above the other forming a concord with the greatest justness.'

When it came time for d'Entrecasteaux to head home, the Lyluequonny people walked for two days around Recherche Bay to farewell them.

Ten years later the British, fearing the French might beat them to it, sent a settlement party from Sydney to the Derwent River, north of Recherche Bay, to take over Tasmania by force. Within days of their arrival, instead of sharing handshakes and songs, the redcoats lined up as a peaceful horde of Tasmanians came down the hill waving green branches (a universal sign of peace) and massacred them: men, women and children. This was the beginning of a civil war.

I am not so naive as to think that a French settlement of Tasmania would have ended better – it would also have come with military force. Yet the visits of d'Entrecasteaux's ships to Recherche Bay in 1792 and 1793 threw a spotlight on the better side of human nature and our keenness to understand and even celebrate 'others' rather than to repel them, lock them up or simply shoot them down.

In a world pockmarked by battlefields, where cruelty, murder and the intended destruction of others as well as heroism are honoured, Recherche Bay can and should be celebrated as a peacefield.

How many Australians, let alone French or other global citizens, have heard of that remarkable event more than two centuries ago when the foreign visitors mingled with their Australian hosts and then sailed happily away without so much as raising a flag of possession?

There was one moment of violence at Recherche Bay. The French ships had more than 200 men aboard – and one woman. Madame Louise Girardin, a young widow from Brest disguised as a male, had signed on as a steward. Repeatedly taunted for her 'effeminacy' and lack of beard stubble on the long, rough crossing of the Southern Ocean to Tasmania from Cape Town, she challenged her tormentor to a duel. On the beach at Recherche Bay the gallant but untrained Louise was shot in the shoulder. Subsequent medical examination revealed her sex. Louise recovered and fell in love with one of the *Espérance*'s officers. Alas, both died of a tropical fever in Indonesia on their way back to France.

Like most others, I was pig-ignorant of the Recherche Bay saga until, in the years leading up to 2006, the owners of the north-east peninsula applied to log its forest. Though much disturbed since the British takeover, this forest had been the home of the Lyluequonny for millennia. It had been crisscrossed by the French scientific parties in 1792 and 1793.

In 2003 Paul and I were taken for a bush picnic on the Buckland property of sheep graziers Bob Graham and Helen Gee, and I wondered aloud what a boon to saving the peninsula it would be if we could find the French garden of 1792. A couple of weeks later Bob and Helen found the mossy rocks surrounding the garden 70 metres from the shore, exactly as Labillardière had described it 211 years earlier: 'This spot which was well dug for an extent of nine metres by seven had been divided into four sections.'

But in 2005 the bulldozers of logging corporation Gunns began gouging a road across the buttongrass plain near Southport Lagoon in order to log the peninsular forest. Following public protests in Hobart and 1000 people, including local and Aboriginal people, demonstrating on the road near Recherche Bay with flags and banners, a remarkable gift saved the day. Dick and Pip Smith knew Recherche Bay and, after I explained its plight to Dick, he enabled the purchase of the peninsula for $2 million. The Smiths made the vital gift to the Tasmanian Land Conservancy, which had been set up on the model of Bush Heritage Australia to purchase and protect lands of high conservation value in Tasmania.

So, with a stroke of extraordinary philanthropy, the historic Recherche Bay landscape was rescued from disaster. The Tasmanian Government paid for remedial works and compensated Gunns.

While it is easy to idealise the Recherche Bay meetings of the First Tasmanians and their French visitors in 1793 – there were fears and tensions on both sides – that two peoples so unlike and from so far apart on the globe could get together and respect and celebrate each other so wonderfully deserves to be better known. Theirs is a true story offering optimism to the world, which is so often racked by violence over racial, religious, linguistic and other cultural differences and territorial possession.

Battlefields like those at Waterloo, Gettysburg and Gallipoli are depicted and celebrated in our history. So why not equally celebrate the peacefield at Recherche Bay?

The Lyluequonny people farewell d'Entrecasteaux's ships Recherché *and* Espérance, *Recherche Bay, Tasmania 1793* by Ian Hansen

As I began considering retirement in 2011, I wanted to make a gift to Tasmania for returning me to the state and federal parliaments over nearly 30 years. At Cygnet's Lovett Gallery I saw a flyer on the superb maritime paintings of Sydney artist Ian Hansen. He readily agreed to paint the ships *Recherché* and *Espérance* pulling anchor in Recherche Bay to set sail for France.

Ian visited Recherche Bay twice. His oil painting depicts the Lyluequonny people watching the *Recherché* and *Espérance* under sail that sunny morning of 15 February 1793, with the snowy ramparts of Mount La Perouse in the background.

On 14 February 2014, Paul and I, with Ian and his wife, Kaylene, presented the painting to the acting director of the Tasmanian Museum and Art Gallery, Jennifer Storer. First Tasmanians and French representatives spoke at the launch, which was enlivened by period music and a rollicking song about botanist Labillardière by the Recherche Babes.

The Australian National University's emeritus professor John Mulvaney, who was there too, had visited Recherche Bay and helped rescue it. He had recognised the value of keeping its natural face intact:

> The vista for most of the harbour foreshore is little changed from that described with wonderment by the French explorers under d'Entrecasteaux. Given the association of the area with Aboriginal and French contacts in 1792–93 and the scientific experiments undertaken here, this cultural landscape merits World Heritage nomination.

It is hard to picture history without a picture. Let's hope Ian Hansen's beautiful painting will help lift Recherche Bay to its rightful and uplifting place in Australian, French and global history.

30

'I am an environmentalist.'

On 1 December 2009 Tony Abbott beat Malcolm Turnbull by one vote to become leader of the Opposition. Kevin Rudd was prime minister. I wrote this memo after calling, as leader of the Australian Greens, to make Abbott's acquaintance when parliamentary sittings began in 2010.

MEMO.

Monday, 8 February 2010.
Parliament House.

Met with new opposition leader Tony Abbott this afternoon (1) – he had an aide and environment spokesperson Greg Hunt. I took Ben Oquist.

An affable meeting. He began by referring to our public debate in Sydney last year on euthanasia (2) – he thought I was reasonable but Philip Nitschke frightened him!

I gave him *Earth* plus our proposal for extending the Tasmanian Wilderness World Heritage Area (3).

I explained that Greens preferences go 80/20 or 70/30 to Labor, but Labor powerbrokers hate us because we threaten their seats, like Melbourne. However, psephologists say the

Greens will have sole 'balance of power' in the Senate after the next elections (4) and we want to talk with 'both sides' without fear or favour. In Germany the Greens are in Coalition with the Christian Democrats in two states and, while we will always have major differences, we are not pro-Labor or anti-Liberal but are our own party. In fact, we see Labor and Liberal as having most in common with each other. On climate change we rejected Rudd's CPRS bill because it locks in a 5 per cent target (5) for 15 years, so we have put forward our interim proposal for a $20 (in 2005 values, per tonne of carbon dioxide entering the atmosphere) carbon tax and are negotiating with the government in good faith because we are NOT sceptics and are deeply, truly concerned by global warming.

Abbott quickly engaged though, clearly, he has no good knowledge or understanding of the Greens – he remarked that this was the first time we'd ever had a proper conversation.

Hunt raised the fact that Eric Abetz has 'signed on' to Rachel Siewert's bill prohibiting Australian entities from aiding whaling. I recommended we now use our numbers to enforce time in the Senate to pass the bill (6).

I took this opportunity to point out the rapid change in the forest saga in Tasmania, with Gunns (7) jousting with the state government and moving to Forest Stewardship Council certification including dropping charges against the last four 'Gunns 20' defendants. They were surprised.

Abbott: 'I am an environmentalist.' He spoke of the need for human stewardship of the planet.

Hunt later phoned Ben to say Abbott liked the meeting (and us)!

5pm. Coincidentally, Malcolm Turnbull called to thank me for passing on Cornelia Rau's (8) muppet doll to him. She sent two to me – one for him. I told him Cornelia must like him. He is chuffed and asked for her address to send her a 'thank you'. He had just given his highly reported speech declaring he will cross the floor to back the CPRS [Carbon Pollution Reduction Scheme] bill he negotiated as Leader last year with Labor.

1. This was at my request after Tony was elected the Coalition leader.
2. We had been on opposite sides in a public forum, staged by Sydney's St James Ethics Centre on euthanasia. It was recorded by the ABC.
3. *Earth* is my self-published book of 500 words and 40 photos, a homily to the planet. Consultant Geoff Law drew up the World Heritage proposal for me in 2009: it is a booklet with colour photos including the tall forests of Tasmania.
4. These elections were due later in 2010 and the psephologists were correct.
5. This was the low target for reduction in Australia's greenhouse gas emissions: our target was minimum 20 per cent. Our legal advice was that the Rudd formula could not later be lifted without massive taxpayer compensation to the worst polluters.
6. This bill was to prohibit Australian companies assisting the Japanese whaling that had been declared illegal by Australia's Federal Court in 2008. However, when the bill came up for debate in the Senate Abetz overruled Hunt and Abbott or had them change their minds and voted with Labor to reject the bill.
7. The export woodchip corporation that had Liberal and Labor support, but Greens opposition, to building a pulp mill on the Tamar River north of Launceston.
8. Ms Rau had been wrongly detained for some months in Howard government internment centres for refugees.

31
Julia Gillard, PM

CONSIDERING JULIA GILLARD's earlier opinions, we got along very well.

In 2005, long before she became prime minister, Gillard told *Good Weekend* magazine's Fenella Souter:

> Bob Brown is pretty much the most calculating politician in Canberra. He's not an archangel of moral force. He's a bloke who wakes up every day and says: 'How can I chisel a bit of political advantage today' ... I'm not saying he doesn't believe the things he says he believes in ... but he is as hard-nosed and pragmatic ... as any politician you'll ever meet.

In 2008, as she was coming out of Prime Minister Kevin Rudd's office, Julia asked me what I was doing 'to damage the Labor Party today'. And so it went. But in June 2010 Gillard became prime minister and, three months later, she weathered a stormy election campaign in which she had to contend with damaging leaks from her own side, many say from Rudd, as well as barbs from Opposition Leader Tony Abbott and his team.

A few days before the 2010 election, Gillard said:

> while I don't rule out the possibility of legislating a carbon pollution reduction scheme, a market-based mechanism, I

rule out a carbon tax ... while any carbon price would not be triggered until after the 2013 election.

A tough future was in the offing but Gillard had the mettle.

Late on election night 21 August 2010 it became clear that, with 72 seats each, neither she nor Abbott had enough to form government. I was impressed by Gillard's stately grit when she rang me. She told me she wanted to be on the front foot and would like to see me the next day to discuss Labor forming government. She was businesslike but affable. Abbott did not call.

I met the prime minister in Melbourne the next day and she asked me to guarantee supply and the confidence for her government to remain in office. The key to government was the stunning win of the Greens' Adam Bandt in the seat of Melbourne. This was the first time the Australian Greens or any other 'minor' party had won a seat at a national election in at least half a century.

Adam's vote in the House of Representatives was essential. Gillard was aware of his commitment to his electorate that he would not back an Abbott government. She was also aware that, while the record high vote for the Greens meant that our nine senators would hold balance-of-power in the Senate, who we backed as prime minister could well turn that key for the crucial independents in the House – Tony Windsor, Rob Oakeshott and Andrew Wilkie – to open the door to government.

I told Gillard, and made it public, that I would consult the Greens Party Room and that it was my intention to speak with both sides, as I had done after the Tasmanian state elections in 1989.

Tony Abbott did not call me until the following Thursday. We arranged to meet at Parliament House in Canberra on the second Tuesday (31 August) after the election.

Perhaps he thought such a meeting would be a charade – if so, he should not have met me at all. I respected the people's vote and knew how important the process for deciding government would be for Australians. I also knew that Adam Bandt would stick to his commitment. However, a savvy Coalition leader could offer social and environmental outcomes that would not only make backing Labor difficult but would create long-term angst for the Greens if we turned them down. This was his chance and I was determined he should exercise it.

What if Abbott had had the innovative flare to take on a few of our most popular policies: to return Australia's troops from Afghanistan, to protect Tasmania's World Heritage value forests at a time when the export woodchip industry was collapsing, or to offer the guarantee of six months' fully paid parental leave (financed by a new corporate tax) that he was devising anyway? Or he could have gone without Adam Bandt and offered serious incentives to the bush to get the House independents, all of whom were moderate conservatives, on side – he needed only one of the three to block Gillard.

But Tony Abbott lacked the nous to capitalise on the hand he had been dealt by Australia's voters. In Canberra I was ushered through the door by his chief of staff, Peta Credlin, to be greeted by Mr Abbott sitting in his lounge. He had his shoes up on the coffee table.

I sat down opposite him, looking over the soles of his shoes. I assumed this was studied arrogance and that he thought he would be prime minister by Christmas anyway. Whatever the case, I was very relaxed. There was to be no difficult statesmanship or strategy here. It was a poor performance from Abbott, who said that he would talk about anything except a carbon tax in order to get government. But he had no offer and was neither seriously engaged nor up to being seriously engaged. The contrast with meeting John Howard as prime minister (cup of tea, no table in between, simple courtesies) could not have been greater.

The Prime-Minister-Abbott-by-Christmas idea was more than a theory. It would require making the people go back to the polls and the Murdoch media, exasperated by the way Australians had voted, was demanding just that. This would leave no room for the mature, responsible process of negotiating a minority government as practised in countries with more democratic voting systems like Germany, Sweden and Denmark.

Within days of the election, a front-page opinion piece in *The Australian* opened with, 'It's getting to the stage where Julia Gillard, Tony Abbott and the nation would actually be better off if we just went back to the polls.' Actually, it was getting to the stage where it was clear Abbott was not going to win – and Murdoch didn't like it.

Though this was before Rupert Murdoch began tweeting, there is no doubt what the Big Man wanted. Murdoch came out directly in October to admonish the world with 'whatever you do, don't let the bloody Greens mess it up!' His *The Australian* thundered hopefully that 'the Greens must be destroyed at the ballot box'. Abbott took to demanding a new election, with all fingers crossed. But there was no ballot box handy.

The hard right head-bangers were working for a quick disintegration of Gillard's signed agreement with the Greens and independents and a rapid return to the polls. They underestimated my resolve and that of the prime minister and the other signatories that our agreement for government should work.

The next election was three years away.

32

Gillard pre-empts Abbott

AFTER MEETING WITH Julia Gillard and Tony Abbott in the wake of the 2010 election (in Abbott's case, nearly a week after the election), and after I had time to consult my colleagues, I wrote the following memos. My chief of staff, Ben Oquist, stayed in contact with Gillard's staff as we moved towards a solid contract for her to form government.

I was keenly aware that commitments from minority governments must be worked out at the outset and that such commitments must all be on the public record to help guarantee that they are kept. Gillard proved faithful to her commitments.

MEMO.

Monday, 30 August 2010.
Parliament House.

(The federal election was on Saturday 21 August 2010.)

Had dinner with Julia Gillard 7.30–8.45: takeaway Chinese (out of plastic bowls) and a glass of red.

A very good get-together: just us two and a general post-election discourse, discussion of the nastiness of the Murdoch press (1), in particular *The Australian* and *The Telegraph*, and a run through our evolving agreement.

This agreement will be as good as can be without frightening the horses of the good country independents: so no gay marriage clause for example. However I put it to the PM that such be reviewed (she had raised this option before) at the next ALP national conference (end of '11 or early '12) with the aim of getting a conscience vote. This will fit with the lobby groups – and I talked it over with Rodney Croome in Salamanca (2) last Saturday – getting time to raise a public campaign.

We will get a commission to work towards a carbon price and (in a phone conversation today 31st, afternoon (3), she committed to establishment and report by March 2011, legislation in spring '11 and then implementation by July 2012) (4).

Truth in political advertising.

Referenda recognising Indigenous Australians and local government (in the constitution).

Progress in dental health care.

And all the rest to be thrashed out.

I explained that my aim is to see the next three years of the Gillard Government be one of the most productive in Australian history.

MEMO.

Tuesday, 31 August 2010.
Parliament House.

6 pm. Called Julia after meeting Tony Abbott, 5 pm, Room RG 109 (5).

This last was a jangling yet satisfactory affair. His feet up on the coffee table, soles towards us (6).

He made a good pitch – 'I can negotiate ANYTHING (except a carbon price)' – to get us closer. But I was direct in saying I thought we'd have an accommodation with Labor by tomorrow. He said, 'You know I will come out and attack you!'

I diverted to the need, if he becomes PM, for us to meet to get the best out of the Senate rather than obstruction. He came right back to try to discover what we are agreeing on (a carbon price, specially, as he wants to attack this) – but got nowhere. I told him those discussions were confidential.

He thinks [Andrew] Wilkie is still available.

I told him I had no idea, and I don't, of what any of the independents will do.

He looks a bit troubled and it turns out Wilkie is likely to sign up (7) on the Royal Hobart Hospital and pokies tomorrow.

Had a good [Greens] Party Room: six including Adam [Bandt], at 3 pm, and Party Convenor Derek [Schild].

Will go to La Scala (8) now for dinner with fellow Greens.

Julia was thankful at our suggestion we transfer some of the parliamentary reforms to the bailiwick of the independents so they'll have a good package to announce (9). RJB.

1. I raised this issue.
2. At the Retro Cafe, Salamanca Place, Hobart.
3. The memo about the 30th was written on the 31st.
4. The idea of a cross-party commission was put to me by Christine Milne and I was pleasantly surprised when Gillard, independently, had come up with the same proposal.
5. Gillard arranged to meet me first on 22 August, the day after the election. Abbott saw me more than a week later. Whatever he thought about his chances, this was poor strategy.
6. My Chief of Staff Ben Oquist was with me.
7. Gillard had got to all the key independents way ahead of Abbott.
8. An Italian restaurant in Civic, Canberra.
9. For example, in the House of Representatives, the recommittal of votes when a member inadvertently fails to get to the chamber in time, retaining the 'acknowledgement of First Australians and country' at the start of each session, and dedicated time for private members' bills to be debated. Other Greens' ideas included the establishment of a Leaders' Debate commission to review pre-election leaders' debates, the Parliamentary Budget Office to independently cost policies and election promises and the Parliamentary Integrity Commissioner to advise MPs on the use of their entitlements.

33
Agreeing to government

AFTER THE 2010 election the Australian Greens Party Room unanimously backed an agreement supporting Julia Gillard's Labor team for government. Christine Milne had played a pivotal role in formulating the key outcome of this agreement, which was the establishment of a cabinet sub-committee to tackle global warming. The Climate Change Committee was to develop a carbon trading scheme for Australia and to boost Australia's job-rich renewable energy sector in a package paid for by the polluters. In 2014 Abbott, as prime minister, moved to replace this scheme with one in which the polluters are paid by the taxpayers to reduce their carbon discharge into the atmosphere.

As the vital day of reaching agreement unfolded, I took a few minutes to jot down some very sketchy notes.

MEMO.

Wednesday, 8 September 2010.
Parliament House.

Had light breakfast with PM Julia. She is quite remarkable. While obviously tired, her enthusiasm and optimism are real. Real zeal. A premium quality in such demanding circumstances.

I called her two days ago to seek this meeting. Yesterday Katter went Coalition, Oakeshott and Windsor Labor. So it's 76–74!

Breakfast 7.45–8.30 after I'd done Radio National Breakfast (1) and an early cup of coffee with Erin and Prue at Aussie's (2).

Julia and I discussed:

1. Carbon price committee: Garnaut (3) is agreed. We (she first) will seek approach to Malcolm Turnbull. I will think of other participants and Christine is to talk with [Greg] Combet after he becomes minister (tomorrow). I will pursue Adam [Bandt] being on it. Businessperson? Scientist?

2. Referenda. I pursued Indigenous recognition. JG had great idea of involving John Howard – I agree! I will stay closely involved and with Rachel [Siewert].

3. High Speed Rail: I will talk with Albanese: this is a good, positive option and the Opposition has come on side: I will foster.

4. Forests. A thorny one. [Tony] Burke will remain minister. I will seek, now, serious engagement to get Tasmanian outcome. I suggested we get Geoff Gallop (4) involved and JG agrees.

5. Minister for Environment. Peter [Garrett] has had a hard time of it. Suggested 'a Richo' – not necessarily green but necessarily influential and prepared to engage positively with the constituency.

6. Nationals. Assured JG we will take them on in the Senate.

7. Broadband. A winner. I suggested the two country independents be involved in 'roll-out' of this great project. A good morning so far.

Our first Party Room for TEN (Green MPs) is next and I'm looking forward to it!

Today's SMSs after Gillard government established:

Me to JG: 'Congratulations! Bob Brown.'
JG to me: 'and thank you to you and your fellow Greens.'

Me to TA: 'Commiserations. I look forward to discussing the future.'

No reply.

We had an excellent Party Room [meeting] and following press conference.

I'm looking forward to getting home late tonight and (interviews notwithstanding) going round the lambs with Paul in the morning. RJB.

---

1. With host Fran Kelly.
2. My advisers Erin Farley and Prue Cameron, at the Parliament House coffee shop.
3. This was Australian economist and global warming expert Professor Ross Garnaut. The committee, with the status of a cabinet sub-committee, was to be known as the 'Climate Change Committee'.
4. The Labor premier who implemented the trailblazing Western Australian forest agreement. However the government opted for former ACTU head Bill Kelty to take this post.

34

Guardian of Walmadan

THE WORLD HAS a regular turnover of strongarm political leaders who wreak havoc on human and natural heritage for 'progress' in their own time. Cortés, Henry VIII, Mao Zedong, Queensland's Joh Bjelke-Petersen, Tasmania's 'Electric' Eric Reece and, now, Western Australia's premier, Colin Barnett: different in other respects as they are, they have all shown indifference to priceless heritage assets. The former three were recklessly free of the fetters of democracy. The latter three didn't get it all their own way.

Premier Barnett echoed Tasmania's pillaging premier (the 'whispering bulldozer') Robin Gray's 1982 description of the World Heritage Franklin River as 'a brown, leech-ridden ditch' with his 2009 description of the Walmadan (James Price Point) beach area of the Kimberley as 'unremarkable'. He was dead set on imposing Woodside Petroleum's massive gas hub, to process gas from 400 kilometres out to sea, on Walmadan. This proposed hub would comprise the world's largest gas factory, a port with 2.5 kilometres of breakwater, and jetty requiring a trench 5 kilometres long and 300 metres wide dredged from the shore, through corals and seagrass meadows, to accommodate up to 14 pipelines as well as thousands of tanker ships coming to export the gas each year. The millions of tonnes of dredge spoil would be dumped further out to sea.

Here's a short list of the 'unremarkable' items in the Walmadan precinct that were threatened by Woodside's planned industrial complex straddling the shore: the world's largest dinosaur footprints and tracks from more than a dozen species of dinosaurs; the living Songlines (oral history) of the Goolarabooloo people with a history stretching back into the Dreamtime; their stone tool workshop, women's birthing place and sand-dune burial sites; the largest humpback whale nursery on Earth; the stunning blood-red pindan coastal cliffs; rare monsoon vine thickets and tropical bats in the dunes; dugongs, flatback turtles and five species of dolphins offshore; and an unexpected colony of bilbies right where the factory was due to go.

In this age of rampant Materialism, these items have a problem: they are priceless. On the other hand, the gas hub was to initially cost $30 billion (this blew out to an estimated $80 billion) and the processed gas had a predicted sale price of $200 billion. So that's zero dollars against many, many billions. You can see why Barnett was eager. His enthusiasm was infectious; by early 2010 Woodside was declaring a 95 per cent chance that the James Price Point (Walmadan) development would proceed.

However, most of the 15,000 people of the resort town of Broome, set to be the centre for this 'gas boom', did not want their relaxed and visitor-friendly lifestyle overrun by a massive industrial juggernaut. There were three other factors Barnett did not count upon: the Goolarabooloo resistance, the national outrage and the concern of Woodside's venture partners, Shell, Chevron and BHP Billiton, for their reputation.

Barnett also underestimated the stocky Goolarabooloo elder Joe Roe, grandson of the famous patriarch of Walmadan, Paddy Roe. Joe Roe spurned the $1.4 billion (less than 1 per cent of the gas sales income) offered by Woodside over 30 years, though this was accepted by the Kimberley Land Council to develop Indigenous services. He courted influential visitors like former Federal Court chief justice Murray Wilcox and former economic adviser to Prime Minister John Howard, Geoffrey Cousins, both from Sydney. Local and national environmental groups helped spread the word and Australian musicians like John Butler, Missy Higgins and Xavier Rudd drew crowds to 'Save the Kimberley' gatherings around the nation, including 5000 in Melbourne and 20,000 in Perth.

Defiantly, Joe Roe argued that the state and federal governments should pay for better health, education and other services and business opportunities for Aboriginal people – they should not have to depend on gas royalties. 'Do we have to kill our country for what is the birthright of all Australians?' he argued. 'It's wrong, very wrong.'

In Canberra in 2010 Western Australian Greens Senator Rachel Siewert introduced me to Walmadan 'law bosses', including Joe Roe, who asked me to visit the Kimberley after both Wilcox and Cousins had told me about the plight of Walmadan. So I flew up to Broome. This is my memo from Sunday 16 October 2010:

> On Tuesday I flew with Alison Hetherington to Perth and Broome where we caught up with Rachel [Siewert] and Scott Ludlam and Environs Kimberley (EK) campaigner Emma Belfield (who has been in Tasmania and organised my 2007 election campaign) and EK Director Martin Pritchard, a delightful Welshman-Australian and encyclopedia of things Kimberley. We had dinner with EK members at a local pub.
>
> On Wednesday morning we drove 60 kilometres north to Price Point. Nearly there, we were met by three happy local botanists for a quick introduction to the monsoon vine thicket, a rare ecological community and rainforest remnant upon which the gas hub will be plonked. We were to return.
>
> Hot. Cloudy. The red road a little wet after yesterday's downpour. But, mercifully, no mosquitos or gnats.
>
> We soon arrived at Price Point (I apologise for not having the Aboriginal name here and intend to school myself in it)

to be met by Neilo (Neil McKenzie), Joseph (Joe) Roe and a photographer, and a TV camera (for WIN and ABC). Another photographer and *Sydney Morning Herald* journalist Paul McGeough soon arrived too.

In the following two hours I struck up a sudden and embracing friendship with Joe.

I first met Joe, with Neilo and Albert (a younger and very impressive man) when they came to Canberra some weeks ago, met me with Rachel, and asked me to join them in speaking on stage before a John Butler concert at the Canberra Convention Centre – and I committed to coming up.

Joe showed me some dinosaur footprints on the seashore rock faces, and we could see two drilling rigs (and two service boats) offshore just south – testing the rock for the soon-to-be 5 or 7 kilometres dredged channel to facilitate thousands of ships to the gas hub each year: largely to take the liquid natural gas to the world for Woodside (and Shell, BHP Billiton, Chevron). Premier Barnett is compulsorily acquiring Price Point.

The point is stunning deep-red pindan. Neilo pointed out the pink around yellow sandy holes in the sub-tidal beach zone where fresh water is exuded via the sub-beach-dwelling molluscs' holes after the tide leaves. A huge centipede was climbing up the native morning glory that was festooning the red cliff face. A sea eagle floated over us, south to north. Frigate birds. Crabs. Rockpool fish.

But towering above the scene of living beauty facing Woodside's transmogrification are its Songlines – the Aboriginal connectedness: ancient, vibrant, globally significant for modern *Homo sapiens* and, with a gas hub, doomed.

Here, with Joe Roe, I was sturdily introduced to the men's oral history and being with Earth – timeless attachment ignorantly smashed in most places south, including Tasmania.

We drove a little south and stopped at another watering place – no water now as there's been no recent digging to keep the hole patent – and then past vandalised bollards where vandals have driven over eternal Aboriginal rights, and the bollards, to conquer the beach. A tiny incursion, strewn with beer cans, to notify the World's Biggest Gas Processing Factory is now on its way courtesy of the Western Australian premier, Woodside and, unless we make it otherwise, the community of modern Australia.

Over the dune crest, some hundreds of metres ploughing our boots (Joe in red shirt and thongs) through soft white sand, we knelt on a westerly face of a vegetation-topped dune where a dry and friable bone, a fragment of a clavicle or pelvis I think, lay out on the sun-warmed surface slope.

This is a fragment of the 'old man we buried here'. Joe had me, with him, dig our fingers into the sand and have our hands go beyond wrist-deep to touch other bones of the old man. He was laid here, west–east, in line with the waterhole, half of him in adjacent clan's country. Our 12 or so companions watched. No photographs or film.

On/in yonder dunes are two women, including the old man's wife. The gas hub will extrude or crush her too.

There are disputes in the community about legitimacy. In this extraordinary act of bestowing of honour but also deep human appeal, Joe dispatched that dispute. We walked back together after our eyes met in mutual recognition of both the past human universe of this place, the present unforgivably arrogant notice of trespass and our immediate, coming struggle to keep the gas hub out.

As we neared the cars we talked circumcision: mine before memory and for no good reason; his the initiation rite conveying to a next generation the key to the world a thousand before have inhabited – the opening of the door to life.

Joe told me he doesn't watch TV. We talked about knowing country. He is a PhD with no limit: I, as a boy from the bush (luckily), have a primary school education in the planet. Take it from the child and they'll never have it.

I was riveted by this man's stories. I can no longer look at the stars ablaze at night without seeing among them the Emu Man (his head is the 'coal sack' next to the Southern Cross) who came down and formed Earth and whose three-toed tracks along the Walmadan shore are attributed to dinosaurs in our own culture.

That evening, at a packed public meeting in Broome, I joined in the commitment to the campaign to save Walmadan. I flew east determined to add my voice to those of Western Australian Greens senators Rachel Siewert and Scott Ludlam in the national parliament.

The more people who experienced Walmadan the more would go out of their way to fight for it. This had to become a national campaign because, as the Franklin River dam only was prevented after it became an issue north of Bass Strait, so the Kimberley Coast would be saved from this gas factory and port only if it became an issue east of the Nullarbor Plain.

I put the alternatives to Prime Minister Gillard and, with adviser Alison Hetherington, had a long and straight-talking meeting with Minister for Resources and Energy Martin Ferguson. He told us that moving the gas hub from Walmadan was 'not on'.

I visited Walmadan again and caught up with Joe and his brother Phillip and Richard Hunter before retiring from the Senate in June 2012. In August I flew back to lead Sea Shepherd Australia's 'Operation Kimberley Minimbi' to the Walmadan coast for the humpback whale calving season. SSA's Jeff Hansen had suggested this at a public meeting in Perth and Sea Shepherd's founder, Paul Watson, then detained in Germany, enthusiastically agreed. SSA's *Steve Irwin* headed from Melbourne, via Papua New Guinea, to the Kimberley.

Joe Roe and the Goolarabooloo had formalised an invitation to their 'sea country' and *Steve Irwin* arrived with a flourish, showing hundreds of people, including journalists, the nursing whales and calves off the long, red coastline north of Broome. This put the lie to the contention of factory proponents, including Western Australian government environmental experts, that the whales would not be significantly affected by the factory and port. With volunteer on-shore scientists also counting thousands of whales moving in and through the proposed port precinct, it was bleedingly obvious that the Woodside project would cut the whale nursery in half.

Meanwhile there had been hundreds of people – including two very determined older women – arrested for blocking Woodside's way to Walmadan. The giant corporation was said to have spent $1 billion proving-up the site and on preliminary works that involved a bevy of private security guards to complement the planeful of police that Premier Barnett had sent up from Perth.

The chair of Woodside's board, Michael Chaney, agreed to see me but when he read that I was to lead Sea Shepherd Australia's 'Operation Kimberley Minimbi' he churlishly wrote to say he wouldn't after all. Speculation was rising that, despite the gas factory having the support of the Gillard government and its environment minister, Tony Burke, its major partner in the venture, Shell Australia, had dug in its heels in favour of processing the gas from a floating platform at its source, 400 kilometres out to sea.

This was crucial. There is nothing more inimical to a destructive project than a better option, especially if that option is cost-competitive and carries less cultural and environmental risk.

In Perth, Premier Barnett proceeded to compulsorily acquire the Aborigines' Walmadan and, in Canberra, Tony Burke excluded it from the Western Kimberley area that he listed on the Register of the National Estate.

Even so, Woodside finally gave way to the growing local, national and international opposition. On 12 April 2013 it withdrew from Walmadan.

Aged just 47, the hero of this story, the warrior of Walmadan, died of a heart attack less than a year later. He had lived to see his homeland saved and his spirit for Earth prevail. Along with his Goolarabooloo successors, and the Kimberley environmentalists, those of us who were enfolded by that spirit will continue his watch as the guardians of Walmadan.

35

Ambush in the Senate

ACCORDING TO THE Roman historian Suetonius, the emperor
Caligula:

> invited King Ptolemy to visit Rome, welcomed him with
> appropriate honours, and then suddenly ordered his execution
> because, at Ptolemy's entrance into the amphitheatre during
> a gladiatorial show, the fine purple cloak he wore attracted
> universal admiration.

Enmity is a killer, whether it is fired up by purple or green.

Eric Abetz has headed up Tony Abbott's Coalition in the Senate
since 2010, and he harbours more than a little enmity towards the
Greens.

So, when President of the Senate John Hogg (Labor) rose to his
feet at 24 minutes to four, just after Abetz had entered the almost
empty chamber one sunny afternoon in spring 2011, I sensed enmity
in the air.

A tipped-off Murdoch journalist hurried into the gallery
to perch like a vulture above the rail. President Hogg never did
explain how this journalist had been told about his decision while
I had not.

Here is Hansard's record of President Hogg's announcement:

The PRESIDENT (15.36): …. The matter concerns a possible relationship between Senator Bob Brown and Mr Graham [sic] Wood and whether, on the one hand, Senator Brown sought a benefit from Mr Wood in the form of political donations on the understanding that he would act in Mr Wood's interests in the Senate or, on the other hand, whether Mr Wood, through large political donations, improperly influenced Senator Brown and other Australian Greens senators, including Senator Milne, in the discharge of their duties as senators, including by the asking of questions without notice.

The president finished his speech with an invitation for Eric Abetz's colleague, Senator Helen Kroger, who had raised the issue, to move that the matter be referred to the Committee of Privileges and Members' Interests.

Eric Abetz is, like Christine Milne and me, from Tasmania. That's where the likeness ends. The humanitarian founder of the website Wotif, Graeme Wood, had raised Abetz's hackles when he donated $1.6 million to the Australian Greens for the 2010 federal election campaign. In that election Adam Bandt won the House of Representatives seat of Melbourne and new Greens senators were elected in South Australia (Sarah Hanson-Young), Queensland (Larissa Waters), New South Wales (Lee Rhiannon) and Victoria (Richard Di Natale).

A year later, Wood and fellow philanthropist Jan Cameron purchased Tasmania's oldest export woodchip mill at Triabunna on the island's scenic east coast. Woodchips from the logging of native forests had been shipped to Japan's paper mills since the Triabunna operation began in 1971. The new owners of the mill announced that it would never again be used to smash up trees from the world's tallest flowering forests, which grew in Tasmania's interior.

There had been a powerful campaign to have the state government back the loggers' bid, using millions of dollars of taxpayers' money, for the Triabunna mill. That bid fell through.

The 'crime' Abetz and Kroger wanted the powerful Privileges Committee to investigate was their invented contention that Christine and I had accepted Graeme Wood's 2010 donation to the Greens on the condition that we support his purchase of the woodchip mill.

But the mill, owned by the notorious logging company Gunns, had not been for sale in 2010.

When the mill did come up for sale in 2011, we backed leaving the sale to the open market. Graeme Wood never flagged his bid with Christine or me.

Abetz supported government largesse for the loggers. As Minister for Fisheries, Forestry and Conservation under Prime Minister John Howard in 2004, Abetz had doled out hundreds of millions of dollars of taxpayers' money in an effort to prop up Tasmania's job-losing logging industry.

Never before had senators been referred to the Privileges Committee under the provisions of the *Parliamentary Privileges Act 1987*. The committee was made up of seven senators, only one of whom (Scott Ludlam from Western Australia) was a Green.

Christine Milne and I took the matter seriously. If convicted we could be sent to prison. We declared that we would take the matter to the High Court if the committee were to find us guilty. We were signalling that the committee's job was legal, not political. Also at stake was the reputation of Graeme Wood, who had more regard for proper process and decency than a brace of parliamentary presiding officers.

We engaged a fine legal team. Hobart solicitor Roland Browne instructed Melbourne barrister and former Federal Court judge Ron Merkel QC assisted by Frances Gordon.

Meanwhile Rupert Murdoch's flagship newspaper, *The Australian*, ran the story about the Abetz-backed putsch on the Greens in the

Senate without mentioning Abetz. Its headline was 'Bob Brown faces privileges committee inquiry over Wotif donor'. I was reminded of Oscar Wilde's observation: 'In olden days they had the rack but nowadays they have the press!'

In very olden days they had more than the rack. In Rome, Suetonius reports that Caligula,

> being anxious that one particular senator should be torn to pieces, persuaded some of his colleagues to challenge him as a public enemy when he entered the House, stab him with their pens, and then hand him over for lynching to the rest of the senate; and was not satisfied till the victim's limbs, organs and guts had been dragged through the streets and heaped up at his feet.

In Canberra, senators are not enticed to (literally) stab each other with their pens. But the Privileges Committee meets in secret. They took in our legal submission, never letting us appear before them.

After the ambush I wrote to President Hogg pointing out the absurdity of his judgement. He did not foresee that the Privileges Committee, no matter what the accusatory Eric Abetz thought, would have to throw the accusations out.

I may as well have written to the trolley boy. President Hogg had acted without consulting us and was not about to listen now. Hogg would stick with his mistake until, months later, Mr Merkel's written advice to the Privileges Committee demolished the Coalition's proposition.

A member of the Privileges Committee was Queensland senator George Brandis who, these days, is the nation's attorney-general. In the Senate he sat next to Eric Abetz. Well before the Hogg decision, Brandis had made a similar accusation in the Senate to that of the Kroger motion. He had pre-judged the matter. Nevertheless he did not recuse himself from the committee until early 2012, and only after a letter pointing out this legal indiscretion had been dispatched to the committee, indicating our willingness to have the issue of Senator Brandis's participation decided by the High Court if necessary.

On 19 March 2012, the committee reported to the Senate that it had found 'no evidence' to back the accusation and concluded that 'no question of contempt arises with respect to the matter referred'. The committee recommended that:

> in the future it would be appropriate, where the President makes a statement in relation to a matter of privilege which names or appears to involve senators, for the President to inform those senators that such a statement will be made.

Sometimes common sense has to be codified.

Unlike in Caligula's time, in modern Australia political assassination is illegal and senators don't even consider it, I presume. But hard feelings are not so easily proscribed.

'How do you put up with it?' a friend asked me when I told her about the ambush in the Senate and that Christine and I were left with a bill of $70,000 while senators Abetz, Brandis and Kroger didn't spend a cent.

'Worse things have happened,' I told her, recalling Suetonius's stories. Unlike the one in Rome, the Australian Senate has excellent standing orders to eventually protect senators from seething enmity, bumbling presidents and pen stabbings.

And while Eric Abetz might not like it, I'd rather be innocent and $70,000 out of pocket at the hands of President Hogg than have been innocent and had my entrails dumped at the feet of Emperor Caligula.

36
Ambush in the Great Hall

It is a good thing to be mindful of older people whose bones ache if they are left standing. So on 21 October 2012, when a slightly stooped elderly lady in a blue dress came slowly my way in a huge crowd, I looked about for a chair.

There was none. The throng got thicker and I was being pushed sideways from where I stood. The old lady was in danger of being swept right off her feet and left with broken bones on the floor.

As she got closer, people near me started to elbow each other. The crowd surged forward and, seeing her plight, I said to Paul, 'Oh, no! I wish we hadn't come.'

But we couldn't leave. By arrangement, Her Majesty Queen Elizabeth II, Queen of Australia, was coming over to see us. Burly security men were painstakingly clearing her way through the throng.

Months earlier, at one of our weekly meetings, Prime Minister Julia Gillard had told me that the Queen of England, Australia's non-Australian head of state (my description, not the PM's) was to spend a few days in Australia. As the leader of the Australian Greens, I asked Julia to place me in the official welcoming party at Parliament House along with the leader of Her Majesty's Opposition, Tony Abbott. This request was turned down. Instead, it was arranged for me to meet the Queen when the welcoming ceremony was over. Oh well!

I was to stand near the front of the Great Hall, on the right-hand side, and wait until HM was brought over. So there waited Paul and I as she came down off the dais and very slowly approached us. Neither the magnificent trumpet fanfare nor the welcoming speeches matched the sheer beauty of Geoffrey Gurrumul Yunupingu's song for HM during the dais procedures.

After a series of ambushes from the crowd, the little lady in blue, with her coiffure of white wavy hair, arrived before me … I mean, I stood before her. We began to chat. I told her that I led the Australian Greens and was a senator from Tasmania, where her 1964 walk on Wineglass Bay beach (after being boated ashore from the Royal Yacht *Britannia*) is a legend.

A man behind me was shouting but, above the din, the Queen responded cheerily that she was unable to make it to Tasmania this trip as she didn't have the yacht with her.

The shouter got louder. A backward glance revealed him to be one of Tony Abbott's most senior senators. 'He's a republican! He's a republican! He's a republican!' the man was yelling, as if to alert HM to some terrible disease. The greatest threat to her royal personage was his assault on her eardrums.

I repressed my disgust at this oaf's behaviour and HM didn't turn a hair. After a couple of minutes and a parting exchange of smiles, she was moved along to the next bout of small talk. The shouting stopped and I was overtaken by a wave of sympathy for this intelligent and lively octogenarian who is uniquely imprisoned by tradition, the hazards of milling crowds, and silly monarchists.

Sadly, one crucial bit of the tradition has gone: there was no throne. Not even a chair. There was only the imaginary throne usurped by a shouting monarchist who thought he was back in the chamber shouting at the Greens: instead we were in the Great Hall of Parliament House and he was abusing her, in the real sense of that word.

If this is the lot of the Queen of Australia, approaching 90 years of age, what hope is there of preventing elder abuse in the hoi polloi?

When Australia becomes a republic there will be no more trips for HM to the other side of the planet to put up with unruly Aussie dignitaries. I'm all in favour of that – and our exchange of smiles left me thinking HM wouldn't mind either!

37
Little strangers

One wintry afternoon in Canberra the Senate debated a Greens bill to ban junk food advertising in children's television viewing hours.

The bill was backed by a powerful line-up of doctors and other child health experts, but opposed by the fast food corporations. It was about to be voted down by Labor and the Coalition.

The Senate president, Labor's John Hogg, was also about to show how children were to be tolerated in the chamber.

Previously members of Parliament such as Mark Latham, Jackie Kelly, Anna Burke, Natasha Stott Despoja, Jacinta Collins, Winston Crane and Sarah Hanson-Young had brought one, two or three children to sit briefly with them while debates proceeded. On each occasion the mood of the chambers had been lifted by the appearance of the little 'strangers in the house'.

Here is the Hansard record of proceedings from that Thursday 18 June 2009. I was concluding the debate.

Senator **BOB BROWN** – How can we allow millions of children every day to be exposed to junk food purveyors pushing food at these children which injures their health ... to increase profit lines against the interests of the health of children? This bill is all about the public interest and it should be supported.

The vote was about to be taken. The division bells rang, and Senator Hanson-Young, who had her two-year-old daughter, Kora, with her outside the Senate chamber, brought the child in while the count took place.

> **The PRESIDENT** – Senator Hanson-Young, you will have to take the child outside for a division. We cannot allow children to be in here for a division.
>
> **Senator BOB BROWN** – I request that you provide a childminder for the division so that Senator Hanson-Young has somebody to provide the care that you insist she gets. Senator Hanson-Young, I want you to stay here.
>
> **The PRESIDENT** – I think the action is being taken. Someone is going to mind the child.
>
> **Senator BOB BROWN** – I object. President, there is no such rule as the one you have just employed. Although it is in the form of a request, I ask you to come back to this chamber on this ruling that I object to, and object to in the strongest terms.

Hansard then records the voting senators' names. There were five 'ayes', from the five Greens. There were 43 'noes' from the other parties' benches. Twenty-eight senators from other parties and independent Senator Xenophon did not vote. So the bill was voted down. I then moved dissent from President Hogg's ruling that Senator Hanson-Young's daughter be evicted and that the issue be brought back to the Senate when it next sat:

> **Senator BOB BROWN** – Mr President, I ask that the matter be put on the Notice Paper for debate at the next day of sitting.
>
> **Senator BOYCE** – I would like to support Senator Brown's call. Children have come into this chamber in the past, and it is a situation that needs to be debated so that people have a sense of what they can do and what they cannot do.

Senator FIELDING — Mr President, very quickly on the same point: I have the utmost respect for your position and the role but I also support Senator Brown. There could have been a better handling of that.

President Hogg agreed that debate be adjourned until the following Monday. However his order to evict the child had led the Senate from peace to pandemonium. Kora went from happily sitting beside her mother to a bewildered and screaming child as she was evicted. Greens Whip's Clerk Emma Bull, watching events unfold on in-house television, rushed to the Senate to take Kora in her arms before the doors were locked. With this sudden separation, both mother and child were in tears.

As Senator Hanson-Young explained to the Senate on the next day of sitting:

> When we are in Canberra, [my daughter] Kora comes into Parliament House where the nanny cares for her ... I had taken my daughter, Kora for a quick walk around the building to say goodbye to her before she left with the nanny back to Adelaide to spend the next few days with her father. They were leaving at 4.55 pm. This goodbye ritual is something the two of us do every Thursday before she flies back to Adelaide ... The bells started ringing during this time and I realised I would not be able to drop Kora back upstairs to my office ...
>
> Knowing that the vote would only take a few minutes and I was about to not see Kora for a day or so, I simply brought her onto the chamber floor to sit quietly next to me while my vote was counted ...
>
> I am not arguing ... that children ... should be present during the normal proceedings of parliament. I do not believe it is appropriate for the Senate to become a crèche — far from it. I have never suggested that we all bring our kids into the

chamber for debates, or while we give speeches, or during question time. But on rare occasions … surely allowing a little flexibility to a small child who is caught spending a few short minutes with their mum or their dad when the only thing the parent needs to do is sit on the right side of the chamber and be counted is not such a bad thing.

Well, yes it was. Outside the Senate the Mother Grundys went into conniptions! The radio shock-jocks' phones were running hot.

National Party Senate Leader Barnaby Joyce proclaimed on the national airwaves that it was a Green stunt! Never mind that he had been absent from the Senate for the debate, the division and the vote and missed the whole event because 'it was a motion about junk food that we knew did not have legs and I had an interview at the time with some people'.

Joyce was coat-tailing on the usual right-wing smashers, the new political correctness brigade, who know they are right without having to think about it. They were appearing from under every rock. Here's Wendy Hargreaves in Murdoch's *Sunday Herald Sun*: 'this week's wah-wah effort by Greens senator Sarah Hanson-Young takes political mewling to an all-time low'. She goes on: 'I've been through the trauma of hearing my children cry as I leave for work … It's the ultimate bad mummy guilt.' With seamlessly selfish illogic, she concludes: 'so why should this politician – an employee of the people – be able to carry her young child into the Australian Senate for a voting session?'

Over at Murdoch's *The Australian*, David Penberthy raged with enmity: 'Sarah Hanson-Young is the pin-up girl for the work–life balance brigade'. He notes that the parliament had a child-care centre and fumed, irrelevantly,

> throw in the gymnasium, the pool, the free tennis courts and walking tracks that ring the building, and federal parliament is pretty much the equivalent of Club Med for mums and dads,

which makes Hanson-Young's star turn as Sally Field in *Not Without My Daughter* all the more ridiculous.

Anne Summers in *The Sunday Age* injected some common sense into the furore, and she had done some research:

> In January 2007, as Nancy Pelosi was sworn in as Speaker in the US House of Representatives before a packed chamber that included more than 100 children, she invited some of these children to join her at the podium. As the votes for her were tabulated, she held an infant in her arms and was surrounded by children. She ended her inaugural speech by saying: 'For these children, and for all of America's children, the House will come to order.' It wouldn't happen in Canberra.

Summers noted that children had previously been brought into the Australian Parliament and asked:

> So why all the fuss? It is obvious that Senate president John Hogg handled the matter badly. He should have been aware that children have been in the chamber before and he should have been more sympathetic. Instead he opted to order the child removed so that the nation was confronted with the sight of a screaming toddler being ejected from the place where the nation's laws are made. What has been most instructive about this brouhaha is how it has brought into the open the still archaic attitudes towards mothers in the workplace. The response was predictable – and savage.

Back in the Senate on Monday 22 June Deputy President Alan Ferguson, a Liberal Senator, was upbeat: 'I have never seen online polling on such an issue, where 85 per cent of the population do not agree with Senator Hanson-Young's action …'

Ferguson then spilled the beans:

As it so happens – I do not think the President would mind me saying this – he and I had a discussion about the very matter the night before this occurred, because of the fact that Senator Hanson-Young had unexpectedly brought a child into the chamber on a previous occasion.

So the president and his deputy had had their heads together and predetermined that the child would be thrown out if she was brought into the chamber again. The conniving men gave the young mother no warning.

However, faced with the motion of dissent, President Hogg had thought again. After I spoke to him informally and he then sought good advice outside the chamber, he returned to the Chair later that Thursday to say that he could have handled the situation better. That is, he had got it wrong. I withdrew the motion of dissent.

A benefit has flowed from little Kora's eviction from the Senate. Since 2009 no presiding officer has expelled a child from any Australian parliament. Over at Strasbourg, in the European Parliament, Italian MP Licia Ronzulli has had her toddler sitting with her at the sessions since she was born and the sky has not fallen in.

However, Labor, the Liberals and the National Party continue to block the Greens' efforts to protect children from junk food advertisers, and childhood obesity in Australia is epidemic.

Big Junk Food's right to advertise should not trump a child's right to be healthy and, as with Big Tobacco, it is only a matter of time before its wings are clipped and the Greens' policy becomes law.

38

The New Political Correctness

'POLITICAL CORRECTNESS' (PC) was a sneering term devised in the US by right-wing critics, to hurl at progressive thinkers in the 1990s. 'Oh, that's so PC!' was their dismissive cry against advocates of human rights. 'Typical of the PC brigade!' they would taunt people who spoke out against racist, sexist, homophobic or other discriminatory behaviour. It worked.

In Australia, the tide against 'political correctness' helped cover the rise of the racist politics of Pauline Hanson from 1996 and the failure of Prime Minister John Howard to take her on at the outset, and then his adoption of some of her policies. Howard took to calling the nation's formative history 'black armband history'. This prime minister was doing all he could to make the destruction of thousands of Indigenous Australians and their cultures, a fact of the British takeover of Australia, an offensive topic unfit for public discussion.

That was racist but few dared to say so, even after a brave group of Aborigines at the Reconciliation Convention in Melbourne in 1997 turned their backs on Howard in protest at his policies. The mood against 'political correctness' paralleled the underlying appeal to racism that has boosted the electoral stocks of successive governments that have dished out inhumane treatment to genuine asylum seekers coming by boat (but not by plane) to seek refuge in Australia.

Who can forget the children and parents locked up, to the point of permanent mental trauma, behind razor wire in Howard's desert refugee camps? That led to the so-called 'Pacific Solution': concentration camps where decent, loving people are now locked up interminably in inhumane conditions outside Australia and without access to Australian law. There will be more of it – under the cover of deterring people smugglers, who are rarely locked up, and never interminably – because in 2013 most Australians voted for more.

The 'Pacific Solution' is a prime example of the New Political Correctness (NPC) in which the sneering dismissal of human rights has moved on to legislative action to erode, remove or pre-empt those rights.

NPC is action-oriented and its success comes of its reckless simplicity: if you're (to the) right you are right. If you're left, you are (to be) left. Society's laws are being altered to reflect and enforce this new correctness and protect the advantaged – and those who advocate equality, socialism (quelle horreur!), ecological wisdom or for the compensation of disadvantage must be sneered down and excoriated. Never engage in a debate of ideas; after all, you are right. Always go for the jugular: smash the intellectuals, sandal-footed do-gooders (including those advocating Jesus's compassion) and whingers (people who don't work, haven't schooled themselves properly, or who are born black – it's all their own problem). NPC is a greedy, dominating, hard right, me-now view of life that resonates wonderfully with Materialism and the worship of Growth.

In Australia, NPC's simplest success has been to suborn the word 'liberal'. Tony Abbott is the head sherang of Australian Liberalism.

NPC's legislative successes are paired with the bludgeoning of public advocates of civil rights, the environment, Aboriginal sovereignty and democratic reform. Debate about a bill of rights for Australia, to have us catch up with other democracies such as the USA, UK and South Africa, has gone off the two bigger parties' agendas.

Instead, in an example of NPC illogic, in 2004 the Howard government, inveigled by Labor, went out of its way to legislate a pre-emptive ban on same-sex marriages. On 12 August 2004 this amendment to the *Marriage Act 1961* was pushed through the Senate 38 votes to 6. I refused the Chair's demand that I withdraw my description of the amendment as 'hateful'.

Besides eroding international laws protecting refugees, NPC thinking ensured that a blind eye was turned to egregious breaches of the Geneva Protocols against torture at Guantanamo Bay, in Iraq and Afghanistan and elsewhere as determined by the Bush administration's criminal policy of rendition. Recognition of President Bush's US Military Tribunals in Australian law was passed by the national Parliament.

The environment has been relegated to the chaff bag and laws to protect it, now sneeringly dismissed as 'green tape', are being dismantled across the country.

In an ambitious move to pull the rug from under the World Heritage Convention, signed by the Whitlam government and strongly backed by the Fraser, Hawke and Keating governments, the Abbott government followed through on an election promise of 2013 to remove World Heritage status from the tallest flowering forests on Earth, in Tasmania. No other government in the world has sought to have World Heritage status removed from one of its environmental icons in this way. But that's the popular NPC in Australia today.

There are four pillars of Greens political philosophy: social justice, democracy, peace, and ecological well-being, and the political mood in Australia was swinging against all four. It was not a bad time, I thought, to swing in the opposite direction, starting with democracy.

I gave the 2012 Green Oration in the Hobart Town Hall and focused on the need for global democracy. I was particularly pleased to be advocating democracy because these orations celebrate the first Greens party meeting in the world. That meeting took place on 23 March 1972.

Despite mounting local, national and international clamour in 1972, all Labor and Liberal members of the Tasmanian House of Assembly had voted for the Hydro-Electric Commission's Middle Gordon Scheme, a set of three dams that was to flood and obliterate the magnificent Lake Pedder National Park. Lake Pedder, with its 2-kilometre long, fine pink sandy beach, was a bushwalkers' mecca nestled 300 metres high in the western Tasmanian wilderness mountains. In 1971, Dr Richard Jones, his foot on a Central Plateau boulder, had seen the pointlessness of pursuing ecological wisdom with the old parties and proposed to his companions that a new party based on ecological principles should be formed.

The Hobart Town Hall was packed at that first meeting. When Jones called for a vote on the idea, it was shouted down by the pro-dam gentlemen (according to the rules of NPC, one must not refer to the right-wing disrupters as radicals, whether they are in Hobart Town Hall or outside Parliament House in Canberra under banners reading 'Julia Gillard: Bob Brown's Bitch') who had come for that purpose.

The savvy Jones then took a meticulous hand count; the majority said yes, and so the world's first Greens party (then called the United Tasmania Group or 'UTG') was set up. I arrived in Tasmania a month later and quickly fell in with the UTG radicals and, three years later, Jones asked me to stand with him on the UTG's Senate ticket. We didn't win a seat but he got 1028 votes and I scored 199 of the 246,694 votes cast.

Forty years later and 26 years after Jones's death, I let rip on the grand view that humanity's common future on Earth will be best managed through global democracy.

The NPC brigade, led by the Murdoch media, went into orbit.

39

He sounds like John Lennon

IN 2014, TWO years after the Green Oration in the Hobart Town Hall in which I talked about our unique place in the Universe and advocated a global parliament, Murdoch's syndicated NPC attack-dog, Piers Akerman, was still in high dudgeon:

> Less than two years ago, then Greens leader Bob Brown delivered an hubristic address in which he proclaimed: 'Fellow Earthians, never before has the Universe unfolded such a flower as our collective human intellect, so far as we know.' We can only hope and pray he was not including members of the loopy Greens party in that intelligent collective.

Akerman's main target this time, however, was Acting Greens Leader Richard Di Natale, who had made a call for an end to the recital of the Lord's Prayer at the start of parliamentary sittings in Canberra every day. This idea had evinced howls of horror, but also some ecclesiastical support, when I first floated it in 1998. In the quote above Akerman drops a clue as to what he prays for but he does not reveal which of his trespasses he asks God to forgive. He went on to say that questioning the parliamentary prayer session is 'an offensive topic' – that is, should not be allowed. So much for free speech. So very NPC.

My earlier foray into that topic brought me one of the most treasured letters of my years in the Senate. It was written by an anonymous believer on a torn piece of paper, in biro, and is a gem of brevity and unintended irony:

> Senator Bob Brown. Who the HELL are you to stop the Lords Prayer for guidance, publicly recited by the Senate President. All the garbage in this country and you'd like to kill the only right thing that's probably ever been done. You piece of SHIT.

This devout scribe's last word was repeatedly underlined.

Despite being very upset by the Lord's Prayer debate, Akerman's great horror was at the idea of global democracy, which I canvassed in that Green Oration in the Hobart Town Hall on 23 March 2012, commemorating that first Greens Party meeting, held in the same hall 40 years earlier. After some musings on life in the Universe, I went on to outline the case for global democracy.

The NPC brigade of the right-wing media, none of which was among the very fine audience that had filled the town hall, was apoplectic. As if no-one had opened up in public before about humankind's place in the Universe, let alone a global polity, their outrage went on for weeks and has simmered ever since.

The more they have screwed up their hankies in indignation, the more confident I have become. Without their unrelenting condemnation the speech would have been quickly forgotten, but now I feel very happy with it: it has even drawn some international (if not intergalactic) attention. I will share it with you in the coming pages.

But first, let's go back to some of the NPC outrage in 2012. The Murdoch media was beside itself. Its fusillades began in *The Australian*, with Amos Aikman complaining, 'Senator Brown repeatedly attacked corporations and rich people.' The broadsheet was still roiled a week later when Chris Kenny derided the speech as 'ravings' and demanded to know why 'the ABC, which usually pays great attention to the Greens, has failed to seriously analyse and discuss this speech'.

A very good question. But Jon Faine at Melbourne ABC Radio heard the call and talked right over the top of guest Christine Milne. She had been at the Green Oration and told Faine my speech was 'actually a celebration of life on Earth and collective human intelligence'. Faine was not listening: 'I thought his website must have been hacked … has Bob Brown lost it completely? This is just crazy stuff isn't it?' he ranted before cutting off Milne's reply. *The Australian* breathlessly reprinted Faine's interview while more of its columnists joined in the frenzy, labelling the speech 'wacky', 'batty' and 'barking mad'.

The *Herald Sun*'s Patrick Carlyon was in orbit, calling me an 'oddball in the Senate' who 'is known to detest the Murdoch media, which he has labelled the "hate media"'. Carlyon added another old complaint for good measure: 'In recent years he has called for the halt of coal exports.' He then fired his most devastating salvo: I had 'sounded like a latter-day John Lennon'!

I shared a bottle of Tasmanian bubbly with friends to help relieve the hurt.

A few days later the *Herald Sun*'s Alan Howe caught up, describing my 'extravagantly absurd Green Oration' as 'bonkers' and 'vulgar theatre'. His stablemate Andrew Bolt was worried the speech might even be banned: 'read this while it is still legal', he urged his flock, because it might 'finally wake up the dozy to his unreason and intolerance'.

Up in Sydney, the *Daily Telegraph*'s Miranda Devine thought 'the Greens leader must really be smoking something'. Ms Devine said the speech was 'the true nature of the Greens in all its loopy glory'. She refrained from repeating her earlier suggestions that environmentalists should be bashed or strung up from lampposts.

Over in Adelaide, in Murdoch's *Advertiser*, David Penberthy had spotted that I was 'subverting the dominant paradigm'. The speech was 'dippy enviro-spiritualism' and 'words of madness', though he quoted none of its substance.

Perhaps Carlyon had thrown the most light on the Murdoch camp's mentality with his sad opinion that global democracy would not work because 'we humans collectively don't like each other very much'.

Maybe that's where I am off the rails. I like human beings a great deal and think that seeing the good in others is better than this bitter, accusative NPC mindset.

Piers Akerman is not alone in keeping up the rage from 2012. *The Australian*'s cartoonist Bill Leak began 2014 with a cartoon, out of the blue, titled 'Keeping a finger on the pulses and legumes'. It depicts me ambling down a street with Christine Milne and, ignoring the 'Hobart Hotel' on one side of the street, telling her that the 'Earthians' Vegetarian Cafe', on the other side, is the place to 'gauge the public mood'.

Maybe the news of the day was too hard for Leak to lampoon. In Sydney the Liberal state government was announcing new laws to curb hotel drinking hours in the wake of a young man being pointlessly punched to death while, in Perth, farmer Steve Marsh was taking court action after his organic farmland was contaminated by a Monsanto GM pollutant from a neighbour's farm.

I enjoy a beer and am not a vegetarian, but the world would be a better place if there was a little less alcohol consumption and a lot more organic 'Earthians' Vegetarian Cafes'!

If you want to avoid my 'barking mad' Green Oration, skip the next few chapters. Otherwise, here are a couple of other comments to sweeten the way. *The Age*'s Michelle Grattan wrote, 'Brown thinks not just about the here and now but a century hence.' Commenting in Crikey, Susan Winstanley thought that 'the knuckle-draggers at News [Limited] think they are being funny ... but they miss Bob Brown's light and gracious humour'.

And, to set the scene, let me quote Aboriginal poet Kevin Gilbert (1933–1993): 'Creation flows to me, through me, within me ... the Universe is part of me as I am part of it.'

40

Third Green Oration:
We people of the Earth …

Hobart Town Hall – 23 March 2012

Fellow Earthians,

Never before has the Universe unfolded such a flower as our collective human intelligence, so far as we know.

Nor has such a one-and-only brilliance in the Universe stood at the brink of extinction, so far as we know.

We people of the Earth exist because our potential was there in the Big Bang, 13.7 billion years ago, as the Universe exploded into being.

So far it seems like we are the lone thinkers in this vast, expanding Universe.

However recent astronomy tells us that there are trillions of other planets circling Sun-like stars in the immensity of the Universe, millions of them friendly to life. So why has no-one from elsewhere in the Cosmos contacted us?

Surely some people-like animals have evolved elsewhere. Surely we are not, in this crowded reality of countless other similar planets, the only thinking beings to have turned up. Most unlikely! So why isn't life out there contacting us? Why aren't the intergalactic phones ringing?

Here is one sobering possibility for our isolation: maybe life has often evolved to intelligence on other planets with biospheres and every time that intelligence, when it became able to alter its environment, did so with catastrophic consequences. Maybe we have had many predecessors in the Cosmos, but all have brought about their own downfall.

That's why they are not communicating with Earth. They have extincted themselves. They have come and gone. And now it's our turn.

Whatever has happened in other worlds, here we are on Earth altering this bountiful biosphere which has nurtured us from newt to Newton.

Unlike the hapless dinosaurs which went to utter destruction when that rocky asteroid plunged into Earth 65 million years ago, this accelerating catastrophe is of our own making.

Just as we are causing that destruction, we could be fostering its reversal. Indeed nothing will save us from ourselves but ourselves.

We need a strategy. We need action based on the reality that this is our own responsibility – everyone's responsibility.

So democracy – ensuring that everyone is involved in deciding Earth's future – is the key to success.

For comprehensive Earth action, an all-of-the-Earth representative democracy is required. That is, a global parliament.

In his Gettysburg address of 1859 Abraham Lincoln proclaimed: 'We here highly resolve … that government of the people, by the people, and for the people, shall not perish from the Earth.'

One hundred and fifty-three years later, let us here in Hobart, and around the world, highly resolve that through global democracy we shall save the Earth from perishing.

For those who oppose global democracy the challenge is clear: how else would you manage human affairs in this new century of global community, global communications and shared global destiny?

Recently, when I got back to bed at Liffey after ruminating under the stars for hours on this question, Paul inquired, 'Did you see a comet?'

'Yes', I replied, 'and it is called 'Global Democracy.'

A molten rock from space destroyed most life on the planet those 65 million years ago. Let us have the comet of global democracy save life on Earth this time.

41

Third Green Oration: Plutocracy or democracy?

NINE YEARS AGO, after the invasion of Iraq which President George W. Bush ordered to promote democracy over tyranny, I proposed to the Australian Senate a means of expanding democracy without invasion. Let Australia take the lead in peacefully establishing a global parliament. I explained that this ultimate democracy would decide international issues. I had in mind nuclear proliferation, international financial transactions and the plight of our one billion fellow people living in abject poverty.

In 2003 our other Greens senator, Kerry Nettle, seconded the motion but we failed to attract a single other vote in the 76-seat chamber. The four other parties – the Liberals, the Nationals, Labor and the Democrats – voted 'no'! As he crossed the floor to join the 'noes' another senator called to me: 'Bob, don't you know how many Chinese there are?'

Well, yes I did. Surely that is the point. There are just 23 million Australians among seven billion equal Earthians. Unless and until we accord every other citizen of the planet, friend or foe, and regardless of race, gender, ideology or other characteristic, equal regard, we, like them, can have no assured future.

Twenty-five hundred years ago the Athenians, and 180 years ago the British, gave the vote to all men of means. After Gettysburg, the United States made the vote available to all men, regardless of means. One man, one vote.

But what about women, Louisa Lawson asked in 1889: 'Pray, why should one half of the world govern the other half?'

So, in New Zealand, in 1893, followed by South Australia in 1895, and the new Commonwealth of Australia in 1901, universal suffrage – the equal vote for women as well as men – was achieved.

In this second decade of the twenty-first century, most people on Earth get to vote in their own countries. Corruption and rigging remain commonplace, but the world believes in democracy.

As Winston Churchill observed in 1947,

> many forms of government have been tried in this world of sin and woe. No one pretends that democracy is perfect or all-wise. Indeed, it has been said that democracy is the worst form of government except all those other forms that have been tried from time to time.

Yet in Australia and other peaceful places which have long enjoyed domestic democracy, establishing a global democracy – the ultimate goal of any real democrat – is not on the public agenda.

Exxon, Coca-Cola, BHP Billiton and News Corporation have much more say in organising the global agenda than the planet's five billion mature-age voters without a ballot box.

Plutocracy, rule by the wealthy, is democracy's most insidious rival. It is served by plutolatry, the worship of wealth. But on a finite planet, the rule of the rich must inevitably rely on guns rather than the ballot box – though, I hasten to add, wealth does not deny a good heart. All of us here are amongst the world's wealthiest people but I think none of us worship wealth to the exclusion of democracy.

We instinctively know that democracy is the only vehicle for creating a fair global society in which freedom will abound but the extremes of gluttony and poverty will not. Mahatma Ghandi observed that the world has enough for everyone's need but not for everyone's greed.

So what's it to be: democracy or guns? I plunk for democracy.

42

Third Green Oration:
A global parliament

THE CONCEPT OF world democracy goes back centuries, but since 2007 there has been a new movement towards an elected representative assembly at the United Nations in parallel with the unelected, appointed, General Assembly. This elected assembly would have none of the General Assembly's powers but would be an important step along the way to a future popularly elected and agreeably empowered global assembly.

Two Greens motions in the Australian Senate to support this campaign for a global people's assembly have been voted down. However similar motions won support in the European Parliament and, in India, 40 MPs including a number of ministers have backed the proposal. I will move for the world's 100 Greens parties to back it too at the third Global Greens conference in Senegal next week. It fits perfectly with the Global Greens Charter adopted in Canberra in 2001.

We Earthians can develop rosier prospects. We have been to the Moon. We have landed eyes and ears on Mars. We are discovering planets hundreds of light years close which are ripe for life. We are on a journey to endless wonder in the Cosmos and to realising our own remarkable potential.

To give this vision security we must get our own planet in order.

The political debate of the twentieth century was polarised between capitalism and communism. It was about control of the economy in the narrow sense of material goods and money. A free market versus state control.

Bitter experience tells us that the best outcome is neither, but some of both. The role of democracy in the nation state has been to calibrate that balance.

In this twenty-first century the political debate is moving to a new arena. It is about whether we expend Earth's natural capital as our population grows to ten billion people in the decades ahead, with average consumption also growing.

We have to manage the terrifying facts that Earth's citizenry is already using 120 per cent of the planet's productivity capacity – its renewable living resources; that the last decade was the hottest in the last 1300 years (if not the last 9000 years); that we are extincting our fellow species faster than ever before in human history; and that to accommodate ten billion people at American, European or Australasian rates of consumption we will need two more planets to exploit within a few decades.

It may be that the Earth's biosphere cannot tolerate ten billion of us big-consuming mammals later this century. Or it may be that, given adroit and agreeable global management, it can. It's up to us.

Once more the answer lies between the poles: between the narrow interests of the mega-rich and a surrender to the nihilist idea that the planet would be better off without us.

It will be global democracy's challenge to find the equator between those poles, and it is that equator which the Greens are best placed to reach.

One great difference between the old politics and Green politics is the overarching question which predicates all our political decisions: 'Will people one hundred years from now thank us?'

In thinking one hundred years ahead we set our community's course for one hundred thousand years: that humanity will not perish at its own hand but will look back upon its twenty-first century ancestry with gratitude.

And when the future smiles, we can smile too.

That query, 'Will people a hundred years from now thank us?' should be inscribed across the door of Earth's Parliament.

So let us resolve
that there should be established
for the prevalence and happiness of humankind
a representative assembly
a global parliament
for the people of the Earth
based on the principle of
one person one vote one value;
and to enable this outcome
that it should be a bicameral parliament
with its house of review
having equal representation
elected from every nation.

An Earth parliament for all. But what would be its commission? Here are four goals:

Economy
Equality
Ecology
Eternity.

To begin with: economy, because that word means managing our household. The parliament would employ prudent resource management to put an end to waste and to better share Earth's plenitude. For example, it might cut the trillion dollar annual spending on armaments. A cut of just 10 per cent would free up the money to guarantee every child on the planet clean water and enough food, as well as a school to attend to develop her or his best potential. World opinion would back such a move, though I suppose Boeing, NATO, the People's Liberation Army and the Saudi Arabian royal family might not.

The second goal is equality. This begins with equality of opportunity – as in every child being assured of a school where lessons are in her or his own first language and a health clinic to attend. Equality would ensure, through the fair regulation of free enterprise, each citizen's wellbeing, including the right to work, to innovate, to enjoy creativity and to understand and experience and contribute to defending the beauty of Earth's biosphere.

Which brings me to the third goal: ecology. Ecological wellbeing must understrap all outcomes so as to actively protect the planet's biodiversity and living ecosystems. 'In wildness,' wrote Thoreau, 'is the preservation of the world.' Wild nature is our cradle and the most vital source for our spiritual and physical wellbeing yet it is the world's most rapidly disappearing resource. And so I pay tribute to Miranda Gibson, 60 metres high on her tall tree platform tonight as the rain and snow fall across central Tasmania. In Miranda's spirit is the saving of the world.

And lastly, eternity. Eternity is for as long as we could be. It means beyond our own experience. It also means 'forever' if there is no inevitable end to life. Let's take the idea of eternity and make it our own business.

I have never met a person in whom I did not see myself reflected. Some grew old and died, and I am now part of their ongoing presence on Earth.

Others have a youthful vitality which I have lost and will soon give up altogether. These youngsters will in turn keep my candle, and yours, if you are aged like me, alight in the Cosmos. In this stream of life where birth and death are our common lot, the replenishment of humankind lights up our own existences. May it go on and on and on …

The pursuit of eternity is no longer the prerogative of the gods: it is the business of us all, here and now.

43

Third Green Oration: One person, one vote, one value, one planet

DRAWING ON THE best of our character, Earth's community of people is on the threshold of a brilliant new career in togetherness. But we, all together, have to open the door to that future using the powerful key of global democracy.

I think we are intelligent enough to get there. My faith is in the collective nous and caring of humanity, and in our innate optimism. Even in its grimmest history, the optimism of humanity has been its greatest power. We must defy pessimism as well as the idea that there is any one of us who cannot turn a successful hand to improving Earth's future prospects.

I am an optimist. I'm also an opsimath: I learn as I get older. And I have never been happier in my life. Hurtling to death, I am alive and loving being Green.

I look forward in my remaining years to helping spread a contagion of confidence that, together, we people of Earth will secure a great future. We can and will retrieve Earth's biosphere. We will steady ourselves – this unfolding flower of intelligence in the Universe – for the long, shared, wondrous journey into the enticing centuries ahead.

Let us determine to bring ourselves together, settle our differences and shape and realise our common dream for this joy ride into the future. In that pursuit, let us create a global democracy and parliament under the grand idea of one person, one vote, one value, one planet.

We must, we can, we will.

Thank you all!

Bob Brown.

(After the speech diva Claire Dawson sang 'Earth Song', with Rod Thomson playing the grand Hobart Town Hall organ. A Greens' fortieth birthday cake was cut as the celebrations continued.)

44
Ingrid

AFTER BEING ELECTED to the Senate in 1996 I had a strong desire to give back to the Greens which, by then, had 70 parties around the world. One goal was to get all those parties together. Due to the extraordinary work of Margaret Blakers, my senior policy adviser who took a year off to make it happen, the first Global Greens Conference was held in Canberra in April 2001. It was a cracker. Eight hundred delegates arrived and the cardinal achievement, with Christine Milne in the chair, was the adoption of the Global Greens Charter that now binds all the world's Greens parties together. (It can be viewed at www.greens.org).

Gathering global contributions to draft this historic charter had been the spare-time job of Dr Louise Crossley, Australia's Antarctic base leader on Macquarie Island, which is halfway between Hobart and Antarctica.

Opening the conference, I pointed out that:

when 1500 scientists, including 100 Nobel Laureates, petitioned the world in 1995 that serious remedies were required to halt the destruction of the living fabric of the Earth, their warning was ignored. Had it been 1500 economists warning of a stock market crash it would have got banner headlines and emergency government action.

Two remarkable women stole the show. The first was the Kenyan forest protector and tree-planter extraordinaire Wangari Maathai who was soon to be awarded the Nobel Peace Prize for her work.

The second was Colombia's Oxygen Green Party Senator Ingrid Betancourt. In her fiery speech to the assembly at the Canberra Convention Centre, Ingrid laid out the urgent need for action and received a foot-stamping standing ovation. She said:

> The salvation of the planet, the right to live, is nothing else than a fight for values. These values are ones that we human beings all share, regardless of the colour of our skin or of the name that we give to our God. And because they are essential values, they are not negotiable. To outline a new economic order, a new social pact, is not seeking a utopia. It is simply outlining the basic thing, the minimum thing for us to continue working as societies in a globalised world. I say this with force and with anguish because I feel that we cannot waste any more time. We still have time to stop the self-destruction that is imposed on us. But this will depend on our will, on our character, on our commitment, and not on what power they choose to grant us.

Within 12 months Senator Betancourt, the Greens' candidate for the Colombian presidential elections, was utterly powerless. She had responded to calls for help from Greens supporters in San Vicente as the town came under bombardment in a battle between the Colombian army and 'left-wing' FARC (Revolutionary Armed Forces of Colombia) guerrillas. En route to San Vicente by car on 23 February 2002 – the president had bumped her from an arranged helicopter flight – Ingrid was kidnapped at gunpoint by the guerrillas and taken deep into the jungle. She was kept in inhumane conditions – after one escape attempt she was shackled by the neck to a tree for months – over the next six long years.

Ingrid's kidnap put her out of election contention, though her campaign was continued. Taking account of the warnings against travel to Colombia, I flew to Bogota to join Ingrid's Greens team and add attention to her plight. I was met at the airport by Australia's nearest ambassador, from Venezuela, who asked me to quit and return home.

There were ten bodyguards outside my little hotel in Bogota and, when I joined the Greens for an election walk down a city thoroughfare carrying a cardboard cut-out of Ingrid Betancourt, we had an armed phalanx of plain-clothes police officers walk with us.

Thousands of people were slaughtered in the war with FARC and the bodies of prisoners were dumped all over the country. So our fears for Ingrid's life and wellbeing were real and were heightened when her captors sent out a videotape showing her gaunt figure in captivity.

There was a global movement for her release, centred in France, and one attempt to find her involved a plane landing in Brazil near the Colombian border: this led to diplomatic recriminations between France and Brazil. The release of other high-profile hostages through the intervention of President Hugo Chavez of Venezuela early in 2008 raised hopes for Ingrid's release.

Accompanied by Paul, I diverted our flight plans to Sao Paulo for the Second Global Greens Conference (once again Margaret Blakers was a key organiser) in May 2008. We spent three days in Caracas to lobby the Chavez government to negotiate Ingrid's release with the FARC. While I got to see the leader of the Venezuelan army and give him a letter for the president – we knew he was a close friend of Chavez – this effort was in vain.

In Sao Paulo, after a replay of her Canberra speech, there was another standing ovation, this time in support of a motion for Ingrid's release. But her cause seemed hopeless, not least because successive Colombian presidents seemed content to let her rot in the jungle. Suddenly, that changed.

On 2 July 2008 Ingrid was kidnapped again. A huge 'FARC' helicopter landed in the jungle and the prisoners in the camp were bundled aboard. When it got into the air the armed 'FARC' personnel who had arrived in the helicopter revealed they were government soldiers. They quickly overwhelmed the FARC guards who had got aboard with the prisoners, equally deceived by this extraordinary ruse, and set the astonished prisoners, including Ingrid, free.

Her spirit was indomitable. In Paris three weeks later she made this call to the commander of the FARC guerrillas, Alfonso Cano:

See this Colombia. See the extended hand of President Uribe and understand that it is time to stop the bloodshed. It is time to drop those weapons and change them for roses. Substitute them with tolerance, respect, and as the brothers we all are, find a way so that we can all live together in the world.

French President Sarkozy awarded her the Legion of Honour.

Ingrid came to Australia in 2012 and we had an onstage conversation in the packed Hobart Town Hall. The crowd was enthralled by the spirit of this remarkable woman. On the historic Town Hall organ, Rod Thomson played the song 'Ingrid, can you see the flowers?' which I had written to her while she was imprisoned in the jungle. We all shed a few tears.

Early in 2014 there was speculation that Ingrid would lead the Greens' team for the next Colombian elections. I called her at Oxford University and she told me she had declined the invitation. She had written an account of her six years of captivity – *Even Silence Has an End* – and an adventure novel and was planning a doctorate on liberation theology. The same passion and concern for her home country and the world came through.

Ingrid Betancourt had lit up the first Global Greens Conference where she proclaimed:

If the great people of history defeated adversity, if those who changed the course of events did so although they were predicted to fail, if it is true that faith moves mountains and that David conquered Goliath, then our fight should be victorious. To defend the right to live, today as in the past, implies heroism, temper and courage. Let us not deceive ourselves. To be Green in this millennium we have to take on the uniform of the new samurai, to defend our values ... the survival of the whole of humanity, its history, its dignity, its accumulated cultural richness, its diversity. This is our new frontier.

Her spirit can never be shackled.

45

'I have never advocated violence.'

SIX HUNDRED YEARS ago Machiavelli warned that if you want to change the world, get ready to be crushed by those who already hold the power and the money.

In the twenty-first century, the rich and powerful are the multinational corporations. They have realised Abraham Lincoln's nineteenth-century fear that corporations would seize the throne of power from democracy.

The corporate domination of the public discourse and of political lobbying, and its strident New Political Correctness (NPC) eroding democratically evolved rights and laws, aims to throttle progress towards real human equality or respect for our Earth's sustaining biosphere.

A simple example of this high-handed disdain for fairness came in the form of Murdoch firebrand (and doyenne of NPC) Miranda Devine of *The Sunday Telegraph* and her reaction to my recollection of her 1995 advocacy of violence against environmentalists.

She headlined her piece on 13 January 2013 'Bob Brown has it wrong – I do not advocate violence against greenies'. Here is the opening paragraph of her tirade:

I can't say I was surprised when Bob Brown had a shot at me in *The Sydney Morning Herald* last week. Still, even though he is a Green, you'd think he'd have more integrity than to lie about me.

Then, after a below-the-belt swipe at Jonathan Moylan, the campaigner against coal mining who has a regard for life on the planet beyond Miranda's comprehension, she gets to the point – herself.

> Which brings us to me. Australian eco-activists are 'committed to non-violence', Bob wrote. But no such commitment exists on 'the other side'.
>
> 'Just read Miranda Devine's advocacy of violence against environmentalists in *The Daily Telegraph*.'
>
> It's not true, Bob. I have never advocated violence.
>
> Bob did try to get me sacked for a column I wrote in the *Herald* in 2009, a week after Victoria's Black Saturday bushfires killed 173 people.

Miranda then quotes herself blaming 'the power of green ideology' for killing those people and her conclusion that 'if politicians are intent on whipping up a lynch mob to divert attention from their own culpability, it is not arsonists who should be hanging from lamp-posts but greenies'.

Having written that, she absolved herself with this absurdity: 'No reasonable person would have read my column as advocating violence, or hanging greenies from lamp-posts.'

I sent a reply to *The Sunday Telegraph* but my letter was not printed. They can't have a copy of the Journalists' Code of Ethics down at Murdoch's Sydney HQ. When the Press Council took up my complaint the newspaper's editor phoned me and asked if I would drop the matter if the letter was printed. I agreed. Here it is as it appeared the following Sunday.

Dear Editor,

With her usual grace, Miranda Devine calls me a liar and says that she has never advocated violence even though she admits she wrote 'it is not arsonists who should be hanging from lamp-posts but greenies'.

She makes the extraordinary claim that 'no reasonable person would have read my column as advocating violence, or hanging greenies from lamp-posts'.

She would have been on stronger ground had she ended that claim after the first eight words.

Miranda is a repeat offender. Let me quote, for example, from her column in *The Daily Telegraph-Mirror* of the 16th February 1995:

'It may not be palatable to say so publicly, but violence can sometimes be good. When a forestry worker named "Steve" this week lost his temper and punched an eco-protester in the face at a logging camp near Bega, he was using a technique for settling disputes that is as old as mankind. Brutal though it is, a short sharp punch to the nose can achieve a lot more than years of appeasement, diplomacy and compromise.'

She added that 'there comes a point in any disagreement when diplomacy ceases to be of any use. That is when violence has its place'.

When next Miranda insists that she never advocates violence, someone with a fire extinguisher should keep a close eye on her trousers.

Yours sincerely,
Bob Brown

(Hand in hand with NPC is deception. While under threat of a Press Council finding against *The Sunday Telegraph* the editor printed my letter; a year later Miranda Devine's article remains on the paper's website with no sign of my reply so that readers might judge for themselves. Such brazen unfaithfulness to the public is the seed of NPC's own self-destruction.)

46

High tea with Miranda

Tasmania Police never discovered who gelignited and burned the three cars of the East Picton forest blockaders in 1993, who lit the fire that raged up onto the Great Western Tiers before the first Jackeys Marsh Forest Festival, or who put the match to the Liffey River Reserve the day after Bush Heritage Australia opened a new public walking track.

So it followed suit that no-one was brought to book after a fire was deliberately lit from a loggers' road in the Styx River valley in central Tasmania in 2013. There was no inquiry under way when I wrote to the Commissioner of Police pointing out that the arsonist could have killed a young woman living nearby.

Here's my letter:

Dear Commissioner,

On Tuesday evening, 5th March 2013, a fire was lit southwest of Maydena. Media reports yesterday and today are that Forestry Tasmania believes the fire may have been deliberately lit.

The circumstances lead me to believe that a person or persons lit the fire to burn out the nearby forest platform which, since 14th December 2011, was occupied by Miranda Gibson. If that is right, it is a matter of intended homicide.

A police officer attended the site of Ms Gibson's tree on Wednesday 6th March. I ask you to take all immediate and necessary action to discover who lit the fire.
Yours sincerely,
Dr Brown

Within six hours I received this reply:

I refer to the attached email forwarded to the Commissioner of Police in which you request action in relation to a fire southwest of Maydena. This matter has been referred to me as I have responsibility for the Crime and Operations portfolio. I can advise that I am seeking an operational assessment of this matter and will determine if a subsequent investigation is warranted. I will advise you accordingly in due course.
Regards,
Donna ADAMS
Assistant Commissioner
CRIME AND OPERATIONS

I had good reason to get involved.

In the spring of 2011 Miranda Gibson had called me to ask what I thought about her sitting on a platform in a tall tree to protest against the logging of Tasmania's World Heritage value forests. A few days later, at my Senate office in Hobart, we talked it over. She was resolute, her plan was well thought out and she had a good back-up crew. With my sit on Mount Wellington 35 years earlier in mind, I supported her (while advising strongly that she never contemplate fasting!) and, on the first day of her sit, flew over her tree in a helicopter with a television camera crew and photographers, making sure she wore her red raincoat so she could be seen in the sea of green forest.

Miranda, a schoolteacher, had spent a lot of time camped in the Tasmanian forests, including with the Upper Florentine blockaders who had survived attacks by pro-logging vigilantes. One day those vigilantes smashed the body and windows of a disabled car with a sledgehammer while Miranda and a fellow forest defender, Nishant Datt, sat huddled inside through the terrifying experience.

Miranda climbed more than 60 metres – about 20 storeys high – to her wooden platform where she had a tiny shelter and solar-powered computer from which she emailed and Skyped the world. She quickly made the plight of the forests of Tasmania, which were being logged and sold for a pittance as woodchips to make paper in Japan, a cause célèbre.

Her eucalypt tree towered above a ridge running down from Mount Mueller. The mountaintop was in the Tasmanian Wilderness World Heritage Area, but not her tree and the magnificent forest below. Her tree-sit added enduring testimony and international attention to the negotiations taking place back in the cities over future protection of the forests, including the Styx River's Valley of the Giants just south of her tree.

Miranda was visited by her mother, father and sister, and a steady flow of friends and intrigued journalists, as well as an array of birds, including giant Tasmanian wedge-tailed eagles and yellow-tailed black cockatoos – all of which she photographed to illustrate the beautifully written accounts of her vigil that she sent back to the ground-dwelling world.

Paul baked a fruitcake and we took it out for morning tea, slipping and sliding along the muddy trail leading from the nearest public road to Miranda's remote perch. When we arrived at her tree, we were each hauled aloft with the aid of a pulley system and ropes. Paul went first. When it was my turn, I sat on a plank the size of a child's swing seat and tried to stave off panic. As I rose I bumped against the massive trunk and then swung, twisting, out over the fern-spangled forest until I reached the trapdoor through which visitors had to clamber, stretching every shoulder muscle, onto Miranda's little deck.

The view over the hills and forests was astounding. We sat in our socks, cross-legged in Miranda's tiny living space, as she brewed tea and Paul cut the cake. I studied the seemingly fragile strap that was the main tether for her platform to the trunk, not much assured by her insistence that it was strong and safe. We were there on a sunny, still morning but Miranda had to endure days and nights of gales, blizzards piling snow on her platform, hail and driving rains. In high winds such great trees sway back and forth and rotate to and fro as well: they are remarkable towers of natural engineering.

Some nights friends in her support group camped by the tree: they could send aloft a hot vegetarian dinner or breakfast. But often she was alone for days with just the scampering of wallabies, potoroos and Tasmanian devils in the undergrowth far below. A hefty pro-logging protester drew much-valued publicity to Miranda's tree-sit when he camped at the base of the tree in winter but he went home to his heated house after just four nights.

The highlight of many talks I gave to audiences around Australia during Miranda's 15 months aloft was to dial her mobile phone and, signal permitting, have her tell everyone how she was going by holding my phone next to the microphone. In the middle of winter, up to a thousand people in a warm city theatre would listen, enraptured, to Miranda's quiet, unassuming voice as she described her remote universe, alone for the night in the wilds of central Tasmania. It left audiences clapping, whistling and hollering applause for a remarkable young champion of Earth's fast-disappearing forests and wildlife.

Miranda made a real difference. During her treetop vigil, negotiations on protecting one quarter of Tasmania's state forests proceeded, with the very disturbing concession from environmental negotiators that 'significant' forest protests should be abandoned. Miranda stayed put. In February 2013 Gillard's federal government sent its nomination for the enlargement of Tasmania's Wilderness World Heritage Area by 10 per cent, to include the tallest flowering forests on Earth, to the World Heritage Bureau in Paris. In June the nomination was accepted.

However, the summer of 2012–13 had scorched Tasmania with record high temperatures. On 4 January, Hobart – Australia's southernmost city – recorded a record high temperature of 41.8 degrees Celsius, and destructive bushfires burned more than a hundred homes to the east of the capital. Miranda had confided to me that two things would bring her down: a severe electrical storm or a bushfire.

An arsonist was set to strike.

One hot night in March, Miranda's friend Jenny Weber called me to say that a bushfire had 'broken out' close to Miranda's tree. I called Miranda and backed her decision to come down, although the protective World Heritage nomination had not yet been ratified. Next morning a group of her supporters, including Jenny and I, joined journalists at the base of the towering tree as Miranda descended on the same ropes she had climbed 447 days earlier. Smoke was pluming from the bushfire, which had been lit beside a loggers' road less than 2 kilometres away. Another extremely hot day with dangerous winds had been forecast, and common sense dictated that Miranda leave before her exit was impossible.

Luckily Miranda's tree was spared by the bushfire, before quenching rains doused it a week or so later. The worst of it was the decision by the authorities not to pursue the arsonist. My letter to the commissioner, which I made public, led to a belated investigation but the culprit was not arrested and is still abroad, matches in pocket.

Miranda Gibson and Jenny Weber remain at the forefront of the campaign to save Tasmania's unprotected forests. However, in September 2013, the voters of Australia elected the government of Prime Minister Tony Abbott – whose very low platform included a promise to remove the World Heritage protection from 74,000 hectares of Tasmanian forests, but not including that towering tree in which Miranda had made her home.

The day is not yet done when a few men wielding chainsaws and matches go to work, with most voters' approval and subsidies, to destroy the living lungs of Earth. The day has yet to come when the public gives sufficient backing to the courage and dedication of the Miranda Gibsons and Jenny Webers of the world to save what is left of its wild forests.

47
Horizontal hail

On a late winter's day in 2013 my nephew Jock Brown picked me up at Launceston Airport and, with the rain falling, we headed west through the gloaming to the picturesque village of Stanley on the Bass Strait coast, in advance of an early-morning drive into the Tarkine. Stormy weather was predicted.

A recent opinion poll had indicated that three out of four people in Tasmania's north-west wanted mines in the Tarkine. The mood was decidedly anti-environmentalist. So it was reassuring to have the young woman who served us dinner at the pub whisper, 'Good luck tomorrow!' Her good wishes also made it obvious that everyone in the pub knew that we were there and why.

The local Tarkine protection group, Save the Tarkine, had asked me to join them at a vigil site where the Shree Minerals bulldozers had moved into the Tarkine Protected Area to start clearing woodlands for an open-pit mine more than 1 kilometre long and 200 metres deep. There was to be a well-publicised cavalcade of pro-mining people descending on the vigil the next day, a Sunday, and I was keen to support this brave little band of Tarkine defenders.

Leading the vigil, and the Save the Tarkine group, was Scott Jordan. He had been born in the famous old mining city of Zeehan on the Tarkine's southern margin. Scott's father had been a miner and Scott had begun his own working life in the mines. However, he had also spent much of his childhood in the Tarkine's rainforest, swimming in its clear pools and exploring along its southern backtracks. He was now the spokesman for keeping the Tarkine's wildness intact. We had arranged to meet him at the vigil camp midmorning.

The day broke full of promise. Sheets of cold rain were sweeping across Stanley, the gutters were running swiftly and the weather forecast had ramped up: local floods, possible thunder, gale-force winds and an ocean swell rising above 8 metres. To share our enjoyment of these spectacles, 'extreme sports' enthusiasts from countries around the world, including Germany, Peru and Japan, had gathered for a day of action on the Tarkine coastline. These daredevils watch for wild weather around the planet and, if there is time, fly in to test their skills. Some days earlier they had spotted an enormous storm forming west of Tasmania. A German surf-somersaulter later enthused to television cameras that he had never seen such monstrous seas in Europe.

As Jock drove us down the Tarkine coast the roaring forties were blasting in from the south-west. For kilometres out to sea, giant waves were tossing their white manes high in the air. A series of heavy-cloud squalls were interspersed with sunny breaks and rainbows bursting over the land.

Through the sand dunes we could see flocks of seabirds occasionally lifting up from the beaches to duck and weave in the maelstrom before quickly coming down again.

We arrived at the inland vigil camp on schedule. Flags were flapping from steel poles. A couple of dozen men and women were gathered on a cleared space where the road to the mine site headed north from the road to the coast. In the centre of the group was a metal drum containing a wood fire.

We greeted each other as the next squall hit. It swept in from the south-west with horizontal hail stinging faces and blasting against sturdy raincoats. We pulled down our woollen beanies and leaned away from the wind. As suddenly as the squall arrived, it left. Within a few minutes the morning sky turned brilliant blue and another rainbow was shimmering over the Tarkine's coastal plain to the east. Then the police arrived.

There were four or five police cars and vans. The policewoman in charge was friendly and a little apprehensive but assured us that the main pro-mining cavalcade, now nearing us, was to drive past without stopping. The first pro-mining cars pulled up and 15 or 20 people got out, one with a hastily drawn cardboard poster proclaiming 'We want the Shree mine and jobs'. The three Aboriginal people on our side of the road unfurled their second Aboriginal flag next to a white banner with SAVE THE TARKINE in big red letters.

The two groups filmed each other across the gravel road. Another squall hit and again winter hail lashed our coats and faces. The people over the road disappeared into their cars. A television camera crew arrived and made a first sally out into the wild weather. Once again the squall left as abruptly as it had come and a short sunny break brought our opponents back out of their cars as the main cavalcade arrived. Two to three hundred vehicles, mostly four-wheel drives, came up the hill from the west and drove very slowly past our little group of Tarkine defenders before heading east under the watchful eyes of the police.

One man came across the road to vent his spleen and was escorted back by a constable. 'You fucking poofter Brown, you fucking poofter!' screamed another from his passing car window. As if he had just one idea in life, he kept yelling until another police officer strode down the road, fronted the gentleman and moved him along. 'Go back to the mainland, you bastard, go back to the mainland, why don'ya?' another mining backer demanded of Scott, who was born locally. Apparently, this savant was unaware that he was backing a foreign mining company. No-one from Shree Minerals turned up and no-one on our side of the road got personal.

The TV interviewer, in high heels, did her best. As I talked with her about the wildness of the Tarkine in a largely tamed-and-samed world, a magnificent streak of lightning hit the heathland behind her, followed by a roar of thunder and the sudden downpour of the next squall. The Aboriginal flags fluttered in the wind.

Far away in air-conditioned anonymity, plans were being finalised to dig up yet another natural corner of this noisy, overpopulated planet.

In 2013 CNN declared that Tasmania's Tarkine was number one on their list of the world's ten most desirable places to visit. It may suffer some damage in the meantime, but the world is coming to the Tarkine's rescue.

48

A toast to Australia
'Ne na!'

NATIONAL DAYS ARE good opportunities for celebration and social bonding. The idea of Australia Day is fine but the date, 26 January, is not. It rubs in the grief of First Australians so that instead of a uniting celebration our country is left with deliberate division.

Many Aboriginal Australians call 26 January Invasion Day. Tasmanian Aboriginal leader Ruth Langford asked me to speak at her community's rally to 'Change the Date' of Australia Day outside Parliament House in Hobart in 2014.

As Jimmy Everett went up the steps to the microphone, Michael Mansell yelled, 'Go Jimmy, you tell them Jimmy!' And tell them he did. Everett summed up the murder, rape and dispossession of the 8000 or so of his ancestors, the Australians who lived in Tasmania when the British arrived in 1803–1804. It was a powerful speech underscoring the fact that his people had never ceded sovereignty of this land.

At the back of her book *Pride against Prejudice*, Aboriginal Aunty Ida West appended extracts from the nineteenth-century historian James Bonwick's description of the hunt for the First Tasmanians. Horrifying as it is for most of us to think of two centuries later, British settlers in Tasmania organised hunting parties to go out and shoot the Aboriginal people. Bonwick wrote:

One man was shot; he sprang up, turned round like a whipping top, and fell dead. The party then went up to the fires, found a great number of waddies and spears, and an infant sprawling on the ground, which one of the party pitched into the fire.

And this:

Two men went out shooting birds. Some Natives [Tasmanians] seeing them approach, hastily fled. A woman, far advanced in pregnancy, unable to run with the rest, climbed up a tree, and broke down the branches around her for concealment. But she had been observed by the sportsmen. One of those proposed to shoot her, but the other objected. The first, however, dropped behind, and fired at the unfortunate creature. A fearful scream was heard, and then a new-born infant fell out of the tree.

It was a sunny morning in Hobart and the Union Jack dominated the Tasmanian flag (which also has a British lion on it but nothing Tasmanian) fluttering over Parliament House at Salamanca Place. I spoke in the wake of Jimmy Everett.

Australians are the wealthiest people on Earth, ever.

We are second to none in our innovation, hard work, zest for life and entertainment and our performance in music, the arts and sporting challenges.

And we have been here 60,000 years. Well may we argue that we have the oldest living culture on the planet.

All of us, without exception, are immigrants or the descendants of immigrants, though some so long ago.

Our land broke from the supercontinent Gondwana millions of years ago and so even the most ancient of our citizens are relative newcomers.

Yet in our limited human thinking, we have been here through a vast history which saw not one early and one late great overtaking of the land, but successive waves of people measured first in ice ages and now in a constant, regulated stream.

We do not know whether the pre-European waves of immigration, spaced thousands of years apart, caused an upheaval for the earliest settlers, or whether there was easy assimilation.

We do know that the latest wave of settlement, which began on 26th January 1788, was followed by devastation of the settled life of the half-million or more Australians who were already here and who were bonded to the driest inhabited continent's unique environment.

The continent and its seas were not handed away. As it became clear that the British, the new Australians, were for taking the established Australians' lands by force, the owners and occupiers fought back in defence of their birthright.

From 1788 to 1938 a civil war, with massacres, ensued. In Tasmania alone, more than 200 new settlers and 1000 original Tasmanians were killed in this civil war – that is, as many Australians as died at Gallipoli in the Battle of Lone Pine and more than died in Vietnam.

All wars are barbaric. In Tasmania the terrible death toll of the civil war included men, women, children and babies. Thousands more died from the ravages of diseases brought with the new invasion.

Across the continent hundreds of thousands of First Australians died in horrible circumstances. If we are not moral cowards we will not allow this reality to be ignored as 'black-armband history'. It is our history, our civil war and we must own it. Denying it leaves ourselves hollow.

There can be no genuine settlement and closure from Australia's civil war while the First Australians' prior sovereignty is ignored. There cannot be a hand-back and eviction of us 23 million new-wave settlers. But a treaty, acknowledging that the land was taken and acknowledging that, in the main, it cannot and will not be given back needs to be settled. The logical consequence is to give just compensation which, above all, recognises the civil war and its toll and gives an agreed return to the original owners on the riches being taken from the land. For example, why should not a tithe – of even 1 per cent – of the profits or royalties from logging of native forests and their replacement plantations, or of fisheries or gas and minerals extraction, go back to the traditional owners of the lands and seas?

We are the inheritors of 60,000 years of human history in this land and not just 226 years.

Australian culture, distinguished around the world, comes from that 60,000 years. Aboriginal art, music and story, along with our natural heritage, highlight Australia's unique character in a world of 200 nations. This mantle of our special place in the world can be worn with pride if we latecomers fairly and honestly recognise the burden of dispossession of Australia's early-comers. We can't do that by making a national holiday out of the day the dispossession began.

Here are three better options.

Why not 15th May, recollecting that on that day in 1967 Australians voted overwhelmingly to guarantee First Australians the right to vote? This rings of reconciliation.

What about midwinter's day, 1st July, the day in 1983 when the High Court judgement saved the Franklin River after a national campaign in which Aboriginal power in Tasmania was central to success? This rings of love of country.

My preference is the first day of spring, 1st September. A day of renewal and resurgence. This is already Australia's green and gold day, officially designated as Wattle Day. More widely pitched, it opens us all up to an inclusive celebration of being strong, confident and free in the modern Great South Land.

Leave 26th January as First Fleet Day. Let's move on to an Australia Day we can enjoy together: so we can all toast each other and our nation, as Aunty Ida would have, with a 'ne na!' – 'amen!' or 'to you!'

49
Killers on the loose

In 1961 our family took the Bruce Highway north from Brisbane – long stretches of it gravel – to my oldest brother's wedding at Mackay. It was a happy holiday although nearly everyone got seasick on the pre-wedding trip to Brampton Island. And sharks were in the headlines. Just before we arrived a young woman was attacked and killed as she waded in the waves at Slade Point and her fiancé, who went to her aid, lost one of his legs. It was a horrifying event and, to bring further reality to the horror, some huge sharks were caught and hung on hooks above the beach. Crowds flocked to see the bloody spectacle.

But there was more to come. My brother, the groom, took our youngest brother and me south to a creek near the coast to fish. It was a tidal creek and we arrived at low tide when the wide sandy bed, lined either side with mangroves, was exposed except for the narrow central channel perhaps 10 metres across. It was hot and we had a swim in the channel. Then, in water up to our armpits, we drew a net across the current to catch some small baitfish.

This region has big tides. Soon the tide came swirling in with a first creek-wide wave half a metre high. As a series of waves swept up from the coast, the broad creek bed was quickly covered and soon there was a metre and then two metres of swirling water above it. We rowed out in the 12-foot (4-metre) dinghy, which, with three hefty blokes aboard, floated just a few inches above the waterline. With baited hooks we waited for the lines to zing.

Suddenly the creek erupted. An astonishingly beautiful sailfish flew up in an arc 2 or 3 metres high and, with a mighty splash, re-entered the creek 20 metres from our dinghy. Behind it came a bronze whaler shark. This monster, much longer than our dinghy, rocketed up out of the creek, full length, in pursuit of its prey. It came back down with a terrifying splash where we had been swimming half an hour earlier, creating a wave that rocked more than the vessel we sat in.

What if the fleeing sailfish turned and came back over our dinghy? What if the bronze whaler's next target was us? We rowed to shore. We had that singular feeling of being caught defenceless in the lair of a ruthless predator we could not see.

It was good to get back on the creek bank.

There had been another fatal shark attack further south at Noosa. The Queensland government responded to the public outcry by putting baited hooks chained to drums along the coastline near popular beaches. This official cull involves the killing of sharks of more than 2 metres in length and has made a contribution to the 90 per cent decline in global shark populations since 1961.

After five fatal shark attacks in three years, the Western Australian government followed suit in 2014 with baited drums and the requirement that designated sharks of more than 3 metres in length be shot and their carcasses dumped out to sea.

Perhaps the greatest monster of the deep is the great white shark (*Carcharodon carcharias*). It grows even bigger than the bronze whaler. It is found in all the oceans and can grow to weigh more than 2 tonnes and measure more than 6 metres in length.

Great whites follow migrating fish and have no trouble cruising between Australia and South Africa. They often target the same seal slipways each year just as the seal pups are leaving land to begin feeding in the sea. Not a few people have been killed swimming or diving near seal colonies.

However, more Australians die each year in road smashes (in excess of 1000 on average) or from drowning (more than 100) and in floods and fires than from shark attacks (fewer than five). Worldwide, fewer than 100 humans are eaten by sharks each year but we eat 100 million of them.

Like all the monsters on Earth, the great white is a pale threat when compared to the planet's most colourful killer, *Homo sapiens*. Our herd of more than 7 billion large omnivorous mammals is outdoing the remaining 3500 great white sharks in every department, including the killing of each other and the ransacking of the food stocks in the ocean. We are destroying all the other top predators as well, from arctic bears to tropical tigers – along with their habitats.

Sharks have swum Earth's oceans for 400 million years. They saw the dinosaurs come and go, but now we human beings are giving them the drum roll.

Yet there has been a popular backlash. In early 2014 protests against the Putin-like effrontery of Western Australia Premier Colin Barnett, who announced his shark cull while fingering a huge barbed hook for the television cameras, drew big crowds to beach protests around Australia. Seven thousand people turned out against Barnett's baited hooks chained to drums off Perth's Cottesloe Beach.

While the Perth daily, *The West Australian*, kept in lockstep with its conservative premier, the media elsewhere reflected the changed Australian sentiment. Hobart's *Mercury* headed its editorial 'Shark cull indefensible' and quoted shark expert and historian Chris Black:

> the ocean isn't a hotel swimming pool, it's a wild place … we don't have an unassailable right to feel safe in the ocean, we can't just exterminate every animal that we see as being dangerous.

Perhaps the watershed in thinking about our extermination of other predators came in 1993 when philosopher Val Plumwood survived a crocodile's ambush in Kakadu National Park. Plumwood had been canoeing alone, looking for Aboriginal art sites. A huge reptile attacked her canoe and dragged her under the water and through three death rolls. Nearly unconscious, she made an astonishing escape in heavy rain and, with gaping leg wounds, was rescued late that night by a search party.

Recovering in the Darwin Hospital, Plumwood stoked world headlines by calling for the consequent crocodile hunt to be stopped. She had trespassed into its territory and accepted the consequences. She got the nation talking. She noted that we are outraged by the notion of being eaten but eat billions of other animals each year ourselves.

Plumwood went on to talk around the world about our 'illusion of invulnerability' as the 'experience of being prey is eliminated from the face of the Earth'. She stressed 'our failure to perceive human vulnerability, the delusion of our view of ourselves as rational masters of a malleable nature' and the arrogance of the idea that 'we ourselves cannot be food for worms and certainly not meat for crocodiles'.

Where philosophers go fishermen may follow.

In 2002 recreational fisher Rex Brereton caught a 4.8-metre-long great white shark in his net off Tasmania's Maria Island. He told Chris Black:

I was cautious about cutting the net ... as soon as that last cut was made in the net I knew it was free and so did the shark. It was an eerie feeling ... and it didn't kick back when I was cutting away real close to its nose or mouth, it didn't try to do anything, but as soon as that last cut was made and I pulled the net back – that's when it went!

In his book *White Pointer South*, Black says:

white sharks ... are an important environmental factor in the regulation of the fur seal population. As such, their presence in the wild benefits fishermen, who often find themselves in conflict with seals that opportunistically compete for the catches in their nets ... the removal of even a single sexually mature female white shark from the breeding stock is likely to have potentially serious ramifications for a species of such comparatively low fecundity. Unlike other shark species ... *Carcharodon* typically bears litters of less than ten pups, perhaps as infrequently as every three years.

Since that summer of 1961, Queensland has killed hundreds of great whites and other sharks of more than 2 metres that have been snagged on its hooks. It has also jagged thousands of smaller sharks, fish and birds and snared in its nets whales, dugongs (more than 80 per cent of these drowned in horrific circumstances) and dolphins. But this carnage of sea dwellers has been more than satisfactory for the invaders from the land: since the culls started, only one person has been attacked by a shark in any of the cull areas.

The calamity of removing or otherwise putting out of action the other top predators of the world is licensed by every one of us who does nothing about it as we replace life-filled marine ecosystems with deadened ones that are shark free and surf-ski dominated.

However the change in the public mood since 1961 is monumental. There is an intelligent revolt under way. Professional fisherman Robert Cunningham caught a great white in his net in 1999: he took risks to cut the huge shark free and it is, hopefully, still alive in the deeps. Cunningham told Black:

As far as the big sharks go, for sure ... if it's possible to free them, let them go. You always do. They're just not worth the hassle, plus I'd rather see them swim. I surf, dive and swim, and the way I look at it, you take your chances in their world.

50
White goshawks

'Bold and fearless when attacking but otherwise timid and skulking.'

That is what my bird book has to say about goshawks – and it is wrong, at least as far as the white goshawks that live near my old home, Oura Oura, in the Liffey Valley, are concerned. A pair of them – the female is bigger – have their nest of sticks high up in a stringybark tree on the southern face of the Cluan Tiers across the valley.

White goshawks (*Accipiter novaehollandiae*) mostly keep their distance but one day I was out walking where one sat on a branch at the forest edge under Taytitikitheeker (Drys Bluff). She was in a wattle tree less than 10 metres up, her brilliant red eyes peering down as I stopped on the track below.

The book says this look is 'fierce'. I would call it pulverising. While I moved my ground she stayed stock-still on her branch. I think she was less interested in me than a nearby mouse-hole, but it was an intimidating experience even for this too-big mammal caught out in the open. Not one feather of this bird was 'timid and skulking'.

These pure white raptors, with their sturdy yellow legs, black claws and beaks, and those pulverising red eyes, command attention. And they are smart: a friend told me he was watching a flying flock of white cockatoos in the Tasmanian Midlands one day when one peeled off to pounce down on a grounded target. It was a hunting white goshawk using the white cockatoo flock as cover.

The book calls them 'grey goshawks' because that is their usual colour on the mainland of Australia – with the exception of the Kimberley region, as far from Tasmania as you can get. Like white cockatoos, clouds give the white goshawks camouflage. Tasmania and the Kimberley have high rainfall with months of cloudy white skies each year. A goshawk blends with the clouds as it drops from the skies on each hapless marsupial or chicken morsel or, these days, well-fed racing pigeon.

From across the Liffey Valley their flashing white trajectory is an instant eye-catcher. Like a single snowflake driven horizontally through the dark green forest tops, the white goshawk's flight is spectacularly distracting.

Yet it may soon be another item of Earth's lost natural wonder.

Scientists warn that if current projections of the increasing impact of global warming and the increasing spread of human occupation of the wilds hold, 25 per cent of Australia's birds will be extinct by 2100 and 75 per cent of Earth's birds by 2200. There are perhaps 100 pairs of white goshawks left in Tasmania. Who in the prime minister's office knows or cares if there are any there at all?

The goshawk in a wattle tree is no match for a bullet, although it is a fair guess that this species can survive the threat of humans hunting in the wilds. Global warming and more bushfires are another thing. Then there are the powerlines that cut through flight paths in their hunting grounds and, deadlier still, the loggers.

Logging roads and clearfelling destroy the wilds. Worse than shooters, they open the forests and woodlands to fires, feral cats and chainsaws. They destroy the goshawks' nesting sites and bring more competitors to their feeding grounds. No nests, no birds.

Birds of prey like eagles, owls and hawks inspire our imagination. To the ancients they were gods. They have inspired aviation as far back as the unfortunate Icarus and have been purloined as national emblems.

Who would volunteer to be a national emblem? Emblematic status is more likely if you are rare, facing extinction or extinct.

Australia's emblematic emu was shot to extinction in Tasmania faster than the Tasmanian tiger. It has been eradicated from much of its range across the mainland. A remaining stronghold in coastal northern New South Wales is currently being cut in two by a new multi-lane Pacific Highway. We will zing past, oblivious.

Victoria's faunal emblem is the cute little Leadbeater's possum: this emblem is totally dependent on the old-growth mountain ash (*Eucalyptus regnans*) forests of that state's Central Highlands. These forests are 97 per cent gone, and the possums face extinction as logging and burning proceeds. The disastrous Victorian bushfires of 2009 burnt half the possums' remaining habitat forests: the Victorian government compensated by increasing the rate of logging in the other half.

Many birds of paradise are going or gone. The dodo is done for. So is New Zealand's moa and its predatory Haast's eagle which, until the Maoris arrived in 1500 or so, was the world's largest eagle.

More recently New Zealand attempted a rescue. The Norfolk Island Boobook owl was down to one last live specimen, a female. Two near-relative male boobooks were flown in from Aotearoa in a forlorn attempt to keep the unique Norfolk Island genes alive and kicking.

Hundreds of bird species face imminent extinction from the devastation of their nesting and feeding places. Poignantly, almost-extinct birds have responded to heroic efforts by ornithologists in the countries that have the biggest footprints trampling Earth's biosphere. These include North America's bald eagle, the Californian condor and, in Australia, the Lord Howe Island woodhen.

What will become of Tasmania's white goshawk? If the remaining native forests, woodlands and adjacent natural fields are protected from destruction and if, as predicted, global warming does not reduce Tasmania's cloudiness, they will be fine.

But the fight for the white goshawk's shrinking habitat has ramped right up. Voters across Australia and in Tasmania have just elected governments in favour of winding back action on global warming and increasing native forest and woodland destruction, as well as a developer-led round of private 'eco-friendly' tourist intrusions into national parks. That means fewer nesting and hunting sites for the birds.

In a twist of fate, it may be that global warming actually comes to the Tasmanian white goshawks' rescue. In human affairs, money rules. And in Tasmania, logging and burning of native forests for the export woodchip industry has, in recent decades, injected more carbon and methane into Earth's atmosphere than all other Tasmanian sources – such as factories, farms, transport and shipping – combined.

Nations other than Australia are taking increasing action to offset their greenhouse gas emissions. Inventories show that the tall eucalypt forests of southeastern Australia (those occupied by the Leadbeater's possum in Victoria and the white goshawk in Tasmania, for example) are the most carbon-rich on Earth. The value of keeping these forests intact will outstrip the dollars to be pocketed from logging and burning them. If so, the forests will be at a premium as 'offsets' to allow carbon pollution elsewhere. If market theory is correct they will be kept upright as 'carbon banks'.

The forests will not be protected by the birds, so much as the birds will be protected by the forests.

But not yet. The white goshawks and a galaxy of other birds and animals face destruction from renewed industrial logging in Tasmania's wild and scenic forests. Post-election in 2013 and 2014, the conservative federal and Tasmanian governments are striving to hand over 74,000 hectares (74,000 soccer fields) of the World Heritage forests to the loggers who backed them into office.

The Tasmanian Liberal government, elected in March 2014, not only told voters it would get the loggers back into the World Heritage forests, it also promised draconian punishment for citizens who go out to those forests and peacefully get in the way of the chainsaws and bulldozers. That punishment involves mandatory $10,000 fines for first offences and three-month jail sentences thereafter.

What's it to be for the wondrous white goshawk: bold and fearless or timid and skulking?

When the vandals return to ransack Tasmania's World Heritage and world-famous cathedrals of nature, I will be there in defence of that fierce red eye.

51
The good work of Cynthia

It is Christmas Eve, 2013, and I have just received the fourth Christmas card in as many days from my old friend Cynthia. She is in an aged care unit near Melbourne. On the front of the cards is a white Christmas tree on a red background. Beneath the tree is a red 'Merry Christmas' on a band of sparkly white. There is an advertisement for medical research on the back.

In her first card Cynthia's rickety writing simply said 'Dearest Bob' above the printed words 'Best wishes for the season and throughout the new year'. Then she had written 'And do be careful!! Love, Cynthia.' I presumed she had read that I am helping Sea Shepherd Australia's mission to Antarctica to save the whales from Japanese harpoons and thought that I was aboard one of the ships.

Her second card began more purposefully: 'To dear Bob, Keep up the wonderful work but KEEP SAFE!!!' Curiously, inside this card was a different inscription from the others: 'Wishing you the brightest Christmas and a fun-filled new year.' After the inscription Cynthia wrote that she thought she may have sent another card: 'Love, Cynthia (Another card may turn up – I am in a fearful confusion & muddle here.)'

Cynthia enclosed a plain blue pamphlet about her nursing home with her second card. She had overwritten the pamphlet with the words 'Here 2 years now – one survives!!'

Cynthia was in Tasmania during the 1990s campaigns to save the island's wild forests. When hundreds of people took part in the blockade of logging World Heritage forests at Mother Cummings Peak, Cynthia was there every second day with a large, fresh pot of stew. She helped edit the Tasmanian Greens' magazine, *The Daily Planet*. I enjoyed her gentle but powerful intellect, not least her persuasive atheism. She believed in the ability of people to get together to change the world for the better. She needed no prop.

Existence is inscrutable. The very fact that we go about our daily lives untroubled by our inability to know or understand what we are doing here, where we come from, or where we are going to, is a tribute to the evolution of a very capable denial mechanism in our brains.

Many people put their existence down to God who, conveniently, is beyond the reach of our reasoning. Their faith in God makes the unanswerable questions once-removed and therefore less concerning. For the rest of us the best hope of getting the answers lies in human inquiry and our expanding knowledge of the Universe. That hope depends upon *Homo sapiens* staying alive and prospering on and from our Earth for thousands of years to come. Our job is to ensure that all the people yet to come will have a safe and liveable planet upon which such inquiry can flourish.

Believers depend on faith, reasoners on hope. In both cases, present wellbeing depends on future wellbeing. And vice versa.

I honour anyone's belief in God. It is an understandable belief. And faith is a worthwhile way of leaving to that God the questions that dog the inscrutableness of our very being. Faith is not just a cop-out. It is a logical option for getting along happily in life while having no idea of what, beyond God, if anything, existence is about.

Faith shelters sanity. It saves us from the very real possibility that there is no reason, justification or divine purpose in anything, including any of us. Faith is putty patching up the black hole of pointlessness. It bolsters happiness. So I like it.

However faith is not always benign. When cardinals, mullahs or witch doctors become middlemen between the faithful and the divine, and direct how faith must express itself, there can be awful consequences, like the Spanish (Christian) Inquisition.

What amazes me is that the faith I needed so badly as a youngster has evaporated and yet I am getting along quite happily. In fact I'm happier than before. In Launceston Cynthia and I used to talk about how we both came to be faithlessly well-adjusted human beings.

When I was 13, I raised the fundamental question of God with my school friend Judy Henderson, who also attended St Andrew's Presbyterian Sunday School at Bellingen in northern New South Wales. She doesn't remember that conversation outside the church hall but I do: I was stonkered when she told me that God didn't necessarily exist. It wasn't that I had a particular devotion to God Himself. He was as scary as he was (reported to be) loving. My panic was that I could not imagine how anyone could remain sane if God did not exist. I believed in God because it was untenable not to. The prospect of pointlessness was too shocking.

Not long after that philosophical foray with Judy, I was rocked by hearing on the radio that song of rollicking Biblical skepticism 'It ain't necessarily so!' from the musical *Porgy and Bess*. I didn't know whether to laugh, cry or simply await the wrath of God. The wrath didn't arrive but I never forgot those words.

At the age of 18 I was doggedly hanging on to the illogical idea that God might be, as the Church insisted, both almighty and all good. However, the sheer incongruity of this duo of characteristics, in a world in which there is so much bad, was bursting my brain.

I was studying medicine at Sydney University, and these were the formative years of the 'Permissive Society'. Nearly 200 years after Charles Darwin had published his theory of evolution, Western society's popular thinking was moving swiftly from Christian dogma to scientific inquiry and godlessness.

At Sydney University the middle ground was occupied by bioethics lecturer Professor Charles Birch, who postulated God's Blueprint. It was the theory that a non-interfering God had laid down a blueprint for the Universe and was content to let it unfold without getting involved in the day-to-day minutiae, including human affairs. We are left to sort out the details. Helpful as this idea was, it left God Himself in the 'unsorted' basket. Being hands-off was not the same as being the God of Love, which had previously made Him so worthwhile.

Charles Birch was a fine thinker and an asset to the university. He also provided me with an event of considerable embarrassment. A commercial channel put him on late-night television to talk to the wider 1960s adult audience about how the world worked. I phoned my mother to let her know that my favourite lecturer would be on telly on Thursday night. After the ten o'clock news I settled back to watch his presentation and was thunderstruck when he revealed that his topic for the week would be 'the human testicle'. Graciously, my mother never mentioned the program afterwards. As I had not yet made the transition to easy conversation about sexual matters that many of my fellow students were enjoying, nor did I.

But on another Thursday evening I crossed the Rubicon. I went along to a Presbyterian Fellowship Bible class in suburban Earlwood and the young woman leading the class had a Bible that had red underlinings on every page. My question was simple: 'Is it true that the South Sea Islanders who had never heard the name of Jesus, because they lived before Captain Cook arrived, all went to Hell?'

So was her answer: 'Yes, that is so!' she confidently replied, flicking towards the relevant New Testament text.

I didn't make any fuss. The problem was mine, not hers. I was annoyed with myself that I had gone along with this absurdity for so long. I got up quietly and left the Church of the Loving God, never to return.

Dogma, not just the religious variety, is dangerous – especially when it sweeps up the masses – as those who suffered Mao's Cultural Revolution or Hitler's holocaust attest.

So years later, when I told the celebrated Tasmanian author of *Hook's Mountain*, James McQueen (who was writing an article on the Franklin River campaign for *Playboy* magazine), that had I been in Germany in the 1930s I would have joined a Hitler Youth group, I was being as honest as I could about the dangers of youthful gullibility and acquiescence, not least my own. Decades later, that bit of honest self-analysis was read out, disparagingly, to the Australian Senate, after I had left it, by one of Tony Abbott's senior senators – a Christian, and reader of *Playboy*, from Queensland.

Cynthia hinted in her third card that she worried about those who want to save the planet: 'For dearest Bob & all fellow workers, (Best wishes for the season and throughout the new year) Love from Cynthia & <u>do</u> take care in your dangerous work!!!'

Her fourth card was waiting in my post office box today, Christmas Eve. She has changed from blue ink to black.

> Dearest Bob and All the 'family', Thinking of you all with love … (Best wishes for the season and throughout the new year). I'm now in full retirement in permanent care at the above address – brain VERY DICEY and last bit of independent mobility. Think of you all heaps – some good work, we did! Love and good wishes, Cynthia

Some good work she did, indeed.

What a grand Earth spirit. She's handing on the baton. When I call Cynthia I will tell her that if I am in any danger, it is because friends like her have made me bolder, that I love her, and that her caring intellect, as well as her good wishes, is sailing south with the defenders of the whales on those Sea Shepherd Australia ships.

There will be no divine intervention in the destruction of Earth's biosphere. The onus is ours, and the spirit of Cynthia goes with us.

52
Saving the whales

PAUL WATSON FOUNDED Sea Shepherd in 1977 with the ideology that we should not compromise on Earth's living biosphere, not least the oceans, which cover three quarters of Earth's surface.

He could be a tycoon. He has intelligence, drive, ambition, determination and strategic nous – all attributes for success in business. Instead he is the world's top defender of our ocean ecosystems without which, Watson makes plain, we human beings cannot survive.

In Australia's Senate I advocated the majority public opinion that our nation should defend the whales from the annual slaughter when the Japanese whaling fleet comes south each summer to invade the Southern Ocean Whale Sanctuary in our own backyard.

Many of the whales are born in Australia. They are nurtured off our east and west coasts, where herds of minke and humpback whales calve each winter before heading south to their summer feeding seas off Antarctica.

In 2008 I backed Sea Shepherd's right to ram the harpoon ships if necessary in order to defend the whales. With Sea Shepherd's ships calling into Hobart, I met Watson and heard his cool, calm argument in favour of direct action, avoiding harm to people, to intervene between the whales and the grenade-tipped harpoons of their killers. Watson's line of command was simple: he said he took his cue from the whales themselves and not from those who aided or abetted or did nothing to stop the slaughter.

Also in 2008, Australia's Federal Court ruled in favour of Humane Society International's claim that the whaling was illegal. The court issued an injunction against future whaling, but Tokyo kept sending the fleet south as if nothing had happened.

This underscored the timidity of Australia's politicians in the face of the combined might of Tokyo and those Australian corporations that trade with Japan. If you or I ignored an injunction of the Federal Court we would be arrested and jailed, pronto. But not the whale killers: they flouted Australia's Federal Court with impunity.

This further stoked the rising public anger, and the Greens actively took Sea Shepherd's case into Parliament. In 2010 Prime Minister Kevin Rudd, urged on by Minister for the Environment Peter Garrett, took the option of challenging Japan's whaling in the International Court of Justice in The Hague. The case was finally heard in 2013 and in 2014, by 12 judges to four, the court found the whaling to be illegal, because it was commercial and not for scientific purposes, and ordered Japan to put an immediate halt to it.

Two factors paved the way to this victory: the tide of public opinion and political action, and the relentless campaign by Sea Shepherd, whose winning strategy was to get film of the gruesome whale killings to the world.

As Machiavelli warns, the already rich and powerful will do all they can to crush reformers. So Japan, the law-breaker, used its global might to 'imprison' Watson, the upholder of the law. By the end of 2012, Watson was on the high seas and unable to land anywhere in the world for fear of being arrested and extradited to Tokyo, where he would be tried not according to international law but according to the commercial interests he had so clearly offended. If Tokyo could get him, he faced years in solitary confinement.

In a pincer movement Japan used the courts of the US to effectively close down the Sea Shepherd Conservation Society there. It had been the key source of funds for previous Antarctic whale defence funds.

While the admirable Watson was confined I was set free – after 16 years of service, I resigned from the Senate.

Nature abhors a vacuum. I had got to know and also admire Sea Shepherd Australia's operations manager, Jeff Hansen. He had instigated the successful mission to help save the Kimberley coast from Woodside Petroleum's proposed gas factory. Now free to take up new roles, I first took on the leadership of the Kimberley mission and then the chair of the board of Sea Shepherd Australia as it became obvious we would have to take on the Japanese whalers in the absence of both Watson and the Sea Shepherd Conservation Society.

I had an easy prescription for the job – Watson's own philosophy – and helped steer the rapidly growing organisation as it prepared for summer operations, with the help of Sea Shepherd's global supporters outside the US, to save the whales from the slaughter. It was an honour to be Watson's surrogate.

It is a multimillion-dollar effort to have three or four ships with more than 100 crew, mostly volunteers, go south in hazardous circumstances and confront the whale butchers. The more I got to see of these ships and their captains – in 2013–2014 they were Peter Hammarstedt (on the *Bob Barker*) from Sweden, Siddharth Chakravarty (on the *Steve Irwin*) from India and Adam Meyerson (on the *Sam Simon)* from the US – and their international crews, the more I admired Watson's nous. His decades of devotion to the living oceans had made the whole operation happen, persist, grow and become unstoppable in its mission to end the Antarctic bloodshed.

Time will tell. Japan defied the Australian Federal Court with impunity, so why not find a way to thwart the International Court of Justice? After all Australia's new prime minister, Tony Abbott, opposed at the outset the court action that led to Japan's conviction. But if the Japanese whaling fleet ever does sail south again Sea Shepherd Australia will be there, waiting for it, in defence of the whales.

There are good global laws to protect the biosphere but no global green police contingent to enforce those laws. Criminal behaviour plundering forbidden resources, not least in the oceans, is rampant in the age of Materialism.

In the southern summers of 2012–2013 and 2013–2014 alone, Sea Shepherd Australia's gallant ships saved more than 1500 whales from a cruel and bloody death. These great mammal cousins of ours are alive to re-enter Australia's continental waters and have their calves, enjoy the warmer subtropical seas over the winter months, and bring delight to the increasing thousands of people who go out to greet them with binoculars, cameras and cries of joy rather than harpoons and grenades.

Paul Watson is now safely ashore in the US, but the Japanese whalers' harassment of him in the US courts continues.

In the court of global public opinion, and in the annals of environmental history, Captain Watson will be a champion long after the last Japanese factory ship finds its resting place in the museum of selfish disregard for the living Earth upon which we all depend.

53

Pitfalls in the night

'You do come home!' I said as Paul came in the door after dark.

I got him a beer from the fridge. He had been searching the nooks and crannies in the far top paddock for a lamb that had separated from its mother. 'I wonder if the wedge-tailed eagle got it?' I asked. The eagles sometimes take a dead or sickly lamb.

In the lambing season Paul goes around his flock every morning and evening. I like to tag along and stroke the ewes' brows while he attends to any birthing problems. So the next morning we headed off to do the rounds, ending up in that far top paddock.

Though this was only the second morning of spring by the calendar, there was no frost, fog or dew. It was unseasonably warm with hardly a cloud in the sky. A few white flecks of snow remained on the distant mountains. Paul's steep-terrain farm overlooks the sea, and the rising Sun threw long shadows across the hillsides from the skyline trees. As we walked up to the furthest corner an eagle came out of the western woods and floated 50 metres over our heads, hardly a feather moving in its effortless morning surveillance flight. It turned north and disappeared over the ridge.

We walked back down the gully that drains the paddock. The gully starts with a high marshy flat and ends, 500 metres downhill, in a small creek running through a copse of blackwood trees and ferns, which then flows into a cool, deep green pond. Most of the watercourse is grassy but, here and there, since the earth-binding forest was removed a century ago, holes appear where the creek has eroded underground for a little way before surfacing again.

Paul reckoned the lamb might have ended up in one of those holes.

It hadn't. However, our search led to a miraculous rescue.

'I'll need your help!' Paul suddenly called to me as he knelt and reached to full stretch below the paddock. I hurried over to where, with his own eagle's eye, Paul had spotted white wool in a deep shadowy hole amongst the clumps of reeds in the gully.

Paul hauled a ewe up from the depths. Her head appeared above the ground and, clutching the thick winter wool of her flank, I helped him lift her back onto the paddock. She stood stock still, silent, dripping some mud, bewildered by her underground experience. But she hadn't been alone. 'Her lamb must be down there too,' said Paul as he lay flat on his belly and reached deeper into the black cavern beneath. And there it was.

Paul lifted high a dirty but very lively lamb. Within seconds the lamb was under its mother for a revival drink and then, in the warm morning sunlight, the rescued pair headed downhill to rejoin their flock in greener pastures.

During the night the unsuspecting lamb must have fallen into the hole. In my mind's eye I could see the ewe desperately searching for her lamb bleating below – and suddenly falling in too. There they would have stayed and died had it not been for our search for the first lamb, whose own minor miracle was about to unfold.

High up on the hill, near the thistle patch where a giant eucalypt had fallen in the cyclonic storm of 2009, Paul found his lost lamb. Abandoned by mother and flock, she was hungry but in good health. Paul took her to her ewe, who was now on the next hill, but the mother was determined to reject her. Luckily, Paul had a more enthusiastic mother-in-waiting called Billie Raffety.

Billie, the 12-year-old daughter of friends, had telephoned a fortnight earlier to put in an order for any female lamb that was orphaned. So Paul took the lamb home, gave her a bottle of warm milk and called to let Billie know he had a lamb that needed her care. The lucky lamb spent the rest of the sunlight hours keeping us entertained – not least when she came in the door and jumped up onto the office couch as if to demonstrate her ancestral link with mountain goats.

The Raffetys arrived before dark and Billie couldn't have been happier. She bottle-fed the lamb with the skill of a veteran and took her off to her own greener pastures. Not every lamb spends one night abandoned beside wildlife-filled woods and the next in a garden home with an attentive new mother.

There are pitfalls in the night but the Sun never fails to rise, and fate works its surprises in both directions.

Epilogue

THE SENATE IS sitting and so am I. Seven hundred kilometres north of here it is question time and the urgent issue of the day – it's front page across the nation – is an investigation into an assistant minister's possible indiscretion: did he or did he not gain an improper monetary advantage?

Down here (or rather 'up here', because I'm sitting on a lichen-encrusted sandstone cliff) there is total indifference to the saga gripping the press gallery. Not one tree is leaning north to listen.

However there is a local kerfuffle going on: the scrubtits are making a racket in the native cherry tree. The sandy colour of the usually black tiger snake that crawled quietly under a fallen tree trunk as I came striding up here showed that it has just shed a skin to enable it to grow even bigger – maybe that's what caused the little birds' commotion. In the dip below are the scant remains of a Bennett's wallaby with a telltale eagle's feather nearby. One eucalypt tree is creaking and groaning – and occasionally shrieking – over another as they sway in the gentle mountain breeze. And the echidna that was scratching away under a rock on the slope above me has left the ants in a disorganised welter.

For all of that, I feel much more relaxed here than I ever did in question time. It was a privilege to be there but I'm not missing Parliament one bit.

Up here I'm feeling relaxed and optimistic, thanks to old Alison Cox and young Richard Chin who got together to buy these woods and the riverside paddock below from farmer Tom when he sold up a decade or so ago. Nearly 70 years ago Alison and her husband, Geoff, from Springbanks near Longford, had their honeymoon picnic on the sandstone boulder by the river, near the footbridge, at the upstream end of the paddock.

Last year Alison died and now her sons, Bill and Jamie, and Richard have on-sold the block to Bush Heritage Australia, the guardian of one million hectares of Australian bush and wildlife habitat, which began right here in the Liffey Valley in 1990. I know she would be delighted.

I sure am because, with my old property, Oura Oura, which Paul and I gave to Bush Heritage in 2011, the Cox-Chin block sets aside a lovely tract of riverside paddocks and forest adjoining the Great Western Tiers as a picnic and rambling nature spot for visitors for centuries to come.

I suppose no-one else has sat here on this hidden cliff since last I did some 25 years ago, but I know there'll be plenty more long after I, like Alison, have gone. It's a good feeling.

Optimism, like pessimism, feeds on itself and, having tried the latter for a decade or so when I was younger, I recommend optimism any time. Besides being more enjoyable, it gets things done.

We don't know what the world has in store for us, or us for it, but common sense says we should tread carefully on Earth and share it well – not least to ensure our fellow species their own living room and to guarantee we leave the world the better for those of our own species who will follow us.

It's time for me to go back down through the woods and across the paddock for a dip in the river with Paul, who is down there working on the paddock, before we head off into Launceston tonight where I'm showing films about the Tarkine and Antarctica at a 'Spirituality over Supper' night at the Pilgrim Uniting Church.

I've finished this book of anecdotes on time, with Paul helping out all along the way, and in a fortnight I'll hand it over to Pam Brewster at the publishers, Hardie Grant, in Melbourne. Then Paul and I are driving north to see some of Bush Heritage Australia's mainland treasures near the western borders of New South Wales and Queensland. We plan to sleep out under the stars.

I hope you have enjoyed these stories from my life's adventure and that you and your progeny (even down to the fifth generation!) will get to sit on plenty of hilltops or sand dunes or boulders – perhaps even this one – and, just like me, feel at peace with this magnificent Earth and all the life upon it.

Acknowledgements

My mother and father, brothers and sister and their families lit my way; my school friends and work fellows carried me along; the kindness and inspiration of so many people living and dead gave me joy; and the persistence and forbearance of so many others I came to know, or know about, who rose above the indignity and injustice others dealt them, have made my life seem blessed.

This book comes from them all.

I thank editor Allison Hiew who made the book much the better, Anna Reynolds who assisted me with research, archivist Eve Phillips, Pam Brewster (who approached me with the concept of a book of anecdotes) and her colleagues at Hardie Grant.

The book is dedicated to Rosario Godoy who never got to write her story. Rosario loved life and spoke out for justice but in the days of Guatemala's right-wing assassins she ended up dead in a roadside ditch with her infant child beside her. Her defiant optimism inspires all my days.

It is also dedicated to Ben Oquist, my friend and confidant and senatorial chief of staff, whose strategic brilliance has been a core factor in the Greens becoming the third largest party in Australian politics. His optimism has been a game changer.

Above all my special thanks to my good companion and partner, Paul Thomas, for his technical assistance, patience, good advice and endless encouragement. My optimism has flourished in his company.

Bob Brown
26 April 2014

Index